ANNUAL EDITIONS

American Government 11/12
Forty-First Edition

EDITOR

Bruce Stinebrickner
DePauw University

Bruce Stinebrickner is the Leonard E. and Mary B. Howell Professor of Political Science at DePauw University in Greencastle, Indiana, and has taught American politics at DePauw since 1987. He has also taught at Lehman College of the City University of New York (1974–1976), at the University of Queensland in Brisbane, Australia (1976–1987), and in DePauw programs in Argentina (1990) and Germany (1993). He served fourteen years as chair of his department at DePauw after heading his department at the University of Queensland for two years. He earned his BA *magna cum laude* from Georgetown University in 1968, his MPhil from Yale University in 1972, and his PhD from Yale in 1974.

Professor Stinebrickner is the coauthor (with Robert A. Dahl) of *Modern Political Analysis,* sixth edition (Prentice Hall, 2003), and has published articles on the American presidential selection process, American local governments, the career patterns of Australian politicians, and freedom of the press. He has served as editor of thirty-three earlier editions of this book as well as fourteen editions of its *State and Local Government* counterpart in the McGraw-Hill Contemporary Learning Series. His current research interests focus on government policies involving children (e.g., schooling, child custody, adoption, and foster care). In both his teaching and his writing, Professor Stinebrickner applies insights on politics gained from living, teaching, and lecturing abroad, as well as from serving on the school board and Redevelopment Commission in Greencastle, Indiana.

ANNUAL EDITIONS: AMERICAN GOVERNMENT, FORTY-FIRST EDITION

Published by McGraw-Hill, a business unit of The McGraw-Hill Companies, Inc., 1221 Avenue
of the Americas, New York, NY 10020. Copyright © 2012 by The McGraw-Hill Companies, Inc. All
rights reserved. Previous edition(s) 2009, 2010, 2011. No part of this publication may be reproduced
or distributed in any form or by any means, or stored in a database or retrieval system, without the
prior written consent of The McGraw-Hill Companies, Inc., including, but not limited to, in any
network or other electronic storage or transmission, or broadcast for distance learning.

Some ancillaries, including electronic and print components, may not be available to customers
outside the United States.

Annual Editions® is a registered trademark of The McGraw-Hill Companies, Inc.

Annual Editions is published by the **Contemporary Learning Series** group within the
McGraw-Hill Higher Education division.

1 2 3 4 5 6 7 8 9 0 QDB/QDB 1 0 9 8 7 6 5 4 3 2 1

ISBN 978-0-07-805082-4
MHID 0-07-805082-0
ISSN 0891-3390 (print)
ISSN 2158-3218 (online)

Managing Editor: *Larry Loeppke*
Developmental Editor II: *Debra A. Henricks*
Permissions Coordinator: *Lenny J. Behnke*
Marketing Specialist: *Alice Link*
Senior Project Manager: *Joyce Watters*
Design Specialist: *Margarite Reynolds*
Buyer: *Susan K. Culbertson*
Cover Graphics: *Kristine Jubeck*

Compositor: Laserwords Private Limited
Cover Image: S. Meltzer/PhotoLink/Getty Images (inset); S. Meltzer/PhotoLink/Getty Images
(background)

www.mhhe.com

Editors/Academic Advisory Board

Members of the Academic Advisory Board are instrumental in the final selection of articles for each edition of ANNUAL EDITIONS. Their review of articles for content, level, and appropriateness provides critical direction to the editors and staff. We think that you will find their careful consideration well reflected in this volume.

ANNUAL EDITIONS: American Government 11/12
41st Edition

EDITOR

Bruce Stinebrickner
DePauw University

ACADEMIC ADVISORY BOARD MEMBERS

Preface

In publishing ANNUAL EDITIONS we recognize the enormous role played by the magazines, newspapers, and journals of the public press in providing current, first-rate educational information in a broad spectrum of interest areas. Many of these articles are appropriate for students, researchers, and professionals seeking accurate, current material to help bridge the gap between principles and theories and the real world. These articles, however, become more useful for study when those of lasting value are carefully collected, organized, indexed, and reproduced in a low-cost format, which provides easy and permanent access when the material is needed. That is the role played by ANNUAL EDITIONS.

American Government 11/12 is the forty-first edition in an *Annual Editions* series that has become a mainstay in many introductory courses on the American political system. The educational goal is to provide a readable collection of up-to-date articles that are informative, interesting, and stimulating to students beginning their study of the American political system.

Everyone reading this book no doubt knows, in January 2009 Democrat Barack Obama was sworn in as president of the United States. That same month the 111th Congress convened, with both houses having substantial Democratic majorities. The forty-fourth president of the United States entered the White House facing a daunting array of challenges. Succeeding Republican George W. Bush, Obama became president amidst a severe economic recession that many Americans feared would become a second Great Depression. U.S. military forces had been fighting in Iraq and Afghanistan for most of the decade, and many Americans thought it was time to reduce the two wars' toll on American lives and pocket books and try to restore the nation's tattered image in the world. President Obama and the country faced other major challenges too. These included skyrocketing health care costs while millions of Americans were left without insurance and timely access to appropriate medical care, shortcomings in financial institutions and regulations that had led to the economic meltdown, the threat of climate change thought by many to imperil the entire human race, the long-simmering problem of millions of undocumented immigrants living in the United States, and large budget deficits leading to mounting national debt.

No one should be surprised that, as I write this preface in early September, 2010, President Obama and the 111th Congress have *not* solved all the problems and challenges noted in the preceding paragraph. Some of these problems have been addressed during the first 20 months of the Obama administration, with the long-term results unknowable at this time; some have been intentionally put aside for later consideration; and some policy initiatives have ground to a halt, at least for now. All in all, the first twenty months of the Obama administration have been extraordinarily interesting, and the Obama presidency may well turn out to be, for better or worse, a truly historic period in American history.

Immediately on taking office, President Obama faced decisions about how to spend the remaining $350 billion dollars of Troubled Asset Relief Program (TARP) funds. This amount was left from the TARP law passed in October 2008, a bipartisan attempt under President Bush to bail out teetering financial institutions that had precipitated the economic crisis. One key TARP decision was whether—and, if so, how and to what extent—to try to save General Motors and Chrysler, two U.S. automakers that for decades had been stalwarts of the American economy, but which were on the verge of bankruptcy when President Obama took office. The Obama administration developed a plan to use TARP money to try to save the two car manufacturers, and, in time-honored Keynesian fashion, also urged quick congressional passage of a mammoth stimulus

bill aimed at combating the recession. In February 2009, the president signed a $787-billion-dollar stimulus package into law. A week or so later, wearing his commander-in-chief hat, Obama announced an August 2010 deadline for withdrawing U.S. combat troops from Iraq. In March, he announced a new strategy for U.S. military activities in Afghanistan, and in May replaced the U.S. commander in that theatre of war.

After the flurry of decisions and events during the first half of 2009 outlined in the preceding paragraph, the 111th Congress began its more public phase of considering major health care reform, with support from the president in this potentially historic endeavor. By October, five different congressional committees had approved five different versions of health care reform. On November 7, 2009, the House of Representatives passed its $1.1 trillion health care reform bill by a five-vote margin. In late December, the Senate passed a somewhat different health care bill. Political leaders and observers alike expected a conference committee comprising selected members of each chamber—the usual mechanism used when the two houses of Congress pass different bills on the same topic—to address differences in the two bills and produce a compromise bill that would then be passed by each house of Congress early in 2010.

But American politics can take surprising twists and turns. In January 2010, Republican Scott Brown won a special election to fill the Massachusetts Senate seat vacated by the death of long-serving Democrat Ted Kennedy and thereafter filled on an interim basis by an appointed Democrat. Brown's election raised the total of Republicans in the Senate to 41, which meant that Senate Republicans could mount a successful filibuster against passage of any House-Senate compromise health care reform bill. In another surprising turn of events in March 2010, congressional Democrats used a somewhat obscure procedural route ("reconciliation") to bypass a threatened Republican filibuster and enact a set of historic health care reform measures that President Obama promptly signed into law.

In June 2009, the House of Representatives passed an Obama-supported cap-and-trade bill aimed at restricting greenhouse gas emissions in the United States. Three months later, a bill on the same topic was introduced in the Senate and then got stalled in committee. Despite the April 2010 explosion at the Deepwater Horizon oil well in the Gulf of Mexico that killed 11 workers and initiated a three-month flow of oil into the Gulf, efforts to pass a comprehensive energy and environment bill in the Senate foundered. By August, Senate majority leader Harry Reid had announced that he was abandoning the attempt to pass such legislation in the 111th Congress.

The summer of 2010 did produce one noteworthy legislative accomplishment. In July, Congress passed the Dodd-Frank Wall Street Reform and Consumer Protection Act. Supported by President Obama, this law was the most comprehensive set of financial reforms and new regulations since the New Deal, and was aimed at preventing the dysfunctions of the financial markets that precipitated the financial crisis in mid-2008.

Primarily on account of tax cuts enacted early in the Bush administration and the financial meltdown and resulting recession late in President Bush's second term, large budget deficits were already a concern when President Obama took office. Even in that context, many observers were alarmed when the budget deficit for the fiscal year ending 30 September 2009 amounted to the biggest percentage of the nation's economic output since the last years of World War II. Unsurprisingly, the budget deficit for the fiscal year ending a year later will also be of alarming proportions, and substantial deficit spending is foreseeable for years to come. Moreover, retiring members of the baby boomer generation (the first baby boomers will turn 65 in 2011) will put increasing demands on both the Social Security trust fund and Medicare, a coming fiscal challenge readily apparent for decades and for which American national government has done relatively little to prepare.

On the national security front, in late 2009 President Obama announced a new military strategy in Afghanistan, which included sending thousands of additional American troops to the country that harbored Osama bin Laden when the 9/11 terrorist attacks were launched. By June 2010, the added U.S. troops were in place, but it remained to be seen whether the new strategy would succeed. The American public's support for military involvement in Afghanistan had declined amidst mounting U.S. casualties and perceived lack of progress on the ground as well as longstanding corruption in the Afghanistan government, and it is unclear how that decline in support will affect U.S. military options in the future. On a brighter note, in August 2010 the last contingent of American combat troops withdrew from Iraq, consistent with a commitment that President Obama had made as a presidential candidate a withdrawal plan that had been announced early in his presidency.

About two months after I finish writing this preface, Americans will go to the polls to elect all 435 members of the House of Representatives and 37 senators. Those November 2010 mid-term elections will almost certainly bring big Republican gains in both houses of Congress, but whether the current minority party will gain a majority in either chamber is unclear. The impact of the Tea Party movement on the outcome of these elections will also be interesting to watch, especially since Tea Partiers seem to have affected the outcome of several key Republican primaries that have served as preliminaries to the coming general election.

As I have written in prefaces to earlier editions of this book, "every time I work on the preface for a new edition of this book, I am led to write that the coming year will be another interesting one for students of American politics." The past year has certainly proved no exception to this general rule. Yet many of the elements in any overall narrative of President Obama's first term in the White House remain incomplete. Will President Obama be able to work with the 112th Congress, which will convene in January 2011, to deliver the sort of "change" of which he spoke during his 2008 election campaign? Just how badly will Democratic congressional candidates fare in November 2010? Will the tepid—some would say *very* tepid—economic recovery develop into more robust economic growth that produces more satisfactory levels of employment? Will the health care reform legislation passed in early 2010, once fully implemented, make quality medical care accessible to all Americans and help contain escalating health care costs? In the aftermath of the historic Gulf oil spill and the failure to enact comprehensive energy and environment legislation in 2010, will the United States under President Obama's leadership take any major steps to combat climate change or achieve greater energy self-sufficiency? How successful will the Wall Street Reform and Consumer Protection Act be in preventing recurrence of the financial markets' excesses of recent years and the resulting financial and economic meltdown?

The next year will likely provide answers or partial answers to some of the questions just posed, as well as others like them. Careful observation of American politics as it unfolds on a day-to-day basis can teach us a great deal about regularities and unpredictable aspects of the American political system. The selections in this book should help readers comprehend and even anticipate what will happen in the year to come and, more importantly, enhance their understanding of the characteristic functioning of the contemporary American political system.

The systems approach provides a rough organizational framework for this book. The first unit focuses on ideological and constitutional underpinnings of American politics from both historical and contemporary perspectives. The second unit treats the major institutions of the national government. The third covers the "input" or "linkage" mechanisms of the system—political parties, elections, interest groups, and media. The fourth and concluding unit shifts the focus to policy choices that confront the government in Washington and resulting "outputs" of the political system.

Each year thousands of articles about American politics appear, and deciding which to reprint in a collection of readings such as this can be difficult. Articles are chosen with an eye toward providing viewpoints from left, right, and center. Nearly half of the selections in this book are new to this year's edition, a reflection of continuing efforts to help keep those who read this book abreast of important contemporary developments in the American political system. Also new to this edition are two new learning features to aid you in your study. Located at the beginning of each unit, *Learning Outcomes* outline the key concepts that you should focus on as you are reading the material. *Critical Thinking* questions at the end of each article allow you to test your understanding of the key concepts.

Next year will bring another opportunity for change, and you, the reader, are invited to participate in the process. Please complete and return the postage-paid *article rating form* on the last page of the book and let us know what you think.

Bruce Stinebrickner

Bruce Stinebrickner
Editor

Contents

UNIT 1
Foundations of American Politics

The concepts in bold italics are developed in the article. For further expansion, please refer to the Topic Guide.

UNIT 2
Structures of American Politics

The concepts in bold italics are developed in the article. For further expansion, please refer to the Topic Guide.

The concepts in bold italics are developed in the article. For further expansion, please refer to the Topic Guide.

UNIT 3
Process of American Politics

The concepts in bold italics are developed in the article. For further expansion, please refer to the Topic Guide.

The concepts in bold italics are developed in the article. For further expansion, please refer to the Topic Guide.

UNIT 4
Products of American Politics

The concepts in bold italics are developed in the article. For further expansion, please refer to the Topic Guide.

The concepts in bold italics are developed in the article. For further expansion, please refer to the Topic Guide.

Correlation Guide

The *Annual Editions* series provides students with convenient, inexpensive access to current, carefully selected articles from the public press. **Annual Editions: American Government 11/12** is an easy-to-use reader that presents articles on important topics in the study of American Government. For more information on *Annual Editions* and other *McGraw-Hill Contemporary Learning Series* titles, visit www.mhhe.com/cls.

This convenient guide matches the units in **Annual Editions: American Government 11/12** with the corresponding chapters in three of our best-selling McGraw-Hill American Government textbooks by Harrison/Harris and Losco/Baker.

Annual Editions: American Government 11/12	American Democracy Now, 2/e by Harrison/Harris	A More Perfect Union, 1/e by Harrison/Harris	AM GOV 2010, 2/e by Losco/Baker
Unit 1: Foundations of American Politics	**Chapter 1:** People, Politics, and Participation **Chapter 2:** The Constitution **Chapter 3:** Federalism **Chapter 4:** Civil Liberties **Chapter 5:** Civil Rights	**Chapter 1:** People, Politics, and Participation **Chapter 2:** The Constitution **Chapter 3:** Federalism **Chapter 4:** Civil Liberties **Chapter 5:** Civil Rights	**Chapter 1:** Citizenship in Our Changing Democracy **Chapter 2:** The Constitution: The Foundation of Citizens' Rights **Chapter 3:** Federalism: Citizenship and the Dispersal of Power **Chapter 4:** Civil Liberties: Expanding Citizens' Rights **Chapter 5:** Civil Rights: Toward a More Equal Citizenry
Unit 2: Structures of American Politics	**Chapter 11:** Congress **Chapter 12:** The Presidency **Chapter 13:** The Bureaucracy **Chapter 14:** The Judiciary	**Chapter 11:** Congress **Chapter 12:** The Presidency **Chapter 13:** The Bureaucracy **Chapter 14:** The Judiciary	**Chapter 11:** Congress: Doing the People's Business **Chapter 12:** The Presidency: Power and Paradox **Chapter 13:** Bureaucracy: Citizens as Owners and Consumers **Chapter 14:** The Courts: Judicial Power in a Democratic Setting
Unit 3: Process of American Politics	**Chapter 6:** Political Socialization and Public Opinion **Chapter 7:** Interest Groups **Chapter 8:** Political Parties **Chapter 9:** Elections, Campaigns, and Voting **Chapter 10:** The Media	**Chapter 6:** Political Socialization and Public Opinion **Chapter 7:** Interest Groups **Chapter 8:** Political Parties **Chapter 9:** Elections, Campaigns, and Voting **Chapter 10:** The Media	**Chapter 6:** Public Opinion: Listening to Citizens **Chapter 7:** Political Participation: Equal Opportunities and Unequal Voices **Chapter 8:** Interest Groups in America **Chapter 9:** Parties and Political Campaigns: Citizens and the Electoral Process **Chapter 10:** Media: Tuning In or Turning Out
Unit 4: Products of American Politics	**Chapter 15:** Economic Policy **Chapter 16:** Domestic Policy **Chapter 17:** Foreign Policy and National Security	**Chapter 15:** Economic Policy **Chapter 16:** Domestic Policy **Chapter 17:** Foreign Policy and National Security	**Chapter 15:** Public Policy: Responding to Citizens **Chapter 16:** Foreign and Defense Policy: Protecting American Interests in the World

Topic Guide

This topic guide suggests how the selections in this book relate to the subjects covered in your course. You may want to use the topics listed on these pages to search the Web more easily.

On the following pages a number of websites have been gathered specifically for this book. They are arranged to reflect the units of this Annual Editions reader. You can link to these sites by going to www.mhhe.com/cls

All the articles that relate to each topic are listed below the bold-faced term.

xv

Internet References

The following Internet sites have been selected to support the articles found in this reader. These sites were available at the time of publication. However, because websites often change their structure and content, the information listed may no longer be available. We invite you to visit www.mhhe.com/cls for easy access to these sites.

Annual Editions: American Government 11/12

General Sources

Plain Blog About Politics
plainblogaboutpolitics.blogspot.com

"I'm a political scientist blogging about American politics, especially the presidency, Congress, parties, and elections." So reads Jonathan Bernstein's description of his blog. Go see for yourself.

The Monkey Cage
www.themonkeycage.org

"Democracy is the art of running the circus from the monkey cage." (H.L. Mencken) Despite its humorous name and epigram, this is a serious blog written by political scientists to relate political science research to current political happenings.

The Atlantic: Andrew Sullivan
andrewsullivan.theatlantic.com

Political and social commentary by award-winning editor, journalist, and author Andrew Sullivan, with links to other useful sources.

National Review: The Corner
www.nationalreview.com/corner

Part of National Review Online, this blog addresses a whole range of political issues in a timely fashion and from a conservative perspective.

Think Progress
www.thinkprogress.org

Part of the Center for American Progress, this blog addresses a whole range of political issues in a timely fashion and from a liberal perspective.

Fact-checking
www.factcheck.org
www.opensecrets.org
www.politifact.com

If you are not sure you believe what a politician, blogger, television commentator, or organization is saying, here are three sites dedicated to fact-checking political assertions.

UNIT 1: Foundations of American Politics

National Archives and Records Administration (NARA)
www.archives.gov

This official site of the NARA, which oversees the management of all records of the national government, offers easy access to background information for students interested in the policy-making process, including a search function for federal documents and speeches, and much more.

Library of Congress
www.loc.gov/rr/program/bib/ourdocs/NewNation.html

The Library of Congress holds many of the most important documents in United States history, especially those that relate to the founding of the nation. Here you will find not only the original documents, but also a wealth of supplemental material such as correspondence among the founders, copies of relevant proceedings, and events taking place on key dates in the adoption of those documents.

The American Scene
www.theamericanscene.com

Open this site for access to political, cultural, and Web commentary on a number of issues from a conservative political viewpoint.

The Pew Center for the People and the Press
people-press.org

The Pew Center conducts research on attitudes toward politics, the press, and public policy issues. This site contains a wealth of interesting information on what people in the United States and other nations are thinking.

UNIT 2: Structures of American Politics

United States House of Representatives
www.house.gov

The official website of the House of Representatives provides information about current and past House members and agendas, the legislative process, and more. You can learn about events on the House floor as they happen.

United States Senate
www.senate.gov

The Senate website provides information about current and past Senate members and agendas, legislative activities, and committees.

White House
www.whitehouse.gov

The White House website contains presidential speeches, press briefings, and issue positions of the incumbent president.

United States Supreme Court
www.supremecourt.gov

The official website of the Supreme Court contains recent opinions, biographies of the nine justices, and some background information on the Court.

Department of State
www.state.gov

View this site for understanding of the workings of a major executive branch department. Links explain what the department does, what services it provides, and what it says about U.S. interests around the world. Generally similar information about other executive branch departments can be found at their official websites (e.g., www.usda.gov, www.energy.gov, and www.usdoj.gov).

Federal Reserve System
www.federalreserve.gov

Consult this site to learn the answers to FAQs about the structure of the Federal Reserve System, monetary policy, and more. It provides links to speeches and interviews as well as essays and articles presenting different views on the Fed.

Internet References

UNIT 3: Process of American Politics

The Gallup Organization
www.gallup.com

Open this Gallup Organization home page for links to an extensive archive of public opinion poll results and special reports on a variety of topics related to American society, politics, and government.

FiveThirtyEight
fivethirtyeight.blogs.nytimes.com

More than a polling site with a liberal bent, FiveThirtyEight includes fascinating detail about the science and limitations of polling and critiques of data from other sites. It provided perhaps the most accurate predictions of state and national elections in 2008. FiveThirtyEight (which refers to the number of votes in the Electoral College) originally had its own site, but is now hosted by *The New York Times*.

Poynter Online
www.poynter.org

This site of the Poynter Institute for Media Studies provides extensive links to information and resources about the media, including media ethics and reporting techniques. Many bibliographies and websites are included.

Real Clear Politics
www.realclearpolitics.com

This site presents, in a timely and easily accessible manner, the latest published poll results on a variety of political topics, including, of course, how candidates are faring during election campaigns. There are also commentaries from a range of sources about campaigns and American politics more generally. Like FiveThirtyEight.com, it is a popular and authoritative source for so-called political junkies.

Tech President
techpresident.com

This site began as a "crosspartisan group blog covering how the 2008 presidential candidates were using the web, and . . . how content generated by voters affected the campaign." It has now expanded to how candidates and government offices at all levels are using the web and how voters are responding.

UNIT 4: Products of American Politics

American Diplomacy
www.unc.edu/depts/diplomat

American Diplomacy is an online journal of commentary, analysis, and research on U.S. foreign policy and its results around the world.

Cato Institute
www.cato.org

Conservative commentary on American politics.

Ezra Klein
voices.washingtonpost.com/ezra-klein

Liberal commentary on American politics.

Foreign Affairs
www.foreignaffairs.org

This website of the well-respected foreign policy journal is a valuable research tool. It allows users to search the journal's archives and provides indexed access to the field's leading publications, documents, online resources, and more. Links to dozens of other related websites are available.

Paul Krugman
krugman.blogs.nytimes.com

A Nobel Prize winning economist, *New York Times* columnist, and a liberal, Paul Krugman discusses mostly economic issues.

Tax Foundation
www.taxfoundation.org

The Tax Foundation (or what some commentators call the "Anti-Tax" Foundation) provides critical analysis of your tax bill and taxes in general.

UNIT 1

Foundations of American Politics

Unit Selections

Learning Outcomes

After reading this unit you should be able to:

- Distinguish—and provide examples of—*empirical* writings about politics, which focus on what is (or was), and *normative* writings about politics, which focus on what ought to be.

- Compare and contrast the relative persuasiveness of normative writings that address the same political topic (e.g., the U. S. Supreme Court's *Citizens United v. F.E.C.* decision in 2010) from different, even completely opposite, perspectives.

- Compare and contrast the relevance and applicability of historic writings from a century or more ago with the relevance and applicability of contemporary writings about American politics.

- Assess how important for the functioning of the contemporary American political system historic writings and contemporary normative writings actually are, and defend your assessment.

- Analyze how important various constitutional and legal issues are for the actual functioning of the contemporary American political system, and defend your conclusions on the matter.

- Appraise the extent to which various political writings, including historic documents like the Declaration of Independence and the U. S. Constitution, are conservative or liberal, as those words are used in the American political system today.

- Determine whether the Constitution of the United States is a force for democratic government (as *The Federalist Papers* argue) or contains many troublesome undemocratic elements (as "It Is Time to Repair the Constitution's Flaws" contends), and explain why.

- Investigate whether fundamental ideas and ideals that appear in the Declaration of Independence, the *Preamble* to the Constitution, and *Federalist Papers 51* and *10* reappear in contemporary writings about American politics "Can America Fail?" "The Purposes of Political Combat," "The Crisis Comes Ashore," and "A Triumph for Political Speech."

Student Website
www.mhhe.com/cls

This unit treats some of the less concrete aspects of the American political system—historic ideals, contemporary ideas and values, and constitutional and legal issues. These dimensions of the system are not immune to change. Instead, they interact with the wider political environment in which they exist, and are modified accordingly. Usually this interaction is a gradual process, but sometimes events foster more rapid change.

Human beings can be distinguished from other species by their ability to think and reason at relatively high levels of abstraction. In turn, ideas, ideals, values, and principles can and do play important roles in politics. Most Americans value ideals such as democracy, freedom, equal opportunity, and justice. Yet, the precise meanings of these terms and the best ways of implementing them are the subject of much dispute in the political arena. Such ideas and ideals, as well as disputes about their "real" meanings, are important elements in the practice of American politics.

Although the selections in this unit span more than 200 years, they are related to one another. Understanding contemporary political viewpoints is easier if the ideals and principles of the past are also taken into account. In addition, we can appreciate the significance of historic documents such as the Declaration of Independence and the Constitution better if we are familiar with contemporary ideas and perspectives. The interaction of different ideas and values plays an important part in the continuing development of the "foundations" of the American political system.

The first section of this unit includes several historic documents from the eighteenth century. The first is the Declaration of Independence. Written in 1776, it proclaims the Founders' views of why independence from England was justified and, in doing so, identifies certain "unalienable" rights that "all men" are said to possess. The second document, the Constitution of 1787, remains in effect to this day. It provides an organizational blueprint for the structure of American national government, outlines the federal relationship between the national government and the states, and expresses limitations on what government can do. Twenty-seven amendments have been added to the original Constitution in two centuries. In addition to the Declaration of Independence and the Constitution, the first section includes two selections from *The Federalist Papers,* and a series of newspaper articles written in support of the proposed new Constitution. Appearing in 1787 and 1788, *The Federalist Papers* addressed various provisions of the new Constitution and argued that putting the Constitution into effect would bring about good government. The second section treats contemporary political ideas and viewpoints. As selections in this section illustrate, efforts to apply or act on political beliefs in the context of concrete circumstances often lead to interesting commentary and debate. "Liberal" and

© Library of Congress, Prints and Photographs Division

"conservative" are two labels often used in American political discussions, but political views and values have far more complexity than can be captured by these two terms.

Selections in the third section show that constitutional and legal issues and interpretations are tied to historic principles as well as to contemporary ideas and values. It has been suggested that throughout American history almost every important political question has, at one time or another, appeared as a constitutional or legal issue.

The historic documents and the other selections in this unit might be more difficult to understand than the articles in other units. Some of them may have to be read and reread carefully to be fully appreciated. But to grapple with the important material treated here is to come to grips with a variety of conceptual foundations of the American political system. To ignore the theoretical issues raised would be to bypass an important element of American politics today.

Internet References

National Archives and Records Administration (NARA)
   www.archives.gov
Opinion, Inc.: The Site for Conservative Opinion on the Web
   www.opinioninc.com
Smithsonian Institution
   www.si.edu

The Declaration of Independence

THOMAS JEFFERSON

When in the Course of human events, it becomes necessary for one people to dissolve the political bands which have connected them with another, and to assume among the powers of the earth, the separate and equal station to which the Laws of Nature and of Nature's God entitle them, a decent respect to the opinions of mankind requires that they should declare the causes which impel them to the separation.—We hold these truths to be self-evident, that all men are created equal, that they are endowed by their Creator with certain unalienable Rights, that among these are Life, Liberty and the pursuit of Happiness.—That to secure these rights, Governments are instituted among Men, deriving their just powers from the consent of the governed.—That whenever any Form of Government becomes destructive of these ends, it is the Right of the People to alter or to abolish it, and to institute new Government, laying its foundation on such principles and organizing its powers in such form, as to them shall seem most likely to effect their Safety and Happiness. Prudence, indeed, will dictate that Governments long established should not be changed for light and transient causes; and accordingly all experience hath shewn, that mankind are more disposed to suffer, while evils are sufferable, than to right themselves by abolishing the forms to which they are accustomed. But when a long train of abuses and usurpations, pursuing invariably the same Object evinces a design to reduce them under absolute Despotism, it is their right, it is their duty, to throw off such Government, and to provide new Guards for their future security.—Such has been the patient sufferance of these Colonies; and such is now the necessity which constrains them to alter their former Systems of Government. The history of the present King of Great Britain is a history of repeated injuries and usurpations, all having in direct object the establishment of an absolute Tyranny over these States. To prove this, let Facts be submitted to a candid world.—He has refused his Assent to Laws, the most wholesome and necessary for the public good.—He has forbidden his Governors to pass Laws of immediate and pressing importance, unless suspended in their operation till his Assent should be obtained; and when so suspended, he has utterly neglected to attend to them.—He has refused to pass other Laws for the accommodation of large districts of people, unless those people would relinquish the right of Representation in the Legislature, a right inestimable to them and formidable to tyrants only.—He has called together legislative bodies at places unusual, uncomfortable, and distant from the depository of their public Records, for the sole purpose of fatiguing them into compliance with his measures.—He has dissolved Representative Houses repeatedly, for opposing with manly firmness his invasions on the rights of the people.—He has refused for a long time, after such dissolutions, to cause others to be elected; whereby the Legislative powers, incapable of Annihilation, have returned to the People at large for their exercise; the State remaining in the meantime exposed to all the dangers of invasion from without, and convulsions within.—He has endeavoured to prevent the population of these States; for that purpose obstructing the Laws for Naturalization of Foreigners; refusing to pass others to encourage their migrations hither, and raising the conditions of new Appropriations of Lands.—He has obstructed the Administration of Justice, by refusing his Assent to Laws for establishing Judiciary powers.—He has made Judges dependent on his Will alone, for the tenure of their offices, and the amount and payment of their salaries.—He has erected a multitude of New Offices, and sent hither swarms of Officers to harass our people, and eat out their substance. He has kept among us, in times of peace, Standing Armies without the Consent of our legislatures.—He has affected to render the Military independent of and superior to the Civil power.—He has combined with others to subject us to a jurisdiction foreign to our constitution, and unacknowledged by our laws; giving his Assent to their Acts of pretended Legislation:—For quartering large bodies of armed troops among us:—For protecting them, by a mock Trial, from punishment for any Murders which they should commit on the Inhabitants of these States:—For cutting off our Trade with all parts of the world:—For imposing Taxes on us without our Consent:—For depriving us in many cases, of the benefits of Trial by Jury:—For transporting us beyond Seas to be tried for pretended offences:—For abolishing the free System of English Laws in a neighboring Province, establishing therein an Arbitrary government, and enlarging its Boundaries so as to render it at once an example and fit instrument for introducing the same absolute rule into these Colonies:—For taking away our Charters, abolishing our most valuable Laws and altering fundamentally the Forms of our Governments:—For suspending our own Legislatures, and declaring themselves invested with power to legislate for us in all cases whatsoever.—He has abdicated Government here, by declaring us out of his Protection and waging War against us.—He has plundered our seas, ravaged our Coasts, burnt our towns, and destroyed the lives of our people.—He is at this time transporting large Armies of foreign Mercenaries to compleat the works of death, desolation and tyranny, already begun with circumstances of Cruelty & perfidy scarcely paralled in the most barbarous ages, and totally unworthy the Head of a civilized nation.—He has constrained our fellow Citizens taken Captive on the high Seas to bear Arms against their Country, to become the executioners of their friends and Brethren, or to fall themselves by their Hands.—He has excited domestic insurrections amongst us, and has endeavoured to bring on the inhabitants of our frontiers, the merciless Indian Savages, whose known rule of warfare, is an undistinguished destruction of all ages, sexes and conditions. In every stage of these Oppressions We have Petitioned for Redress in the most humble terms: Our repeated Petitions have been answered only by repeated injury. A Prince, whose character is thus marked by every act which may define a Tyrant, is unfit to be the ruler of a free people. Nor have We been wanting in attentions to our British brethren. We have warned them from time to time of attempts by their legislature to extend an unwarrantable jurisdiction over us. We have reminded them of the circumstances of our emigration and settlement here. We have appealed to their native justice and magnanimity, and we have conjured them by the ties of our common kindred to disavow these usurpations, which would inevitably interrupt our connections and correspondence. They too have been deaf to the voice of justice and of consanguinity. We must, therefore, acquiesce in the necessity, which denounces our Separation, and hold them, as we hold the rest of mankind, Enemies in War, in Peace Friends.—

WE, THEREFORE, the Representatives of the UNITED STATES OF AMERICA, in General Congress, Assembled, appealing to the Supreme Judge of the world for the rectitude of our intentions, do, in the Name, and by Authority of the good People of these Colonies, solemnly publish and declare, That these United Colonies are, and of Right ought to be FREE AND INDEPENDENT STATES; that they are Absolved from all Allegiance to the British Crown, and that all political connection between them and the State of Great Britain, is and ought to be totally dissolved; and that as Free and Independent States, they have full Power to levy War, conclude Peace, contract Alliances, establish Commerce, and to do all other Acts and Things which Independent States may of right do.—And for the support of this Declaration, with a firm reliance on the protection of divine Providence, we mutually pledge to each other our Lives, our Fortunes and our sacred Honor.

Critical Thinking

1. What are the three inalienable rights outlined in the Declaration of Independence?

2. Break down the main arguments for independence as outlined in the document.

3. From where do governments draw their power, according to the Declaration of Independence?

The History of the Constitution of the United States

Constitution of the United States. The Articles of Confederation did not provide the centralizing force necessary for unity among the new states and were soon found to be so fundamentally weak that a different political structure was vital. Conflicts about money and credit, trade, and suspicions about regional domination were among the concerns when Congress on February 21, 1787, authorized a Constitutional Convention to revise the Articles. The delegates were selected and assembled in Philadelphia about three months after the call. They concluded their work by September.

The delegates agreed and abided to secrecy. Years afterward James Madison supported the secrecy decision writing that "no man felt himself obliged to retain his opinions any longer than he was satisfied of their propriety and truth, and was open to the force of argument." Secrecy was not for all time. Madison, a delegate from Virginia, was a self-appointed but recognized recorder and took notes in the clear view of the members. Published long afterward, Madison's Journal gives a good record of the convention.

The delegates began to assemble on May 14, 1787, but a majority did not arrive until May 25. George Washington was elected President of the Convention without opposition. The lag of those few days gave some of the early arrivals, especially Madison, time to make preparations on substantive matters, and Gov. Edmund Jennings Randolph presented a plan early in the proceedings that formed the basis for much of the convention deliberations. The essentials were that there should be a government adequate to prevent foreign invasion, prevent dissension among the states, and provide for general national development, and give the national government power enough to make it superior in its realm. The decision was made not merely to revise the articles but to create a new government and a new constitution.

One of the most crucial decisions was the arrangement for representation, a compromise providing that one house would represent the states equally, the other house to be based on popular representation (with some modification due to the slavery question). This arrangement recognized political facts and concessions among men with both theoretical and practical political knowledge.

Basic Features. Oliver Wendell Holmes, Jr., once wrote that the provisions of the Constitution were not mathematical formulas, but "organic living institutions *[sic]* and its origins and growth were vital to understanding it." The constitution's basic features provide for a supreme law—notwithstanding any other legal document or practice, the Constitution is supreme, as are the laws made in pursuance of it and treaties made under the authority of the United States.

The organizational plan for government is widely known. Foremost is the separation of powers. If the new government were to be limited in its powers, one way to keep it limited would have been executive, legislative, and judicial power [given] to three distinct and non-overlapping branches. A government could not actually function, however, if the separation meant the independence of one branch from the others. The answer was a design to insure cooperation and the sharing of some functions. Among these are the executive veto and the power of Congress to have its way if it musters a super-majority to override that veto. The direction of foreign affairs and the war power are both dispersed and shared. The appointing power is shared by the Senate and the president; impeaching of officers and financial controls are powers shared by the Senate and the House.

A second major contribution by the convention is the provision for the judiciary, which gave rise to the doctrine of judicial review. There is some doubt that the delegates comprehended this prospect but Alexander Hamilton considered it in *Federalist* No. 78: "The interpretation of the laws is a proper and peculiar province of the Courts. . . . Wherever a particular statute contravenes the Constitution, it will be the duty of the judicial tribunals to adhere to the latter and disregard the former."

Another contribution is the federal system, an evolution from colonial practice and the relations between the colonies and the mother country. This division of authority between the new national government and the states recognized the doctrine of delegated and reserved powers. Only certain authority was to go to the new government; the states were not to be done away with and much of the Constitution is devoted to insuring that they were to be maintained even with the stripping of some of their powers.

It is not surprising, therefore, that the convention has been called a great political reform caucus composed of both revolutionaries and men dedicated to democracy. By eighteenth-century standards the Constitution was a democratic document, but standards change and the Constitution has changed since its adoption.

Change and Adaptation. The authors of the Constitution knew that provision for change was essential and provided for it in Article V, insuring that a majority could amend, but being restrictive enough that changes were not likely for the "light and transient" causes Jefferson warned about in the Declaration of Independence.

During the period immediately following the presentation of the Constitution for ratification, requiring assent of nine states to be effective, some alarm was expressed that there was a major defect: there was no bill of rights. So, many leaders committed themselves to the presentation of constitutional amendments for the purpose. Hamilton argued that the absence of a bill of rights was not a defect; indeed, a bill was not necessary. "Why," he wrote, in the last of *The Federalist Papers,* "declare things that shall not be done which there is no power to do?" Nonetheless, the Bill of Rights was presented in the form of amendments and adopted by the states in 1791.

Since 1791 many proposals have been suggested to amend the Constitution. By 1972 sixteen additional amendments had been adopted. Only one, the Twenty-first, which repealed the Eighteenth, was ratified by state conventions. All the others were ratified by state legislatures.

Even a cursory reading of the later amendments shows they do not alter the fundamentals of limited government, the separation of powers, the federal system, or the political process set in motion originally. The Thirteenth, Fourteenth, Fifteenth, and Nineteenth amendments attempt to insure equality to all and are an extension of the Bill of Rights. The others reaffirm some existing constitutional arrangements, alter some procedures, and at least one, the Sixteenth, states national policy.

Substantial change and adaptation of the Constitution beyond the formal amendments have come from national experience, growth, and development. It has been from the Supreme Court that much of the gradual significant shaping of the Constitution has been done.

Government has remained neither static nor tranquil. Some conflict prevails continually. It may be about the activities of some phase of government or the extent of operations, and whether the arrangement for government can be made responsive to current and prospective needs of society. Conflict is inevitable in a democratic society. Sometimes the conflict is spirited and rises to challenge the continuation of the system. Questions arise whether a fair trial may be possible here or there; legislators are alleged to be indifferent to human problems and pursue distorted public priorities. Presidents are charged with secret actions designed for self-aggrandizement or actions based on half-truths. Voices are heard urging revolution again as the only means of righting alleged wrongs.

The responses continue to demonstrate, however, that the constitutional arrangement for government, the allocation of powers, and the restraints on government all provide the needed flexibility. The Constitution endures.

Adam C. Breckenridge, University of Nebraska-Lincoln

The Constitution of the United States

We the People of the United States, in Order to form a more perfect Union, establish Justice, insure domestic Tranquility, provide for the common defence, promote the general Welfare, and secure the Blessings of Liberty to ourselves and our Posterity, do ordain and establish this Constitution for the United States of America.

Article. I.

SECTION. 1. All legislative Powers herein granted shall be vested in a Congress of the United States, which shall consist of a Senate and House of Representatives.

SECTION. 2. The House of Representatives shall be composed of Members chosen every second Year by the People of the several States, and the Electors in each State shall have the Qualifications requisite for Electors of the most numerous Branch of the State Legislature.

No Person shall be a Representative who shall not have attained to the age of twenty five Years, and been seven Years a Citizen of the United States, and who shall not, when elected, be an Inhabitant of that State in which he shall be chosen.

Representatives and direct Taxes shall be apportioned among the several States which may be included within this Union, according to their respective Numbers, which shall be determined by adding to the whole Number of free Persons, including those bound to Service for a Term of Years, and excluding Indians not taxed, three fifths of all other Persons. The actual Enumeration shall be made within three Years after the first Meeting of the Congress of the United States, and within every subsequent Term of ten Years, in such Manner as they shall by Law direct. The Number of Representatives shall not exceed one for every thirty Thousand, but each State shall have at Least one Representative; and until such enumeration shall be made, the State of New Hampshire shall be entitled to chuse three, Massachusetts eight, Rhode-Island and Providence Plantations one, Connecticut five, New York six, New Jersey four, Pennsylvania eight, Delaware one, Maryland six, Virginia ten, North Carolina five, South Carolina five, and Georgia three.

When vacancies happen in the Representation from any State, the Executive Authority thereof shall issue Writs of Election to fill such Vacancies.

The House of Representatives shall chuse their Speaker and other Officers; and shall have the sole Power of Impeachment.

SECTION. 3. The Senate of the United States shall be composed of two Senators from each State, chosen by the Legislature thereof, for six years; and each Senator shall have one Vote.

Immediately after they shall be assembled in Consequence of the first Election, they shall be divided as equally as may be into three Classes. The Seats of the Senators of the first Class shall be vacated at the Expiration of the second Year, of the second Class at the Expiration of the fourth Year, and of the third Class at the Expiration of the sixth Year, so that one third may be chosen every second year; and if Vacancies happen by Resignation, or otherwise, during the Recess of the Legislature of any State, the Executive thereof may make temporary Appointments until the next Meeting of the Legislature, which shall then fill such Vacancies.

No Person shall be a Senator who shall not have attained to the Age of thirty Years, and been nine Years a Citizen of the United States, and who shall not, when elected, be an Inhabitant of that State for which he shall be chosen.

The Vice President of the United States shall be President of the Senate, but shall have no Vote, unless they be equally divided.

The Senate shall chuse their other Officers, and also a President pro tempore, in the Absence of the Vice President, or when he shall exercise the Office of President of the United States.

The Senate shall have the sole Power to try all Impeachments. When sitting for that Purpose, they shall be on Oath or Affirmation. When the President of the United States is tried the Chief Justice shall preside: And no Person shall be convicted without the Concurrence of two thirds of the Members present.

Judgment in Cases of Impeachment shall not extend further than to removal from Office, and disqualification to hold and enjoy any Office of honor, Trust or Profit under the United States: but the Party convicted shall nevertheless be liable and subject to Indictment, Trial, Judgment and Punishment, according to Law.

SECTION. 4. The Times, Places and Manner of holding Elections for Senators and Representatives, shall be prescribed in each State by the Legislature thereof; but the Congress may at any time by Law make or alter such Regulations, except as to the Places of chusing Senators.

The Congress shall assemble at least once in every Year, and such Meeting shall be on the first Monday in December, unless they shall by Law appoint a different Day.

SECTION. 5. Each House shall be the Judge of the Elections, Returns and Qualifications of its own Members, and a Majority of each shall constitute a Quorum to do Business; but a smaller Number may adjourn from day to day, and may be authorized to compel the Attendance of absent Members, in such Manner, and under such Penalties as each House may provide.

Each House may determine the Rules of its Proceedings, punish its Members for disorderly Behaviour, and, with the Concurrence of two thirds, expel a Member.

Each House shall keep a Journal of its Proceedings, and from time to time publish the same, excepting such Parts as may in their Judgment require Secrecy; and the Yeas and Nays of the Members of either House on any question shall, at the Desire of one fifth of those Present, be entered on the Journal.

Neither House, during the Session of Congress, shall, without the Consent of the other, adjourn for more than three days, nor to any other Place than that in which the two Houses shall be sitting.

SECTION. 6. The Senators and Representatives shall receive a Compensation for their Services, to be ascertained by Law, and paid out of the Treasury of the United States. They shall in all Cases, except Treason, Felony and Breach of the Peace, be privileged from Arrest during their Attendance at the Session of their respective Houses, and in going to and returning from the same; and for any Speech or Debate in either House, they shall not be questioned in any other Place.

No Senator or Representative shall, during the Time for which he was elected, be appointed to any civil Office under the Authority of the United States, which shall have been created, or the Emoluments whereof shall have been encreased during such time; and no Person holding any Office under the United States, shall be a Member of either House during his Continuance in Office.

SECTION. 7. All Bills for raising Revenue shall originate in the House of Representatives; but the Senate may propose or concur with amendments as on other Bills.

Every Bill which shall have passed the House of Representatives and the Senate, shall, before it become a Law, be presented to the President of the United States; If he approve he shall sign it, but if not he shall return it, with his Objections to that House in which it shall have originated, who shall enter the Objections at large on their Journal, and proceed to reconsider it. If after such Reconsideration two thirds of that House shall agree to pass the Bill, it shall be sent, together with the Objections, to the other House, by which it shall likewise be reconsidered, and if approved by two thirds of that House, it shall become a Law. But in all such Cases the Votes of both Houses shall be determined by Yeas and Nays, and the Names of the Persons voting for and against the Bill shall be entered on the Journal of each House respectively. If any Bill shall not be returned by the President within ten Days (Sundays excepted) after it shall have been presented to him, the Same shall be a Law, in like Manner as if he had signed it, unless the Congress by their Adjournment prevent its Return, in which Case it shall not be a Law.

Every Order, Resolution, or Vote to which the Concurrence of the Senate and House of Representatives may be necessary (except on a question of Adjournment) shall be presented to the President of the United States; and before the Same shall take Effect, shall be approved by him, or being disapproved by him, shall be repassed by two thirds of the Senate and House of Representatives, according to the Rules and Limitations prescribed in the Case of a Bill.

SECTION. 8. The Congress shall have Power To lay and collect Taxes, Duties, Imposts and Excises, to pay the Debts and provide for the common Defence and general Welfare of the United States; but all Duties, Imposts and Excises shall be uniform throughout the United States;

To borrow Money on the credit of the United States;

To regulate Commerce with foreign Nations, and among the several States, and with the Indian Tribes;

To establish an uniform Rule of Naturalization, and uniform Laws on the subject of Bankruptcies throughout the United States;

To coin Money, regulate the Value thereof, and of foreign Coin, and fix the Standard of Weights and Measures;

To provide for the Punishment of counterfeiting the Securities and current Coin of the United States;

To establish Post Offices and post Roads;

To promote the Progress of Science and useful Arts, by securing for limited Times to Authors and Inventors the exclusive Right to their respective Writings and Discoveries;

To constitute Tribunals inferior to the supreme Court;

To define and punish Piracies and Felonies committed on the high Seas, and Offences against the Law of Nations;

To declare War, grant Letters of Marque and Reprisal, and make Rules concerning Captures on Land and Water;

To raise and support Armies, but no Appropriation of Money to that Use shall be for a longer Term than two Years;

To provide and maintain a Navy;

To make Rules for the Government and Regulation of the land and naval Forces;

To provide for calling forth the Militia to execute the Laws of the Union, suppress Insurrections and repel Invasions;

To provide for organizing, arming, and disciplining, the Militia, and for governing such Part of them as may be employed in the Service of the United States, reserving to the States respectively, the Appointment of the Officers, and the Authority of training the Militia according to the discipline prescribed by Congress;

To exercise exclusive Legislation in all Cases whatsoever, over such District (not exceeding ten Miles square) as may, by Cession of Particular States, and the Acceptance of Congress, become the Seat of the Government of the United States, and to exercise like Authority over all Places purchased by the Consent of the Legislature of the State in which the Same shall be, for the Erection of Forts, Magazines, Arsenals, dock-Yards, and other needful Buildings;—And

To make all Laws which shall be necessary and proper for carrying into Execution the foregoing Powers, and all other Powers vested by this Constitution in the Government of the United States, or in any Department or Officer thereof.

SECTION. 9. The Migration or Importation of such Persons as any of the States now existing shall think proper to admit, shall not be prohibited by the Congress prior to the Year one thousand eight hundred and eight, but a Tax or duty may be imposed on such Importation, not exceeding ten dollars for each Person.

The Privilege of the Writ of Habeas Corpus shall not be suspended, unless when in Cases of Rebellion or Invasion the public Safety may require it.

No Bill of Attainder or ex post facto Law shall be passed.

No Capitation, or other direct, Tax shall be laid, unless in Proportion to the Census or Enumeration herein before directed to be taken.

No Tax or Duty shall be laid on Articles exported from any State.

No Preference shall be given by any Regulation or Commerce or Revenue to the Ports of one State over those of another; nor shall Vessels bound to, or from, one State, be obliged to enter, clear or pay Duties in another.

No Money shall be drawn from the Treasury, but in Consequence of Appropriations made by Law; and a regular Statement and Account of the Receipts and Expenditures of all public Money shall be published from time to time.

No Title of Nobility shall be granted by the United States: And no Person holding any Office of Profit or Trust under them, shall, without the Consent of the Congress, accept of any present Emolument, Office, or Title, of any kind whatever, from any King, Prince, or foreign State.

SECTION. 10. No State shall enter into any Treaty, Alliance, or Confederation; grant Letters of Marque and Reprisal; coin Money; emit Bills of Credit; make any Thing but gold and silver Coin a Tender in Payment of Debts; pass any Bill of Attainder, ex post facto Law, or Law impairing the Obligation of Contracts, or grant any Title of Nobility.

No State shall, without the Consent of the Congress, lay any Imposts or Duties on Imports or Exports, except what may be absolutely necessary for executing its inspection Laws: and the net Produce of all Duties and Imposts, laid by any State on Imports or Exports, shall be for the Use of the Treasury of the United States; and all such Laws shall be subject to the Revision and Controul of the Congress.

No state shall, without the Consent of Congress, lay any Duty of Tonnage, keep Troops, or Ships of War in time of Peace, enter into any Agreement or Compact with another State, or with a foreign Power, or engage in War, unless actually invaded, or in such imminent Danger as will not admit of delay.

Article. II.

SECTION. 1. The executive Power shall be vested in a President of the United States of America. He shall hold his Office during the Term of four Years, and, together with the Vice President, chosen for the same Term, be elected as follows.

Each State shall appoint, in such Manner as the Legislature thereof may direct, a Number of Electors, equal to the whole Number of Senators and Representatives to which the State may be entitled in the Congress: but no Senator or Representative, or Person holding an Office of Trust or Profit under the United States, shall be appointed an Elector.

The Electors shall meet in their respective States, and vote by Ballot for two Persons, of whom one at least shall not be an Inhabitant of the same State with themselves. And they shall make a List of all the persons voted for, and of the Number of Votes for each; which List they shall sign and certify, and transmit sealed to the Seat of Government of the United States, directed to the President of the Senate. The President of the Senate shall, in the Presence of the Senate and House of Representatives, open all the Certificates, and the Votes shall then be counted. The Person having the greatest Number of Votes shall be the President, if such Number be a Majority of the whole Number of Electors appointed; and if there be more than one who have such Majority, and have an equal Number of Votes, then the House of Representatives shall immediately chuse by Ballot one of them for President; and if no Person have a Majority, then from the five highest on the List the said House shall in like Manner chuse the President. But in chusing the President,

the Votes shall be taken by States, the Representation from each State having one Vote; a quorum for this Purpose shall consist of a Member or Members from two thirds of the States, and a Majority of all the States shall be necessary to a Choice. In every Case, after the Choice of the President, the Person having the greatest Number of Votes of the Electors shall be the Vice President. But if there should remain two or more who have equal Votes, the Senate shall chuse from them by Ballot the Vice President.

The Congress may determine the Time of chusing the Electors, and the Day on which they shall give their Votes; which Day shall be the same throughout the United States.

No Person except a natural born Citizen, or a Citizen of the United States, at the time of the Adoption of this Constitution, shall be eligible to the Office of President; neither shall any person be eligible to that Office who shall not have attained to the Age of thirty five Years, and been fourteen Years a Resident within the United States.

In Case of the Removal of the President from Office, or of his Death, Resignation, or Inability to discharge the Powers and Duties of the said Office, the Same shall devolve on the Vice President, and the Congress may by Law provide for the Case of Removal, Death, Resignation or Inability, both of the President and Vice President, declaring what Officer shall then act as President, and such Officer shall act accordingly, until the Disability be removed, or a President shall be elected.

The President shall, at stated Times, receive for his Services, a Compensation, which shall neither be encreased nor diminished during the Period for which he shall have been elected, and he shall not receive within that period any other Emolument from the United States, or any of them.

Before he enter on the Execution of his Office, he shall take the following Oath or Affirmation:—"I do solemnly swear (or affirm) that I will faithfully execute the Office of President of the United States, and will to the best of my Ability, preserve, protect and defend the Constitution of the United States."

SECTION. 2. The President shall be Commander in Chief of the Army and Navy of the United States, and of the Militia of the several States, when called into the actual Service of the United States; he may require the Opinion, in writing, of the principal Officer in each of the executive Departments, upon any Subject relating to the Duties of their respective Offices, and he shall have Power to grant Reprieves and Pardons for Offences against the United States, except in Cases of Impeachment.

He shall have Power, by and with the Advice and Consent of the Senate, to make Treaties, provided two thirds of the Senators present concur; and he shall nominate, and by and with the Advice and Consent of the Senate, shall appoint Ambassadors, other public Ministers and Consuls, Judges of the supreme Court, and all other Officers of the United States, whose Appointments are not herein otherwise provided for, and which shall be established by Law: but the Congress may by Law vest the Appointment of such inferior Officers, as they think proper, in the President alone, in the Courts of Law, or in the Heads of Departments.

The President shall have Power to fill up all Vacancies that may happen during the Recess of the Senate, by granting

Commissions which shall expire at the End of their next Session.

SECTION. 3. He shall from time to time give to the Congress Information of the State of the Union, and recommend to their Consideration such Measures as he shall judge necessary and expedient; he may, on extraordinary Occasions, convene both Houses, or either of them, and in Case of Disagreement between them, with Respect to the Time of Adjournment, he may adjourn them to such Time as he shall think proper; he shall receive Ambassadors and other public Ministers; he shall take Care that the Laws be faithfully executed, and shall Commission all the Officers of the United States.

SECTION. 4. The President, Vice President and all civil Officers of the United States, shall be removed from Office on Impeachment for, and Conviction of, Treason, Bribery, or other high Crimes and Misdemeanors.

Article. III.

SECTION. 1. The judicial Power of the United States, shall be vested in one supreme Court, and in such inferior Courts as the Congress may from time to time ordain and establish. The Judges, both of the supreme and inferior Courts, shall hold their Offices during good Behaviour, and shall, at stated Times, receive for their Services, a Compensation, which shall not be diminished during their Continuance in Office.

SECTION. 2. The judicial Power shall extend to all Cases, in Law and Equity, arising under this Constitution, the Laws of the United States, and Treaties made, or which shall be made, under their Authority;—to all Cases affecting Ambassadors, other public Ministers and Consuls;—to all Cases of admiralty and maritime Jurisdiction;—to Controversies to which the United States shall be a Party;—to Controversies between two or more States;—between a State and Citizens of another State;—between Citizens of different States;—between Citizens of the same State claiming Lands under Grants of different States, and between a State, or the Citizens thereof, and foreign States, Citizens or Subjects.

In all Cases affecting Ambassadors, other public Ministers and Consuls, and those in which a State shall be Party, the supreme Court shall have original Jurisdiction. In all the other Cases before mentioned, the supreme Court shall have appellate Jurisdiction, both as to Law and Fact, with such Exceptions, and under such Regulations as the Congress shall make.

The Trial of all Crimes, except in Cases of Impeachment, shall be by Jury; and such Trial shall be held in the State where the said Crimes shall have been committed; but when not committed within any State, the Trial shall be at such Place or Places as the Congress may by Law have directed.

SECTION. 3. Treason against the United States, shall consist only in levying War against them, or in adhering to their Enemies, giving them Aid and Comfort. No Person shall be convicted of Treason unless on the Testimony of two Witnesses to the same overt Act, or on Confession in open Court.

The Congress shall have Power to declare the Punishment of Treason, but no Attainder of Treason shall work Corruption of Blood, or Forfeiture except during the Life of the Person attained.

Article. IV.

SECTION. 1. Full Faith and Credit shall be given in each State to the public Acts, Records, and judicial Proceedings of every other State. And the Congress may by general Laws prescribe the Manner in which such Acts, Record and Proceedings shall be proved, and the Effect thereof.

SECTION. 2. The Citizens of each State shall be entitled to all Privileges and Immunities of Citizens in the several States.

A Person charged in any State with Treason, Felony, or other Crime, who shall flee from Justice, and be found in another State, shall on Demand of the executive Authority of the State from which he fled, be delivered up, to be removed to the State having Jurisdiction of the Crime.

No Person held to Service or Labour in one State, under the Laws thereof, escaping into another, shall, in Consequence of any Law or Regulation therein, be discharged from such Service or Labour, but shall be delivered up on Claim of the Party to whom such Service or Labour may be due.

SECTION. 3. New States may be admitted by the Congress into this Union; but no new State shall be formed or erected within the Jurisdiction of any other State; nor any State be formed by the Junction of two or more States, or Parts of States, without the Consent of the Legislatures of the States concerned as well as of the Congress.

The Congress shall have Power to dispose of and make all needful Rules and Regulations respecting the Territory or other Property belonging to the United States; and nothing in this Constitution shall be so construed as to Prejudice any Claims of the United States, or of any particular State.

SECTION. 4. The United States shall guarantee to every State in this Union a Republican Form of Government, and shall protect each of them against Invasion; and on Application of the Legislature, or of the Executive (when the Legislature cannot be convened) against domestic Violence.

Article. V.

The Congress, whenever two thirds of both Houses shall deem it necessary, shall propose Amendments to this Constitution, or, on the Application of the Legislature of two thirds of the several States, shall call a Convention for proposing Amendments, which, in either Case, shall be valid to all Intents and Purposes, as Part of this Constitution, when ratified by the Legislatures of three fourths of the several States, or by Conventions in three fourths thereof, as the one or the other Mode of Ratification may be proposed by the Congress; Provided that no Amendment which may be made prior to the Year One thousand eight hundred and eight shall in any Manner affect the first and fourth Clauses in the Ninth Section of the first Article; and that no State, without its Consent, shall be deprived of its equal Suffrage in the Senate.

Article. VI.

All Debts contracted and Engagements entered into, before the Adoption of this Constitution, shall be as valid against the United States under this Constitution, as under the Confederation.

This Constitution, and the Laws of the United States which shall be made in Pursuance thereof; and all Treaties made, or which shall be made, under the Authority of the United States, shall be the supreme Law of the Land; and the Judges in every State shall be bound thereby, any Thing in the Constitution or Laws of any State to the Contrary notwithstanding.

The Senators and Representatives before mentioned, and the Members of the several State Legislatures, and all executive and judicial Officers, both of the United States and of the several States, shall be bound by Oath or Affirmation, to support this Constitution; but no religious Test shall ever be required as a Qualification to any Office or public Trust under the United States.

New Hampshire	JOHN LANGDON
	NICHOLAS GILMAN
Massachusetts	NATHANIEL GORHAM
	RUFUS KING
Connecticut	Wm. SAML JOHNSON
	ROGER SHERMAN
New York . . .	ALEXANDER HAMILTON
New Jersey	WIL: LIVINGSTON
	DAVID BREARLEY
	Wm. PATERSON
	JONA: DAYTON
Pennsylvania	B FRANKLIN
	THOMAS MIFFLIN
	ROBt MORRIS
	GEO. CLYMER
	THOs. FITZSIMONS
	JARED INGERSOLL
	JAMES WILSON
	GOUV MORRIS
Delaware	GEO: READ
	GUNNING BEDFORD jun
	JOHN DICKINSON
	RICHARD BASSETT
	JACO: BROOM
Maryland	JAMES McHENRY
	DAN OF St THOs. JENIFER
	DANL CARROLL
Virginia	JOHN BLAIR
	JAMES MADISON Jr.
North Carolina	Wm. BLOUNT
	RICHd. DOBBS SPAIGHT
	HU WILLIAMSON
South Carolina	J. RUTLEDGE
	CHARLES COTESWORTH PINCKNEY
	CHARLES PINCKNEY
	PIERCE BUTLER
Georgia	WILLIAM FEW
	ABR BALDWIN

Article. VII.

The Ratification of the Conventions of nine States, shall be sufficient for the Establishment of this Constitution between the States so ratifying the Same.

Done in Convention by the Unanimous Consent of the States present the Seventeenth Day of September in the Year of our Lord one thousand seven hundred and Eighty seven and of the Independence of the United States of America the Twelfth In witness whereof We have hereunto subscribed our Names,

Go. WASHINGTON—Presidt. and deputy from Virginia
In Convention Monday, September 17th 1787.

Present The States of

New Hampshire, Massachusetts, Connecticut, Mr. Hamilton from New York, New Jersey, Pennsylvania, Delaware, Maryland, Virginia, North Carolina and Georgia.

Resolved,

That the preceeding Constitution be laid before the United States in Congress assembled, and that it is the Opinion of this Convention, that it should afterwards be submitted to a Convention of Delegates, chosen in each State by the People thereof, under the Recommendation of its Legislature, for their Assent and Ratification; and that each Convention assenting to, and ratifying the Same, should give Notice thereof to the United States in Congress assembled. Resolved, That it is the Opinion of this Convention, that as soon as the Conventions of nine States shall have ratified this Constitution, the United States in Congress assembled should fix a Day on which Electors should be appointed by the States which shall have ratified the same, and a Day on which the Electors should assemble to vote for the President, and the Time and Place for commencing Proceedings under this Constitution. That after such Publication the Electors should be appointed, and the Senators and Representatives elected: That the Electors should meet on the Day fixed for the Election of the President, and should transmit their Votes certified, signed, sealed and directed, as the Constitution requires, to the Secretary of the United States in Congress assembled, that

Ratification of the Constitution

State	Date of Ratification
Delaware	Dec 7, 1787
Pennsylvania	Dec 12, 1787
New Jersey	Dec 19, 1787
Georgia	Jan 2, 1788
Connecticut	Jan 9, 1788
Massachusetts	Feb 6, 1788
Maryland	Apr 28, 1788
South Carolina	May 23, 1788
New Hampshire	June 21, 1788
Virginia	Jun 25, 1788
New York	Jun 26, 1788
Rhode Island	May 29, 1790
North Carolina	Nov 21, 1789

the Senators and Representatives should convene at the Time and Place assigned; that the Senators should appoint a President of the Senate, for the sole Purpose of receiving, opening and counting the Votes for President; and, that after he shall be chosen, the Congress, together with the President, should, without Delay, proceed to execute this Constitution.

By the Unanimous Order of the Convention
Go. WASHINGTON—Presidt.
W. JACKSON Secretary.

ARTICLES IN ADDITION TO, AND AMENDMENT OF, THE CONSTITUTION OF THE UNITED STATES OF AMERICA, PROPOSED BY CONGRESS, AND RATIFIED BY THE SEVERAL STATES, PURSUANT TO THE FIFTH ARTICLE OF THE ORIGINAL CONSTITUTION.

Amendment I.

Congress shall make no law respecting an establishment of religion, or prohibiting the free exercise thereof; or abridging the freedom of speech, or of the press; or the right of the people peaceably to assemble, and to petition the Government for a redress of grievances.

Amendment II.

A well regulated Militia, being necessary to the security of a free State, the right of the people to keep and bear Arms, shall not be infringed.

Amendment III.

No Soldier shall, in time of peace be quartered in any house, without the consent of the Owner, nor in time of war, but in a manner to be prescribed by law.

Amendment IV.

The right of the people to be secure in their persons, houses, papers, and effects, against unreasonable searches and seizures, shall not be violated, and no Warrants shall issue, but upon probable cause, supported by Oath or affirmation, and particularly describing the place to be searched, and the persons or things to be seized.

Amendment V.

No person shall be held to answer for a capital, or otherwise infamous crime, unless on a presentment or indictment of a Grand Jury, except in cases arising in the land or naval forces, or in the Militia, when in actual service in time of War or public danger; nor shall any person be subject for the same offence to be twice put in jeopardy of life or limb; nor shall be compelled in any criminal case to be a witness against himself, nor

be deprived of life, liberty, or property, without due process of law; nor shall private property be taken for public use, without just compensation.

Amendment VI.

In all criminal prosecutions, the accused shall enjoy the right to a speedy and public trial, by an impartial jury of the State and district wherein the crime shall have been committed, which district shall have been previously ascertained by law, and to be informed of the nature and cause of the accusation; to be confronted with the witnesses against him; to have compulsory process for obtaining witnesses in his favor, and to have the Assistance of Counsel for his defence.

Amendment VII.

In Suits at common law, where the value in controversy shall exceed twenty dollars, the right of trial by jury shall be preserved, and no fact tried by a jury, shall be otherwise re-examined in any Court of the United States, than according to the rules of the common law.

Amendment VIII.

Excessive bail shall not be required, nor excessive fines imposed, nor cruel and unusual punishments inflicted.

Amendment IX.

The enumeration in the Constitution, of certain rights, shall not be construed to deny or disparage others retained by the people.

Amendment X.

The powers not delegated to the United States by the Constitution, nor prohibited by it to the States, are reserved to the States respectively, or to the people.

Amendment XI.

(Adopted Jan. 8, 1798)

The Judicial power of the United States shall not be construed to extend to any suit in law or equity, commenced or prosecuted against one of the United States by Citizens of another State, or by Citizens or Subjects of any Foreign State.

Amendment XII.

(Adopted Sept. 25, 1804)

The Electors shall meet in their respective states and vote by ballot for President and Vice-President, one of whom, at least, shall not be an inhabitant of the same state with themselves; they shall name in their ballots the person voted for as President, and in distinct ballots the person voted for as Vice-President, and they shall make distinct lists of all persons voted for as President, and of all persons voted for as Vice-President, and of the number of votes for each, which lists they shall sign and certify, and transmit sealed to the seat of the government of the United States, directed to the President of the Senate;—The President of the Senate shall, in the presence of the Senate and House of Representatives, open all the certificates and the votes shall then be counted;—The person having the greatest number of votes for President, shall be the President, if such number be a majority of the whole number of Electors appointed; and if no person have such majority, then from the persons having the highest numbers not exceeding three on the list of those voted for as President, the House of Representatives shall choose immediately, by ballot, the President. But in choosing the President, the votes shall be taken by states, the representation from each state having one vote; a quorum for this purpose shall consist of a member or members from two-thirds of the states, and a majority of all the states shall be necessary to a choice. And if the House of Representatives shall not choose a President whenever the right of choice shall devolve upon them, before the fourth day of March next following, then the Vice-President shall act as President, as in the case of the death or other constitutional disability of the President.—The person having the greatest number of votes as Vice-President, shall be the Vice-President, if such number be a majority of the whole number of Electors appointed, and if no person have a majority, then from the two highest numbers on the list, the Senate shall choose the Vice-President; a quorum for the purpose shall consist of two-thirds of the whole number of Senators, and a majority of the whole number shall be necessary to a choice. But no person constitutionally ineligible to the office of President shall be eligible to that of Vice-President of the United States.

Amendment XIII.

(Adopted Dec. 18, 1865)

SECTION 1. Neither slavery nor involuntary servitude, except as a punishment for crime whereof the party shall have been duly convicted, shall exist within the United States, or any place subject to their jurisdiction.

SECTION 2. Congress shall have power to enforce this article by appropriate legislation.

Amendment XIV.

(Adopted July 28, 1868)

SECTION 1. All persons born or naturalized in the United States and subject to the jurisdiction thereof, are citizens of the United States and of the State wherein they reside. No State shall make or enforce any law which shall abridge the privileges or immunities of citizens of the United States; nor shall any State deprive any person of life, liberty, or property, without due process of law; nor deny to any person within its jurisdiction the equal protection of the laws.

SECTION 2. Representatives shall be apportioned among the several States according to their respective numbers, counting the whole number of persons in each State, excluding Indians not taxed. But when the right to vote at any election for the choice of electors for President and Vice President of the United States, Representatives in Congress, the Executive and Judicial officers of a State, or the members of the Legislature thereof, is denied to any of the male inhabitants of such State, being twenty-one years of age, and citizens of the United States, or in any way abridged, except for participation in rebellion, or other crime, the basis of representation therein shall be reduced in the proportion which the number of such male citizens shall bear to the whole number of male citizens twenty-one years of age in such State.

SECTION 3. No person shall be a Senator or Representative in Congress, or elector of President and Vice President, or hold any office, civil or military, under the United States, or under any State, who, having previously taken an oath, as a member of Congress, or as an officer of the United States, or as a member of any State legislature, or as an executive or judicial officer of any State, to support the Constitution of the United States, shall have engaged in insurrection or rebellion against the same, or given aid or comfort to the enemies thereof. But Congress may by a vote of two-thirds of each House, remove such disability.

SECTION 4. The validity of the public debt of the United States, authorized by law, including debts incurred for payment of pensions and bounties for services in suppressing insurrection or rebellion, shall not be questioned. But neither the United States nor any State shall assume or pay any debt or obligation incurred in aid of insurrection or rebellion against the United States, or any claim for the loss or emancipation of any slave; but all such debts, obligations and claims shall be held illegal and void.

SECTION 5. The Congress shall have power to enforce, by appropriate legislation, the provisions of this article.

Amendment XV.

(Adopted March 30, 1870)

SECTION 1. The right of citizens of the United States to vote shall not be denied or abridged by the United States or by any State on account of race, color, or previous condition of servitude.

SECTION 2. The Congress shall have power to enforce this article by appropriate legislation.

Amendment XVI.

(Adopted Feb. 25, 1913)

The Congress shall have power to lay and collect taxes on incomes, from whatever source derived, without apportionment among the several States, and without regard to any census or enumeration.

Amendment XVII.

(Adopted May 31, 1913)

The Senate of the United States shall be composed of two Senators from each State, elected by the people thereof, for six years; and each Senator shall have one vote. The electors in each State shall have the qualifications requisite for electors of the most numerous branch of the State legislatures.

When vacancies happen in the representation of any State in the Senate, the executive authority of such State shall issue writs of election to fill such vacancies: Provided, That the legislature of any State may empower the executive thereof to make temporary appointments until the people fill the vacancies by election as the legislature may direct.

This amendment shall not be so construed as to affect the election or term of any Senator chosen before it becomes valid as part of the Constitution.

Amendment XVIII.

(Adopted Jan. 29, 1919)

SECTION 1. After one year from the ratification of this article the manufacture, sale or transportation of intoxicating liquors within, the importation thereof into, or the exportation thereof from the United States and all territory subject to the jurisdiction thereof for beverage purposes is hereby prohibited.

SECTION 2. The Congress and the several States shall have concurrent power to enforce this article by appropriate legislation.

SECTION 3. This article shall be inoperative unless it shall have been ratified as an amendment to the Constitution by the legislatures of the several States, as provided in the Constitution, within seven years from the date of the submission hereof to the States by the Congress.

Amendment XIX.

(Adopted Aug. 26, 1920)

The right of citizens of the United States to vote shall not be denied or abridged by the United States or by any State on account of sex.

Congress shall have power to enforce this article by appropriate legislation.

Amendment XX.

(Adopted Feb. 6, 1933)

SECTION 1. The terms of the President and Vice President shall end at noon on the 20th day of January, and the terms of Senators and Representatives at noon on the 3d day of January, of the years in which such terms would have ended if this article had not been ratified; and the terms of their successors shall then begin.

SECTION 2. The Congress shall assemble at least once in every year, and such meeting shall begin at noon on the 3d day of January, unless they shall by law appoint a different day.

SECTION 3. If, at the time fixed for the beginning of the term of the President, the President elect shall have died, the Vice President elect shall become President. If a President shall not have been chosen before the time fixed for the beginning of his term, or if the President elect shall have failed to qualify, then the Vice President elect shall act as President until a President shall have qualified; and the Congress may by law provide for the case wherein neither a President elect nor a Vice President elect shall have qualified, declaring who shall then act as President, or the manner in which one who is to act shall be selected, and such person shall act accordingly until a President or Vice President shall have qualified.

SECTION 4. The Congress may by law provide for the case of the death of any of the persons from whom the House of Representatives may choose a President whenever the right of choice shall have devolved upon them, and for the case of the death of any of the persons from whom the Senate may choose a Vice President whenever the right of choice shall have devolved upon them.

SECTION 5. Sections 1 and 2 shall take effect on the 15th day of October following the ratification of this article.

SECTION 6. This article shall be inoperative unless it shall have been ratified as an amendment to the Constitution by the legislatures of three-fourths of the several States within seven years from the date of its submission.

Amendment XXI.

(Adopted Dec. 5, 1933)

SECTION 1. The eighteenth article of amendment to the Constitution of the United States is hereby repealed.

SECTION 2. The transportation or importation into any State, Territory, or possession of the United States for delivery or use therein of intoxicating liquors, in violation of the laws thereof, is hereby prohibited.

SECTION 3. This article shall be inoperative unless it shall have been ratified as an amendment to the Constitution by conventions in the several States, as provided in the Constitution, within seven years from the date of the submission hereof to the States by the Congress.

Amendment XXII.

(Adopted Feb. 27, 1951)

SECTION 1. No person shall be elected to the office of the President more than twice, and no person who has held the office of President, or acted as President, for more than two years of a term to which some other person was elected President shall be elected to the office of the President more than once. But this Article shall not apply to any person holding the office of President when this Article was proposed by the Congress, and shall not prevent any person who may be holding the office of President, or acting as President, during the term within which this Article becomes operative from holding the office of President or acting as President during the remainder of such term.

SECTION 2. This Article shall be inoperative unless it shall have been ratified as an amendment to the Constitution by the legislatures of three-fourths of the several States within seven years from the date of its submission to the States by the Congress.

Amendment XXIII.

(Adopted Mar. 29, 1961)

SECTION 1. The District constituting the seat of Government of the United States shall appoint in such manner as the Congress may direct:

A number of electors of President and Vice President equal to the whole number of Senators and Representatives in Congress to which the District would be entitled if it were a State, but in no event more than the least populous State; they shall be in addition to those appointed by the States, but they shall be considered, for the purposes of the election of President and Vice President, to be electors appointed by a State; and they shall meet in the District and perform such duties as provided by the twelfth article of amendment.

SECTION 2. The Congress shall have power to enforce this article by appropriate legislation.

Amendment XXIV.

(Adopted Jan. 23, 1964)

SECTION 1. The right of citizens of the United States to vote in any primary or other election for President or Vice President, for electors for President or Vice President, or for Senator or Representative in Congress, shall not be denied or abridged by the United States or any State by reason of failure to pay any poll tax or other tax.

SECTION 2. The Congress shall have the power to enforce this article by appropriate legislation.

Amendment XXV.

(Adopted Feb. 10, 1967)

SECTION 1. In case of the removal of the President from office or of his death or resignation, the Vice President shall become President.

SECTION 2. Whenever there is a vacancy in the office of the Vice President, the President shall nominate a Vice President who shall take the office upon confirmation by a majority vote of both houses of Congress.

SECTION 3. Whenever the President transmits to the President pro tempore of the Senate and the Speaker of the House of Representatives his written declaration that he is unable to discharge the powers and duties of his office, and until he transmits to them a written declaration to the contrary, such powers and duties shall be discharged by the Vice President as Acting President.

SECTION 4. Whenever the Vice President and a majority of either the principal officers of the executive departments or

of such other body as Congress may by law provide, transmit to the President pro tempore of the Senate and the Speaker of the House of Representatives their written declaration that the President is unable to discharge the powers and duties of his office, the Vice President shall immediately assume the powers and duties of the office as Acting President.

Thereafter, when the President transmits to the President pro tempore of the Senate and the Speaker of the House of Representatives his written declaration that no inability exists, he shall resume the powers and duties of his office unless the Vice President and a majority of either the principal officers of the executive department or of such other body as Congress may by law provide, transmit within four days to the President pro tempore of the Senate and the Speaker of the House of Representatives their written declaration that the President is unable to discharge the powers and duties of his office. Thereupon Congress shall decide the issue, assembling within forty-eight hours for that purpose if not in session. If the Congress within twenty-one days after receipt of the latter written declaration, or, if Congress is not in session, within twenty-one days after Congress is required to assemble, determines by two-thirds vote of both Houses that the President is unable to discharge the powers and duties of his office, the Vice President shall continue to discharge the same as Acting President; otherwise, the President shall resume the powers and duties of his office.

Amendment XXVI.

(Adopted June 30, 1971)

SECTION 1. The right of citizens of the United States, who are 18 years of age or older, to vote shall not be denied or abridged by the United States or by any state on account of age.

SECTION 2. The Congress shall have the power to enforce this article by appropriate legislation.

Amendment XXVII.

(Adopted May 7, 1992)

No law, varying the compensation for the services of the Senators and Representatives, shall take effect, until an election of Representatives shall have intervened.

Critical Thinking

1. What is concept of supreme law, and how does it apply to the Constitution?

2. Name the three main branches of government as outlined in the Constitution, and explain how they relate to one another under the concept of separation of powers.

3. What is the federalist system? What powers do individual states retain under the federalist system, if any?

4. What is the Bill of Rights? What are some of the key protections it offers?

Federalist No. 10

JAMES MADISON

To the People of the State of New York

Among the numerous advantages promised by a well-constructed Union, none deserves to be more accurately developed than its tendency to break and control the violence of faction. The friend of popular governments never finds himself so much alarmed for their character and fate, as when he contemplates their propensity to this dangerous vice. He will not fail, therefore, to set a due value on any plan which, without violating the principles to which he is attached, provides a proper cure for it. The instability, injustice, and confusion introduced into the public councils, have, in truth, been the mortal diseases under which popular governments have everywhere perished; as they continue to be the favorite and fruitful topics from which the adversaries to liberty derive their most specious declamations. The valuable improvements made by the American constitutions on the popular models, both ancient and modern, cannot certainly be too much admired; but it would be an unwarrantable partiality, to contend that they have as effectually obviated the danger on this side, as was wished and expected. Complaints are everywhere heard from our most considerate and virtuous citizens, equally the friends of public and private faith, and of public and personal liberty, that our governments are too unstable, that the public good is disregarded in the conflicts of rival parties, and that measures are too often decided, not according to the rules of justice and the rights of the minor party, but by the superior force of an interested and overbearing majority. However anxiously we may wish that these complaints had no foundation, the evidence of known facts will not permit us to deny that they are in some degree true. It will be found, indeed, on a candid review of our situation, that some of the distresses under which we labor have been erroneously charged on the operation of our governments; but it will be found, at the same time, that other causes will not alone account for many of our heaviest misfortunes; and, particularly, for that prevailing and increasing distrust of public engagements, and alarm for private rights, which are echoed from one end of the continent to the other. These must be chiefly, if not wholly, effects of the unsteadiness and injustice with which a factious spirit has tainted our public administrations.

By a faction, I understand a number of citizens, whether amounting to a majority or minority of the whole, who are united and actuated by some common impulse of passion, or of interest, adverse to the rights of other citizens, or to the permanent and aggregate interests of the community.

There are two methods of curing the mischiefs of faction: the one, by removing its causes; the other, by controlling its effects.

There are again two methods of removing the causes of faction: the one, by destroying the liberty which is essential to its existence; the other, by giving to every citizen the same opinions, the same passions, and the same interests.

It could never be more truly said than of the first remedy, that it was worse than the disease. Liberty is to faction what air is to fire, an aliment without which it instantly expires. But it could not be less folly to abolish liberty, which is essential to political life, because it nourishes faction, than it would be to wish the annihilation of air, which is essential to animal life, because it imparts to fire its destructive agency.

The second expedient is as impracticable as the first would be unwise. As long as the reason of man continues fallible, and he is at liberty to exercise it, different opinions will be formed. As long as the connection subsists between his reason and his self-love, his opinions and his passions will have a reciprocal influence on each other; and the former will be objects to which the latter will attach themselves. The diversity in the faculties of men, from which the rights of property originate, is not less an insuperable obstacle to a uniformity of interests. The protection of these faculties is the first object of government. From the protection of different and unequal faculties of acquiring property, the possession of different degrees and kinds of property immediately results; and from the influence of these on the sentiments and views of the respective proprietors, ensues a division of the society into different interests and parties.

The latent causes of faction are thus sown in the nature of man; and we see them everywhere brought into different degrees of activity, according to the different circumstances of civil society. A zeal for different opinions concerning religion, concerning government, and many other points, as well of speculation as of practice; an attachment to different leaders ambitiously contending for pre-eminence and power; or to persons of other descriptions whose fortunes have been interesting to the human passions, have, in turn, divided mankind into parties, inflamed them with mutual animosity, and rendered them much more disposed to vex and oppress each other than to co-operate for their common good. So strong is this propensity of mankind to fall into mutual animosities, that where no substantial occasion presents itself, the most frivolous and fanciful distinctions have been sufficient to kindle their unfriendly passions and excite their most violent conflicts. But the most common and durable source of factions has been the various and unequal distribution of property. Those who hold and those who are without property have ever formed distinct interests in society.

Those who are creditors, and those who are debtors, fall under a like discrimination. A landed interest, a manufacturing interest, a mercantile interest, a moneyed interest, with many lesser interests, grow up of necessity in civilized nations, and divide them into different classes, actuated by different sentiments and views. The regulation of these various and interfering interests forms the principal task of modern legislation, and involves the spirit of party and faction in the necessary and ordinary operations of the government.

No man is allowed to be a judge in his own cause, because his interest would certainly bias his judgment, and, not improbably, corrupt his integrity. With equal, nay with greater reason, a body of men are unfit to be both judges and parties at the same time; yet what are many of the most important acts of legislation, but so many judicial determinations, not indeed concerning the rights of single persons, but concerning the rights of large bodies of citizens? And what are the different classes of legislators but advocates and parties to the causes which they determine? Is a law proposed concerning private debts? It is a question to which the creditors are parties on one side and the debtors on the other. Justice ought to hold the balance between them. Yet the parties are, and must be, themselves the judges; and the most numerous party, or, in other words, the most powerful faction must be expected to prevail. Shall domestic manufactures be encouraged, and in what degree, by restrictions on foreign manufactures? are questions which would be differently decided by the landed and the manufacturing classes, and probably by neither with a sole regard to justice and the public good. The apportionment of taxes on the various descriptions of property is an act which seems to require the most exact impartiality; yet there is, perhaps, no legislative act in which greater opportunity and temptation are given to a predominant party to trample on the rules of justice. Every shilling with which they overburden the inferior number, is a shilling saved to their own pockets.

It is in vain to say that enlightened statesmen will be able to adjust these clashing interests, and render them all subservient to the public good. Enlightened statesmen will not always be at the helm. Nor, in many cases, can such an adjustment be made at all without taking into view indirect and remote considerations, which will rarely prevail over the immediate interest which one party may find in disregarding the rights of another or the good of the whole.

The inference to which we are brought is, that the *causes* of faction cannot be removed, and that relief is only to be sought in the means of controlling its *effects*.

If a faction consists of less than a majority, relief is supplied by the republican principle, which enables the majority to defeat its sinister views by regular vote. It may clog the administration, it may convulse the society; but it will be unable to execute and mask its violence under the forms of the Constitution. When a majority is included in a faction, the form of popular government, on the other hand, enables it to sacrifice to its ruling passion or interest both the public good and the rights of other citizens. To secure the public good and private rights against the danger of such a faction, and at the same time to preserve the spirit and the form of popular government, is then the great object to which our inquiries are directed. Let me add that it is the great desideratum by which this form of government can be rescued from the opprobrium under which it has so long labored, and be recommended to the esteem and adoption of mankind.

By what means is this object attainable? Evidently by one of two only. Either the existence of the same passion or interest in a majority at the same time must be prevented, or the majority, having such coexistent passion or interest, must be rendered, by their number and local situation, unable to concert and carry into effect schemes of oppression. If the impulse and the opportunity be suffered to coincide, we well know that neither moral nor religious motives can be relied on as an adequate control. They are not found to be such on the injustice and violence of individuals, and lose their efficacy in proportion to the number combined together, that is, in proportion as their efficacy becomes needful.

From this view of the subject it may be concluded that a pure democracy, by which I mean a society consisting of a small number of citizens, who assemble and administer the government in person, can admit of no cure for the mischiefs of faction. A common passion or interest will, in almost every case, be felt by a majority of the whole; a communication and concert result from the form of government itself; and there is nothing to check the inducements to sacrifice the weaker party or an obnoxious individual. Hence it is that such democracies have ever been spectacles of turbulence and contention; have ever been found incompatible with personal security or the rights of property; and have in general been as short in their lives as they have been violent in their deaths. Theoretic politicians, who have patronized this species of government, have erroneously supposed that by reducing mankind to a perfect equality in their political rights, they would, at the same time, be perfectly equalized and assimilated in their possessions, their opinions, and their passions.

A republic, by which I mean a government in which the scheme of representation takes place, opens a different prospect, and promises the cure for which we are seeking. Let us examine the points in which it varies from pure democracy, and we shall comprehend both the nature of the cure and the efficacy which it must derive from the Union.

The two great points of difference between a democracy and a republic are: first, the delegation of the government, in the latter, to a small number of citizens elected by the rest; secondly, the greater number of citizens, and greater sphere of country, over which the latter may be extended.

The effect of the first difference is, on the one hand, to refine and enlarge the public views, by passing them through the medium of a chosen body of citizens, whose wisdom may best discern the true interest of their country, and whose patriotism and love of justice will be least likely to sacrifice it to temporary or partial considerations. Under such a regulation, it may well happen that the public voice, pronounced by the representatives of the people, will be more consonant to the public good than if pronounced by the people themselves, convened for the purpose. On the other hand, the effect may be inverted. Men of factious tempers, of local prejudices, or of sinister designs, may, by intrigue, by corruption, or by other means, first obtain the suffrages, and then betray the interests, of the people. The question resulting is, whether small or extensive republics are more favorable to the election of proper guardians of the public weal; and it is clearly decided in favor of the latter by two obvious considerations.

In the first place, it is to be remarked that, however small the republic may be, the representatives must be raised to a certain number, in order to guard against the cabals of a few; and that, however large it may be, they must be limited to a certain number, in order to guard against the confusion of a multitude. Hence, the number of representatives in the two cases not being in proportion to that of the two constituents, and being proportionally greater in the small republic, it follows that, if the proportion of fit characters be not less in the large than in the small republic, the former will present a greater option, and consequently a greater probability of a fit choice.

In the next place, as each representative will be chosen by a greater number of citizens in the large than in the small republic, it will be more difficult for unworthy candidates to practise with success the vicious arts by which elections are too often carried; and the suffrages of the people being more free, will be more likely to centre in men who possess the most attractive merit and the most diffusive and established characters.

It must be confessed that in this, as in most other cases, there is a mean, on both sides of which inconveniences will be found to lie. By enlarging too much the number of electors, you render the representative too little acquainted with all their local circumstances and lesser interests; as by reducing it too much, you render him unduly attached to these, and too little fit to comprehend and pursue great and national objects. The federal Constitution forms a happy combination in this respect; the great and aggregate interests being referred to the national, the local and particular to the State legislatures.

The other point of difference is, the greater number of citizens and extent of territory which may be brought within the compass of republican than of democratic government; and it is this circumstance principally which renders factious combinations less to be dreaded in the former than in the latter. The smaller the society, the fewer probably will be the distinct parties and interests composing it; the fewer the distinct parties and interests, the more frequently will a majority be found of the same party; and the smaller the number of individuals composing a majority, and the smaller the compass within which they are placed, the more easily will they concert and execute their plans of oppression. Extend the sphere and you take in a greater variety of parties and interests; you will make it less probable that a majority of the whole will have a common motive to invade the rights of other citizens; or if such a common motive exists, it will be more difficult for all who feel it to discover their own strength, and to act in unison with each other. Besides other impediments, it may be remarked that, where there is a consciousness of unjust or dishonorable purposes, communication is always checked by distrust in proportion to the number whose concurrence is necessary.

Hence, it clearly appears, that the same advantage which a republic has over a democracy, in controlling the effects of faction, is enjoyed by a large over a small republic,—is enjoyed by the Union over the States composing it. Does the advantage consist in the substitution of representatives whose enlightened views and virtuous sentiments render them superior to local prejudices and to schemes of injustice? It will not be denied that the representation of the Union will be most likely to possess these requisite endowments. Does it consist in the greater security afforded by a greater variety of parties, against the event of any one party being able to outnumber and oppress the rest? In an equal degree does the increased variety of parties comprised within the Union, increase this security. Does it, in fine, consist in the greater obstacles opposed to the concert and accomplishment of the secret wishes of an unjust and interested majority? Here, again, the extent of the Union gives it the most palpable advantage.

The influence of factious leaders may kindle a flame within their particular States, but will be unable to spread a general conflagration through the other States. A religious sect may degenerate into a political faction in a part of the Confederacy; but the variety of sects dispersed over the entire face of it must secure the national councils against any danger from that source. A rage for paper money, for an abolition of debts, for an equal division of property, or for any other improper or wicked project, will be less apt to pervade the whole body of the Union than a particular member of it; in the same proportion as such a malady is more likely to taint a particular county or district, than an entire State.

In the extent and proper structure of the Union, therefore, we behold a republican remedy for the diseases most incident to republican government. And according to the degree of pleasure and pride we feel in being republicans, ought to be our zeal in cherishing the spirit and supporting the character of Federalists.

PUBLIUS

Critical Thinking

1. How does Madison view majority rule?
2. Can the causes of faction, or partisanship, be eliminated? Can its effects be controlled?
3. What, according to Madison, are the two key differences between a democracy and a republic?
4. What are the advantages of a republican form of government? Does Madison advocate a democratic or a republican government? Why?

From *The Federalist No. 10,* 1787.

Federalist No. 51

JAMES MADISON

To the People of the State of New York

To what expedient, then, shall we finally resort, for maintaining in practice the necessary partition of power among the several departments, as laid down in the Constitution? The only answer that can be given is, that as all these exterior provisions are found to be inadequate, the defect must be supplied, by so contriving the interior structure of the government as that its several constituent parts may, by their mutual relations, be the means of keeping each other in their proper places. Without presuming to undertake a full development of this important idea, I will hazard a few general observations, which may perhaps place it in a clearer light, and enable us to form a more correct judgment of the principles and structure of the government planned by the convention.

In order to lay a due foundation for that separate and distinct exercise of the different powers of government, which to a certain extent is admitted on all hands to be essential to the preservation of liberty, it is evident that each department should have a will of its own; and consequently should be so constituted that the members of each should have as little agency as possible in the appointment of the members of the others. Were this principle rigorously adhered to, it would require that all the appointments for the supreme executive, legislative, and judiciary magistracies should be drawn from the same fountain of authority, the people, through channels having no communication whatever with one another. Perhaps such a plan of constructing the several departments would be less difficult in practice than it may in contemplation appear. Some difficulties, however, and some additional expense would attend the execution of it. Some deviations, therefore, from the principle must be admitted. In the constitution of the judiciary department in particular, it might be inexpedient to insist rigorously on the principle: first, because peculiar qualifications being essential in the members, the primary consideration ought to be to select that mode of choice which best secures these qualifications; secondly, because the permanent tenure by which the appointments are held in that department, must soon destroy all sense of dependence on the authority conferring them.

It is equally evident, that the members of each department should be as little dependent as possible on those of the others, for the emoluments annexed to their offices. Were the executive magistrate, or the judges, not independent of the legislature in this particular, their independence in every other would be merely nominal.

But the great security against a gradual concentration of the several powers in the same department, consists in giving to those who administer each department the necessary constitutional means and personal motives to resist encroachments of the others. The provision for defence must in this, as in all other cases, be made commensurate to the danger of attack. Ambition must be made to counteract ambition. The interest of the man must be connected with the constitutional rights of the place. It may be a reflection on human nature, that such devices should be necessary to control the abuses of government. But what is government itself, but the greatest of all reflections on human nature? If men were angels, no government would be necessary. If angels were to govern men, neither external nor internal controls on government would be necessary. In framing a government which is to be administered by men over men, the great difficulty lies in this: you must first enable the government to control the governed; and in the next place oblige it to control itself. A dependence on the people is, no doubt, the primary control on the government; but experience has taught mankind the necessity of auxiliary precautions.

This policy of supplying, by opposite and rival interests, the defect of better motives, might be traced through the whole system of human affairs, private as well as public. We see it particularly displayed in all the subordinate distributions of power, where the constant aim is to divide and arrange the several offices in such a manner as that each may be a check on the other—that the private interest of every individual may be a sentinel over the public rights. These inventions of prudence cannot be less requisite in the distribution of the supreme powers of the State.

But it is not possible to give to each department an equal power of self-defence. In republican government, the legislative authority necessarily predominates. The remedy for this inconveniency is to divide the legislature into different branches; and to render them, by different modes of election and different principles of action, as little connected with each other as the nature of their common functions and their common dependence on the society will admit. It may even be necessary to guard against dangerous encroachments by still further precautions. As the weight of the legislative authority requires that it should be thus divided, the weakness of the executive may require, on the other hand, that it should be fortified. An absolute negative on the legislature appears, at first view, to be the natural defence with which the executive magistrate should be armed. But perhaps it would be neither altogether safe nor alone sufficient. On ordinary occasions it might not be exerted with the requisite firmness, and on extraordinary occasions it might be perfidiously abused. May not this defect of an absolute negative be supplied by some qualified connection between this weaker department and the weaker branch of the stronger department, by which the latter may be led to support the constitutional rights of the former, without being too much detached from the rights of its own department?

If the principles on which these observations are founded be just, as I persuade myself they are, and they be applied as a criterion to the several State constitutions, and to the federal Constitution, it will be found that if the latter does not perfectly correspond with them, the former are infinitely less able to bear such a test.

There are, moreover, two considerations particularly applicable to the federal system of America, which place that system in a very interesting point of view.

First. In a single republic, all the power surrendered by the people is submitted to the administration of a single government; and the usurpations are guarded against by a division of the government into distinct and separate departments. In the compound republic of America, the power surrendered by the people is first divided between two distinct governments, and then the portion allotted to each subdivided among distinct and separate departments. Hence a double security arises to the rights of the people. The different governments will control each other, at the same time that each will be controlled by itself.

Second. It is of great importance in a republic not only to guard the society against the oppression of its rulers, but to guard one part of the society against the injustice of the other part. Different interests necessarily exist in different classes of citizens. If a majority be united by a common interest, the rights of the minority will be insecure. There are but two methods of providing against this evil: the one by creating a will in the community independent of the majority—that is, of the society itself; the other, by comprehending in the society so many separate descriptions of citizens as will render an unjust combination of a majority of the whole very improbable, if not impracticable. The first method prevails in all governments possessing an hereditary or self-appointed authority. This, at best, is but a precarious security; because a power independent of the society may as well espouse the unjust views of the major, as the rightful interests of the minor party, and may possibly be turned against both parties. The second method will be exemplified in the federal republic of the United States. Whilst all authority in it will be derived from and dependent on the society, the society itself will be broken into so many parts, interests and classes of citizens, that the rights of individuals, or of the minority, will be in little danger from interested combinations of the majority. In a free government the security for civil rights must be the same as that for religious rights. It consists in the one case in the multiplicity of interests, and in the other in the multiplicity of sects. The degree of security in both cases will depend on the number of interests and sects; and this may be presumed to depend on the extent of country and number of people comprehended under the same

government. This view of the subject must particularly recommend a proper federal system to all the sincere and considerate friends of republican government, since it shows that in exact proportion as the territory of the Union may be formed into more circumscribed Confederacies, or States, oppressive combinations of a majority will be facilitated; the best security, under the republican forms, for the rights of every class of citizens, will be diminished; and consequently the stability and independence of some member of the government, the only other security, must be proportionally increased. Justice is the end of government. It is the end of civil society. It ever has been and ever will be pursued until it be obtained, or until liberty be lost in the pursuit. In a society under the forms of which the stronger faction can readily unite and oppress the weaker, anarchy may as truly be said to reign as in a state of nature, where the weaker individual is not secured against the violence of the stronger; and as, in the latter state, even the stronger individuals are prompted, by the uncertainty of their condition, to submit to a government which may protect the weak as well as themselves; so, in the former state, will the more powerful factions or parties be gradually induced, by a like motive, to wish for a government which will protect all parties, the weaker as well as the more powerful. It can be little doubted that if the State of Rhode Island was separated from the Confederacy and left to itself, the insecurity of rights under the popular form of government within such narrow limits would be displayed by such reiterated oppressions of factious majorities that some power altogether independent of the people would soon be called for by the voice of the very factions whose misrule had proved the necessity of it. In the extended republic of the United States, and among the great variety of interests, parties, and sects which it embraces, a coalition of a majority of the whole society could seldom take place on any other principles than those of justice and the general good; whilst there being thus less danger to a minor from the will of a major party, there must be less pretext, also, to provide for the security of the former, by introducing into the government a will not dependent on the latter, or, in other words, a will independent of the society itself. It is no less certain than it is important, notwithstanding the contrary opinions which have been entertained, that the larger the society, provided it lie within a particular sphere, the more duly capable it will be of self-government. And happily for the *republican cause,* the practicable sphere may be carried to a very great extent, by a judicious modification and mixture of the *federal principle.*

PUBLIUS

Critical Thinking

1. Explain the concept of checks and balances.
2. Why is a system of independent departments of government with discrete powers necessary?
3. Of the three branches, which does Madison believe to be predominant? Why?
4. What two considerations are particularly relevant to the federal system when designing a system of checks and balances?

From *The Federalist No. 51,* 1787.

Can America Fail?

A sympathetic critic issues a wake-up call for an America mired in groupthink and blind to its own shortcomings.

Kishore Mahbubani

In 1981, Singapore's long-ruling People's Action Party was shocked when it suffered its first defeat at the polls in many years, even though the contest was in a single constituency. I asked Dr. Goh Keng Swee, one of Singapore's three founding fathers and the architect of its economic miracle, why the PAP lost. He replied, "Kishore, we failed because we did not even conceive of the possibility of failure."

The simple thesis of this essay is that American society could also fail if it does not force itself to conceive of failure. The massive crises that American society is experiencing now are partly the product of just such a blindness to potential catastrophe. That is not a diagnosis I deliver with rancor. Nations, like individuals, languish when they only have uncritical lovers or unloving critics. I consider myself a loving critic of the United States, a critic who wants American society to succeed. America, I wrote in 2005 in *Beyond the Age of Innocence: Rebuilding Trust Between America and the World,* "has done more good for the rest of the world than any other society." If the United States fails, the world will suffer too.

The first systemic failure America has suffered is groupthink. Looking back at the origins of the current financial crisis, it is amazing that American society accepted the incredible assumptions of economic gurus such as Alan Greenspan and Robert Rubin that unregulated financial markets would naturally deliver economic growth and serve the public good. In 2003, Greenspan posed this question: "The vast increase in the size of the over-the-counter derivatives markets is the result of the market finding them a very useful vehicle. And the question is, should these be regulated?" His own answer was that the state should not go beyond regular banking regulation because "these derivative transactions are transactions among professionals." In short, the financial players would regulate themselves.

This is manifest nonsense. The goal of these financial professionals was always to enhance their personal wealth, not to serve the public interest. So why was Greenspan's nonsense accepted by American society? The simple and amazing answer is that most Americans assumed that their country has a rich and vibrant "marketplace of ideas" in which all ideas are challenged. Certainly, America has the finest media in the world. No

subject is taboo. No sacred cow is immune from criticism. But the paradox here is that the *belief* that American society allows every idea to be challenged has led Americans to assume that every idea *is* challenged. They have failed to notice when their minds have been enveloped in groupthink. Again, failure occurs when you do not conceive of failure.

The second systemic failure has been the erosion of the notion of individual responsibility. Here, too, an illusion is at work. Because they so firmly believe that their society rests on a culture of individual responsibility—rather than a culture of entitlement, like the social welfare states of Europe—Americans cannot see how their individual actions have undermined, rather than strengthened, their society. In their heart of hearts, many Americans believe that they are living up to the famous challenge of President John F. Kennedy, "Ask not what your country can do for you—ask what you can do for your country." They believe that they give more than they take back from their own society.

There is a simple empirical test to see whether this is true: Do Americans pay more in taxes to the government than they receive in government services? The answer is clear. Apart from a few years during the Clinton administration, the United States has had many more federal budget deficits than surpluses—and the ostensibly more fiscally responsible Republicans are even guiltier of deficit financing than the Democrats.

The recently departed Bush administration left America with a national debt of more than $10 trillion, compared with the $5.7 trillion left by the Clinton administration. Because of this large debt burden, President Barack Obama has fewer bullets to fire as he faces the biggest national economic crisis in almost a century. The American population has taken away the ammunition he could have used, and left its leaders to pray that China and Japan will continue to buy U.S. Treasury bonds.

How did this happen? Americans have justified the erosion of individual responsibility by demonizing taxes. Every candidate for political office in America runs against taxes. No American politician—including

Although individual responsibility is a cherished part of the national creed, Americans have long reaped more in services and benefits from government than they pay in taxes.

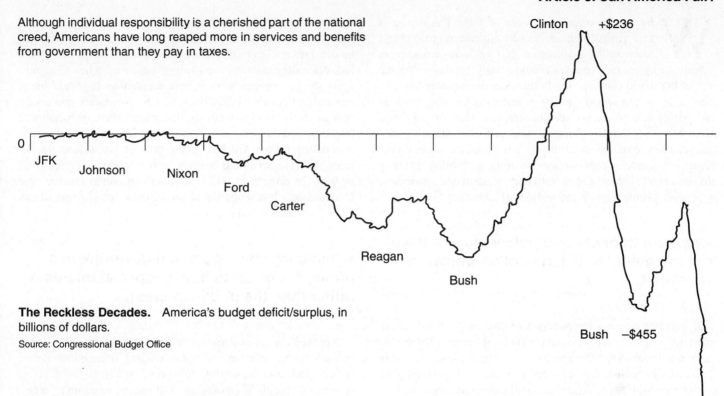

Clinton   +$236

JFK

Johnson

Nixon

Ford

Carter

Reagan

Bush

Bush   −$455

Obama
−$1,2
(projected)

The Reckless Decades.   America's budget deficit/surplus, in billions of dollars.
Source: Congressional Budget Office

President Obama—dares to tell the truth: that no modern society can function without significant taxes. In some cases, taxes do a lot of good. If Americans were to impose a $1 per gallon tax on gasoline (which they could easily afford), they would begin to solve many of their problems, reducing greenhouse-gas emissions, dependence on Middle East oil, and the production of fuel-inefficient cars and trucks.

The way Americans have dealt with the tax question shows that there is a sharp contradiction between their belief that their society rests on a culture of individual responsibility and the reality that it has been engulfed by a culture of individual irresponsibility. But beliefs are hard to change. Many American myths come from the Wild West era, when lone cowboys struggled and survived supposedly through individual ingenuity alone, without the help of the state. Americans continue to believe that they do not benefit from state support. The reality is that many do.

The third systemic failure of American society is its failure to see how the abuse of American power has created many of the problems the United States now confronts abroad. The best example is 9/11. Americans believe they were innocent victims of an evil attack by Osama bin Laden and Al Qaeda. And there can be no doubt that the victims of 9/11 were innocent. Yet Americans tend to forget the fact that Osama bin Laden and Al Qaeda were essentially created by U.S. policies. In short, a force launched by the United States came back to bite it.

During the Cold War, the United States was looking for a powerful weapon to destabilize the Soviet Union. It found it when it created a pan-Islamic force of mujahideen fighters, drawn from countries as diverse as Algeria and Indonesia, to roll back the Soviet invasion of Afghanistan after 1979. For a time, American interests and the interests of the Islamic world converged, and the fighters drove the Soviets out and contributed

to the collapse of the Soviet Union. At the same time, however, America also awakened the sleeping dragon of Islamic solidarity.

Yet when the Cold War ended, America thoughtlessly disengaged from Afghanistan and the powerful Islamic forces it had supported there. To make matters worse, it switched its Middle East policy from a relatively evenhanded one on the Israel-Palestine issue to one heavily weighted toward the Israelis. Aaron David Miller, a longtime U.S. Middle East negotiator who served under both the Clinton and George W. Bush administrations (and is now a public-policy scholar at the Woodrow Wilson Center), wrote recently that both administrations "scrupulously" road-tested every idea and proposal with Israel before bringing it to the Palestinians.

Americans seem only barely aware of the pain and suffering of the Palestinian people, and the sympathy their plight stirs in the world's 1.2 billion Muslims, who hold America responsible for the Palestinians' condition. And tragically, in the long run, a conflict between six million Israelis and 1.2 billion Muslims would bring grief to Israel. Hence, Americans should seriously review their Middle East policies.

The Middle East is only one of many areas in which American policies have harmed the world. From U.S. cotton subsidies, which have hurt poor African farmers, to the invasion of Iraq; from Washington's double standard on nuclear proliferation—calling on non-nuclear states to abide by the Nuclear Non-Proliferation Treaty while ignoring its own obligations—to its decision to walk away from the Kyoto Protocol without providing an alternate approach to global warming, many American policies have injured the 6.5 billion other people who inhabit the world.

Why aren't Americans aware of this? The reason is that virtually all analysis by American intellectuals rests on the assumption that *problems* come from outside America and America provides only *solutions*. Yet the rest of the world can see clearly that American power has created many of the world's major problems. American thinkers and policymakers cannot see this because they are engaged in an incestuous, self-referential, and self-congratulatory discourse. They have lost the ability to listen to other voices on the planet because they cannot conceive of the possibility that they are not already listening. But until they begin to open their ears, America's problems with the world will continue.

American thinkers and policy-makers have lost the ability to listen to other voices on the planet.

It will not be easy for America to change course, because many of its problems have deep structural causes. To an outsider, it is plain to see that structural failures have developed in America's governance, in its social contract, and in its response to globalization. Many Americans still cannot see this.

When Americans are asked to identify what makes them proudest of their society, they inevitably point to its democratic character. And there can be no doubt that America has the most successful democracy in the world. Yet it may also have some of the most corrupt governance in the world. The reason more Americans are not aware of this is that most of the corruption is legal.

In democracies, the role of government is to serve the public interest. Americans believe that they have a government "of the people, by the people, and for the people." The reality is more complex. It looks more like a government "of the people, by special-interest groups, and for special-interest groups." In the theory of democracy, corrupt and ineffective politicians are thrown out by elections. Yet the fact that more than 90 percent of incumbents who seek reelection to the U.S. House of Representatives are reelected provides a clear warning that all is not well. In *The Audacity of Hope* (2006), Barack Obama himself describes the corruption of the political system and the public's low regard for politicians. "All of which leads to the conclusion that if we want anything to change in Washington, we'll need to throw the rascals out. And yet year after year we keep the rascals right where they are, with the reelection rate for House members hovering at around 96 percent," Obama writes. Why? "These days, almost every congressional district is drawn by the ruling party with computer-driven precision to ensure that a clear majority of Democrats or Republicans reside within its borders. Indeed, it's not a stretch to say that most voters no longer choose their representatives; instead, representatives choose their voters."

The net effect of this corruption is that American governmental institutions and processes are now designed to protect special interests rather than public interests. As the financial crisis has revealed with startling clarity, regulatory agencies such as the Securities and Exchange Commission and the Commodity Futures Trading Commission have been captured by the industries they are supposed to regulate. And when Congress opens the government's purse, the benefits flow to special interests rather than the public interest. Few Americans are aware how severely special interests undermine their own national interests, both at home and abroad. The latest two world trade negotiating rounds (including the present Doha Round), for example, have been held hostage by the American agricultural lobbies. To protect 25,000 rich American cotton farmers, the United States has jeopardized the interests of the rest of the 6.8 billion people in the world.

When congress opens the government's purse, the benefits flow to special interests rather than the public interest.

Normally, a crisis provides a great opportunity to change course. Yet the current crisis has elicited tremendous delay, obfuscation, and pandering to special interests. From afar, America's myopia is astounding and incomprehensible. When the stimulus packages of the Chinese and U.S. governments emerged at about the same time, I scanned American publications in search of attempts to compare the two measures. I could not find any. This confirmed my suspicion that American intellectuals and policymakers could not even conceive of the possibility that the Chinese effort may be smarter or better designed than the American one.

An even bigger structural failure that American society may face is the collapse of its social contract. The general assumption in the United States is that American society remains strong and cohesive because every citizen has an equal chance to succeed. Because most Americans believe they have had the same opportunity, there is little resentment when a Bill Gates or a Sergey Brin amasses a great fortune.

This ideal of equal opportunity is a useful national myth. But when the gap between myth and reality becomes too wide, the myth cannot be sustained. Today, research shows that social mobility in the United States has declined significantly. In the 2008 report *The Measure of America,* a research group, the American Human Development Project, notes that "the average income of the top fifth of U.S. households in 2006 was almost 15 times that of those in the lowest fifth—or $168,170 versus $11,352." The researchers also observe that "social mobility is now less fluid in the United States than in other affluent nations. Indeed, a poor child born in Germany, France, Canada, or one of the Nordic countries has a better chance to join the middle class in adulthood than an American child born into similar circumstances."

Behind these statistics are some harsh realities. Nearly one in five American children lives in poverty, and more than one in 13 lives in extreme poverty. African-American babies are more than twice as likely as white or Latino babies to die before reaching their first birthday. People in more than half a million households experience hunger, data from the U.S. Department of Agriculture indicate. The education system is both inegalitarian and ineffective. In a recent international assessment of subject-matter literacy in 57 countries, America's 15-year-olds ranked 24th in mathematics and 17th in science. It should come as no surprise that though the United States ranks second among 177 countries in per capita income, it ranks only 12th in terms of human development.

More dangerously, many of those who have grown wealthy in the past few decades have added little of real economic value to society. Instead, they have created "financial weapons of mass destruction," and now they continue to expect rich bonuses even after they delivered staggering losses. Their behavior demonstrates a remarkable decline of American values and, more important, the deterioration of the implicit social contract between the wealthy and the rest of society. It would be fatal for America if the wealthy classes were to lose the trust and confidence of the broader American body politic. But many of America's wealthy cannot even conceive of this possibility. This explains why so few of the Richard Fulds and John Thains have apologized with any sincerity for the damage they have done.

America's latest responses to globalization also reveal symptoms of a structural failure. Hitherto, Americans have been champions of globalization because they have believed that their own economy, the most competitive in the world, would naturally triumph as countries lowered their trade and tariff barriers. This belief has been an important force driving the world trading system toward greater openness.

Today, in a sign of great danger for the United States and for the world, the American people are losing confidence in their ability to compete with Chinese and Indian workers. More and more American politicians are jumping on the protectionist bandwagon (although almost all of them dishonestly claim they are not protectionists). Even the American intelligentsia is retreating from its once stout defense of free trade. Paul Krugman of Princeton and The *New York Times,* who won the Nobel Prize for Economics in 2008, showed which way the wind was blowing when he wrote, "It's hard to avoid the conclusion that growing U.S. trade with Third World countries reduces the real wages of many and perhaps most workers in this country. And that reality makes the politics of trade very difficult."

At the moment of their country's greatest economic vulnerability in many decades, few Americans dare to speak the truth and say that the United States cannot retreat from globalization. Both the American people and the world would be worse off. However, as globalization and global capitalism create new forces of "creative destruction," America will have to restructure its economy and society in order to compete. It will need to confront its enormously wasteful and inefficient health care policies and the deteriorating standards of its public education system. It must finally confront its economic failures as well, and stop rewarding them. If General Motors, Chrysler, and Ford cannot compete, it will be futile to protect them. They, too, have failed because they could not conceive of failure.

Every problem has a solution. This has always been the optimistic American view. It is just as true in bad times as in good times. But painful problems do not often have painless solutions. This is equally true of the current economic crisis. To deal with it, American leaders must add an important word when they speak the truth to the American people. The word is *sacrifice.* There can be no solution to America's problems without sacrifice.

One paradox of the human condition is that the most logical point at which to undertake painful reform is in good times. The pain will be less then. But virtually no society, and especially no democratic society, can administer significant pain in good times. It takes a crisis to make change possible. Hence, there is a lot of wisdom in the principle, "never waste a crisis."

Let me suggest for purely illustrative purposes three painful reforms the United States should consider now. The goal of these suggestions is to trigger a serious discussion of reform in American discourse.

First, there is a silver bullet that can dispel some of the doom and gloom enveloping the world and admit a little hope. And hope is what we need to get the economic wheels turning in the right direction. As Amartya Sen, another Nobel laureate in economics, said recently, "Once an economy is in the grip of pessimism, you cannot change it just by changing the objective circumstance, because the lack of confidence in people makes the economy almost unrescuable. You have to address the confidence thing, and that requires a different type of agenda than we have." The completion of the Doha Round of world trade talks would go a long way toward restoring that confidence. The good news is that the deal is almost 95 percent cooked. But the last five percent is the most difficult.

One of the key obstacles to the completion of the Doha Round is the resistance of those 25,000 rich American cotton farmers. Millions of their poor West African counterparts will not accept a Doha Round agreement without a removal of the U.S. cotton subsidies that unfairly render their own crops uncompetitive. In both moral and rational terms, the decision should be obvious. The interests of the 6.8 billion people who will benefit from a successful Doha Round are more important than the interests of 25,000 American farmers. This handful of individuals should not be allowed to veto a global trade deal.

America's rich cotton farmers are also in the best position to make a sacrifice. Collectively, they have received more than $3 billion a year in subsidies over the last eight years, a total of about $1 million each. If they cannot make a sacrifice, who in America can? Where is the American politician with the courage to say this?

America has a second silver bullet it can use: a $1 per gallon tax on gasoline. To prevent the diversion of the resulting revenues into pork barrel projects, the money should be firewalled and used only to promote energy efficiency and address the challenge of climate change. Last year, the United States consumed more than 142 billion gallons of gas. Hence, even allowing for

23

a change in consumption, a gas tax could easily raise more than $100 billion per year to address energy challenges.

This sounds like a painful sacrifice, one that America's leaders can hardly conceive of asking, yet it is surprising that Americans did not complain when they effectively paid a tax of well over $1 per gallon to Saudi Arabia and other oil producers when oil prices surged last year. Then, the price at the pump was more than $4 a gallon. Today, with world oil prices hovering around only $40 a barrel, the price per gallon is around half its peak price. A $1 tax would still leave gas relatively cheap.

This brings me to the third silver bullet: Every American politician should declare that the long-term interests of the country are more important than his or her personal political career. As leaders, they should be prepared to make the ultimate political sacrifice in order to speak the truth: The time has come for Americans to spend less and work harder. This would be an extraordinary commitment for politicians anywhere in the world, but it is precisely politics as usual that led the United States to today's debacle.

The latest budget presented to Congress by President Obama offers a great opportunity for change. Instead of tearing the budget apart in pursuit of narrow interests and larding it with provisions for special interests, Congress has the opportunity to help craft a rational plan to help people at the bottom, promote universal health care, and create incentives to enhance American competitiveness.

I know that such a rational budget is almost totally inconceivable to the American body politic. The American political system has become so badly clogged with special interests that it resembles a diseased heart. When an individual develops coronary blockages, he or she knows that the choices are massive surgery or a massive heart attack. The fact that the American body politic cannot conceive of the possibility that its clogged political arteries could lead to a catastrophic heart attack is an indication that American society cannot conceive of failure. And if you cannot conceive of failure, failure comes.

Critical Thinking

1. What does the author present as the three systemic failures of American society?

2. How, according to the author, did groupthink contribute to the financial crisis of 2008–2010?

3. How does the author explain the 9/11 terrorist attacks in the context of American abuse of power?

4. What are some of the ways in which corruption is embedded in the American political system, according to the author?

5. What are the author's three "silver bullet" reforms suggested to trigger dialogue and reform in America?

KISHORE MAHBUBANI, dean of the Lee Kuan Yew School of Public Policy at the National University of Singapore, is the author most recently of *The New Asian Hemisphere: The Irresistible Shift of Global Power to the East* (2008).

From *The Wilson Quarterly,* Spring 2009, pp. 48–54. Copyright © 2009 by Kishore Mahbubani. Reprinted by permission of Kishore Mahbubani.

The Right Bite

There are five maxims the federal government can follow to regain the public confidence it has lost over the past four decades.

WILLIAM A. GALSTON

One of the puzzles of our age is why Americans distrust their own government so deeply. Against the inescapable and well-publicized cases of failure by the federal government must be weighed a remarkable half-century record of accomplishment. The federal government has cleaned up our air and water, improved safety in the workplace, spurred immense amounts of scientific and medical research, and underwritten technological innovations, such as the computer and the Internet, that have transformed our society. It has dramatically reduced poverty among the elderly while ensuring their access to medical care. It has expanded both individual freedom and social inclusion—for women, racial and ethnic minorities, and people with disabilities, among others. The list goes on. Yet despite this record, trust in the federal government now stands at the lowest level ever recorded. That is not merely a riddle for academicians. Without the public's confidence it becomes ever more difficult for government to do its job effectively.

We might be tempted to seek an explanation in recent failures, such as an unpopular war, economic crisis, and the monumentally botched response to Hurricane Katrina. But the decline began long ago. As recently as the mid-1960s, about 70 percent of Americans reported that they trusted the federal government. That number then dropped steadily, with only modest interruptions, before bottoming out at 21 percent in the early 1990s. The peace and prosperity of the Clinton years brought it back up, but only to about 40 percent—little more than half its post–World War II peak. After another rise early in George W. Bush's first term, it has steadily declined and now stands at 17 percent. We are mired, it seems, in a long cycle of diminished trust, decoupled—at least in part—from government's performance. The question is why.

One possibility is that the two decades after World War II are a misleading baseline. Compared with those of other advanced societies, America's public culture is basically antistatist, skeptical at best about concentrated public power. Government's successful response to the Great Depression and the fascist threat shifted the mainstream, this argument goes, but only temporarily. As memories of crisis faded and a generation reached maturity, public sentiment would inevitably have reverted to its deeply rooted default setting, a process accelerated by the Vietnam War, Watergate, and the "Great Inflation" of the 1970s. As Hugh Heclo, a leading scholar of political institutions, puts it, "We are disposed to distrust institutions. That is the basic fact of life we share as modern people. . . . We are compelled to live in a thick tangle of institutions while believing that they do not have our best interests at heart."

While we cannot dismiss this hypothesis out of hand, we must consider that trust in state and local government remained relatively stable even as trust in the federal government plunged. We cannot explain this divergence as a response to the sheer growth of federal activities: By many measures, state and local governments have expanded at least as fast. Nor can it be said that state and local governments are more honest, less self-dealing, or less corrupt. Heclo himself notes that the most logical consequence of America's quasi-libertarian tradition is skepticism about the federal government, not the cynicism that prevails today. It is the move from skepticism to outright cynicism that needs explaining.

One possibility is that the news media's turn from supportive to adversarial during the 1970s exacerbated mistrust by bringing to light mistakes and misdeeds in Washington that would have remained hidden in earlier times. There's something to this, but the withdrawal of public trust was under way well before Bob Woodward and Carl Bernstein broke the Watergate story and made investigative journalism fashionable. The public's response to events—real or perceived—changed the tone of public life and created an opportunity that journalists alertly filled.

The remaining possibility is that something about the qualitative expansion of federal power—about the additional responsibilities the federal government has taken on and the way in which it discharges them—is the reason for its diminished standing. Here there is much to say.

Since the New Deal, Americans have held the federal government accountable for the performance of the economy. In the quarter-century after World War II, this expanded responsibility seemed unproblematic: The economy grew steadily, with low inflation, and Americans at every income level experienced rising living standards. Among officials and citizens alike, confidence grew that Keynesian economics offered the tools needed to mute the inevitable downturns and spur non-inflationary growth whose fruits would be widely shared. But at the moment that complacency peaked (Richard M. Nixon famously declared that "we are all Keynesians now"), new developments—slower growth, higher inflation, increasing inequality, and threats to U.S. manufacturing supremacy—challenged government competence and eroded public confidence.

At roughly the same time, the elite consensus on fundamentals was breaking down. Liberals and conservatives parted ways on economics and foreign policy, and the duopoly that had kept most racial and cultural issues off the federal government's agenda gave way to national action and contestation. When combined with government's expanded reach, rancorous and prolonged disputes among elites further weakened public confidence.

Some have argued that starting with the civil rights and voting rights legislation of the mid-1960s, the federal government's efforts to advance racial equality led to a withdrawal of trust among white Americans. The facts do not support this view. Whites and blacks expressed trust in the federal government at equal (and high) rates until 1968, after which trust declined more rapidly among blacks than among whites for a number of years before measures for the two groups converged again in the late 1970s. It may well be the case, however, that public controversy over government's role in race relations exacerbated the decline across the board.

In civil rights and many other areas, expanding government bypassed the tiered constraints of the federal system and established direct links between Washington and localities, or with the people themselves. The federal government not only created new conflicts with mayors and governors but also assumed responsibilities that often exceeded its ability to act effectively. Although the Elementary and Secondary Education Act of 1965 aimed to reduce inequalities between rich and poor districts, the federal government provided less than 10 percent of total funding for the nation's public schools and had limited authority, at most, to alter local school practices. A gap between promise and performance was inevitable. All too often, the federal government used legislative authorizations to proclaim expansive good intentions while proving unable or unwilling to back up those intentions with commensurate resources.

During the New Deal, a new kind of governance had arisen, as Congress increasingly set only general goals in legislation, leaving it to government agencies to give form and substance to national policies through regulations and other administrative tools. The presidencies of Lyndon B. Johnson and Richard Nixon expanded this strategy into a host of new areas, from workplace safety and racial equity to environmental regulation. While yielding some real accomplishments, the new "administrative state," as political scientists called it, produced unintended harmful consequences. As former Harvard president Derek Bok has argued, federal agencies tended to develop regulations without adequately consulting the people they affected, generating charges that elites and "faceless bureaucrats" were running roughshod over democracy. Litigation surged, slowing the translation of purposes into policy. As agencies with overlapping jurisdictions

issued conflicting directives, compliance costs rose. And many citizens experienced regulations—for example, limiting construction on their property to preserve wetlands—as invasions of what they had long considered their personal rights and liberties.

This was but one instance of a more general problem: As government activities ramified through society, interactions between citizens and the federal government multiplied. All too often, in areas ranging from drivers' licenses and home improvement permits to voter registration, government was slow moving, unresponsive, and maddeningly hard to navigate. Interaction often bred dissatisfaction. As the private sector deployed new technologies to improve customer service, government suffered by comparison.

Even at its best, however, government could not hope to be as flexible as the private sector at its best can be. In the first place, the exercise of public power requires public authorization, direct or indirect, a process that is bound to be more cumbersome than everyday corporate decision-making. Second, government is committed to norms of procedural fairness that tug against efficiency. This fact reflects Americans' historic aversion to concentrated power as well as a more recent mistrust of unchecked administrative discretion. Public infrastructure projects, for example, now must run a gauntlet of public meetings, environmental impact statements, and multilayered policy reviews that can last for a decade—longer than the entire New Deal era. Unless citizens are prepared to relax their guard, they will have to accept a government that moves more slowly than the private sector in making decisions; implementing, reviewing, and adjusting those decisions; and firing incompetent or redundant employees.

Many of the federal government's new responsibilities strained against the limits of its effectiveness. The key issue, however, turned out to be qualitative, not quantitative. For example, though large and increasingly costly, Social Security proved relatively straightforward to administer: Government collected payroll taxes at a flat rate, kept records of contributions, and made payments to retirees based on a clear formula that left little room for bureaucratic discretion. Every month, the Social Security Administration, with only 62,000 employees, efficiently dispenses billions of dollars in benefits to 55 million Americans. To the extent that it involved more than writing checks, winning the Johnson-era "war on poverty" turned out to be far more difficult. And it proved impossible to honor the new commitment to eliminate racial segregation in public education; residential mobility defeated efforts of bureaucrats and courts to establish and maintain racially balanced jurisdictions.

Government is now called upon to exercise a degree of foresight that exceeds its competence.

Citizens' enlarged expectations make matters worse. Government is now called upon to exercise a degree of foresight—about the performance of the economy, the future costs of present commitments, the behavior of adversaries, and much else—that exceeds its competence (indeed, anyone's competence).

Contingency and risk are built into social life. Beyond a certain point, the effort to increase security becomes futile, even self-defeating.

Nor is it possible wholly to avoid administrative error, a fact that legislators and the news media often overlook. When officials fear that they will be pilloried for isolated mistakes, they will manage defensively, impairing government innovation and effectiveness. Although the cost of excessive caution is harder to measure than that of recklessness, it is no less real. After a period in which home loan standards were relaxed to an absurd degree, we are in danger of lurching to the other extreme, making mortgages inaccessible to all but gold-plated borrowers. We would do well to remember the old maxim that a loan officer who never makes a bad loan is a bad loan officer, and adapt it to government: An administrator who never makes a mistake is probably too cautious.

So what is to be done? There is no manual for improving government's performance, let alone the public's assessment of it. But heeding a few simple (at least simple to state) maxims would make matters better over time.

The first is to focus on the basics. The people expect the national government to keep the economy on an even keel, exercise a measure of foresight, win the wars it decides to wage, and deal effectively with disasters. In recent years, government has done poorly in all these areas. The new administration and Congress must do better.

Second, federal officials in every branch of government must be more conscious of the need to align their promises with the limits of feasible performance. While we can reasonably hope to move our transportation system away from fossil fuels during the next generation, "energy independence" is beyond reach. The constant use of that phrase does nothing to reduce public cynicism.

Third, leaders must be more honest about the costs as well as benefits of the measures they support. In the debate over how to reduce greenhouse-gas emissions, for example, many elected officials prefer a "cap-and-trade" strategy rather than a carbon tax because they think the public would rebel against a new tax. But most specialists agree that a cap-and-trade system would drive up consumers' costs just as much as the tax, albeit indirectly, and might also invite corruption in the distribution of pollution quotas. The deliberate attempt to obscure the link between a policy decision and its consequences will exacerbate mistrust without improving performance.

Fourth, pay attention to institutional design. After the end of the Cold War, Washington reduced the effectiveness of our public diplomacy by abolishing the independent U.S. Information Agency and folding its functions into the State Department, where its old mission of promoting American ideas and values conflicted with Foggy Bottom's culture of conflict avoidance and diplomacy. Incorporating the Federal Emergency Management Agency into the new, behemoth Department of Homeland Security contributed to the federal government's disastrous response to Hurricane Katrina. Conversely, as the United States imports increasing quantities of food from countries around the world, the failure to establish a single, unified agency to oversee food safety has been steadily increasing risks, some of which are already becoming realities. High-profile consternation over the adulteration of Chinese-manufactured powdered milk is a warning sign that we should not ignore.

Fifth, as Elaine Kamarck, the director of the National Performance Review during the Clinton administration, has argued, policies should be designed with effective implementation firmly in mind: Pick the right means to each end. For any particular initiative, policymakers can choose to use reformed bureaucracies, networks, or market mechanisms to accomplish their goals. For some purposes, moving away from public institutions to contracts with the private sector or nonprofit institutions may work best. (This is one of the principal arguments in favor of President George W. Bush's faith-based initiative, which President Barack Obama has pledged to continue.) For others—environmental regulation and health insurance are frequently cited examples—it may make sense to use public power to create market mechanisms. In every case, however, employing public power and resources requires effective mechanisms of oversight and accountability. "Contracting out" will not achieve its intended purpose if contract recipients misappropriate funds or do shoddy work, and public confidence will be further weakened.

Policymakers must stop the vicious circle in which mistrust breeds inaction and thus exacerbates mistrust. We need to set in motion a virtuous circle of reform.

Public policies cannot succeed in democracies without sustainable public support. In order to restore public confidence in government, policymakers must stop the vicious circle in which mistrust breeds inaction and thus exacerbates mistrust. We need to set in motion a virtuous circle of reform. That means adopting measures that make people's lives better, step by step, without violating their intuitive sense of how much government should try to do and how it should go about doing it.

Critical Thinking

1. What are some possible reasons that Americans have become increasingly distrustful of the federal government, especially in comparison to state and local government?

2. How does government compare unfavorably to the private sector?

3. What are the five maxims suggested by the author to improve government performance?

WILLIAM A. GALSTON is a senior fellow at the Brookings Institution, where he holds the Ezra Zilkha Chair in Governance Studies. A former deputy assistant for domestic policy to President Bill Clinton, he is the author most recently of *Public Matters: Politics, Policy, and Religion in the 21st Century* (2005).

From *The Wilson Quarterly,* Winter 2009, pp. 50–54. Copyright © 2009 by William A. Galston. Reprinted by permission of William A. Galston.

The Purposes of Political Combat

Why Obama Has Been Blindsided by the Strength and Vitality of His Opposition

John Podhoretz

O My America, how partisan you have become! How difficult you have made it for visionary politicians who want nothing more than to improve you!

You have been paralyzed into stasis by the status quo, which has injected its subtle toxins into your bloodstream by means of radio frequencies between 530 and 1700 kilohertz and a lone television cable-news channel, whose incomprehensible power overruns the combined effect of two others like it: nightly newscasts on three broadcast channels, and the vast majority of newspapers and magazines in the United States. Rallies of surly citizens claiming the mantle of Revolutionary War Bostonians in the spring of 2009 and rude questioners at political gatherings with elected officials home from Washington in the summer of 2009 were harbingers of the inexplicable political reversal that has since been made flesh by electoral defeats in Virginia, New Jersey, and Massachusetts, and polling numbers suggesting a catastrophe in the offing for President Barack Obama's party come November, when elections for all 435 House seats and 33 Senate seats take place.

How can this be, my America? You had given Obama and the Democrats a nearly free hand; not since 1977 had the political balance in Washington been tilted so completely to the advantage of one of the two parties. Seventy million cast their ballots for Obama, and on that same night, Democrats won a 50-seat majority in the House of Representatives and (after much recounting) the 60 seats in the Senate they needed to enact legislation almost at will. Under such circumstances, partisanship should no longer have had any meaning or held any sway, for, O my America, you asked for change, and you gave the change agents the power they needed to enact change; but after only a few months, the works got all gummed up. It will now require procedural tricks and sleights of hand to effect the very change you sought—and in effecting it, and thereby following your will, Democrats may seal their own fate in this election year. Thus has partisanship worked its ugly dark magic, turning the political system upon itself when the verdict of the electorate in November 2008 should have been final.

The preceding paragraphs represent a distillation of liberal thought about the political circumstances of the present moment. The degree of bafflement liberals express at the surprisingly perilous position in which Barack Obama and the Democrats find themselves is understandable; after all, such peril was nearly unimaginable to everyone just a year ago. The results of the 2008 election had been so decisive, the condition of the post-Bush Republican party so parlous, and the double wound to the Right caused by the difficulties of the Iraq war and the financial meltdown so infected that Obama and his party appeared to have an all but free hand.

Indeed, the combined effects of a war gone sour and the capitalist system's apparent self-immolation seemed to Obama and his team to have brought a decisive end to one ideological era and inaugurated a new period in which the American people were now consciously and explicitly seeking liberal activism from their politicians.

It was by no means an unreasonable presumption. The 2008 election, with its 53-46 margin in favor of Obama, and Democratic Senate victories in the unlikely states of Virginia, North Carolina, and Indiana followed on the 2006 midterms, in which Democrats crushed Republicans and regained control of both chambers for the first time in 12 years. Both elections were cast as, and indeed seemed to be, referenda on the failures of the Right—not just standard political failures, but failures on a grand scale that invalidated the modern conservative governing project.

Those failures were considered moral ones, expressed in the political and personal corruption in which Republican politicians had engaged and around which much of the 2006 elections seemed to revolve. They were seen as economic, with Republicans shouldering the blame for the economic meltdown of 2008. And they were thought managerial, in the decision to go to war partly on the basis of nonexistent weapons of mass destruction and then the failure to do what was necessary to win that war. Liberals and leftists were tireless in arguing that these failures were not coincidental but linked, that they shared a common root—the essential heartlessness and soullessness of the Republican party and the conservative movement. And the electorate appeared to respond exactly as they had hoped it would.

It therefore seemed only logical that the thoroughgoing rejection of the Right was pretty much the same thing as an endorsement of the ideas and policies of the anti-Right. After all, liberals had had to concede as much when things had gone against them, hadn't they? For years following the 1994 congressional election, a common presumption in political circles was that the United States had proved itself to be a "Center-Right nation," at least as far as the voting public was concerned. Leftist thinkers like Thomas Frank found themselves compelled to devise a theory to explain why Americans chose to vote in ways injurious to their own supposed best interests. "The matter with Kansas," Frank said in his bestselling 2004 analysis, was that its people had been conditioned to respond to hot-button cultural stimuli on matters like abortion rather than to support redistributionist economic policies designed to improve their own well-being. The same line of argument had been offered a decade earlier about Southern and urban ethnic voters by the reporters Thomas and Mary Edsall in their 1992 book, *Chain Reaction*—only in that case, the Edsalls said, the stimuli had been primarily racial.

It had further become axiomatic in liberal circles from the 1970s onward that the Right had secured the superior political posture on matters of security, regarding both crime at home and America's position abroad, by ginning up (knowingly in a state of cynicism, or desperately due to personal neurosis, or innocently as a result of stupidity) a state of peril in relation to supposed threats that were little or no threat at all—Cuba, Nicaragua, and the Soviet Union. The terrorist attacks on the United States in 2001 came as an almost undisguised blessing for the Right, according to one version of this theory popularized in Michael Moore's *Fahrenheit 9/11;* they became a means of generating new security fears, most especially fear of Iraq, which made possible the engagement in an unnecessary war whose purpose was to rally people 'round the flag and the Republican president—until things went horribly wrong.

Bombarded by these various catalysts, the argument ran, the American people had entered into a period of unreason in which they reacted to averse changes in their lives and communities by embracing symbols of power and authority rather than insisting on concrete and specific political changes that would make their lives better and easier. The most telling statement of this theme came from Barack Obama during his run for the Democratic nomination in early 2008, when he said of rural voters that

> our challenge is to get people persuaded that we can make progress when there's not evidence of that in their daily lives. You go into some of these small towns in Pennsylvania, and like a lot of small towns in the Midwest, the jobs have been gone now for 25 years and nothing's replaced them. And they fell through the Clinton administration, and the Bush administration, and each successive administration has said that somehow these communities are gonna regenerate and they have not. So it's not surprising then that they get bitter, they cling to guns or religion or antipathy to people who aren't like them or anti-immigrant sentiment or anti-trade sentiment as a way to explain their frustrations.

These words were revealing not only in the condescension he displayed toward the very people he insisted his campaign was designed to help but also in the way they expressed Obama's—and, by extension, the specific Left-liberal attitude he both embodies and exemplifies—distrust of and contempt for politics itself.

I am using the word *politics* to describe the arena of public policy, in which matters involving the direction of the United States are hashed out. Players in the arena range in size and import from the president to an individual voter, from the Senate majority leader to a school-board member in his home state of Nevada, and from Charles Krauthammer to a commenter on a blog or a caller to a radio show. The arena is host to conflicts over matters large (weapons systems) and small (the food pyramid), bitterly disputed (abortion) and barely discussed (depreciation schedules), of historical import (war) and entirely evanescent (a la carte cable pricing). But conflicts are what they are, and politics is how they are adjudicated.

The great military strategist Clausewitz once said that "war is the continuation of politics by other means," but the opposite is true as well. In a stable republic like the United States, in the 145 years since the end of the Civil War, Americans have managed *not* to war with each other because we have come to accept implicitly that we handle our disagreements in the arena of politics.

And that has led to another implicit acceptance, which is that the system cannot afford to have us arguing, as Henry Kissinger described North Vietnamese negotiating tactics, over the shape of the table. So with very few exceptions, we operate by consensus on the legitimacy of the essential architecture of the government. And because time is finite and there are limits even to the natural human drive to disagree, our politics actually function with a great deal of overall consensus, a consensus driven by the overall stability of the body politic. Among elected politicians, even the pacifistically inclined find it necessary to vote for increases in the defense budget, while those inclined toward libertarianism will support Social Security increases and extensions of unemployment insurance. That may not be their inclination, but they are compelled to it by the logic of a stable political system.

When a stable political system finds itself in imbalance, however, something more complicated and unpredictable begins to happen. Principled differences will tend to crystallize every now and then around one or two events or issues or pieces of proposed legislation. The crystallization almost always occurs when one party or ideological tendency attempts, or is thought by the other party or ideological tendency to be attempting, to extend the bounds of the consensus in such a way that it shifts into something else. Once the conflict crystallizes, all bets are off, and the games in the arena begin.

This is what politics is at its core. Now, elections are the primary vehicle for the conduct of politics, because they are adjudicated at a given time and place and feature a winner and a loser. The methods used to win elections and defeat rivals are always in low odor in a democracy, because they are confrontational and impolite and lack nuance. But those methods work, and so they are used. The odd part is that the people who use them successfully, politicians and their staffs and consultants, often want to limit these methods exclusively to election seasons; they want to believe that there is a time to run for office and a time to govern, and the time for governing ought to function under different rules. According to this way of thinking, "politics" is something low, while governing is something high; you engage in politics because you have to in order to secure the power to engage in governing, which is your sworn and devoted duty.

People who use political tools to win elections often want to limit the use of those tools to election seasons; to them, "politics" is something low, while governing is something high.

Thus it was that Barack Obama could invite his 2008 rival, John McCain, to a health-care summit in February 2010 and greet McCain's criticisms of the president's health-care bill by saying, "Let me just make this point, John. Because we're not campaigning anymore. The election is over. We can spend the remainder of the time with our respective talking points going back and forth. We were supposed to be talking about insurance."

McCain wanted to discuss the particulars of the health-care legislation passed by the House and Senate. The purpose of the health-care event was to create some form of momentum that would help Obama and his vision for health-care reform carry the day. Nonetheless, Obama had determined that the conversation at that point was to be about "insurance." He was annoyed at McCain's effort to introduce political considerations into the discussion. Such a thing was lowering, the stuff of campaigning. "The election is over," said the president. Two weeks later, speaking heatedly before a crowd in Pennsylvania, he insisted that "the time for talk is over."

Talk is politics. Governing is action.

By saying "the time for talk is over," Obama was echoing his own words a year earlier about the $787 billion economic-stimulus proposal he was then trying to work through the legislative process: "The time for talk is over, the time for action is now." At every step of the way in the course of pushing his relentlessly ambitious domestic agenda, Obama has invoked this duality: His opponents want to fight; he wants to do. They are playing politics; he is above politics.

The obvious objection to my argument here is that Obama doesn't mean this; in belittling his opponents and their propensity to talk, he is playing politics himself, attempting to throw them on the defensive. But the habitual nature of his response, and the response of those who support him, to the populist uprisings against his agenda over the past year suggests he is not the least bit disingenuous.

Obama really does seem to believe that the opposition to his core policies—the creeping nationalization of health care, the effective nationalization of the American automotive industry, the imposition of onerous regulations on energy production, and the expiry of tax cuts that will lead to gigantic effective increases—is not principled. Rather, such opposition deserves to be dismissed as bad faith—the efforts of the status quo, big business, and the politicians in their pockets. Or it is to be explained away as evidence of psychological or spiritual impairment created by the wounds inflicted upon sorry and ignorant souls who are being manipulated by forces beyond their control.

How is it that Obama can fail to see that changes of the magnitude he is seeking would compel those who believe that those changes are dangerous—who honestly believe that they are bad for the country and whose belief is grounded in powerful ideas about how society should be ordered—to marshal their forces to do whatever is in their power to prevent them from taking place? And that it would be wise not to dismiss or belittle the energy and resolve of the opposition, but rather to take their full measure and plan accordingly?

Obama's failure may reside in his contempt for politics. For the national counter-assault against Obama is a manifestation of democratic politics as they ought to work. A rather vague promise of change during his presidential campaign morphed afterward into an agenda of astonishing size with an astonishing price tag. The passage of a $700 billion bank bailout supported by Obama before the election was followed by his $787 billion stimulus package. No sooner had that $1.5 trillion been committed than the president began advocating cap-and-trade legislation that would cost $800 billion through the election in 2012. And then came health care, with a cost of, at the barest minimum, $900 billion over 10 years, and very likely double that or more.

Americans did not take this grandiose and ruinously destructive plan on faith, nor should they have. A majority of them may have voted for change, but that change was change *from something,* from George W. Bush primarily, and not necessarily change *toward something,* toward a wholesale revision of the relation between the state and the economy. In response to Obama's call for an end to talk and a time for action, an engaged and concerned citizenry used whatever political means were at hand—from spontaneous rallies following a financial consultant's call on a little-watched cable-TV show for a revival of the Boston Tea Party, to a Senate victory in Massachusetts for a candidate promising to be the 41st vote to block health care.

In using politics to slow down and thwart him, Obama's rivals are not simply talking. They are acting as citizens in a democratic republic. When challenged by their president, they, too, decided that the time for talk was over and the time for action had begun.

Critical Thinking

1. Why were Democrats so confident following the 2008 Presidential election?

2. What is the function of consensus in American politics? How does imbalance affect consensus?

3. How does President Obama's approach to politics negatively impact his ability to implement change, according to the author?

JOHN PODHORETZ is editor of Commentary.

These People Have No Shame

SENATOR BERNIE SANDERS

Today we find ourselves in a momentous and pivotal moment in American history. We are facing the biggest economic challenge since the Great Depression of the 1930s. Millions of our brothers and sisters have lost their jobs. When you look across the country, you see factories now turning to rust that used to produce meaningful products and pay their workers a decent wage. Dairy farmers who have worked on their land for generations are now being thrown off the land because of the disastrously low prices they're getting for their milk.

As a result of the greed and irresponsibility and illegal behavior of Wall Street, we are plunged into a horrendous crisis today that has disrupted the lives of millions of people from all walks of life.

Think about the working elderly, people sixty to sixty-five, who have worked their entire lives to put away a few bucks for a dignified retirement. As a result of the crash on Wall Street, that retirement is gone and some of them are now packing groceries in supermarkets and are wondering how they are going to heat their homes this winter or provide for their basic necessities.

Think about the millions of American workers who have lost their homes because of the scandalous behavior of Wall Street, and all of those mortgage companies that ripped off people from one end of this country to another.

And think about the young people who were looking forward to going to college, and one day, maybe when they were a senior in high school, their mother or father had to say to them, "Sorry, we no longer have the money to send you to college."

The financial crisis of Wall Street comes on the heels of a long trend in which the middle class has continued to decline. It didn't start a year ago. It's just an exacerbation of what's been happening for 30 years.

Now I remember there was a guy in the White House for eight years. He told us the fundamentals of the economy were strong. And then a few months before he left office, he said, it appears we made a slight mistake. The fundamentals of the economy are not so strong, he said. In fact, he told us, if Congress doesn't give us $700 billion in a couple weeks, the financial system of the United States of America and that of the world is going to collapse.

We made a slight mistake. We said to our friends on Wall Street, "We trust you. We love you. We know that you're going to act in the best interests of the American people. So we're going to take away all restrictions. We're going to allow investment banks to merge with commercial banks to merge with insurance companies."

The great crisis facing our country is not going to be cured by any single piece of legislation. The great cause of this crisis is the incredible greed and selfishness that exist in the ruling elite of America. These people have no shame. For years, the CEOs on Wall Street were only making $10 million, $20 million, $50 million a year, at a time when America had the highest rate of childhood poverty in the industrial world, but that was not enough for them. They needed $1 billion a year running hedge funds. They needed to come up with exotic, nonunderstandable financial instruments so that Wall Street became a casino.

And after their slicing and dicing, after their greed, after their recklessness, after their illegal behavior, they plunged this country into a terrible recession. Have you heard one of these people come before the American people and say, "I'm sorry"? Not only have they not apologized after they've taken hundreds of billions of your dollars. They're back to doing today what they were doing before the collapse of Wall Street.

That is unacceptable. That has got to change.

In the 1930s, we had a President who understood that if you explain the issues to the American people, and if you pointed out who was responsible for the crisis, and if you rallied the working class around a progressive agenda, not only could he change public policy, but he would win reelection.

Barack Obama is a good friend of mine. But he has got to learn the lessons of FDR. He has got to stand with the working families of this country and take on the big money interests. And when he points the finger at Wall Street, at the insurance companies, at the drug companies, and at the military and defense contractors ripping off the taxpayers and those people who are putting their money into the Cayman Islands, he will have the vast majority of the American people fighting at his side for progressive change.

We need a thorough investigation of how Wall Street caused this crisis, and we need to hold those people accountable. And instead of giving them bonuses of $100 million a year, some of those people deserve to find out what our penal system is all about.

For years some of us have worked on dealing with the outrage of usury in America. Usury is not about lending money. Usury is about ripping off people and taking advantage of vulnerable people by charging them 20, 30, or 40 percent on their credit cards.

We need a usury law in America.

And we need something else. A 100 years ago, Teddy Roosevelt had a pretty good idea. He looked around and he saw monopoly after monopoly after monopoly, and he said, "Let's break them up." When Bush came to the American people for a bank bailout, we were told that some of these Wall Street firms were too big to fail. Well, if they're too big to fail, they're too big to exist. Let's start breaking them up.

And when we talk about the economy, and why the middle class is shrinking, and why poverty is increasing, and why America has the most unequal distribution of wealth and income of any major industrialized country on Earth, with the top 1 percent owning more wealth than the bottom 90 percent, there is another issue we need to throw on the table, and that is our disastrous trade policy.

It is not acceptable to me that corporate America throws millions of Americans out on the street and runs to China, pays people there 50 cents an hour, and then brings their products back to this country. We need corporate America to start investing here.

Brothers and sisters, the only way we ever win is when working class people, middle class people, and lower income people come together to fight for justice, to fight for the rights of all our people.

On the other side, there are folks who are spending unbelievable sums of money in Washington. And they own much of the media. It's not going to be easy.

But at the end of the day, if we stand together around a progressive agenda, and if we make sure that every working person in this country votes for their own interests, and not for the interests of Wall Street or the insurance companies, there is no limit to what we can accomplish as a nation.

If we are prepared to fight, there is not a doubt in my mind that the world we will leave to our kids and grandchildren will be a better world than we have today.

Critical Thinking

1. What does Sanders view as the primary cause of the economic crisis facing America in 2010?

2. How does Sanders advise President Obama to address the crisis?

3. What is usury? How should the term be applied in the context of the financial crisis, according to the author?

SENATOR BERNIE SANDERS is an Independent from Vermont. This article is adapted from his speech at Fighting Bob Fest in Baraboo, Wisconsin, on September 12.

The Crisis Comes Ashore

Why the oil spill could change everything.

A L G ORE

The continuing undersea gusher of oil 50 miles off the shores of Louisiana is not the only source of dangerous uncontrolled pollution spewing into the environment. Worldwide, the amount of man-made CO_2 being spilled every three seconds into the thin shell of atmosphere surrounding our planet equals, in tons, the highest current estimate of the amount of oil spilling from the Macondo well every day. Indeed, the average U.S. coal-fired power plant gushes more than three times as much global-warming pollution into the atmosphere each day—and there are over 1,400 of them.

Just as the oil companies told us that deep-water drilling was safe, they also tell us that it's perfectly all right to dump 90 million tons of CO_2 into the air of the world every 24 hours. Even as the oil spill continues to grow—even as BP warns that the flow could increase multifold, to 60,000 barrels per day, and that it may continue for months—the head of the American Petroleum Institute, Jack Gerard, says, "Nothing has changed. When we get back to the politics of energy, oil and natural gas are essential to the economy and our way of life." His reaction reminds me of the day Elvis Presley died. Upon hearing the tragic news, Presley's manager, Colonel Tom Parker said, "This changes nothing."

However, both the oil spill in the Gulf of Mexico and the CO_2 spill in the global atmosphere are causing profound and harmful changes—directly and indirectly. The oil is having a direct impact on fish, shellfish, turtles, seabirds, coral reefs, marshes, and the entire web of life along the Gulf Coast. The indirect effects include the loss of jobs in the fishing and tourism industries; the destruction of the health, vitality, and rich culture of communities in the region; imminent bankruptcies; vast environmental damage expected to persist for decades; and the disruption of seafood markets nationwide.

And, of course, the consequences of our ravenous consumption of oil are even larger. Starting 40 years ago, when America's domestic oil production peaked, our dependence on foreign oil has steadily grown. We are now draining our economy of several hundred billion dollars per year in order to purchase foreign oil in a global market dominated by the huge reserves owned by sovereign states in the Persian Gulf. This enormous and increasing transfer of wealth contributes heavily to our trade and current-account deficits, and it enriches regimes in the most unstable region of the world, helping to finance both terrorism and Iran's relentless effort to build a nuclear arsenal.

The profound risk to our national and economic security posed by the prospect of the world's sudden loss of access to Persian Gulf oil greatly contributed to the strategic miscalculations and public deceptions that led to our costly invasion of Iraq, including the reckless diversion of military and intelligence assets from Afghanistan before our mission there was accomplished.

I am far from the only one who believes that it is not too much of a stretch to link the ongoing wars in Iraq, Afghanistan, and northwestern Pakistan—and even the recent attempted bombing in Times Square—to a long chain of events triggered in part by our decision to allow ourselves to become so dependent on foreign oil.

Here at home, the illusion that we can meaningfully reduce our dependence on foreign oil by taking extraordinary risks to develop deep reserves in the Outer Continental Shelf is illuminated by the illustration. The addition to oil company profits may be significant, but the benefits to our national security are trivial. Meanwhile, our increasing appetite for coal is also creating environmental and human catastrophes. The obscene practice known as "mountaintop mining," for instance, is not only defacing the landscape of Appalachia but also destroying streams throughout the region and poisoning the drinking water of many communities.

The direct consequences of burning these vast and ever-growing amounts of oil and coal are a buildup of heat in the atmosphere worldwide and the increased acidity of the oceans. (Although the world has yet to focus on ocean acidification, the problem is terrifying. Thirty million of the 90 million tons of CO_2 being spilled each day end up in the oceans as carbonic acid, changing the pH level by more than at any time in the last many millions of years. This inflicts every form of life in the ocean that makes a shell or a reef with a kind of osteoporosis—interfering with their ability to transform calcium carbonate into the hard structures upon which their lives depend—that threatens the survival of many species of zooplankton at the base of the ocean food chain.)

But rising global temperatures and increasing acidification in the ocean are only the beginning. These processes have triggered a cascading set of other impacts:

- The melting of virtually all of the mountain glaciers in the world—already well underway—threatening the supplies of fresh water for drinking and agriculture in many parts of the world.

- The prospective disappearance of the North Polar ice cap, which, for most of the last three million years, has covered an area roughly the size of the continental United States. Approximately, 25 percent to 30 percent of this ice cap (measured by the area that it used to cover) has disappeared in the last 30 years during summer. The thickness of the remaining ice has also sharply diminished.
- The melting of the two largest masses of ice on the planet—on top of Greenland and Antarctica (especially West Antarctica, where the bottom of the ice rests under the sea atop submerged islands)—is already accelerating far beyond earlier estimates, threatening catastrophic increases in sea levels worldwide.
- As the seas rise more rapidly, many millions of climate refugees will be forced to flee from areas they have long called home. Indeed, thousands have already been forced to move from low-lying island nations. The government of the Maldives has included a new line item in this year's budget for a fund to buy a new country. That option will not be available to Bangladesh.
- Deeper and longer droughts in mid-continent regions, as soil moisture evaporates more rapidly with higher temperatures.
- More and larger forest fires, as drier vegetation becomes kindling for lightning—which, according to researchers at the University of Tel Aviv, is also predicted to increase at the rate of 10 percent with each additional degree of temperature.
- The migration of tropical diseases to temperate latitudes, as new ecological niches invite the intrusion of viruses and bacteria and the mosquitoes, ticks, and other "vectors" that carry these diseases. This process is also already underway.
- An accelerated extinction rate which, according to E.O. Wilson and other biologists, threatens to reach levels that are not seen since the dinosaurs were wiped out 65 million years ago.
- The increased destructive power of tropical storms coming off the ocean (hurricanes, cyclones, and typhoons—all different names for the same phenomenon). Though the number of these storms is not predicted to grow, their destructive power is due to increases in wind speeds and moisture content.
- Increasingly large downpours of both rain and snow—with a steady shift from snow to rain—resulting in a higher frequency of large floods on every continent.

This last phenomenon—long understood by scientists to be one of the most confidently predictable consequences of global warming—hit home for many of my neighbors recently when Nashville, the city where I live, suffered what the Army Corps of Engineers described as "a 1,000 year rain event" that caused horrendous flooding—mostly in neighborhoods that had no flood insurance—because homeowners there had been assured that they lived well outside the historic flood plain. The tragic loss of many lives was accompanied by the ruination of thousands of homes and property damages that Mayor Karl Dean estimated at $1.5 billion dollars.

Scientists are always careful in the way they describe the cause-and-effect relationship between global warming and such events. It is a mistake, they say, to attribute any single extreme weather event only to global warming, because there is large natural variability in weather, but the odds of extremely large downpours, scientists repeatedly insist, are steadily increasing with global warming, and such events are predicted to become far more common with each passing decade because, when water evaporates from the warmer oceans, warmer air holds more of it. Average humidity worldwide has already increased by 4 percent since 1970, and each additional degree Fahrenheit increases it by another 3 percent to 4 percent. The range of increase in global average temperature during this century is estimated at between 2°F and 11.5°F. The high end of this range would be utterly catastrophic, threatening the survival of civilization as we know it.

Even now, the hydrological cycle of the entire globe is being radically altered. The timing and predictability of rainfall are changing in ways that are already beginning to disrupt agriculture—particularly subsistence agriculture in developing countries. Crop failures and food insecurity are increasing ominously in many regions where farmers are no longer able to rely on the clockwork intervals of rainy seasons and dry seasons they learned from previous generations.

The record snowfalls last winter in the northeastern United States also fit into the same pattern. Indeed, the Northeast has long been included among the regions of the world predicted to experience the most dramatic increases in precipitation.

Unusual changes in precipitation patterns are now being observed in many regions throughout the world. Last month, British scientists working near the North Pole were astonished by an unprecedented April rainfall. David Phillips, a senior climatologist in Canada, described the event as "bizarre," adding, "This is up there among fish falling from the sky or Niagara Falls running dry."

Temperatures inside the Arctic Circle are increasing far more rapidly than in the rest of the world because the progressive melting of ice and snow leads to a radical change in the amount of heat absorbed by the surface of the uncovered tundra and Arctic Ocean. Incoming solar radiation is no longer reflected by the ice and snow. Arctic researchers from the University of Washington have documented the beginning of significant releases of methane caused by the rapid thawing of permafrost in Alaska and Siberia.

One important difference between the oil spill and the CO_2 spill is that petroleum is visible on the surface of the sea and carries a distinctive odor filling the nostrils of people onshore. Carbon dioxide, on the other hand, is invisible, odorless, tasteless, and has no price tag. It is all too easily put "out of sight and out of mind." Because the impacts of global warming are distributed worldwide, they often masquerade as an abstraction. And, because the length of time between causes and consequences is longer than we are used to dealing with, we are vulnerable to the illusion that we have the luxury of time before we begin to respond.

But neither assumption is correct. Most of the heat trapped by greenhouse gases is stored in the oceans and reemerges over time into the atmosphere. As a result, we are capable—through inaction—of making truly disastrous consequences that are inevitable long before the worst impacts are manifested. Our perception of the dangers of the climate crisis therefore relies on our ability to understand and trust the conclusions reached by the most elaborate and impressive scientific assessment in the history of our civilization.

In other words, rather than relying on visceral responses, we have to draw upon our capacity for reasoning, communicating clearly with one another, forming a global consensus on the basis of science, and making a choice in favor of preventive action on a global scale.

Over the last 22 years, the Intergovernmental Panel on Climate Change has produced four massive studies warning the world of the looming catastrophe that is being caused by the massive dumping of global-warming pollution into the atmosphere. Unfortunately, this process has been vulnerable to disruption and paralysis by a cynical and lavishly funded disinformation campaign. A number of large carbon polluters, whose business plans rely on their continued ability to freely dump their gaseous waste products into the global atmospheric commons—as if it were an open sewer—have chosen to pursue a determined and highly organized campaign aimed at undermining public confidence in the accuracy and integrity of the global scientific community. They have attacked the scientists by financing pseudo-studies aimed at creating public doubt about peer-reviewed science. They have also manipulated the political and regulatory processes with outsized campaign contributions and legions of lobbyists (there are now four anti-climate lobbyists for every single member of the House and Senate).

This epic contest between the broad public interest and a small but powerful special interest has taken place during a time when U.S. democracy has grown sclerotic. The role of money in our politics has exploded to a dangerous level. Our democratic conversation is now dominated by expensive 30-second TV commercials, which consume two-thirds of the campaign budgets of candidates in both political parties. The only reliable source of such large sums of campaign cash is business lobbies. Most members of the House and Senate facing competitive election contests are forced to spend several hours each day asking special interests for money to finance their campaigns. Instead of participating in committee hearings, floor debates, and Burkean reflections on the impact of the questions being considered, they spend their time as supplicants. Though many struggle to resist the influence that their donors intend to have on the decision-making process, all too frequently, human nature takes its course.

Their constituents now spend an average of five hours per day watching television—which is, of course, why campaigns in both political parties spend most of their money on TV advertising. Viewers also absorb political messages from the same special interests that are wining and dining and contributing to their elected officials. For the last 17 years, the largest carbon polluters have sought to manipulate public opinion with a massive and continuing propaganda campaign, using TV advertisements and all other forms of mass persuasion. It is a game plan spelled out in one of their internal documents, leaked to an enterprising reporter, that stated: "reposition global warming as theory rather than fact." In other words, they have mimicked the strategy pioneered by the tobacco industry, which undermined the scientific consensus linking the smoking of cigarettes with diseases of the lung and heart—successfully delaying appropriate health measures for almost 40 years after the landmark surgeon general's report of 1964.

Meanwhile, many other countries—including China—have developed national strategies for leading the historic shift from oil and coal to renewable forms of energy, higher levels of efficiency, smart grids, fast trains, and sustainable agriculture and forestry.

Here in the United States, the House has passed a meaningful plan to move the country in the same direction and reestablish our capacity to provide leadership in the global community on the most important issue facing the world today. The Senate, however, has struggled for the last 17 months to find enough votes to take up its own version of the same legislative plan. The unpleasant reality now spilling onto the shores of the Gulf Coast is creating public outrage and may also be generating a new opportunity to pass legislation, just as the oil spill 20 years ago from the *Exxon Valdez* created public momentum sufficient to overcome the anti-environment special interests. There is new hope that, by the time we stanch the gusher from the bottom of the Gulf of Mexico, we will also have capped carbon emissions from the burning of oil and coal.

The crisis in the Gulf of Mexico is a consciousness-shifting event. It is one of those rare clarifying moments, an opportunity to take the long view.

It is understandable that the Obama administration is focused on the immediate crisis in the Gulf of Mexico. But this is a consciousness-shifting event. It is one of those clarifying moments that brings a rare opportunity to take the longer view. Unless we change our present course soon, the future of human civilization will be in dire jeopardy. Just as we feel a sense of urgency in demanding that this ongoing oil spill be stopped, we should feel an even greater sense of urgency in demanding that the much larger and more dangerous ongoing emissions of global-warming pollution must also be halted to make the world safe from the climate crisis that is building all around us.

Critical Thinking

1. What are the primary consequences of increased U.S. consumption of oil and gas?

2. What are some of the second-order impacts of global warming?

3. How have certain corporate interests campaigned against the scientific community and its view on global warming?

4. How does the Gulf of Mexico oil spill crisis put the issue of the global warming in perspective for the American public and policymakers?

AL GORE, former vice president of the United States, is chairman of the Alliance for Climate Protection.

Over Time, a Gay Marriage Goundswell

ANDREW GELMAN, JEFFREY LAX, AND JUSTIN PHILLIPS

Gay marriage is not going away as a highly emotional, contested issue. Proposition 8, the California ballot measure that bans same-sex marriage, has seen to that, as it winds its way through the federal courts.

But perhaps the public has reached a turning point.

A CNN poll this month found that a narrow majority of Americans supported same-sex marriage—the first poll to find majority support. Other poll results did not go that far, but still, on average, showed that support for gay marriage had risen to 45 percent or more (with the rest either opposed or undecided).

That's a big change from 1996, when Congress passed the Defense of Marriage Act. At that time, only 25 percent of Americans said that gay and lesbian couples should have the right to marry, according to an average of national polls.

The more important turning points in public opinion, however, may be occurring at the state level, especially if states continue to control who can get married.

According to our research, as recently as 2004, same-sex marriage did not have majority support in any state. By 2008, three states had crossed the 50 percent line.

Today, 17 states are over that line (more if you consider the CNN estimate correct that just over 50 percent of the country supports gay marriage).

In 2008, the year Proposition 8 was approved, just under half of Californians supported same-sex marriage. Today, according to polls, more than half do. A similar shift has occurred in Maine, where same-sex marriage legislation was repealed by ballot measure in 2009.

Support in the States for Same-Sex Marriage, from Least to Most in 2010

Since 1996, 30 states (■) have passed constitutional amendments banning same-sex marriage. It is currently allowed in five states (□), but support has risen across the country, even in relatively conservative states.

■
SELECTED STATES

	1994–6	**2010**		1994–6	**2010**		1994–6	**2010**		1994–6	**2010**		1994–6	**2010**
■ Utah	12%	22%	■ Tex	24%	35%	W.Va.	21%	41%	■ Ariz.	25%	48%	■ Hawaii	28%	54%
■ Okla.	16	26	■ Neb.	20	35	■ Fla.	26	41	Ill.	26	48	Me.	29	55
■ Ala.	17	26	■ La.	23	36	■ Va.	24	42	N.M.	24	49	N.J	27	55
■ Miss.	17	27	N.C.	21	36	□ Iowa.	24	44	Del.	29	50	□ N.H.	30	55
■ Ark.	17	29	■ Kan.	24	37	■ Wis.	26	44	■ Nev.	26	50	■ Calif.	32	56
■ Tenn.	19	31	■ Mo.	26	37	■ Alaska	23	45	Md.	29	51	□ Conn.	34	57
■ Ky.	18	31	Ind.	22	37	■ Ohio	24	45	Pa.	27	51	N.Y.	36	58
■ S.C	21	32	Wyo.	19	37	■ Mont.	23	45	■ Ore.	26	52	□ Vt.	32	59
■ Idaho	17	33	■ S.D.	23	38	■ Mich.	26	46	■ Colo.	27	52	R.I.	34	60
■ Ga.	21	34	■ N.D.	22	38	Minn.	26	47	Wash.	29	54	□ Mass.	33	62

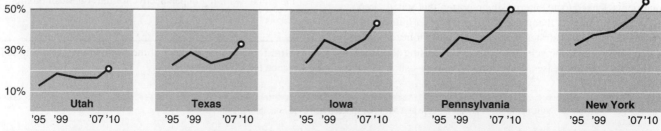

Note: We use a statistical technique for generating state estimates from national polls. Public opinion is estimated in small demographic categories within each state, and then these are averaged using census information to get state-level summaries. For 2010 estimates, we projected from 2008 state-level estimates using an aggregate national estimate of 45 percent (or 50 percent) support for gay marriage.

In both New York and New Jersey, where state legislatures in the past have defeated proposals to allow same-sex marriage, a majority now support it.

And support for same-sex marriage has increased in all states, even in relatively conservative places like Wyoming and Kentucky. Only Utah is still below where national support stood in 1996.

Among the five states that currently allow same-sex marriage, Iowa is the outlier. It is the only one of those states where support falls below half, at 44 percent.

This trend will continue. Nationally, a majority of people under age 30 support same-sex marriage. And this is not because of overwhelming majorities found in more liberal states that skew the national picture: our research shows that a majority of young people in almost every state support it. As new voters come of age, and as their older counterparts exit the voting pool, it's likely that support will increase, pushing more states over the halfway mark.

Critical Thinking

1. Have public attitudes toward same-sex marriage changed between 1996 and 2010? How?

2. Is the trend of growing support for same-sex marriage limited to traditionally liberal states?

3. What are the likely impacts of changing demographics on the same-sex marriage issue?

The authors are professors of political science at Columbia University.

It Is Time to Repair the Constitution's Flaws

SANFORD LEVINSON

In 1987 I went to a marvelous exhibit in Philadelphia commemorating the bicentennial of the drafting of the U.S. Constitution. The exhibit concluded with two scrolls, each with the same two questions: First, "Will You Sign This Constitution?" And then, "If you had been in Independence Hall on September 17, 1787, would you have endorsed the Constitution?" The second question emphasized that we were being asked to assess the 1787 Constitution. That was no small matter inasmuch as the document did not include *any* of the subsequent amendments, including the Bill of Rights. Moreover, the viewer had been made aware in the course of the exhibit that the Constitution included several terrible compromises with slavery.

Even in 1987, because of those compromises I tended to regard the original Constitution as what the antislavery crusader William Lloyd Garrison so memorably called "a covenant with death and an agreement with hell." So why did I choose to sign the scroll? I was impressed that Frederick Douglass, the great black abolitionist, after an initial flirtation with Garrison's rejectionism, endorsed even the antebellum Constitution. He argued that, correctly understood, it was deeply antislavery at its core.

The language of the Constitution—including, most importantly, its magnificent preamble—allows us to mount a critique of slavery, and much else, from within. The Constitution offers us a language by which we can protect those rights that we deem important. We need not reject the Constitution in order to carry on such a conversation. If the Constitution, at the present time, is viewed as insufficiently protective of such rights, that is because of the limited imagination of those interpreters with the most political power, including members of the Supreme Court. So I added my signature to the scroll endorsing the 1787 Constitution.

On July 3, 2003, I was back in Philadelphia to participate in the grand opening of the National Constitution Center. The exhibit culminated in Signers' Hall, which featured life-size (and lifelike) statues of each of the delegates to the constitutional convention. As one walked through the hall and brushed against James Madison, Alexander Hamilton, and other giants of our history, one could almost feel the remarkable energy that must have impressed itself on those actually in Independence Hall.

As was true in 1987, the visitor was invited to join the signers by adding his or her own signature to the Constitution. Indeed, the center organized a major project during September 2003 called "I Signed the Constitution." Sites in all 50 states were available for such a signing. Both the temporary 1987 exhibit and the permanent one that remains at the National Constitution Center leave little doubt about the proper stance that a citizen should take toward our founding document.

This time, however, I rejected the invitation to re-sign the Constitution. I had not changed my mind that in many ways it offers a rich, even inspiring, language to envision and defend a desirable political order. Nor did my decision necessarily mean that I would have preferred that the Constitution go down to defeat in the ratification votes of 1787–88. Rather, I treated the center as asking me about my level of support for the Constitution *today* and, just as important, whether I wished to encourage my fellow citizens to reaffirm it in a relatively thoughtless manner. As to the first, I realized that I had, between 1987 and 2003, become far more concerned about the inadequacies of the Constitution. As to the second, I had come to think that it is vitally important to engage in a national conversation about its adequacy rather than automatically to assume its fitness for our own times.

My concern is only minimally related to the formal rights protected by the Constitution. Even if, as a practical matter, the Supreme Court reads the Constitution less protectively with regard to certain rights than I do, the proper response is not to reject the Constitution but to work within it by trying to persuade fellow Americans to share our views of constitutional possibility and by supporting presidential candidates who will appoint (and get through the Senate) judges who will be more open to better interpretations. Given that much constitutional interpretation occurs outside the courts, one also wants public officials at all levels to share one's own visions of constitutional possibility—as well, of course, as of constitutional constraints. And that is true even for readers who disagree with me on what specific rights are most important.

So what accounts for my change of views since 1987? The brief answer is that I have become ever more despondent about many structural provisions of the Constitution that place almost insurmountable barriers in the way of any acceptable contemporary notion of democracy. I put it that way to acknowledge that "democracy" is most certainly what political theorists call an "essentially contested concept." It would be tendentious to claim that there is only one understanding—such as "numerical majorities always prevail"—that is consistent with "democracy." Liberal constitutionalists, for example, would correctly place certain constraints on what majorities can do to vulnerable minorities.

That being said, I believe that it is increasingly difficult to construct a theory of democratic constitutionalism, *applying our own 21st-century norms,* that vindicates the Constitution under which we are governed today. Our 18th-century ancestors had little trouble integrating slavery and the rank subordination of women into their conception of a "republican" political order. *That* vision of politics is blessedly long behind us, but the Constitution is not. It does not deserve rote support from Americans who properly believe that majority rule, even if tempered by the recognition of minority rights, is integral to "consent of the governed."

I invite you to ask the following questions:

1. Even if you support having a Senate in addition to a House of Representatives, do you support as well giving Wyoming the same number of votes as California, which has roughly 70 times the population? To the degree that Congress is in significant ways *unrepresentative,* we have less reason to respect it. It is not a cogent response, incidentally, to say that any such inequalities are vitiated by the fact that the House of Representatives is organized on the basis of population, putting to one side issues raised by partisan gerrymandering. The very nature of our particular version of bicameralism, after all, requires that both houses assent to any legislation. By definition, that means that the *Senate can exercise the equivalent of an absolute veto power* on majoritarian legislation passed by the House that is deemed too costly to the interests of the small states that are overrepresented in the Senate, especially those clustered together in the Rocky Mountain area and the upper Midwest.

2. Are you comfortable with an Electoral College that, among other things, has since World War II placed in the White House five candidates—Truman, Kennedy, Nixon (1968), Clinton (1992 and 1996), and Bush (2000)—who did not get a majority of the popular vote? In at least two of those elections—in 1960, for which evidence exists that Nixon would have won a recount, and in 2000—the winners did not even come in first in the popular vote. The fact is that presidential candidates and their campaign managers are not necessarily trying to win the popular vote, except as an afterthought. Instead they are dedicated to putting together a coalition of states that will provide a majority of the electoral votes.

3. Are you concerned that the president might have too much power, whether to spy on Americans without any Congressional or judicial authorization or to frustrate the will of a majority of both houses of Congress by vetoing legislation with which he disagrees on political, as distinguished from constitutional, grounds? At the very least, it should be clear from recent controversies that the present Constitution does not offer a clear understanding of the limits of presidential power, particularly during times of presidentially perceived emergencies.

4. Are you concerned about whether the country is well served by the extended hiatus between election day and the presidential inauguration some 10 weeks later, during which lame-duck presidents retain full legal authority to make often controversial decisions? Imagine if John Kerry had won the 2004 election, and President Bush had continued to make decisions about policy on Iraq, Iran, and North Korea that would have greatly affected his administration. Much of the hiatus is explicable only with regard to the need for the Electoral College to operate (which serves as an additional reason to eliminate that dysfunctional institution).

5. Are you satisfied with a Constitution that, in effect, maximizes the baleful consequences of certain kinds of terrorist attacks on the United States? If a successor to United Flight 93 were to succeed in a catastrophic attack on the House of Representatives and the Senate, we could find ourselves in a situation where neither institution could operate—because the Constitution makes it impossible to replace disabled (as distinguished from dead) senators or to fill House vacancies by any process other than an election. That would contribute to the overwhelming likelihood of a presidential dictatorship. The Constitution is written for what is termed "retail" vacancies, which occur only occasionally and are easily subject to being handled by the existing rules. Should "wholesale" vacancies occur, however, the present Constitution is nothing less than a ticking time bomb.

6. Do you really want justices on the Supreme Court to serve up to four decades and, among other things, to be able to time their resignations to mesh with their own political preferences as to their successors?

7. Finally, do you find it "democratic" that 13 legislative houses in as many states can block constitutional amendments desired by the overwhelming majority of Americans as well as, possibly, 86 out of the 99 legislative houses in the American states? No other country—nor, for that matter, any of the 50 American states—makes it so difficult to amend its constitution. Article V of our Constitution constitutes an iron cage with regard to changing some of the most important aspects of our political system. But almost as important is the way that it also constitutes an iron cage with regard to our imagination. Because it is so difficult to amend the Constitution—it seems almost utopian to suggest the possibility, with regard to anything that is truly important—citizens are encouraged to believe that change is almost never desirable, let alone necessary.

One might regard those questions as raising only theoretical, perhaps even "aesthetic," objections to our basic institutional structures *if* we feel truly satisfied by the outcomes generated by our national political institutions. But that is patently not the case. Consider the results when samples of Americans are asked whether they believe the country is headed in the right or the wrong direction. In April 2005, a full 62 percent of the respondents to a CBS poll indicated that they believed that the country was headed in "the wrong direction." A year later, a similar CBS poll found that 71 percent of the respondents said that the country was "on the wrong track," with unfavorable ratings for Congress and the president, and only a slim majority approving of the Supreme Court. Surely that comprehensive sense of dissatisfaction is related for most Americans to a belief that our political institutions are *not* adequately responding to the issues at hand. Serious liberals and conservatives increasingly share an attitude of profound disquiet about the capacity of our institutions to meet the problems confronting us as a society.

To be sure, most Americans still seem to approve of their particular members of Congress. The reason for such approval, alas, may be the representatives' success in bringing home federally financed pork, which scarcely relates to the great national and international issues that we might hope that Congress could confront effectively. In any event, we should resist the temptation simply to criticize specific inhabitants of national offices. An emphasis on the deficiencies of particular officeholders suggests that the cure for what ails us is simply to win some elections and replace those officeholders with presumptively more virtuous officials. But we are deluding ourselves if we believe that winning elections is enough to overcome the deficiencies of the American political system.

We must recognize that substantial responsibility for the defects of our polity lies in the Constitution itself. A number of wrong turns were taken at the time of the initial drafting of the Constitution, even if for the best of reasons given the political realities of 1787. Even the most skilled and admirable leaders may not be able to overcome the barriers to effective government constructed by the Constitution. In many ways, we are like the police officer in Edgar Allen Poe's classic *The Purloined Letter,* unable to comprehend the true importance of what is clearly in front of us.

If I am correct that the Constitution is both insufficiently democratic, in a country that professes to believe in democracy, and significantly dysfunctional, in terms of the quality of government that we receive, then it follows that we should no longer express our blind devotion to it. It is not, as Thomas Jefferson properly suggested, the equivalent of the Ark of the Covenant. It is a human creation open to criticism and even to rejection. You should join me in supporting the call for a new constitutional convention.

Critical Thinking

1. In what way is the current structure of the U.S. Congress unrepresentative of the population?
2. Why should the Electoral College be abolished, according to the author?
3. How are the Constitution's current provisions for replacement of members of Congress a potential problem in the face of a catastrophic attack?
4. Why is Article V of the Constitution problematic?
5. What does the author suggest as a potential remedy to the flaws in the Constitution?

SANFORD LEVINSON is a professor of law at the University of Texas Law School. This essay is adapted from *Our Undemocratic Constitution: Where the Constitution Goes Wrong (And How We the People Can Correct It),* by Oxford University Press. Copyright © 2006 by Oxford University Press.

Is Judicial Review Obsolete?

Stuart Taylor Jr.

The big decision on June 26 that the Second Amendment protects an individual right to keep a loaded handgun for self-defense at home is the high-water mark of the "original meaning" approach to constitutional interpretation championed by Justice Antonin Scalia and many other conservatives. At the same time, the decision may show "originalism" to be a false promise.

Scalia's 64-page opinion for the five-justice majority was a tour de force of originalist analysis. Without pausing to ask whether gun rights is good policy, Scalia parsed the Second Amendment's 27 words one by one while consulting 18th-century dictionaries, early American history, the 1689 English Bill of Rights, 19th-century treatises, and other historical material.

And even the lead dissent for the Court's four liberals—who are accustomed to deep-sixing original meaning on issues ranging from the death penalty to abortion, gay rights, and many others—all but conceded that this case should turn mainly on the original meaning of the 217-year-old Second Amendment. They had little choice, given the unusual absence of binding precedent.

But in another sense, *District of Columbia v. Heller* belies the two great advantages that originalism has been touted as having over the liberals' "living Constitution" approach. Originalism is supposed to supply first principles that will prevent justices from merely voting their policy preferences and to foster what Judge Robert Bork once called "deference to democratic choice." But the gun case suggests that originalism does neither.

Even though all nine justices claimed to be following original meaning, they split along liberal-conservative lines perfectly matching their apparent policy preferences.

First, even though all nine justices claimed to be following original meaning, they split angrily along liberal-conservative lines perfectly matching their apparent policy preferences, with the four conservatives (plus swing-voting Anthony Kennedy) voting for gun rights and the four liberals against.

These eight justices cleaved in *exactly* the same way—with Kennedy tipping the balance from case to case—in the decision the same day striking down a campaign finance provision designed to handicap rich, self-funded political candidates; the June 25 decision barring the death penalty for raping a child; the June 12 decision striking down the elected branches' restrictions on judicial review of Guantanamo detainees' petitions for release; and past decisions on abortion, affirmative action, gay rights, religion, and more.

This pattern does not mean that the justices are *insincerely* using legal doctrines as a cover for politically driven votes. Rather, it shows that ascertaining the original meaning of provisions drafted more than 200 years ago, in a very different society, is often a subjective process on which reasonable people disagree—and often reach conclusions driven consciously or subconsciously by their policy preferences. And some of us have trouble coming to confident conclusions either way.

I wrote approvingly of the federal Appeals Court opinion striking down the District of Colombia's strict handgun ban 15 months ago, and found Scalia's argument for the same result equally persuasive. But then I studied the dissents by liberal Justices John Paul Stevens and Stephen Breyer, and found them pretty persuasive too. Scalia and the two dissenters all made cogent arguments while papering over weaknesses in their positions. I think that Scalia may have won on points. But more study might tip me the other way.

The reason is that the justices' exhaustive analyses of the text and relevant history do not definitively resolve the ambiguity inherent in the amendment's curious wording: "A well-regulated militia, being necessary to the security of a free state, the right of the people to keep and bear arms, shall not be infringed."

And even if there is a clear right answer evident to people more discerning than I, the voting pattern suggests that conservative and liberal justices will never agree on what it is. More broadly, even when there is no dispute as to original meaning, it is often intolerable to liberals and conservatives alike. For example, no constitutional provision or amendment was ever designed to prohibit the federal government from discriminating based on race (or sex). This has not stopped conservatives from voting to strike down federal racial preferences for minorities (by seeking to extend liberal precedents) any more than it stopped liberals from striking down the federal laws that once discriminated against women.

Second, the notion that originalists would defer more to democratic choices than would the loosey-goosey liberals has come to ring a bit hollow. The originalists began with a compelling critique of the liberals' invention of new constitutional rights to strike down all state abortion and death-penalty laws, among others. But the current conservative justices have hardly been models of judicial restraint.

They have used highly debatable interpretations of original meaning to sweep aside a raft of democratically adopted laws. These include federal laws regulating campaign money and imposing monetary liability on states. And in last year's 5-4 decision striking down two local school-integration laws, the conservative majority came close to imposing a "colorblind Constitution" vision of equal protection that may be good policy but which is hard to find in the 14th Amendment's original meaning.

In the gun case, as Justice Breyer argued, "the majority's decision threatens severely to limit the ability of more knowledgeable, democratically elected officials to deal with gun-related problems." (Of course, Breyer's solicitude for elected officials disappears when the issue is whether they should be able to execute rapists of children or ban an especially grisly abortion method.)

If originalism does not deliver on its promises to channel judicial discretion and constrain judicial usurpations of elected officials' power, what good is it?

Indeed, it seems almost perverse to be assessing what gun controls do allow based not on examining how best to save lives but on seeking to read the minds of the men who ratified the Bill of Rights well over 200 years ago.

The originalist approach seems especially odd when it comes down to arguing over such matters as whether 18th-century lawyers agreed (as Scalia contends) that "a prefatory clause does not limit or expand the scope of the operative clause" and whether (as Stevens contends) the phrase " 'bear arms' most naturally conveys a military meaning" and "the Second Amendment does not protect a 'right to keep *and* to bear arms,' but rather 'a right to keep and bear arms' " (emphasis in original). The justices may as well have tried reading the entrails of dead hamsters.

Is the answer to embrace liberals' "living Constitution" jurisprudence, which roughly translates to reading into the 18th-century document whichever meaning and values the justices consider most fundamental?

By no means. Rather, in the many cases in which nothing close to consensus about the meaning of the Constitution is attainable, the justices should leave the lawmaking to elected officials. To borrow from an article I wrote in 1986: "Those who work so hard to prove that the Constitution cannot supply the values for governance of modern society seem to think that judges must do it, with a little help from their friends in academia. But the argument rebounds against the legitimacy of judicial review itself. Bork poses a question for which they have no good answer: 'If the Constitution is not law [that] tells judges what to do and what not to do—. . . what authorizes judges to set at naught the majority judgment of the American people?' "

Now it seems that the originalist view of the Constitution is indeed incapable of telling today's judges what to do—not, at least, with any consistency from one judge to the next. So is judicial review itself obsolete?

Not quite. Judicial review remains valuable, perhaps indispensable, because it helps provide the stability and protection for liberty inherent in our tripartite separation of powers, with the legislative, executive, and judicial branches serving as the three legs of a stool and with each potent enough to check abuses and excesses by the others.

The June 12 decision rebuffing President Bush's (and Congress's) denial of fair hearings to Guantanamo detainees proclaiming their innocence is a case in point. But the broad wording of Kennedy's majority opinion, joined by the four liberals, went too far by flirting with a hubristic vision of unprecedented judicial power to intrude deeply into the conduct of foreign wars. *(See my column, 6/21/08, p. 15.)*

For better or worse, what Scalia has called the imperial judiciary—sometimes liberal, sometimes conservative—seems here to stay.

Indeed, not one of the nine justices seems to have a modest understanding of his or her powers to set national policy in the name of enforcing the Constitution. But the other branches, and most voters, seem content with raw judicial policy-making—except when they don't like the policies. For better or worse, what Scalia has called "the imperial judiciary"—sometimes liberal, sometimes conservative—seems here to stay.

Given this, the best way to restrain judicial imperialism may be for the president and the Senate to worry less about whether prospective justices are liberal or conservative and more about whether they have a healthy sense of their own fallibility.

Critical Thinking

1. What is "originalism," or the "original meaning" approach to interpreting the Constitution?

2. What is the "living Constitution" approach to interpreting the Constitution?

3. When there is no consensus on the interpretation and application of the Constitution, what does the author believe should be done?

4. Why is the process of judicial review valuable?

A Triumph for Political Speech

An Important Supreme Court Decision May Mark the End of Misbegotten Campaign-Finance "Reform"

JENNIFER RUBIN

The United States Supreme Court has come under fire in recent decades for what many critics have condemned as a hunger to subsume the policymaking functions of Congress and the executive branch. But this January, the Court rocked the political landscape by performing what is indisputably its core function: serving as the constitutional guardian of fundamental rights that elected leaders have blithely disregarded in pursuit of political advantage or in the name of a misbegotten policy goal.

In *Citizens United v. Federal Election Commission,* the Court struck down a key provision of the Bipartisan Campaign Reform Act of 2002—commonly known by the monikers of its two principal authors, "McCain-Feingold." The provision in question "prohibits corporations and unions from using their general treasury funds" to make independent expenditures for speech that either is an "electioneering communication" or that expressly advocates the election or defeat of a candidate.

In declaring this provision unconstitutional by a 5-to-4 margin, the Court affirmed the right of labor unions and corporations to expend their own funds to engage in political speech. The specific matter before the Court was a documentary film called *Hillary: The Movie,* which had been produced by a nonprofit corporation called Citizens United. The film harshly criticized Hillary Clinton, then a presidential candidate, and, in effect, urged voters not to elect her. McCain-Feingold effectively outlawed the release of the film, and the Court found that to be an unconstitutional abridgment of free speech.

But the shock waves from the decision shot through the political landscape, unleashing curious political alliances and exposing the precarious nature of fundamental rights in a hyper-politicized culture.

Federal campaign-finance law has a long and tortured history, but it really began garnering widespread attention only in the mid-1970s, when the Watergate abuses led to major legislative action—action that has since been the subject of several major Supreme Court rulings and congressional revisions, of which McCain-Feingold was the most far-reaching. The purpose of campaign-finance law has always been to combat corruption. But over the years, the definition of corruption has expanded from unvarnished influence-peddling and vote-buying to far more vague worries about the influence of the "rich."

The first approach was to control the use of "hard money"—dollars donated and spent in the explicit effort to secure a candidate's victory—by limiting contributions to a set amount. Then came efforts to restrict political parties' use of so-called soft money, money not used expressly to advocate the election or defeat of specific candidates and therefore not subject to specific fundraising or spending restrictions. Controls have also been sought on independent, third-party groups, which legally should have no ties whatsoever to campaigns or parties.

McCain-Feingold restricted the amount of soft money that national parties could collect. As a result, cash began to pour into less visible independent groups, the 527s (so named after the section of the federal tax code that governs them). That fact, in turn, begat regulations on the issue advertising produced by those groups. The course of campaign-finance reform offers an object lesson in the dangers of the administrative state and the way in which good intentions give way to bureaucratic accretions and the heavy hand of regulation.

The political class had become accustomed to restricting political speech in the name of rooting out corruption and purifying American electioneering. Justice Anthony Kennedy's majority opinion represents a sharp break with that precedent. It is a bold rejection of the notion that government officials can micromanage speech in the hopes of leveling the political playing field. No longer will they be allowed to pick favorites among political speakers. Kennedy's far-reaching decision overturned two previous Supreme Court rulings, one from 2003 and another from 1990, and explained exactly why such a sweeping approach was necessary. "The law before us is an outright ban, backed by criminal sanctions," making it, Kennedy wrote, "a felony for all corporations—including nonprofit advocacy corporations—either to expressly advocate the election or defeat of candidates or to broadcast electioneering communications within 30 days of a primary election and 60 days of a general election."

Given these facts, he continued, "the following acts would all be felonies":

> The Sierra Club runs an ad, within the crucial phase of 60 days before the general election, that exhorts the public to disapprove of a Congressman who favors logging in national forests; the National Rifle Association publishes a book urging the public to vote for the challenger because the incumbent U.S. Senator supports a handgun ban; and the American Civil Liberties Union creates a website telling the public to vote for a Presidential candidate in light of that candidate's defense of free speech. These prohibitions are classic examples of censorship.

Quite simply, then, the law's "prohibition on corporate independent expenditures is thus a ban on speech." Courts have allowed electioneering restrictions, citing Congress's constitutional authority to "make or alter" the rules regulating "the Times, Places and Manner of holding Elections for Senators and Representatives." Kennedy pointed out that if the restriction on corporate or union speech "applied to individuals, no one would believe that it is merely a time, place, or manner restriction on speech. Its purpose and effect are to silence entities whose voices the Government deems to be suspect." And in stirring words that came as a torrent of icy water in the faces of those good-government advocates who fancy themselves defenders of democracy, he wrote:

> Speech is an essential mechanism of democracy, for it is the means to hold officials accountable to the people. . . . The right of citizens to inquire, to hear, to speak, and to use information to reach consensus is a precondition to enlightened self-government and a necessary means to protect it. . . . Political speech must prevail against laws that would suppress it, whether by design or inadvertence. Laws that burden political speech are "subject to strict scrutiny," which requires the Government to prove that the restriction "furthers a compelling interest and is narrowly tailored to achieve that interest."

This was as bold a stroke as the usually measured Kennedy has ever delivered from the bench. Political expenditures are equivalent to speech. Speech cannot be censored. The government cannot pick and choose among those speakers it wishes to be heard. With a thud, much of the foundation of campaign-finance reform has been exposed as constitutionally illegitimate. "Premised on mistrust of governmental power, the First Amendment stands against attempts to disfavor certain subjects or viewpoints," Kennedy wrote. "Prohibited, too, are restrictions distinguishing among different speakers, allowing speech by some but not others."

The political establishment was horrified. Editorial boards and pundits thundered that this was the end of democracy as we know it. The *New York Times*'s editors bellowed, "With a single, disastrous 5-to-4 ruling, the Supreme Court has thrust politics back to the robber-baron era of the 19th century." Ruth Marcus of the *Washington Post* pronounced

it "an intellectually dishonest power grab" and decried "the audacity of the result it has inflicted on the political process." Howard Fineman took to MSNBC to call the decision "an amazing piece of alleged jurisprudence" and warned that power companies and other corporate interests would take out Democrats in "Red states."

Politicians threatened that we would see corporate leviathans control our political system. "The Supreme Court's divided opinion," said Senator Patrick Leahy, "is likely to change the course of our democracy and could threaten the public's confidence in the Court's impartiality."

Self-appointed government-reform advocates were beside themselves. Long-time campaign-finance champion Fred Wertheimer proclaimed: "Today's Supreme Court decision in the *Citizens United* case is a disaster for the American people and a dark day for the Supreme Court. The decision will unleash unprecedented amounts of corporate 'influence-seeking' money on our elections and create unprecedented opportunities for corporate 'influence-buying' corruption."

And then, in an unprecedented bit of grandstanding from a former constitutional-law professor, President Barack Obama announced at the State of the Union:

> Last week, the Supreme Court reversed a century of law to open the floodgates for special interests—including foreign corporations—to spend without limit in our elections. Well, I don't think American elections should be bankrolled by America's most powerful interests, or worse, by foreign entities. They should be decided by the American people, and that's why I'm urging Democrats and Republicans to pass a bill that helps to right this wrong.

A "century of law" has not been reversed. The ban on contributions and expenditures by foreign corporations remains, in Section 441e of the statute. As Senate Minority Leader Mitch McConnell, a former litigant in the overturned case and the Senate's primary opponent of McCain-Feingold, succinctly put it: "Contrary to what the President and some of his surrogates in Congress say, foreign persons, corporations, partnerships, associations, organizations, or other combination of persons are strictly prohibited from any participation in U.S. elections, just as they were prohibited before the Supreme Court's *Citizens United* decision."

But the president's comments—however inaccurate—perfectly encapsulated the rage and fear that gripped many in the political establishment who had spent decades trying to control the speech of certain speakers. And the fix the president called for seemed to exemplify the indifference to the constitutional niceties the Court was emphatically reasserting.

The president's comments encapsulated the rage and fear that gripped many in the establishment who had spent decades trying to control the speech of certain speakers.

Any law professor or first-year law student knows that it is quite dicey for Congress simply "to pass a bill" that countermands a Supreme Court's constitutional ruling. Nevertheless, Senator Charles E. Schumer and Representative Chris Van Hollen promptly trotted out their proposed solution, a bevy of onerous reporting regulations for corporations, an attempt to ban speech by those corporations that conduct business with the government, a redefinition of "foreign corporation" as entities with as little as 20 percent ownership based abroad, and a jury-rigging of advertising regulations to ensure that politicians get the "lowest unit" rate to respond to corporate ads.

Noteworthy was the absence of any concern about the political expenditures of unions, which had also been unshackled by the Court decision. Many prominent unions, such as the United Auto Workers and the Service Employees International, have noncitizen members, yet there was no suggestion from Schumer and Van Hollen that *these* noncitizens might unduly influence elections. Instead, the liberal establishment concentrated on corporations they feared might now run ads, thereby managing somehow to hijack American democracy from unwitting voters. But when the AFL-CIO announced a $53 million campaign aimed at saving Democratic congressional seats, the same *Citizens United* critics fell mute.

The vast majority of those groups defined as "corporations" by the law do not resemble ExxonMobil or AT&T but instead are small proprietorships. More to the point, the sort of corporation most likely to participate in campaigns is of the nonprofit variety, such as the Sierra Club or the National Rifle Association. However, the suggested legislative "fixes" would go after all incorporated entities, just as the eviscerated McCain-Feingold act had done.

The proposed end around of the Court's ruling could very well be struck down if it is signed into law. As government contracts constitute a large and important segment of America's corporate sector, any broad attack on them would most likely provoke strong objections. The Court also left open the door to legal challenges to onerous regulations that are styled as mere disclosure requirements if, in their application, they impermissibly intimidate those who wish to participate in campaigns. One legislative proposal, for example, would require corporations to list the names of the five top contributors to their ads, thereby subjecting members of private-interest groups to harassment or attack ads, as was the case when donors to Proposition 8 (the gay-marriage ban) in California had their names released.

Campaign-Finance reform creates an odd divide in the political landscape, one that does not break down neatly along ideological lines as a split between conservatives and liberals. Conservative think tanks, the ACLU, and a heterogeneous group of special-interest groups—from the liberal feminist political fundraiser Emily's List to the libertarian CATO Institute—have always been aligned against McCain-Feingold. On the other side stand, McCain and Feingold themselves (an odd couple from the Center-Right and far Left), professional reformers, and nearly the entire media establishment. At issue is not merely whether "corporations

should dominate politics" but rather two contrasting views of our political system.

Yet for all the talk of first principles, self-interest has guided much of the debate. Mainstream-media outlets, under the stringent rules of McCain-Feingold, have been operating in a protected realm, sheltered from competition in their ability to influence the outcomes of elections by corporations and unions. If corporations were unshackled and could partake in the political process as editorial pages do, the traditional media would face yet another blow to their authority. And then there are the politicians themselves, from McCain and Feingold outward, who have used legislation to tip the scales toward incumbent protection, inveighing against "attack ads" by special-interest groups that seek to hold them accountable for their voting records.

But there was and remains more at stake than incumbency and the relative influence of the *New York Times* and *Time*. For the reformers, the preservation of democracy in a stratified, industrial polity is a matter of minute balancing and strict attention to evaluating good and bad speech. They do not share the conviction of the nation's Founders that robust, even aggressive speech is fundamental to the country's political health. Campaign-finance reformers believe that large, wealthy forces operating clandestinely behind the scenes are always working to capture the political system and that therefore the only means of counterbalancing their influence is to evaluate political speech itself and orchestrate an elaborate set of rules to make sure no one gets more speech than anyone else.

Campaign-finance reformers do not share the conviction of the nation's Founders that robust, even aggressive speech is fundamental to the country's political health.

Those on the other side of the divide, including the five Supreme Court justices who voted to overturn McCain-Feingold this year, reject this notion. The Constitution, in their view, is not a social or political equalizer but rather a framework for *protecting* free expression and other rights essential to the operation of a democratic system. The remedy for "bad" speech cannot be *less* speech.

Will the *Citizens United* ruling permanently shift the balance in this debate to the side of the free-speech advocates? As is the case when discussing the future of any narrowly decided ruling, changes in the composition of the Supreme Court could revive McCain-Feingold. In the short run, the political class will need to digest the ruling and prepare for still more legislative activity and possibly more constitutional housekeeping by the Supreme Court.

Most Supreme Court observers, however, detect little appetite for eviscerating the limits on corporate donations or addressing the dollar limits on campaign spending more generally, insofar as the Court has previously upheld such limits if they are not so draconian as to prevent voters from expressing support for candidates of their choice.

As for the potential for overweening corporate influence in campaigns, the reaction of the political class and alarmist pundits seems overblown, if not hysterical. Reform groups who argue that the political system is at risk of becoming a corrupt racket in which huge public corporations monopolize campaigns to the benefit of the Republican party were especially loud in denouncing the ruling. But corporations spread their money around; they wish to ensure access to both sides of the aisle. A 2009 study released by the Center for Responsive Politics, for example, showed that 63 percent of corporate donations (by both political-action committees and individual donors) flowed to Democrats. Moreover, more than 20 states permit all manner of corporate contributions and unlimited expenditures. There is scant evidence in states like Virginia and Nebraska that the absence of corporate restrictions has unleashed an avalanche of boardroom political influence or increased corruption. And it is far from clear that corporations with diverse shareholders and an aversion to public controversy would choose to wade into federal campaigns with full-blown ad offensives hawking one candidate or another.

Meanwhile, at least for the foreseeable future, the ultimate goal of the reform clique—public financing of campaigns—may have suffered a serious blow. But the chief culprit for the demise of the idea of completely replacing the private financing of elections with a system in which all expenditures would be funded by the taxpayers was not the Supreme Court or even the Republican party. It was, instead, the idol of most of those who have longed for such a scheme: Barack Obama. It was candidate Obama who undermined the basis for the myriad of restrictions that had accumulated in the post-Watergate years designed to squeeze private money out of politics and replace it eventually with a public-financing plan.

It was candidate Obama who undermined the basis for the myriad of restrictions designed to squeeze private money out of politics and replace it with a public financing plan.

Though he had expressed warm support for public-financing ideas in the past, the massive outpouring of private donations from millions of individuals to his campaign—chiefly through the Internet—trumped such theoretical considerations. Obama's declaration during the 2008 race that he would not make use of the public financing now available to presidential candidates of major parties if they agree to spending limits sounded the death knell for that liberal fantasy.

The irony that it was a liberal Democrat who nailed the lid on the public-financing coffin is not lost on supporters of the idea. Indeed, Obama's example skewered the entire rationale for the belief that only by driving out private money can a long-shot outsider stage a successful charge for the White House. Large numbers of individuals expressed their preference for Obama principally through the giving of money to his campaign—thus illustrating a point conservative opponents of such reforms have long made. Given the success, both financially and electorally, of the Obama campaign's approach, it is doubtful, then, that other well-run campaigns will ever limit themselves to public financing again.

This is not to say that campaign-finance-reform advocates have lost their passion for public financing. Senator Richard Durbin has a proposal to extend public financing to congressional races. But there is a significant impediment: the public overwhelmingly opposes it. Even voluntary support, in the form of a check-off on federal tax returns, has diminished over time. The very notion of funding campaigns with involuntary tax monies would surely raise new constitutional concerns as to whether citizens can be forced through their tax dollars to support candidates whose views they may adamantly oppose.

Money has always been part of democratic politics. No legislation can change that. All legislation can do is funnel the dollars into different structures that will be, as the history of the past four decades has shown, increasingly less transparent. Efforts to game the system will continue, and the Court will have to remain the umpire—an umpire whose only interest should be the maintenance of a political structure in which the government is prohibited from picking winners and losers among political speakers.

Critical Thinking

1. What restrictions did the Bipartisan Campaign Reform Act of 2002 ("McCain-Feingold") impose on political funding?

2. Why did the Supreme Court declare the McCain-Feingold Act unconstitutional?

3. What did critics argue was wrong with the Supreme Court decision against McCain-Feingold? Why do supporters believe the decision will have a positive effect?

4. How might increased corporate spending on political campaigns impact the traditional media?

5. How did the 2008 Obama campaign and its decisions affect the movement to provide public campaign financing to political candidates?

JENNIFER RUBIN, Commentary's contributing editor, writes daily for our blog, Contentions. Her most recent article for the magazine was "Going After Joe Lieberman" (March 2010).

Corporations Aren't Persons; Amend the Constitution

MATTHEW ROTHSCHILD

On February 16, about 200 people gathered on the steps of the Wisconsin state capitol. "It's fitting that we stand out in the cold," said Mike McCabe, executive director of the Wisconsin Democracy Campaign. "That's where the Supreme Court has left us."

He was referring to the court's recent decision in *Citizens United v. Federal Election Commission,* which granted corporations the right to spend unlimited funds on so-called independent expenditures to influence the outcome of elections. The crowd heartily agreed with McCabe. Signs said: "No Corporate Takeover of Elections," "Free Speech, Not Fee Speech," "Money Is Not Speech, Corporations Are Not Persons." And a chant went up: "Overrule the Court."

Ben Manski, executive director of the Liberty Tree Foundation, drew the crowd in with a historical analogy.

"Susan B. Anthony, the great suffragist and abolitionist, was born" on February 15, 1820, he said. "Were she alive now, she would be here, celebrating with us, marching to overrule the Court. On a future day, a multitude will gather on these same steps and look back at what we here dare to do, and they will thank you."

What the crowd was daring to do was nothing less than kick off a nationwide grassroots campaign to amend the Constitution not only to overturn the court's reckless decision but also to state, once and for all, that corporations do not have the same rights as persons.

Make no mistake about it: The court's ruling in *Citizens United,* if left to stand, will destroy whatever hope we may ever have had of democracy in this country. It will entrench corporate power as never before. And the promise of America will be dashed.

Fighting Bob La Follette, the great Senator from Wisconsin and the founder of this magazine, warned throughout his career about the looming threat posed by corporate power. When he ran for President in 1924, he said: "Democracy cannot live side by side with the control of government by private monopoly. We must choose, on the one hand, between representative government, with its guarantee of peace, liberty, and economic freedom and prosperity for all the people, and on the other, war, tyranny, and the impoverishment of the many for the enrichment of the favored few."

Yes, we must choose.

And we must choose now.

To read the 5–4 majority decision in *Citizens United* is to look at a fun-house mirror. The case, most narrowly, concerned whether the rightwing nonprofit group Citizens United, which is partially funded by corporations, could run an anti-Hillary Clinton documentary on cable and whether it could promote the film with ads on TV close to election time. The McCain-Feingold law prohibited corporate-funded independent ads during such a timeframe, and Citizens United challenged the constitutionality of the law as it applied to this particular instance.

But the Court's majority was not interested in ruling narrowly. Justice Anthony Kennedy, writing for the majority, threw out decades of Supreme Court precedents. Writing in the most sweeping way, he declared that "political speech of corporations or other associations" cannot "be treated differently under the First Amendment simply because such associations are not 'natural persons.'"

The logic of the Court's argument would throw out all restrictions on corporate expenditures. "Political speech must prevail against laws that would suppress it, whether by design or inadvertence," it said. This seems to justify unlimited direct gifts to candidates, though the majority didn't quite go there. But it went everywhere else.

The decision asserted, astonishingly and without evidence, that "independent expenditures, including those made by corporations, do not give rise to corruption or the appearance of corruption." It added: "The appearance of influence or access, furthermore, will not cause the electorate to lose faith in our democracy." And it asserted that "no sufficient governmental interest justifies limits on the political speech of nonprofit or for-profit corporations."

Justice John Paul Stevens, at eighty-nine writing eloquently in dissent, warned: "Starting today, corporations with large war chests to deploy on electioneering may find democratically elected bodies becoming much more attuned to their interests." The Court's decision, he added, undermines the integrity of our democratic institutions and "will undoubtedly cripple the ability of ordinary citizens, Congress, and the states to adopt even limited measures to protect against corporate domination of the electoral process."

Stevens cut to the heart of the matter and laid out why corporations should not be treated as persons. "In the context of election to public office, the distinction between corporate and human speakers is significant," he argued. "Although they make enormous contributions to our society, corporations are not actually members of it. They cannot vote or run for office. Because they may be managed and controlled by nonresidents, their interests may conflict in fundamental respects with the interests of eligible voters. . . . Our lawmakers have a compelling constitutional basis, if not also a democratic duty, to take measures designed to guard against the potentially deleterious effects of corporate spending in local and national races." Later, he added, witheringly: "Under the majority's view, I suppose it may be a First Amendment problem that corporations are not permitted to vote, given that voting is, among other things, a form of speech."

Stevens also invoked our Founders. "Unlike our colleagues, they had little trouble distinguishing corporations from human beings, and when they constitutionalized the right to free speech in the First Amendment, it was the free speech of individual Americans that they had in mind," he wrote. "Thomas Jefferson famously fretted that corporations would subvert the Republic," Stevens observed, and in a footnote, he provided the quotation from Jefferson from 1816: "I hope we shall . . . crush in [its] birth the aristocracy of our monied corporations."

By an overwhelming margin, the American people have sided with Justice Stevens and against the Court's majority. According to a *Washington Past*-ABC News poll, 80 percent of the American people oppose the Court's decision, and 65 percent "strongly" oppose it. "The poll shows remarkably strong agreement about the ruling across all demographic groups," noted Dan Eggen of the *Post*. "The poll reveals relatively little difference of opinion on the issue among Democrats (85 percent opposed to the ruling), Republicans (76 percent), and independents (81 percent)."

This represents a huge base of support for overturning the decision. But how to do it?

Some members of Congress are hoping to blunt the effect of the decision legislatively. Senator Sherrod Brown of Ohio introduced a bill that would require corporations to get prior approval of their shareholders before launching political ads. And Senator Charles Schumer of New York and Representative Chris Van Hollen of Maryland began circulating drafts of legislation that would ban independent campaign expenditures by corporations that are more than 20 percent foreign owned. They would also ban such expenditures by any company that receives taxpayer support through either the Troubled Asset Relief Program or through federal contracts. And their bills would require a great deal more disclosure.

"If we don't act quickly, the Court's ruling will have an immediate and disastrous impact on the 2010 elections," Schumer said. "Our goal is to advance the legislation quickly, otherwise the Supreme Court will have predetermined winners of next November's election—it won't be Republicans, it won't be Democrats, it will be corporate America."

But the Democrats in Congress aren't acting quickly on this. And even if they did, they'd run into an unmovable object: The Supreme Court's decision is now the law of the land. The Court would likely strike down any legislation that went against it.

"These are noble efforts on the Hill, but they misdiagnose the problem," says Lisa Graves, executive director of the Center for Media and Democracy. "We shouldn't waste energy on legislation that won't pass a filibuster or won't pass muster with this five-member majority on the court." (Graves, by the way, calls *Citizens United "Bush v. Gore* on steroids. That decision affected only one, or at most two, elections. This will affect many elections to come.")

There's another approach, floated by Ralph Nader and by Robert Weissman, the new president of Public Citizen. While they support legislative efforts, they say the President could issue an executive order refusing to "contract with or provide subsidies, handouts, and bailouts to any company that spends money directly in the electoral arena."

But the Supreme Court could invalidate such an order, as well.

Nader and Weissman also recommend that shareholders pass resolutions requiring their corporations to receive majority permission before spending money on elections.

Ultimately, however, Nader and Weissman favor amending the Constitution. "In the absence of a future court overturning *Citizens United*," they wrote in *The Wall Street Journal* on February 10, "the fundamental response should be a constitutional amendment. We must exclude all commercial corporations and other artificial commercial entities from participating in political activities. Such constitutional rights should be reserved for real people."

On February 2, Representative Donna Edwards, Democrat of Maryland, became the first member of Congress to offer up a constitutional amendment aimed at *Citizens United.* She introduced the following: "The sovereign right of the people to govern being essential to a free democracy, Congress and the States may regulate the expenditure of funds for political speech by any corporation, limited liability company, or other corporate entity." It was co-sponsored by Representatives André Carson, John Conyers, Keith Ellison, Raúl Grijalva, Jesse Jackson Jr., Barbara Lee, Ed Markey, Jim McGovern, Eleanor Holmes Norton, Chellie Pingree, and Betty Sutton.

We need to "take matters into our own hands to enact a constitutional amendment that once and for all declares that we the people govern our elections and our campaigns, not we the corporations," Edwards said, in a great video on the website freespeechforpeople.org. "Imagine a world where corporations could spend the never-ending source of their corporations' treasuries on elections and campaigns and public policy. The people would completely lose our voice. . . . It would be gone."

To illustrate Edwards's point, Jamie Raskin, a Maryland state senator and a law professor at American University, provided the following example on that same video. "In 2008, the Fortune 100 corporations had $600 billion in profits," Raskin said. "Now imagine that those top 100 companies decided to spend a modest 1 percent of their profits to intervene in our politics and to get their way. That would mean $6 billion, or double what the Obama campaign spent, the McCain campaign spent, and every candidate for House and Senate."

On February 24, Senator Chris Dodd of Connecticut introduced his own constitutional amendment, which was co-sponsored by Senator Tom Udall of New Mexico. The amendment would "authorize Congress to regulate the raising and spending of money for federal political campaigns, including independent expenditures, and allow states to regulate such spending at their level," according to a statement from Dodd's office.

"Ultimately, we must cut through the underbrush and go directly to the heart of the problem," said Dodd. "And that is why I am proposing this constitutional amendment: because constitutional questions need constitutional answers. I believe it is the best way to save our democratic system of government from the continued corrosion of special interest influence."

Two progressive coalitions are pushing the effort to amend the Constitution. One is at freespeechforpeople.org. According to the website, "this is a campaign sponsored by Voter Action (voteraction.org), Public Citizen (citizen.org), the Center for Corporate Policy (corporatepolicy.org), and American Independent Business Alliance (amiba.net) to restore the First Amendment's free speech guarantees for the people, and to preserve and promote democracy and self-government. We are joined by a growing wave of people around the country."

The other is movetoamend.org. (Disclosure: I signed its petition.) It's a little broader in scope than just overturning *Citizens United.* Here's how it spells out its goals: "We, the People of the United States of America, reject the U.S. Supreme Court's ruling in *Citizens United*," and move to amend our Constitution to:

"Firmly establish that money is not speech, and that human beings, not corporations, are persons entitled to constitutional rights."

"Guarantee the right to vote and to participate, and to have our votes and participation count."

"Protect local communities, their economies, and democracies against illegitimate 'preemption' actions by global, national, and state governments."

Some of the prime movers behind it are the Liberty Tree Foundation, the Center for Media and Democracy, and the Independent Progressive Politics Network. And it is endorsed by the National Lawyers Guild, Progressive Democrats of America, Women's International League for Peace and Freedom, and the Program on Corporations, Law, and Democracy.

There are two ways to amend the Constitution. One is to start with Congress, pass the amendment by a two-thirds margin in both houses, and then get three-quarters of the states to ratify it. The other way, which has almost never been used, is to get two-thirds of the states to call a constitutional convention, and then get three-quarters to ratify.

The Free Speech for People group favors the traditional way, while some in the Move to Amend coalition lean more toward a constitutional convention.

"I certainly think it would be more effective to build up from the states," says Manski. "It may be that in the process of winning state legislatures over, we'll change the political climate and Congress will respond by taking action. But I'm not going to rely on Congress. For myself, the safest route is to put all of our energy into the state initiatives and go the constitutional convention route."

John Bonifaz, the legal director of Voter Action, believes it would be "dangerous to go down that road." A constitutional convention, he fears, could be a disaster for minority rights. He believes that the right wing might successfully organize to pass an amendment declaring marriage as solely between a man and a woman or anointing English as the official language of the United States.

"What we're about is reclaiming our democracy and advancing the franchise, not moving backwards," he says.

The groups are getting along, fortunately, and working together. And they sense the urgency of the moment.

"The Supreme Court has had its say," Raskin said. "Now it's our turn. Now is the time for us to put in motion a great popular movement to defend democracy against the champions of corporate plutocracy."

But no one has any illusions that it will be easy, as anyone who experienced the heartbreak of the Equal Rights Amendment can attest.

"It's certainly an uphill fight," says Weissman. The court's decision "dealt a severe body blow to our democracy, and we'll have to wait and see whether democracy can rise up or falls to the canvas."

Senator Russ Feingold of Wisconsin calls the ruling "one of the most lawless in the history of the Supreme Court." But ever idiosyncratic, Feingold opposes a constitutional amendment as a remedy. "I think that's unwise, but I certainly understand the sentiment," he told

The Progressive. "The best thing to do is to get new justices, different justices, who will do the right thing."

That may be a shortcut—and it may not.

"Based on the age of some of the justices in the majority, that's suggesting we wait a very long time," says Bonifaz, who has litigated the campaign finance issue at the Supreme Court. "And while a constitutional amendment can take a long time, there have been instances where it took only a few years."

There's one other drawback to hoping for a more enlightened composition of justices, because that leaves the question of corporate personhood up for grabs every time there is a new formation on the Supreme Court.

We need to slay the dragon of corporate personhood once and for all.

To do that, it seems to me, we'll have to put our Susan B. Anthony hats on and get to work.

Critical Thinking

1. Why was the Supreme Court's decision declaring the McCain-Feingold campaign finance reform act unconstitutional problematic in its classification of corporations?

2. What are some of the legislative responses posed by members of Congress to address the Supreme Court decision against McCain-Feingold?

3. What does the author suggest is the best way to mobilize public opinion, which has been overwhelmingly opposed to the Supreme Court's decision?

4. Are the options for amending the Constitution or overturning the decision likely to occur? Why or why not?

MATTHEW ROTHSCHILD is the editor of The Progressive.

Reprinted by permission from *The Progressive*, April 2010, pp. 17–20. Copyright © 2010 by The Progressive, 409 E Main St, Madison, WI 53703. www.progressive.org

A Title IX for Health Care

Despite some setbacks, women can take heart in the many gains health-insurance reform will bring.

Eleanor Smeal

Feminists didn't get everything they wanted in the historic health-insurance reform package passed in March. The lack of a public option and limits on abortion coverage were the most glaring setbacks, and a single-payer system wasn't even considered. But bottom line, an additional 32 million Americans will gain health-care coverage—meaning that the vast majority in the U.S., some 95 percent, will be covered.

Considering the hundreds of millions spent by the health-insurance industry in federal lobbying, the intransigence of the Republican bloc in Congress and the lack of a pro-choice majority in either house, it's a wonder that anything was achieved, let alone historic gains for millions of people, especially women.

First and foremost, what has been little reported is that the legislation essentially contains a "Title IX" for women. It states that, with a few exceptions, an individual cannot "be excluded from participation in, be denied the benefits of, or be subjected to discrimination under any health program or activity, any part of which is receiving federal financial assistance." It explicitly refers to Title IX of the Education Amendments of 1972 (which prohibits sex discrimination), Title VI of the Civil Rights Act of 1964 (prohibiting race discrimination), the Age Discrimination Act of 1975, and the Rehabilitation Act of 1973 (which prohibits disability discrimination). In other words, if a public or private entity receives federal funds—and health-insurance companies do!—it can't discriminate against women or on the basis of race, national origin, ethnicity, age or disability. (The act does permit insurers to charge more on the basis of age, but only up to three times more.)

Secondly, as Speaker Nancy Pelosi said repeatedly, "No longer will being a woman be considered a pre-existing condition." Gender rating—charging women more than men for health insurance—is eliminated for individuals plans and for employer plans covering fewer than 100 employees. This, together with the above prohibition against sex discrimination, is the beginning of the end of all gender rating. Today, in most states, women with individual plans pay as much as 48 percent higher premiums than men for the same coverage.

What's more, the legislation requires that insurers provide maternity coverage; currently, about 80 percent of individual insurance policies do not. Companies with more than 50 employees must also provide breast-feeding mothers reasonable break time and a room to express milk. The act also funds support services for, and education and research on, post-partum depression.

Here are a few more of the gains:

- Starting this year, every new insurance policy is required to include **a basic benefits package of preventive care** without copays or deductibles, including PAP smears, mammograms, and immunizations.
- This year, **pre-existing conditions will be eliminated** for children. In 2014, this will be extended to adults and will include the elimination of domestic violence, pregnancy, and cesarian sections as pre-existing conditions. Meanwhile, adults who cannot obtain health insurance because of pre-existing conditions can enter a temporary high-risk health-insurance pool to obtain coverage.
- **Lifetime caps on coverage will be eliminated** immediately, and annual caps will end in 2014.
- The practice of **recision will be banned** immediately. That means insurers cannot drop someone as soon as an illness is diagnosed or a claim is made.
- Beginning this year, **young people can remain on their parents' health-insurance policy** until age 26 if they are not otherwise covered.
- **Medicare benefits are not reduced and recipients will gain two major benefits.** The "doughnut hole" in Medicare prescription drug programs—the gap between the initial coverage limit and the threshold for receiving catastrophic coverage—will begin to close. And in 2011, recipients will no longer have to share costs for preventive services, including cancer screenings, annual physicals and immunizations.
- **Employers will not be able to give lesser plans to lower-paid workers,** who are more likely to be women and people of color.
- Beginning in 2014, **about 16 million more people will gain access to coverage through medicaid and schip** (the State Children's Health Insurance Program). All people (except undocumented immigrants) living at less than 133 percent of the federal poverty level ($10,830 for an individual; $22,050 for a family of four) will qualify for Medicaid.
- In 2014, **24 million more people will be able to purchase insurance at group rates** through state insurance exchanges. Most citizens and legal residents will be *required* to purchase health insurance, but, initially, more than 75 percent will be eligible for federal subsidies credits because their income is between 133 percent and 400 percent ($88,200 for a family of four) of the federal poverty level.

The Feminist Fight for Health Reform

Hundreds of thousands of feminists and a large coalition of women's rights groups have long been immersed in the struggle to win comprehensive health-care reform that eliminates discrimination against women. As I know only too well, health-insurance companies were one of the major opponents of the Equal Rights Amendment ratification drive.

To achieve this recent legislative victory, which eliminates sex discrimination in pricing and many benefits, women's organizations such as Planned Parenthood Foundation of America, NARAL Pro-Choice America, NOW, Feminist Majority, National Women's Law Center, National Partnership for Women and Families, National Council of Women's Organizations, YWCA USA, National Council of Jewish Women and National Older Women's League worked tirelessly together—attending countless meetings with administration officials and members of Congress, delivering millions of emails, sponsoring lobby days and more.

But we haven't eliminated sex discrimination entirely. Although the heinous Stupak/Pitts amendment, which would have banned abortion coverage entirely and was dictated by the National Conference of Catholic Bishops, was defeated, the harmful Nelson language passed. It goes beyond the current Hyde amendment prohibitions against federal funding of abortion to poor women by restricting private insurance coverage as well.

For years, insurance companies denied discrimination against women and/or put bogus claims to justify it. With the passage of this reform package, the beginning of the end of health-insurance sex discrimination, in both benefits and pricing, is at hand. One attribute, for sure, of the women's movement—we don't take no for an answer when it comes to obtaining women's equality. And we *never* give up or give in.

—E.S.

- Also in 2014, EMPLOYERS WITH MORE THAN 50 EMPLOYEES WILL BE OBLIGATED TO OFFER INSURANCE COVERAGE or pay annual penalties of $2,000 per employee. Small businesses (less than 50 employees) are exempted from this penalty. Plus, some small businesses (less than 25 employees) will receive tax credits for providing coverage.

- The new law PROVIDES FOR "MENTAL HEALTH PARITY" in qualified health plans in the exchange—in other words, therapy will be covered.

Many critics have asserted that with more coverage there won't be enough doctors or nurses. The reform package ADDRESSES THE NATIONAL NURSING SHORTAGE by increasing the number of nursing education slots, providing loan repayment and retention grants and offering grants, for employment and training of family nurse practitioners. The SHORTAGE OF PRIMARY-CARE DOCTORS IS ADDRESSED THROUGH SCHOLARSHIPS, loan programs and bonus payments to private-care physicians and general surgeons practicing in areas with shortages. Moreover, it expands access to health care by adding $11 billion to double the capacity of community health centers. New programs will increase support for school-based and nurse-managed health centers.

Setbacks for Women

On the downside, coverage of abortion cannot be required in the state health exchanges' health-care packages, and abortions cannot be covered by any federal subsidy or funding in accordance with current law (the Hyde amendment). Under the Nelson provision in the health-care reform act, individuals may buy private insurance plans in state exchanges that include abortion coverage, but only if they pay for the abortion coverage with their own money. To "segregate" the payments, the Nelson language requires that the policyholder make two payments, one for the bulk of the plan and a second to an allocation fund that includes abortion coverage. Individual states may opt out of providing plans with abortion coverage, but only if they pass a new law prohibiting their insurance exchange from including such plans. President Obama's executive order on abortion restrictions reinforces provisions already in the act.

Another major blow is the revival of domestic abstinence-only sex education funding to the tune of $250 million over five years. These programs, previously defunded by President Obama, have proven to be ineffectual and harmful. The good news is the health-care reform package includes $375 million over five years for comprehensive sex-education programs based on scientific evidence.

The struggle over this legislation shows us the power of the U.S. Conference of Catholic Bishops [see *Ms.*, Winter 2010] and the blatant fact that pro-choice forces do not have a majority in Congress. But this fight also shows the strength of the women's movement, and has galvanized us not only to repeal the Nelson restrictions but, once and for all, to repeal the Hyde amendment.

Critical Thinking

1. What does the "Title IX" clause of the health care reform legislation of 2010 include?

2. What is the practice of "gender rating" in health insurance? How does the 2010 legislation address it?

3. Under the reform legislation, what are some of the gains for women's health coverage?

4. What were the setbacks for women that were included in the legislation?

ELEANOR SMEAL is president of the Feminist Majority Foundation and publisher of Ms.

UNIT 2

Structures of American Politics

Unit Selections

Learning Outcomes

After reading this unit you should be able to:

- Determine the extent to which "the Constitution provides only a bare skeleton" (to quote from the Unit 2 overview that appears below) of how the presidency, Congress, the Supreme Court, and the bureaucracy function today.

- Compare and contrast the performances of different presidents while in office.

- Appraise and evaluate the performances of different presidents while in office.

- Evaluate praise and criticism of the U.S. Congress presented by Lee Hamilton, William G. Howell and Jon C. Pevehouse, Lawrence Lessig, and Thomas Geoghegan. Appraise the performance of the U.S. Congress.

- Compare and contrast the decisions of the Supreme Court under different chief justices.

- Describe and analyze some of the major roles that the bureaucracy plays in the operation of U.S. government.

- Describe, compare and contrast, and categorize shortcomings of (1) presidents, (2) Congress as a whole and of individual members of Congress, (3) the Supreme Court as a whole and of individual members of the Court, and (4) the bureaucracy as a whole and of individual bureaucrats.

- Describe and evaluate congressional-presidential relations in the following contexts: (1) foreign and military policy-making, and (2) legislating, vetoes by presidents, and veto overrides by Congress.

- Compare and contrast congressional-presidential relations when operating under conditions of "unified" government and "divided" government.

- Identify the single most important point made in Unit 2 selections about each: the presidency, Congress, the Supreme Court, and the bureaucracy. Then explain why you think each of the four points you have identified is the most important point made.

James Madison, one of the primary architects of the American system of government, observed that the three-branch structure of government created at the Constitutional Convention of 1787 pitted the ambitions of some individuals against the ambitions of others. Nearly two centuries later, political scientist Richard Neustadt wrote that the structure of American national government is one of "separated institutions sharing powers." These two eminent students of American politics suggest an important proposition: the very design of American national government contributes to the struggles that occur among government officials who have different institutional loyalties and potentially competing goals.

This unit is divided into four sections. The first three treat the three traditional branches of American government, and the last one treats the bureaucracy. One point to remember when studying these institutions is that the Constitution provides only a bare skeleton of the workings of the American political system. The flesh and blood of the presidency, Congress, judiciary, and bureaucracy are derived from decades of experience and the shared expectations of today's political actors.

A second point to note is that the way a particular institution functions is partly determined by the identities of those who occupy relevant offices. The presidency operates differently with Barack Obama in the White House than it did when George W. Bush was president. Similarly, Congress and the Supreme Court function differently according to who serve as members and who hold leadership positions within the institutions. There were significant changes in the House of Representatives after Democrat Nancy Pelosi succeeded Republican Dennis Hastert as speaker in 2007 and, before that, when Hastert took over from Newt Gingrich in 1999. In the Senate, within a two-year period beginning in January 2001, Republican majority leader Trent Lott was succeeded by Democrat Tom Daschle, who in turn was succeeded by Republican Bill Frist. These changes in Senate leadership brought obvious changes in the operation of the Senate. Changes were evident once again when Democrat Harry Reid succeeded Frist in 2007.

A third point about today's American political system is that in recent decades traditional branch vs. branch conflict has been accompanied, and probably overshadowed by increasing partisanship between the two major parties. In the first 6 years of George W. Bush's presidency, Republican members of Congress seemed to be substantially more influenced by the party affiliation that they shared with President Bush than the institutional loyalties that, in Madison's eyes, would and should pit Congress against the president. In turn, many observers think that during the first 6 years of the twenty-first century, Congress did not satisfactorily perform its traditional function of "checking" and "balancing" the executive branch.

The November 2006 elections brought Democratic majorities to both houses of Congress. For Democrats in the 110th Congress, party affiliation and a belief in institutional or branch prerogatives reinforced one another. Both their party differences with President Bush *and* their belief that Congress is and should be co-equal to the executive branch fueled opposition to the Iraq war and to other Bush actions. And President Bush no doubt had both party loyalties and executive branch prerogatives in mind as he contended with Democratic leaders and Democratic majorities in the 110th Congress. The 2008 elections brought Democratic control to all three elective institutions of the national government (Presidency, House of Representatives, and Senate), a situation that political scientists call "unified government." Some observers of the American political system, Woodrow Wilson among them, have argued that "unified government" is likely to be more effective and efficient than its counterpart, "divided government" (in which neither major party controls all three elective institutions). Others, most notably Professor David Mayhew of Yale University, arguably the most respected living political scientist specializing in the study of American politics, have concluded that "unified governments" vary very little, if at all, from "divided governments" in what they accomplish. For nearly two-thirds of

© fStop/Getty Images

the six decades since World War II, Americans have lived under "divided government." But in January 2009, a new period of "unified government" (under Democratic control) began, and only time will tell how well the country is served.

The first section of this unit contains articles on the contemporary presidency. They include both retrospective assessments of the presidency of George W. Bush and articles addressing the first eighteen months of President Barack Obama's first term. Eight months after Bush became president in the aftermath of the controversial 2000 election, terrorist attacks on the World Trade Center and the Pentagon on September 11, 2001, abruptly transformed his presidency. Americans of both parties rallied around President Bush in his efforts to respond decisively to the attacks, and Congress passed a resolution that authorized President Bush to invade Iraq. The resulting war in Iraq began in early 2003, and within a few weeks President Bush triumphantly declared the success of the invasion that had overthrown the regime of Iraqi president Saddam Hussein.

But the situation in Iraq grew worse instead of better in the next few years, and by the start of 2006, the majority of Americans opposed the Iraq war and disapproved of Bush's performance as president. The 2006 congressional elections gave voters the chance to express their views forcefully on the Bush administration and they did so, handing majority control of both houses of Congress to the Democrats. In November 2008, of course, Democrat Barack Obama won the presidency over Republican John McCain, with widespread disapproval of Bush's performance as president apparently being a key factor in that electoral outcome. Twenty months into Obama's presidency, polls show substantial and growing disapproval of his overall performance in office as well as with many of his policy initiatives. It is in these contexts that articles in the first section of this unit assess the presidencies of both George W. Bush and Barack Obama as well as the presidency more generally.

The second section of this unit treats Congress, which has undergone noteworthy changes in the past four decades after over a half-century of relative stability anchored by the extremely powerful seniority system instituted in the early twentieth century. In the 1970s, reforms in that seniority system brought an enormous degree of decentralization to Capitol Hill. The unexpected Republican takeover of the House of Representatives as a result of the 1994 congressional elections brought even more changes. The new Republican speaker, Newt Gingrich, reduced the power of committees and the importance of the seniority system, imposed term limits on committee chairs, consolidated power in the Speaker's office, and became a prominent figure on the national scene. The 2006 congressional elections, of course, enabled Democrats to regain majority control of both houses. A woman, Representative Nancy Pelosi of California, became Speaker of the House for the first time in history, and Republicans controlled neither house of Congress for the first time in a dozen years. Democrats increased their majorities in both houses of Congress in the 2008 elections, and, of course, a fellow Democrat, Barack Obama, won the White House. For the first year of the 111th Congress, Democrats (joined by two independents) controlled 60 seats in the Senate, making for what was often a "filibuster-proof" majority.

The Supreme Court sits at the top of the U.S. court system, and is the focus of the third section in this unit. The Court is not merely a legal institution; it is a policymaker whose decisions can affect the lives of millions of citizens. The Court's decisive role in determining the outcome of the 2000 presidential election showed its powerful role in the American political system.

Membership of the nine-member Court—and, in turn, operation of the institution as a whole—was unusually stable between 1994 and 2005, one of the longest periods in American history during which no Supreme Court vacancies occurred. In July 2005, Associate Justice Sandra Day O'Connor announced her intention to resign and a few months later Chief Justice William Rehnquist died. President Bush's nominees to fill the two vacancies, John Roberts and Samuel Alito, became chief justice and associate justice, respectively. Less than four months into Barack Obama's presidency, Associate Justice David Souter announced his retirement. President Obama nominated Sonia Sontomayor to replace Souter, and she became the first Hispanic woman to sit on the Court.

In 2010, President Obama nominated Elena Kagan to succeed retiring Associate Justice Stevens, and she became the fourth woman to serve on the Court and brought the number of women justices currently serving to three, an all-time high.

Like all people in high government offices, the chief justice and associate justices have policy views of their own. In turn, observers of the Court pay careful attention to the way the chief justice and the eight associate justices interact with one another in shaping the decisions of the Court.

The bureaucracy of the national government, the subject of the fourth and last section in this unit, is responsible for carrying out policies determined by top-ranking officials. Yet the bureaucracy is not merely a neutral administrative instrument, and it is often criticized for waste and inefficiency. Even so, government bureaucracies must be given credit for many of the accomplishments of American government. Whether we like it or not, government bureaucracies wield great power in the conduct of American national government.

As a response to the September 11 terrorist attacks, Congress in 2002 passed a bill establishing the Department of Homeland Security, the biggest reorganization of the executive branch since the Department of Defense was founded in the aftermath of World War II. In the summer of 2004, the 9/11 Commission issued its report recommending the restructuring of the government's intelligence community. In response, Congress passed a bill later that year that established the position of Director of National Intelligence in an attempt to bring a clearer hierarchy and better communication to the government's intelligence establishment. More effective and efficient functioning of the bureaucracy has clearly become an important concern since the destruction of the World Trade Center, and efforts to improve government bureaucracy's performance in the areas of homeland security and intelligence gathering are continuing.

Some observers have attributed the home mortgage crisis and related credit and banking problems that signaled a dramatic economic downturn in 2008 to ineptly functioning bureaucracies of the national government. Fannie Mae and Freddie Mac, two relatively obscure government-related agencies, began to receive unfavorable scrutiny as the nation's home mortgage system faltered, with catastrophic consequences for Wall Street and the economy as a whole. Critics suggested that too generous lending by banks under the auspices of Fannie Mae and Freddie Mac, in conjunction with a number of unregulated or inadequately regulated Wall Street financial practices, was responsible for the credit problems that touched off the global economic downturn. In July, 2010, Congress passed and the president signed the Dodd-Frank Wall Street Reform and Consumer Protection Act, which established a new government agency, the Bureau of Consumer Financial Protection. According to the U.S. Chamber of Commerce, the mammoth bill directs that bureaucrats formulate 350 rules, conduct 47 studies, and write 74 reports.

Student Website
www.mhhe.com/cls

Internet References

Department of State
www.state.gov

Federal Reserve System
www.federalreserve.gov

Supreme Court/Legal Information Institute
http://supct.law.cornell.edu/supct/index.html

United States House of Representatives
www.house.gov

United States Senate
www.senate.gov

Misremembering Reagan

The Gipper still has lessons to teach—just not the ones we usually hear.

RAMESH PONNURU

"Republicans have attempted to lead with one eye on the rear-view mirror, gazing at the fading reflection of Ronald Reagan. . . . But Ronald Reagan cannot win the victory for Republicans in [the next election], and the party had best get busy finding fresh ideas and new leaders." Ralph Reed wrote those words after the Republicans lost the election—the election of 1998.

Since then, Reagan's reflection has faded still more. Yet the tendency Reed lamented has only gotten stronger. Reagan's death, the reevaluation of his presidency by historians (including liberal historians), and, above all, the political failure of George W. Bush have made conservatives cling to Reagan's memory more fiercely. In 2008, during the first presidential-primary campaign since Reagan died, each of the Republican candidates presented himself as his reincarnation. After Republicans lost the election, conservative activist Phyllis Schlafly offered familiar advice: "Republicans should follow Ronald Reagan's example." Conservative congressman Patrick McHenry is running a PAC that seeks "to return the Republican party to its Ronald Reagan roots." The Heritage Foundation's website seeks to resolve today's policy debates by asking, "What would Reagan do?"

Much of the debate over the Republican party's future concerns Reagan. Should the party return to Reaganism, as the "traditionalists" argue, or move beyond it, as the "reformers" say? At a recent party gathering, Jeb Bush was reported to have thrown in his lot with the reformers and urged the party to let go of Reagan's memory. (There are conflicting accounts of what Bush said.) Several conservatives who had previously been fans of the former Florida governor attacked him lustily and in public for the alleged slight.

Liberals deride the Right's fixation with Reagan, and even some conservatives roll their eyes about it. When invoking Reagan, conservatives are prone to two characteristic vices: hero-worship and nostalgia. To hear some conservatives talk, you would forget that Reagan was a human being who made mistakes, including in office. You would certainly forget that movement conservatives were frequently exasperated with Reagan's administration.

Nostalgia is the more serious charge. Conservatives may be looking for a presidential candidate to present himself as "the next Reagan"—the Republican field in 2008 certainly thought so—but the public at large is not. It has, after all, been more than 20 years since Reagan held office. The country has changed, and many observers say that his agenda and even his political vision are now obsolete. "I love Reagan too," Republican strategist Mike Murphy recently wrote in *Time*. "But demographics no longer do."

Liberals may disdain what they call the "cult of Reagan," but Republicans' affection and respect for the man who won the Cold War seems a lot less cultish than their own infatuation with President Obama. Reagan was the most consequential president of the last 35 years, the most successful Republican president of the last century, and the president most associated with the conservative movement. Of course conservatives should try to learn from his example.

If, that is, they can decide which Reagan to learn from. There are quite a few on offer. There is the sunny, irenic Reagan. At a reception following the unveiling of a statue of Reagan in the Capitol, RNC chairman Michael Steele said, "You never heard a harsh word come out of his mouth." (What about the "evil empire" and "welfare queens"?) There is the libertarian Reagan: Former congressman and media personality Joe Scarborough recently complained that Republicans had gone astray by forgetting the maxim, which he attributed to Reagan, that the government is best that governs least. (This was right after Scarborough complained that Republicans had gone too far in deregulating Wall Street.) The liberals' Reagan, meanwhile, is defined less by his principles than by the compromises he made to them: less by the large tax cuts he won than by the smaller tax increases he accepted.

The conservatives who summon Reagan's ghost for use in today's arguments usually use him as a stand-in for doctrinal purity. He illustrates the alleged axiom that true-blue conservatism—these days we would probably have to say true-red—wins elections. His leadership of his party was bookended by moderate-Republican failure. Presidents Nixon and Ford brought their party so low that in their aftermath it considered changing its name. The elder President Bush wasn't just a one-termer; his vote in successive elections dropped more than that of any president since Hoover (another moderate Republican, as historically minded conservatives will inform you). Many conservatives draw the lesson that the GOP is better-off without its non-Reaganite politicians, now dubbed RINOs, for "Republicans in name only."

Such Republicans regularly put up roadblocks in President Reagan's path, and he was frequently tart about them in his diaries. Yet he never supported primary campaigns against them. He challenged an incumbent Republican in a primary himself, of course, in 1976. But he did not support his former aide Jeffrey Bell in his 1978 primary against New Jersey senator Clifford Case. His White House even supported Jim Jeffords of Vermont. After he won the battle over the basic direction of the party, he seems to have concluded in practice that further intra-party fighting was counterproductive. He may have been on to something. It is melancholy for conservatives to contemplate that yesterday's liberal Republican senators have been replaced far more often by liberal Democrats than by conservative Republicans.

Reagan's practice ran counter to our superficial impressions of him in other respects, too. "It's true hard work never killed anyone," he famously quipped, "but I figure, why take the chance?" Reagan had his reasons for wanting his political career to seem effortless. It can be useful for a politician to be underestimated, and for his utterances to sound like pure expressions of common sense. But we now have an extensive documentary record that shows that Reagan worked extremely hard both on his policies and on his rhetoric.

As a conservative spokesman, the governor of the largest state, and then a presidential-candidate-in-waiting, Reagan had taken and defended positions on a multitude of issues. Compared with some later Republican leaders, such as the first Bush and Sen. John McCain, Reagan cared about a broader range of policies and knew more about them. He didn't make up positions on the fly or go with his gut. He had also honed his explanations of why he sought some reforms and rejected other proposals. Steven Hayward, the second volume of whose excellent history *The Age of Reagan* appears this summer, points out that it took practice and attention as well as talent for Reagan to become the Great Communicator. Reagan could ramble through responses to questions and even occasionally flub his lines. But he concentrated on getting his most important messages across, and doing it succinctly.

Are Reagan's would-be successors willing to follow this example? Bush, Dole, Bush, and McCain didn't. None of them could talk, and some of them seemed to disdain the enterprise. One hopes that Sarah Palin is doing her homework on national policy issues behind the scenes, prepared to reemerge with an unquestioned mastery of them. In her career in national politics, she has given one fine speech, at last year's party convention. Nothing as good has followed.

Contemporary Republican politicians might find two features of Reagan's rhetoric instructive. The first is that when he was not appearing before movement audiences, his conservatism was rarely explicit. He did not advertise his conformity to a school of thought even when he did, in fact, conform. He did not, that is, sell his policies on the basis of their conservatism. Rather the reverse: He used attractive policies to get people to give his conservatism a look. Hayward notes that Reagan's televised speech on behalf of Barry Goldwater's presidential campaign was "quite ideological," but that Reagan presented the choice before Americans as "up or down" rather than "left or right."

The second is that the American Founding loomed large in Reagan's rhetoric. The political scientist Andrew Busch has found that during his presidency Reagan mentioned the Founders more than his four immediate predecessors combined. He mentioned the Constitution ten times in his memoirs, compared with zero for those predecessors. Those of us who believe that our political inheritance from the Founders is what conservatives ought to be trying to conserve will naturally find this fact heartening. No serious student of Reagan can believe that his constitutionalism was other than sincere. It also served him well politically. It promoted unity among his sometimes fractious supporters. It rooted him in American tradition even as his opponents called him a radical. It provided a connective thread, a coherence, a seriousness, and even a nobility to his politics that it might otherwise have lacked.

Reagan's constitutionalism puts him squarely in the "traditionalist" camp of today's intra-conservative debates. Taken in full, though, his record shows how misconceived those debates are. Some of his current admirers make him out to be a supremely gifted exponent of a timeless conservative platform, as though he were merely Barry Goldwater with better public-relations skills. Yet Reagan differed in both his program and, especially, his emphases.

John O'Sullivan has written that "Reaganism was not an innovation in political thought":

> It was conservative common sense applied to the problems that had developed in the 1960s and 1970s. To the stagflation of the economy, it applied tax cuts and the monetary control of inflation; to the market-sharing cartel of OPEC, it applied price decontrol and the "magic of the marketplace"; and to the revived threat from the Soviet Union it applied a military build-up and economic competition.
>
> These policies were what most conservatives would have recommended as answers to these problems at most times in [the 20th] century. The only novel thing about them is that they were actually carried out.

That is not quite right. Reagan was an innovator in key respects. It is true, for example, that most conservatives harbored a preference for lower spending and lower taxes. But the previous conservative orthodoxy was content to wait until some future day when spending was lowered to embark on tax cuts. Hence Goldwater voted against Kennedy's tax reductions. Reagan redefined the conservative orthodoxy on this issue.

I quote O'Sullivan at length because he nonetheless grasps something that other admirers of Reagan have scanted: Reaganism succeeded as state craft because it applied characteristically conservative insights to the challenges of his time. Reagan wanted to reform entitlement programs, just as Goldwater did; but he saw that the country had more pressing needs, such as for tax reduction. The tight connection between Reagan's agenda and the nation's circumstances tends to elude us these days—so much so that we misquote one of his signature lines. Everyone remembers that he said in his first inaugural address that "government is not the solution, government is the problem." Everyone forgets that the line began "In this present crisis." He wasn't saying that government was always "the problem," let alone that it would always be the problem in the same way that it was in 1981.

It is thus a mistake to assume that keeping true to the spirit of Reaganism requires contemporary conservatives to press forward with his administration's program: to keep trying to reduce the top income-tax rate, for example, with the same urgency he brought to the task. A conservative today should share Reagan's conservative preference for lower taxes and a less socially harmful tax code. But he might conclude that, in part because Reagan changed our circumstances, the tax that most needs lowering today is the payroll tax. Or he might conclude that a free-market reform of health care is more important now than any changes to the tax code.

Gov. Mitch Daniels of Indiana says that Republicans must be the party of hope, not the party of memory. Reagan managed to lead both parties simultaneously. George Will, correcting a widespread misunderstanding at the time Reagan took office, said that he did not wish to take the country back to the past: He wanted to restore the past's way of facing the future. Conservatism must constantly adapt. Burke knew it. So did Reagan. He was simultaneously a traditionalist and a reformer. Let all conservatives be so.

Critical Thinking

1. How do Republican "traditionalists" view Reagan's legacy? How do Republican "reformers" view Reagan?

2. Why is Reagan considered to be a model for Republican leadership?

3. What two lessons can modern Republicans learn from Reagan's rhetorical style?

4. How was Reagan an innovator?

From *The National Review*, July 6, 2009, pp. 33–34. Copyright © 2009 by National Review, Inc, 215 Lexington Avenue, New York, NY 10016. Reprinted by permission.

Small Ball after All?

Both supporters and critics of George W. Bush tend to view him as a game-changing president. But it's possible he may be remembered another way—as a comparatively minor figure.

JONATHAN RAUCH

"*W*orst. President. Ever.*"* That succinct judgment, received not long ago via e-mail from a political scientist, sums up a good deal of what conventional wisdom has to say about President Bush. In an unscientific online poll of 109 historians conducted in April and published by the History News Network at www.hnn.us, more than 60 percent rated Bush's presidency as the worst in U.S. history. In his 2007 book, *Second Chance: Three Presidents and the Crisis of American Superpower,* former National Security Adviser Zbigniew Brzezinski titles his chapter on Bush "Catastrophic Leadership." "A calamity," Brzezinski wrote. "A historical failure."

And he was referring to just the Iraq war. The litany of disasters and failures commonly attributed to Bush has grown familiar enough to summarize in checklist format: WMD; Guantanamo; Abu Ghraib; waterboarding; wiretapping; habeas corpus; "Osama bin Forgotten"; anti-Americanism; deficits; spending; Katrina; Rumsfeld; Cheney; Gonzales; Libby. In this view, George W. Bush is at least as destructive as was Richard Nixon, a president whose mistakes and malfeasances took decades to undo.

Though a smaller band, Bush's defenders parry that he will look to history more like Harry Truman, a president whose achievements took decades to appreciate. In this view, Bush will be remembered as the president who laid the strategic groundwork for an extended struggle against Islamist terrorism; who made democratization the centerpiece of foreign policy; who transformed the federal-state relationship in education; who showed that a candidate can touch the "third rail" of Social Security and still get elected (twice).

Antithetical as these two views are, notice what they assume in common: Bush has been a game-changing president. For better or worse, he has succeeded in his ambition of being a transformative figure rather than one who plays "small ball," in Bush's own disdainful phrase. Hasn't he?

Perhaps not. Today's debate overlooks another possibility: Bush may go down in history as a transitional and comparatively minor figure. His presidency, though politically traumatic, may leave only a modest policy footprint. In that sense—though by no means substantively or stylistically—Bush's historical profile may resemble Jimmy Carter's more than Truman's or Nixon's. Recall that in 1980 many people wondered if the country would ever recover from Carter. Five years later, he was all but forgotten.

In other words, Bush may have accomplished something that seemed out of the question in January 2002, when he touched greatness, and in January 2007, when he touched bottom. Bush may have achieved mediocrity.

If that hypothesis sounds snide, it is not intended to. Had Bush left office at the beginning of last year, his tenure might indeed have gone down as calamitous. Winding up in the middling ranks, then, would be no mean accomplishment. Far from being happenstance, such a finish would reflect an unusual period of course correction that might be thought of as Bush's third term.

From Uniter to Divider

Odd as it may sound today, this president entered office as a proponent of bipartisanship. In his December 13, 2000, victory speech after Vice President Gore conceded the election, Bush called for a new politics of conciliation. Speaking from the chamber of the Texas House of Representatives, he said, "The spirit of cooperation I have seen in this hall is what is needed in Washington, D.C."

To be sure, Bush was capable of aggressive partisanship and brusque unilateralism, as when in 2001 he pushed through large tax cuts with little Democratic support and tore up an assortment of treaties. But in the early days, he also brought off a bipartisan education reform, and after the September 11 terrorist attacks, he did what even his critics agreed was a masterful job of rallying the country. His public approval rose to a dizzying 90 percent.

The fruits of this early period of two-party government were considerable: a new campaign finance law, the USA PATRIOT Act's revisions to domestic-security law, the Sarbanes-Oxley corporate accountability law, the creation of the Homeland

Security Department, and more. "Seventeen major legislative acts were passed in the first two years of the Bush presidency—the second-highest among first-term presidents in the post-World War II period," writes Charles O. Jones, a presidential historian.

Had Bush left office in January 2003, his reputation as our era's Truman might have been assured. His successor would have inherited not only the aforementioned laws but also a successful military campaign in Afghanistan, a set of broadly accepted policies for combating terrorism, and a United Nations still following America's lead in efforts to confront Iraq's Saddam Hussein.

But 2002 also marked the Bush administration's transition to a more rigidly partisan governing style. That January, Karl Rove, Bush's top political adviser, signaled that Republicans would "make the president's handling of the war on terrorism the centerpiece of their strategy to win back the Senate," as *The Washington Post* reported. This represented a distinct change in tone: "Until now," *The Post* noted, "Bush has stressed that the fight against terrorism is a bipartisan and unifying issue for the country."

It was in this period, says Steven Schier, a political scientist at Carleton College and the author of a forthcoming book on Bush's presidency, that "you get the idea of permanent political advantage based on national security, which becomes intoxicating to Republicans." That year's midterm election, which gave Republicans control of the Senate and consolidated their margin in the House, vindicated their strategy but also trapped the party within it.

In firm control of both branches, Bush and congressional Republicans embarked on an experiment in one-party government. Thanks to superbly honed party discipline, the plan worked for a while, but the price was high. Republicans had to govern from the center of their party, rather than the center of the country; Democrats were absolved from responsibility for the results.

What followed was a period of substantive excess and stylistic harshness that came to define Bush's presidency in the public's mind, obliterating memories of the "compassionate conservative." The list of setbacks in this period is long, merely beginning with Iraq's disintegration, North Korea's test of a nuclear bomb, and Iran's growing boldness and influence.

At home, profligate spending and a major Medicare expansion disgusted conservatives. Rising deficits troubled centrists, as did Bush's (unsuccessful) intervention in a dispute over ending the life of Terri Schiavo. His efforts to reform Social Security and immigration policy collapsed embarrassingly; his sluggish response to Hurricane Katrina cratered Americans' faith in his competence. Abroad, Abu Ghraib, Guantanamo, waterboarding, and extrajudicial detentions called the country's basic decency into question. One could go on.

Whatever you may think of the administration's policies on those issues individually, their cumulative effect on Bush and his party are not in doubt. By 2006, the president's approval rating was in the 30 percent range and falling. The Democrats swept control of Congress in November. If Bush's presidency

had ended in January 2007, his reputation as our era's Nixon might have been assured.

But, of course, Bush did not leave office then. Instead he embarked on what history may come to regard as the most surprising and interesting period of his presidency. Many presidents have had good first terms and troubled second ones; the pattern is conventional, and Bush's presidency approximately fits it. But Bush has used his last two years as, in effect, a third term, behaving as if he were his own successor.

Bush's Third Term

He began with some significant personnel changes. In 2006, Bush replaced the second of two mediocre Treasury secretaries with Henry Paulson Jr., whose performance has been lauded by the likes of House Financial Services Committee Chairman Barney Frank, D-Mass., and New York City Mayor Michael Bloomberg—neither of them Bush fans.

Shortly afterward, ending what seemed an interminable wait, Bush got around to replacing the dysfunctional Donald Rumsfeld at the Defense Department with the far more adept Robert Gates. At Justice, Michael Mukasey, a respected federal judge, set about re-professionalizing a department whose independence and credibility had been compromised under Alberto Gonzales. At State, the president gave Condoleezza Rice her head, a trust that her predecessor, Colin Powell, had never been allowed.

"There was unquestionably a sharp change in their approach to the world and in their policies," says Kenneth Pollack, a senior fellow at the Brookings Institution's Saban Center for Middle East Policy. Frequently cited examples include:

- **The Iraq surge.** Against conventional wisdom, the administration sent more troops to Iraq and gave them a new commander with a new strategy. Even Bush's critics now acknowledge that Iraq is in far better shape than it was two years ago. The gains may or may not be sustainable, but if they can be preserved, Iraq has a shot at peace and stability. That seemed a pipe dream before the surge.
- **Iran.** Bush has been patient but, many critics have said, rigid in his dealings with this charter "axis of evil" member. Lately, however, he has softened his posture and attempted to cultivate new openings, notably by authorizing what *The New York Times* called "the most significant American diplomatic contact with Iran since the Islamic revolution in 1979."
- **The Israeli-Palestinian conflict.** After years of keeping his distance from what he seemed to regard as a morass, Bush changed course in 2007, authorizing Rice to pursue diplomacy vigorously and presiding over a relaunch of Israeli-Palestinian peace talks last November.
- **North Korea.** Over hawks' objections, Bush struck a denuclearization deal with Pyongyang much like the one that conservatives, including some Bushies, derided the Clinton administration for making. "That

is the really dramatic example of Bush doing toward the end of his presidency something he would never have contemplated or tolerated early on," says Strobe Talbott, who was deputy secretary of State in the Clinton administration and is now the president of Brookings.

- **Global warming.** Repudiating the Kyoto climate treaty was among Bush's first presidential acts, and he maintained his disengagement from the issue through most of his presidency. But in July he joined the other major industrial countries in promising to halve greenhouse-gas emissions by 2050. A European environmental official told *The Washington Post,* "President Bush has moved considerably over the past one to two years."

What changed? "I think we learned a bit," Stephen Hadley, Bush's national security adviser, told reporters in June. He was speaking of U.S. forbearance in dealing with the always obstreperous North Koreans, but to outsiders the statement appears to have broader applicability. Liberals say that the administration became more flexible because it ran out of alternatives, conservatives that its resolve weakened, Kremlinologists that (as one aide told Carla Anne Robbins of *The New York Times*) "Condi wins."

Ever protective of Bush's trademark steadfastness, the White House takes issue with any talk of U-turns. "I think there's actually remarkable continuity," says Tony Fratto, the deputy press secretary. He asserts that reality has caught up with the administration rather than the other way around. It took time to draw China, India, and other major emerging economies into global-warming negotiations, a prerequisite for any ambitious U.S. commitment; it took time to persuade China to lean on the North Koreans to make a nuclear deal; it took time to weather leadership changes and factional struggles so that Middle East peace negotiations could resume. The surge in Iraq, Fratto says, "was clearly a change of course. It was a new strategy." Elsewhere, he argues, the administration has been reaping the fruits of patient effort.

Whatever the explanation (the various versions may all be partially right), in the past couple of years Bush has significantly changed the starting point for his successor. He now hands President McCain or President Obama a healing rather than a broken Iraq, diplomatic processes rather than deadlocks in the Middle East and the Korean Peninsula, and a position on global warming that is widely viewed as moving the United States past obstructionism. Both Republican John McCain and Democrat Barack Obama, it seems fair to guess, would rather follow than precede Bush's late-term adjustments. Whatever you may think of Bush's abilities as a sailor, he has proved pretty good at bailing.

Meanwhile, despite his abysmal popularity and the Democrats' control of Congress, Bush managed to win approval, on essentially his own terms, of a new wiretapping law and funding for the war in Iraq, the last things anyone expected a Democratic Congress to give him. "I think what you see here is a guy who has learned to be as effective as possible in reduced circumstances," says Schier, the Carleton College political

scientist. Paradoxically, this chief executive who prided himself on assertive, even aggressive, leadership proved to be a weak strong president but a surprisingly strong weak one.

Back to the Future

To what end?

That Bush has improved his legacy over the past couple of years is an easy case to make. True, the economy has declined, oil prices have risen, and the mortgage crisis has loosed a Category 4 storm on Wall Street. But the economy and oil prices are not under Bush's control, and both he and Congress have leaned aggressively into the financial gale, adopting a bipartisan stimulus package and intervening forcefully to support the mortgage market. With unemployment rising and Wall Street wondering where the mortgage fallout may end, no one much likes the economy's condition today, but not many people would trade the *policies* of late 2008 for the *policies* of late 2006.

The harder question is where Bush will leave matters after eight years, not after just the past two. The only honest answer is: It depends. What do you measure? How do you think a President Gore would have done? Those are the sorts of questions that keep historians and journalists in business. You will find no definitive answers here.

But you will find a hypothesis, one at odds with the prevailing wisdom that Bush, whatever you think of him, has been a president of major consequence. Consider, again, the five problems mentioned earlier, this time comparing their likely status in January 2009 with where things stood in January 2001.

- **Iraq.** The situation in January 2001 was unstable and dangerous but not critical. Then, for a time, affairs in Iraq became critical, verging on catastrophic. Now the situation is again unstable and dangerous but not critical. Obviously, Iraq today is a very different kind of problem than it was eight years ago, one more pregnant with both promise and risk. But the U.S. preoccupation with Iraq that Bush inherited in 2001, and that he intended to dispose of once and for all, will instead continue into its fourth presidency, if not beyond. (Iraq will soon have been a sinkhole for U.S. foreign-policy energy for 20 years, almost half the length of the Cold War.)
- **Iran.** This rogue nation was a problem in 2001 and remains a problem now. In the interim, Iran has raced ahead with uranium enrichment, elevated an apocalyptic demagogue to its second-highest office, and expanded its regional influence. At the same time, however, Western powers have edged toward a consensus on confronting Iran, and the United Nations has imposed several sets of sanctions, some of which—the financial ones—appear to be biting.
- **The Israeli-Palestinian conflict.** As Bill Clinton left office, the United States was struggling against long odds to broker a peace deal; as George W. Bush leaves office, the United States is struggling against long odds to broker a peace deal. Whether the situation is more

intractable today than it was eight years ago is an open question, but Bush's reluctant conclusion that the U.S. must mediate an agreement all but guarantees that no future president will try to walk away from the problem. If Bush couldn't walk away, no one can.

- **North Korea.** A tenuous denuclearization agreement was in place eight years ago; a tenuous denuclearization agreement is in place again today. Now, as then, the agreement may or may not be worth the paper it is written on. In the interim, Pyongyang acquired a few more nuclear bombs and tested one, but the two sides are still playing the same game.
- **Global warming.** Eight years ago, the United States had committed itself to reducing greenhouse-gas emissions, though rhetorically rather than substantively; today the United States has again committed itself to reducing greenhouse-gas emissions, though rhetorically rather than substantively. As with the Israeli-Palestinian conflict, Bush's attempt to disengage from the climate-change issue merely established that the United States cannot do so. The next president will pick up more or less where the Clinton-era Kyoto Protocol left off.

Bush may have made these problems harder or easier to solve, a question that partisans can contest to their hearts' delight. What is clear, however, is that all five were large and difficult challenges in 2000 and all five remain large and difficult challenges in 2008.

Two other areas, the war on terrorism and fiscal policy, deserve a closer look. Bush's defenders stake their claims heavily on the former, his detractors on the latter. Has Bush built a lasting architecture for the "long war"? Has he wrecked the country's finances?

The War on Terrorism

September 11, 2001, it is often said, "changed everything." It certainly changed Americans' attitudes, convincing the public that Al Qaeda and its affiliates are a threat rather than a nuisance, and that the United States must apply military as well as civilian tools to confront terrorism. September 11 thereby triggered a cascade of policy changes, ranging from the PATRIOT Act to the Iraq war.

The threat was pre-existing, however, as Bush's supporters tirelessly repeat (adding that the Clinton administration failed to deal with it). The Qaeda-Taliban-jihadi nexus has relocated its headquarters from Afghanistan to the nearby borderlands of Pakistan, but whether and how much it has been weakened is hard to say. The absence of attacks on the American homeland is to the Bush administration's credit, but it seems only fair to guess that a Gore administration would have worked domestic security just as hard. And to the extent that the United States is safer because jihadists shifted their attention to the softer targets of Iraq and Afghanistan, that is not altogether reassuring. Might a different administration have attained better results with less damage to the American brand overseas? Maybe.

A more intellectually interesting question is whether Bush, like Truman, has set up a lasting strategic and institutional architecture for managing the conflict. Bush's defenders argue that a return to either the pinprick responses of the 1990s or the cynical realism of the Cold War is inconceivable. "If we wait for threats to fully materialize, we will have waited too long," Bush said in June 2002. That statement, the core of the Bush Doctrine, is hardly controversial today.

"None of the key elements of the Bush Doctrine—[U.S.] primacy, prevention [of terrorist attacks], coalitions of the willing, and democracy promotion—will be abandoned in practice by successor administrations, whatever their rhetorical recalibrations and tactical adjustments," write Timothy J. Lynch and Robert S. Singh in their new book, *After Bush: The Case for Continuity in American Foreign Policy.* Similarly, the Detainee Treatment Act, the Military Commissions Act, the PATRIOT Act, and the new Foreign Intelligence Surveillance Act have put in place mechanisms that subsequent presidents may revise but will not repudiate.

Such is the strongest upside case for Bush as a turning-point president, and it may well prove correct. The retort, however, is also strong: What was most striking about Bush's attitude toward the long war was his perverse *reluctance* to create a sustainable institutional architecture. In marked contrast to Truman, Bush treated Congress and U.S. allies as afterthoughts, running the war on jihadism as a permanent emergency in which the president could single-handedly make up the rules as he went along. He regarded the war as an opportunity to build a political base, not an institutional one.

Result: It took nearly seven years to finish the first trial of a Guantanamo detainee. The courts have shredded Bush's claim that he could detain almost anyone practically forever, leaving the presidency, in some respects, with less power than it had before. (George H.W. Bush and Bill Clinton both used Guantanamo Bay to hold detainees without judicial oversight; the Supreme Court recently revoked that authority.) The country still lacks coherent and indisputably constitutional structures governing the detention and treatment of terrorism suspects. The sad fact, in this view, is that it will be largely up to the next president to construct the durable, consensus-based structures for the war on terrorism that Bush could and should have built.

As for strategy, this retort continues, what is new about the Bush Doctrine is not sustainable, and what is sustainable is not new. President Gore would likely have moved toward preemption and democratization, but without the rhetorical and military excesses that have widely discredited both approaches. Indeed, Bush has been forced to become a reluctant realist, collaborating with exactly the sorts of tyrannies—in the Middle East, Africa, and Asia—that he has condemned. The Bush Doctrine's worst enemy, in this view, has been Bush.

This argument can't be settled any time soon, if ever. What seems fairly clear, however, is that the jihadist threat is still very much present and that Bush's role has been ambiguous, erecting while also partially discrediting a militarily focused, executive-driven approach that may prove more vigorous than sustainable.

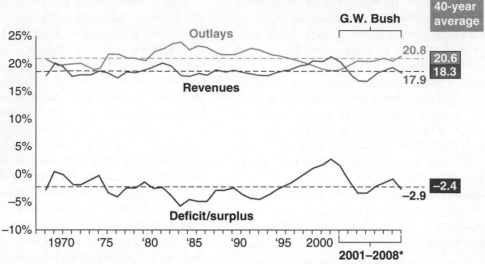

Only Average Federal outlays, revenues and deficit, 1968–2008 (percentage of GDP).

Source: Congressional Budget Office.

Red Ink Rising

Bush's critics, meanwhile, argue that he trashed the country's finances. He cut taxes steeply, waged an expensive war without paying for it, engineered a costly expansion of Medicare (also without paying for it), and untethered federal spending, thus turning healthy surpluses into chronic deficits—all while failing to come to grips with an imminent crisis in entitlement programs.

"We're in much worse fiscal shape today than we were in 2001," says David Walker, who until recently headed the Government Accountability Office and is now president of the Peter G. Peterson Foundation. According to GAO figures, the country's fiscal exposure—the long-term shortfall in its finances, in present-value terms—more than doubled between 2000 and 2007 from $20.4 trillion to $52.7 trillion. Walker says, moreover, "Our $53 trillion hole grows $2 trillion to $3 trillion a year even with a balanced budget," because of rising health care costs, demographic changes (fewer workers supporting more retirees), and accumulating interest on the national debt.

Fiscal recklessness is probably the strongest downside case for Bush as a turning-point president. Here again, however, there is a challenging counterargument.

Thanks mainly to a growing economy, but also partly to tighter budgets, the deficit shrank relative to the economy in Bush's second term. *(See Chart, this page.)* In fiscal 2007, the deficit was 1.2 percent of gross domestic product, which was below the average of the last 40 years. The 2008 deficit will rise to about 2.9 percent of GDP, according to administration projections; but that is still only slightly above the 40-year average, and the cause is primarily cyclical rather than structural, because the economy is slowing down.

For all the talk of runaway spending, moreover, outlays are also right at the 40-year norm. The exceptional federal spending policies were Ronald Reagan's and Bill Clinton's, not Bush's.

As for Bush's tax cuts, viewed in historical perspective they were a blip, not a turning point. Overall, taxes went down early in this decade but then bobbed back up again, though not all the way. In 2007, federal receipts were 18.8 percent of GDP, slightly *above* the 40-year average of 18.3 percent. Even assuming that Bush's tax cuts are all extended when they expire after 2010, *and* assuming that Congress "fixes" the alternative minimum tax by permanently stopping its upward creep, the Congressional Budget Office forecasts that taxes will stay at about 19 percent of GDP.

Bush and Congress, then, didn't smash the revenue base; they just returned it to its well-worn groove. That groove seems to track the public's comfort zone, as suggested by the nonpartisan Tax Policy Center's recent report that Obama's tax program would keep revenues at about 18.4 percent of GDP through 2018—again, right at the historical norm.

As for how the tax burden is allocated, Obama promises to cut taxes at the bottom and increase them at the top. He would raise the top income-tax rate to 39.5 percent, right back where Bill Clinton left it. You can make a plausible case that the end result would approximate what would have been President Gore's tax code.

No question about it: Bush failed to deal with the long-term entitlement problem. He left the ledger in worse shape than he found it, and his botched effort to reform Social Security may have made entitlement reform more difficult politically. "I think we've lost a tremendous opportunity during the Bush period and, really, over the last part of the Clinton period," says Stuart Butler, an analyst at the Heritage Foundation.

Still, as Butler's comment implies, Bush's failure in this regard is not unique. His predecessors ducked the entitlement problem and his would-be successors are all but promising to do the same. McCain's pledges to reduce taxes, and Obama's to increase spending, would likely make the problem worse.

Bush's fiscal failing, in short, arguably lies not in being exceptional but in being all too ordinary.

Disaster, or Detour?

The point of this article is not that the Bush years were uneventful or barren. Far from it. In the realm of foreign policy, the last eight years have seen a nuclear pact with India, a passel of bilateral trade agreements, a redoubled commitment to fight HIV/AIDS, and an innovative foreign-aid program (the Millennium Challenge Account). In social policy, the Bush presidency has brought education reform, restrictions on embryonic-stem-cell research, and incentives for faith-based programs. In finance, the 2002 Sarbanes-Oxley law and the government's current scramble to contain the mortgage-market turmoil have arguably done more to extend Washington's control over Wall Street than anything since the Depression era. The creation of the Homeland Security Department represents the biggest bureaucratic reorganization that Washington has seen in two generations. Bush's two Supreme Court appointments have nudged the Court to the right.

None of those changes is trivial. But few if any are outside the boundaries of ordinary policy-making in an eventful eight-year presidency. It seems fair to guess that most will get sentences or paragraphs, rather than chapters, in the history books.

Indeed, what is most striking about the Bush presidency is not the new problems it has created (though Iraq may yet change that verdict) or the old problems it has solved (though Iraq may yet change that verdict, too). What is striking, rather, is that Bush will pass on to his successor all the major problems and preoccupations he inherited: Iraq, Iran, Israel and the Palestinians, North Korea, global warming, Islamist terrorism, nuclear proliferation, health care, entitlement costs, immigration. What is remarkable, in other words, is not how much Bush has done to reshape the agenda but how little.

Reagan removed inflation from the agenda; he and George H.W. Bush (still sadly underrated) removed the Cold War; Clinton removed welfare and the deficit. Bush, as of now, ends up more or less where he started—not exactly, of course (he resurrected the deficit, for example), but about as close as history's turbulence allows. The biggest surprise of the Bush presidency is its late-breaking bid to join the middling ranks of administrations that are judged not by their triumph or tragedy but by their opportunity cost: What might a greater or lesser president have done with Bush's eight years?

In his recent book *The Bush Tragedy*, Jacob Weisberg, the editor-in-chief of the Washington Post Co.'s Slate Group, mentions the he was "originally going to call this book *The Bush Detour*, thinking of the Bush presidency simply as lost time for the country." His original title may have been closer to the mark. If so, history's ironic judgment on this singularly ambitious president will be that his legacy was small ball, after all.

Critical Thinking

1. What was President George W. Bush's approach to partisan politics at the time of his election and in the early months of his presidency?

2. What were the main characteristics of the Bush administration from 2002 to 2006?

3. What is Bush's so-called "third term" in office? What shifts in policy occurred?

4. What is the "Bush Doctrine" that emerged after the 9/11 terrorist attacks? How did Bush's response to terrorism positively affect his legacy? How did it negatively affect it?

5. What are the negative outcomes of Bush's handling of the country's finances? How can these be viewed in a historical perspective?

6. How did Bush's "third term" impact his legacy? What is the overall view of his eight years in office?

The Founders' Great Mistake

Who is responsible for the past eight years of dismal American governance? "George W. Bush" is a decent answer. But we should reserve some blame for the Founding Fathers, who created a presidential office that is ill-considered, vaguely defined, and ripe for abuse. Here's how to fix what the Founders got wrong—before the next G. W. Bush enters the Oval Office.

GARRETT EPPS

For the past eight years, George W. Bush has treated the White House much as Kenneth Grahame's Mr. Toad treated a new automobile—like a shiny toy to be wrecked by racing the motor, spinning smoke from the tires, and smashing through farmyards until the wheels come off. Bush got to the Oval Office despite having lost the popular vote, and he governed with a fine disdain for democratic and legal norms—stonewalling congressional oversight; detaining foreigners and U.S. citizens on his "inherent authority"; using the Justice Department as a political cudgel; ordering officials to ignore statutes and treaties that he found inconvenient; and persisting in actions, such as the Iraq War, that had come to be deeply unpopular in Congress and on Main Street.

Understandably, most Americans today are primarily concerned with whether Barack Obama can clean up Bush's mess. But as Bush leaves the White House, it's worth asking why he was able to behave so badly for so long without being stopped by the Constitution's famous "checks and balances." Some of the problems with the Bush administration, in fact, have their source not in Bush's leadership style but in the constitutional design of the presidency. Unless these problems are fixed, it will only be a matter of time before another hot-rodder gets hold of the keys and damages the country further.

The historian Jack N. Rakove has written, "The creation of the presidency was [the Framers'] most creative act." That may be true, but it wasn't their best work. The Framers were designing something the modern world had never seen—a republican chief executive who would owe his power to the people rather than to heredity or brute force. The wonder is not that they got so much wrong, but that they got anything right at all.

According to James Madison's *Notes of Debates in the Federal Convention of 1787,* the executive received surprisingly little attention at the Constitutional Convention in Philadelphia. Debate over the creation and workings of the new Congress was long and lively; the presidency, by contrast, was fashioned relatively quickly, after considerably less discussion. One important reason for the delegates' reticence was that George Washington, the most admired man in the world at that time, was the convention's president. Every delegate knew that Washington would, if he chose, be the first president of the new federal government—and that the new government itself would likely fail without Washington at the helm. To express too much fear of executive authority might have seemed disrespectful to the man for whom the office was being tailored.

Washington's force of personality terrified almost all of his contemporaries, and although he said little as presiding officer, he was not always quiet. Once, when an unknown delegate left a copy of some proposed provisions lying around, Washington scolded the delegates like a headmaster reproving careless prep-schoolers, and then left the document on a table, saying, "Let him who owns it take it." No one did.

Even when Washington remained silent, his presence shaped the debate. When, on June 1, James Wilson suggested that the executive power be lodged in a single person, no one spoke up in response. The silence went on until Benjamin Franklin finally suggested a debate; the debate itself proceeded awkwardly for a little while, and was then put off for another day.

Many of the conversations about presidential authority were similarly awkward, and tended to be indirect. Later interpreters have found the original debates on the presidency, in the words of former Supreme Court Justice Robert H. Jackson, "almost as enigmatic as the dreams Joseph was called upon to interpret for Pharaoh."

In the end, the Framers were artfully vague about the extent and limits of the president's powers. Article I, Section 8 of the Constitution, which empowers Congress, runs 429 words; Article II, Section 2, the presidential equivalent, is about half as long. The powers assigned to the president alone are few: he can require Cabinet members to give him their opinions in writing; he can convene a special session of Congress "on extraordinary occasions," and may set a date for adjournment if the two houses cannot agree on one; he receives ambassadors and is commander in chief of the armed forces; he has a veto on legislation (which Congress can override); and he has the power to pardon.

The president also *shares* two powers with the Senate—to make treaties, and to appoint federal judges and other "officers of the United States," including Cabinet members. And, finally, the president has two specific *duties*—to give regular reports on the state of the union, and to "take care that the laws be faithfully executed."

All in all, the text of Article II, while somewhat ambiguous—a flaw that would be quickly exploited—provided little warning that the office of president would become uniquely powerful. Even at the convention, Madison mused that it "would rarely if ever happen that the executive constituted as ours is proposed to be would have firmness enough to resist the legislature." In fact, when citizens considered the draft Constitution during the ratification debates in 1787 and 1788, many of their concerns centered on the possibility that the Senate would make the president its cat's-paw. Few people foresaw the modern presidency, largely because the office as we know it today bears so little relation to that prescribed by the Constitution.

The modern presidency is primarily the intellectual handiwork not of "the Framers" but of one Framer—Alexander Hamilton. Hamilton's idea of the presidency can be found in a remarkable speech he gave to the convention, on June 18, 1787. In it, Hamilton argued that the president should serve for life, name Cabinet members without Senate approval, have an absolute veto on legislation, and have "the direction of war" once "authorized or begun." The president would be a monarch, Hamilton admitted, but an "elective monarch."

Hamilton's plan was so far from the mainstream of thought at the convention that none of its provisions was ever seriously discussed. Nonetheless, Hamilton was and remains the chief theorist of the presidency, first in writing his essays for *The Federalist* and then in serving as George Washington's secretary of the Treasury. In this latter role, acting as Washington's de facto prime minister, Hamilton took full advantage of the vagueness and brevity of Article II, laying the groundwork for an outsize presidency while the war-hero Washington was still in office.

In *The Federalist,* Hamilton had famously proclaimed that "energy in the executive is a leading character in the definition of good government." Just how much energy he favored became clear during America's first foreign crisis, the Neutrality Proclamation controversy of 1793. When Britain and France went to war, many Americans wanted to aid their Revolutionary ally. But Washington and the Federalists were rightly terrified of war with the powerful British Empire. Washington unilaterally proclaimed that the United States would be neutral.

France's American supporters, covertly aided by Thomas Jefferson, fiercely attacked Washington for exceeding his constitutional authority. The power to make treaties, they said, was jointly lodged in the president and the Senate; how could Washington unilaterally interpret or change the terms of the treaty of alliance with France?

Under the pen name "Pacificus," Hamilton wrote a defense of Washington's power to act without congressional sanction. The first Pacificus essay is the mother document of the "unitary executive" theory that Bush's apologists have pushed to its limits since 2001. Hamilton seized on the first words of Article II: "The executive power shall be vested in a President of the United States of America." He contrasted this wording with Article I, which governs Congress and which begins, "All legislative powers herein granted shall be vested in a Congress of the United States." What this meant, Hamilton argued, was that Article II was "a general grant of . . . power" to the president. Although Congress was limited to its enumerated powers, the executive could do literally anything that the Constitution did not expressly forbid. Hamilton's president existed, in effect, outside the Constitution.

That's the Bush conception, too. In 2005, John Yoo, the author of most of the administration's controversial "torture memos," drew on Hamilton's essay when he wrote, "The Constitution provides a general grant of executive power to the president." Since Article I vests in Congress "only those legislative powers 'herein granted'," Yoo argued, the more broadly stated Article II must grant the president "an unenumerated executive authority."

Hamilton's interpretation has proved durable even though there is little in the record of constitutional framing and ratification to suggest that anyone else shared his view. In times of crisis, power flows to the executive; too rarely does it flow back. And while Washington himself used his power wisely (Jeffersonians found out in 1812 that pulling the British lion's tail was poor policy), it was during his administration that the seeds of the "national-security state" were planted.

The system that the Framers developed for electing the president was, unfortunately, as flawed as their design of the office itself. When Madison opened discussion on presidential election in Philadelphia, he opined that "the people at large" were the "fittest" electorate. But he immediately conceded that popular election would hurt the South, which had many slaves and few voters relative to the North. To get around this "difficulty" he proposed using state electors. Electoral-vote strength was based on a state's total population, not on its number of voters—and the South received representation for three-fifths of its slaves both in the House of Representatives and in the Electoral College.

Scholars still debate whether the Framers foresaw the prospect of a contested presidential election, followed by a peaceful shift of power. (Remember that, as Shakespeare pointed out in *Richard II,* kings left office feet first.) Some members of the founding generation believed that a duly elected president would simply be reelected until his death, at which point the vice president would take his place, much like the Prince of Wales ascending to the throne.

Perhaps as a result, the mechanics of presidential election laid out in the Constitution quickly showed themselves to be utterly unworkable. The text of Article II contained no provision for a presidential ticket—with one candidate for president and one for vice president. Instead, each elector was supposed to vote for any two presidential candidates; the candidate who received the largest majority of votes would be president; the runner-up would be vice president. In 1800, this ungainly system nearly brought the country to civil war. Thomas Jefferson and Aaron Burr ran as a team; their electors were expected to vote for both of them. Jefferson assumed that one or two would drop Burr's name from the ballot. That would have given Jefferson the larger majority, with Burr winning the vice presidency. But due to a still-mysterious misunderstanding, all the electors voted for both candidates, producing a tie in the electoral vote and throwing the election to a House vote.

The ensuing drama lasted six days and 36 ballots before Hamilton threw Federalist support to Jefferson (as much as he despised Jefferson, he regarded Burr as "an embryo-Caesar"). This choice began the chain of events that led to Hamilton's death at Burr's hands three years later. More important, the imbroglio exposed the fragility of the election procedure.

In 1804, the Electoral College was "repaired" by the Twelfth Amendment; now the electors would vote for one candidate for president and another for vice president. This was the first patch on Article II, but far from the last—the procedures for presidential election and succession were changed by constitutional amendment in 1933, 1951, 1961, and 1967. None of this fine-tuning has been able to fix the system. In 1824, 1876, 1888, and 2000, the Electoral College produced winners who received fewer popular votes than the losers, and it came startlingly close to doing so again in 2004; in 1824, 1876, and 2000, it also produced prolonged uncertainty and the prospect of civil unrest—or the fact of it.

Even when the election system works passably, a president-elect must endure another indefensible feature of the succession process. In England, a new prime minister takes office the day after parliamentary elections; in France, a newly elected president is inaugurated within a week or two. But when Americans choose a new leader, the victor waits weeks—nearly a quarter-year—to assume office. The presidential interregnum is a recurrent period of danger.

Originally, a new president didn't take office until March 4. This long delay nearly destroyed the nation after the 1860 election. During the disastrous "secession winter," Abraham Lincoln waited in Illinois while his feckless predecessor, James Buchanan, permitted secessionists to seize federal arsenals and forts. By March 1861, when Lincoln took office, the Civil War was nearly lost, though officially it had not even begun.

In 1932, Franklin Roosevelt crushed the incumbent, Herbert Hoover, but had to wait four months to take office. During that period, Hoover attempted to force the president-elect to abandon his proposals for economic reform. Roosevelt refused to commit himself, but the resulting uncertainty led the financial system to the brink of collapse.

The Twentieth Amendment, ratified in 1933, cut the interregnum nearly in half, but 11 weeks is still too long. After his defeat in 1992, President George H. W. Bush committed U.S. troops to a military mission in Somalia. The mission turned toxic, and Bill Clinton withdrew the troops the following year. Clinton was criticized for his military leadership, perhaps rightly—but the Constitution should not have permitted a repudiated president to commit his successor to an international conflict that neither the new president nor Congress had approved.

As the elder Bush did, an interregnum president retains the power of life or death over the nation. As Clinton did, an interregnum president may issue controversial or corrupt pardons. In either case, the voters have no means of holding their leader accountable.

The most dangerous presidential malfunction might be called the "runaway presidency." The Framers were fearful of making the president too dependent on Congress; short of impeachment—the atomic bomb of domestic politics—there are no means by which a president can be reined in politically during his term. Taking advantage of this deficiency, runaway presidents have at times committed the country to courses of action that the voters never approved—or ones they even rejected.

John Tyler, who was never elected president, was the first runaway, in 1841. William Henry Harrison had served only a few weeks; after his death, the obscure Tyler governed in open defiance of the Whig Party that had put him on the ticket, pressing unpopular proslavery policies that helped set the stage for the Civil War.

Andrew Johnson was the next unelected runaway. Politically, he had been an afterthought. But after Lincoln's assassination, Johnson adopted a pro-Southern Reconstruction policy. He treated the party that had nominated him with such scorn that many contemporaries came to believe he was preparing to use the Army to break up Congress

by force. After Johnson rebuffed any attempt at compromise, the Republican House impeached him, but the Senate, by one vote, refused to remove him from office. His obduracy crippled Reconstruction; in fact, we still haven't fully recovered from that crisis.

American political commentators tend to think loosely about exertions of presidential authority. The paradigm cases are Lincoln rallying the nation after Fort Sumter, and Roosevelt, about a year before Pearl Harbor, using pure executive power to transfer American destroyers to embattled Britain in exchange for use of certain British bases. Because these great leaders used their authority broadly, the thinking goes, assertions of executive prerogative are valid and desirable.

Certainly there are times when presidential firmness is better than rapid changes in policy to suit public opinion. Executive theorists in the United States often pose the choice that way—steady, independent executive leadership or feckless, inconstant pursuit of what Hamilton called "the temporary delusion" of public opinion. But not all shifts in public opinion are delusive or temporary. An executive should have some independence, but a presidency that treats the people as irrelevant is not democratic. It is authoritarian.

Lincoln and Roosevelt asserted emergency powers while holding popular mandates. Lincoln had just won an election that also provided him with a handy majority in Congress; Roosevelt was enormously popular, and in 1940 his party outnumbered the opposition 3-to-1 in the Senate and by nearly 100 seats in the House.

But sometimes a president with little or no political mandate uses the office to further a surprising, obscure, or discredited political agenda. Under these circumstances, what poses as bold leadership is in fact usurpation. The most egregious case arises when a president's policy and leadership have been repudiated by the voters, either by a defeat for reelection or by a sweeping rejection of his congressional allies in a midterm election. When that happens, presidents too often do what George Bush did in 2006—simply persist in the conduct that has alienated the country. Intoxicated by the image of the hero-president, unencumbered by any direct political check, stubborn presidents in this situation have no incentive to change course.

When the voters turn sharply against a president mid-term, his leadership loses some or all of its legitimacy, and the result can be disastrous. Clinton was decisively repudiated in November 1994. After the election, the administration and the new Republican Congress remained so far apart on funding decisions that the government had to shut down for 26 days in 1995 and 1996. This episode is now remembered for Clinton's political mastery, but it was actually a dangerous structural failure. (Imagine that the al-Qaeda attacks of September 11, 2001, had happened instead on December 20, 1995, when the stalemate had forced the executive branch to send most of its "nonessential" employees home.)

To sum up, while George W. Bush may have been a particularly bad driver, the presidency itself is, and always has been, an unreliable vehicle—with a cranky starter, an engine too big for the chassis, erratic steering, and virtually no brakes. It needs an overhaul, a comprehensive redo of Article II.

Constitutional change is a daunting prospect. But consider how often we have already changed the presidency; it is the Constitution's most-amended feature. And this is the moment to think of reform—the public's attention is focused on the Bush disaster, and ordinary people might be willing to look at the flaws in the office that allowed Bush to do what he did.

So how should the presidency be changed?

First, voters should elect presidents directly. And once the vote is counted, the president-elect (and the new Congress) should take office within a week. Americans accustomed to the current system will object that this would not allow enough time to assemble a Cabinet—but in England and France, the new chief executive considers ministerial nominations before the election. A shorter interregnum would force the creation of something like the British shadow cabinet, in which a candidate makes public the names of his key advisers. That would give voters important information, and provide the president with a running start.

Next, Article II should include a specific and limited set of presidential powers. The "unitary executive" theorists should no longer be allowed to spin a quasi-dictatorship out of the bare phrase *executive power;* like the responsibilities of Congress, those of the president should be clearly enumerated.

It should be made clear, for example, that the president's powers as commander in chief do not crowd out the power of Congress to start—and stop—armed conflict. Likewise, the duty to "take care that the laws be faithfully executed" needs to be clarified: it is not the power to decide which laws the president wants to follow, or to rewrite new statutes in "signing statements" after Congress has passed them; it is a duty to uphold the Constitution, valid treaties, and congressional statutes (which together, according to the Constitution, form "the supreme law of the land").

After a transformative midterm election like that of 1994 or 2006, the nation should require a compromise between the rejected president and the new Congress. A president whose party has lost some minimum number of seats in Congress should be forced to form the equivalent of a national-unity government. This could be done by requiring the president to present a new Cabinet that includes members of both parties, which the new Congress would approve or disapprove as a whole—no drawn-out confirmation hearings on each nominee. If the president were unwilling to assemble such a government or unable to get congressional approval after, say, three tries, he would have to resign.

This would not give Congress control of the executive branch. A resigning president would be replaced by the vice president, who would not be subject to the new-Cabinet requirement. This new president might succeed politically where the previous one had failed (imagine Al Gore becoming president in 1995, and running in 1996—and perhaps in 2000—as an incumbent). And that possibility would discourage the new congressional majority from simply rejecting the compromise Cabinet. Resignation might be worse for them than approval.

As a final reform, we should reconsider the entire Hamiltonian concept of the "unitary executive." When George Washington became president, he left a large organization (the Mount Vernon plantation) to head a smaller one (the federal government). But today, the executive branch is a behemoth, with control over law enforcement, the military, economic policy, education, the environment, and most other aspects of national life. That behemoth is responsible to one person, and that one person, as we have seen, is only loosely accountable to the electorate.

In other areas, the Framers solved this problem neatly: they divided power in order to protect against its abuse. Congress was split into the House and the Senate to ensure that the legislative process would not be so efficient as to absorb powers properly belonging to the other branches. The problem now is not an overweening Congress but an aggrandized executive branch; still, the remedy is the same. We should divide the executive branch between two elected officials—a president, and an attorney general who would be voted in during midterm elections.

As we are learning from the ongoing scandal of the torture memos, one of the drawbacks of a single executive is that Justice Department lawyers may consider it their job to twist the law to suit the White House. But the president is not their client; the United States is. Justice Department lawyers appointed by an elected attorney general would have no motive to distort law and logic to empower the president, while the White House counsel's office, which does represent the president, would have every incentive to monitor the Justice Department to ensure that it did not tilt too strongly against the executive branch. The watchmen would watch each other.

This arrangement would hardly be unprecedented: most state governments elect an attorney general. The new Article II could make clear that the president has the responsibility for setting overall legal policy, just as governors do today.

None of these changes would erode the "separation of powers." That happens only when a change gives one branch's prerogatives to another branch. These changes refer in each instance back to the people, who are the proper source of all power. The changes would still leave plenty of room for "energy in the executive" but would afford far less opportunity for high-handedness, secrecy, and simple rigidity. They would allow presidential firmness, but not at the expense of democratic self-governance.

It's not surprising that the Framers did not understand the perils of the office they designed. They were working in the dark, and they got a lot of things right. But we should not let our admiration for the Framers deter us from fixing their mistakes.

Our government is badly out of balance. There is a difference between executive energy and autocratic license; between leadership and authoritarianism; between the democratic firmness of a Lincoln and the authoritarian rigidity of a Bush. The challenge we face today is to find some advantage in Bush's sorry legacy. Reform of the executive branch would be a good place to start.

Critical Thinking

1. What powers are unique to the presidency? What powers are shared with the legislative branch? How does the Constitution define the office's duties?

2. How has the vice presidential selection process as originally outlined in the Constitution presented challenges? How have those challenges been addressed?

3. What are the problems associated with the relatively long time span between election results and inauguration day?

4. What specific limits to presidential power does the author suggest?

5. Explain the concept of a "unitary executive." How does the author propose to change that structure?

From *The Atlantic*, January/February 2009, pp. 68, 70–73. Copyright © 2009 by Atlantic Monthly Group. Reprinted by permission of TMS Reprints.

Happy Together?

Americans love to complain about gridlock in Washington and partisan warfare between presidents and Congress. Yet the record suggests that unified party government is no panacea.

DONALD R. WOLFENSBERGER

On the campaign trail, Barack Obama promised to bring change to Washington and a post-partisan, non-ideological approach to governing. In his first post-election press conference on November 7, he reiterated this hope: "I know we will succeed if we put aside partisanship and politics and work together as one nation."

These snowflakes of soothing rhetoric drift slowly down on a Capitol Hill power plant fueled by partisanship and politics. What will happen when the snow hits the furnace—where majority Democrats and their allied interest groups have long been denied their wishes by Republican presidents and Congresses? The question is not whether President Obama can forge an extrapolitical national consensus to solve problems, but how effectively he will be able to govern with his own party in the majority in Congress.

One should not assume that Obama will get everything he wants from congressional Democrats any more than they will succeed in getting him to sign off on all their pent-up demands. Not only does the spike in deficits from the financial bailout and economic recession impose severe constraints, but the history of unified party government suggests that it is no more a guarantor of success than divided government is of failure. Indeed, American chief executives from Harry S. Truman to Ronald Reagan enjoyed some of their greatest successes in periods of divided government. In the end, what the people want and are willing to speak up for usually matters more than all the frantic maneuvering in Washington.

One of the features of the American system that most baffles visitors from parliamentary democracies is the paradox that it can create unified party government without total party unity. They find it hard to believe that our system was intentionally designed with internal checks and balances precisely in order to prevent hasty action and the concentration of too much power in any one place. As James Madison put it, "Ambition must be made to counteract ambition." And the Pennsylvania Avenue axis of power between the White House and the Capitol is aswirl with ambition. Even when politicians belong to the same party, they represent different geographic and demographic constituencies that often put them at odds with one another and their

own party's president. The system was not designed for action. It typically reacts only when required by events, public opinion, and presidential prodding.

That is why the young scholar Woodrow Wilson dismissed the Madisonian system as outmoded. "As at present constituted," he wrote in his 1885 doctoral dissertation, *Congressional Government,* "the federal government lacks strength because its powers are divided, lacks promptness because its authorities are multiplied, lacks wieldiness because its processes are roundabout, lacks efficiency because its responsibility is indistinct and its action without competent direction."

As president, Wilson would reconcile himself to Madison's Constitution as a "living" and "evolving" document. Building on his admiration for the British system of responsible party government, Wilson gave us the first "legislative presidency" as he moved his New Freedom agenda through a Democratic Congress in his first two years. He did so by addressing joint sessions of Congress (a record 22 appearances over eight years); traveling frequently to Capitol Hill to meet with Democratic leaders and their committee lieutenants; holding informal press conferences; and even scheduling forums in the White House on whether he should sign legislation sent to him by Congress.

But the Capitol Hill experiences of the Obama administration are not likely to resemble those of Wilson, nor of the other great examples of "unified" party government, which gave us Franklin D. Roosevelt's New Deal and Lyndon B. Johnson's Great Society.

FDR's presidency occurred under very unusual circumstances (notwithstanding some parallels to today's economic troubles). President Johnson's Great Society successes were made possible in part by the emotional backwash from the assassination of President John F. Kennedy and in part by LBJ's unique mastery of congressional procedures and personalities.

Moreover, Congress as an institution has changed considerably since those periods of presidential dominance. Compared with earlier times, when powerful, autonomy-minded committee chairmen ruled the Hill, the political parties and their leaders in Congress play a much greater role today in directing legislative policy-making. Congress entered this new age in the early 1970s as a result of congressional reforms that produced a resurgence of internal party cohesion and activity to levels not witnessed since the turn of the 20th century. Inspired in part by opposition to the Nixon administration, the Democratically controlled Congress and its members became more assertive, entrepreneurial, and independent of the executive branch.

The more relevant examples of unified party government are the presidencies of Jimmy Carter, Bill Clinton, and George W. Bush—all of whom came to the White House from the governorships of southern states, and all of whom promised to change the way Washington worked. All three experiences provide highly cautionary lessons.

Carter was elected in 1976 after the contentious Nixon years. Although he had a firm working majority of Democrats in both houses—292–143 in the House and 61–38 in the Senate—he never had a firm working partnership with Democrats on the Hill. His arrogant and dismissive attitude toward the Capital establishment offended his own party's leaders in Congress, as did his appointment of Washington neophytes to key staff positions in the White House. (After being refused a common courtesy by the White House, Speaker of the House Thomas "Tip" O'Neill [D.-Mass.] derisively referred to Carter aide Hamilton Jordan as "Hannibal Jerkin.") And Carter's attempt to eliminate pork barrel projects did not endear him to those members of Congress with a taste for that "other white meat."

Carter had a tendency to overload Congress's circuits by submitting many legislative proposals simultaneously, generating sparks and committee power outages. He sent his welfare reform proposal to the Hill, for instance, when the House Ways and Means Committee was already bogged down with his energy and tax reform initiatives. His attempt to enact a comprehensive energy plan faltered in Congress as special interests picked it apart, and it emerged much diminished. Four years of unified party government ended with the economy in dreadful condition and a hostage crisis in Iran (which was beyond Carter's control). The Democrats lost the White House and the Senate.

Bill Clinton took office in 1993 determined not to repeat Carter's mistakes. He made a point to meet with Democratic leaders in Congress prior to his inauguration to map out legislative priorities. He was persuaded to delay his campaign pledge to "eliminate welfare as we know it," and reluctant congressional Democrats agreed to move forward on a deficit reduction package to reassure financial markets in return for his backing of an economic stimulus package.

Clinton eked out narrow victories in both houses on his deficit package after being forced to abandon a hefty BTU energy tax proposal and settle instead for a 4.3-cents-per-gallon gasoline tax increase. His $16 billion economic stimulus club was whittled down in the Senate to a scrawny $840 million twig. The first lady's secret healthcare task force produced a bulky plan that couldn't get off the ground in either house as key congressional committee chairmen who had been shut out of the plan's development were unable to reach consensus.

The Clinton-era experiment with unified government ended ignominiously in 1994 with a Republican electoral sweep of both houses of Congress—which included the first GOP majority in the lower house in 40 years. Some of Clinton's signal achievements, however, were still to come. Even before the GOP takeover, his victory in passing the North American Free Trade Agreement in 1993 depended heavily on Republican support to offset large Democratic defections. Once Republicans took control of Congress, Clinton built on this tactic of "triangulating" between the two caucuses to enact welfare reform and balanced budget legislation.

George W. Bush came to office in 2001 after losing the popular vote and narrowly winning the Electoral College bowl in a sudden-death overtime refereed by the Supreme Court. Notwithstanding widespread press assertions that he had no mandate, he proceeded as if he did, assiduously courting members of both parties to pave the way for his priorities. Even though the Senate flipped to Democratic control in mid-2001 with the defection of Vermont Republican James Jeffords, the GOP still controlled the House. By the end of the year Bush managed to enact his No Child Left Behind education reform with bipartisan support, and his tax cuts with only minimal Democratic support.

Bush failed to achieve two other priorities of his administration, Social Security reform and immigration reform, but it was less party rivalry in Congress than a lack of firm support in the country that did them in. Democrats artfully played his proposal for private accounts in Social Security as an attempt to "privatize" the system, frightening seniors and forcing even Republicans to abandon it. Immigration reform was shot down by members of Bush's own party in Congress, aided by radio and cable shock jocks who claimed he was giving "amnesty" to "illegals."

The Bush presidency was at its apex in the wake of the September 11, 2001, terrorist attacks, when a divided Congress worked together to produce a blizzard of legislation in response. The president's job approval rating shot up to 90 percent, and even Congress briefly enjoyed an unprecedented 84 percent approval rating (more than double its customary level). Five years later, however, in the 2006 elections, Democrats retook control of both houses of Congress as public opinion turned against the Iraq war.

Within Congress itself, unified party government has generally had two less than salutary characteristics. The legislative branch tends to spend more money than it does under divided party government. It is generally more demanding, and presidents more giving (an arrangement that provides new meaning to the term normally used to describe the final review of legislative text before passage—"bill markup"). At the same time, Congress tends to slack off on its oversight responsibilities when its majorities share the president's party label. Under divided party government, however, it is suddenly able to juggle numerous high-level investigative oversight hearings into executive branch activities simultaneously.

Where might an Obama presidency fit in this historical mosaic of unified party governments? Unlike four of the last five presidents, who were governors, Obama is not a stranger to Washington's ways. His four years in the Senate count for something (though he spent most of the last two years running for president). His early picks of experienced hands to run his White House, cabinet departments, and legislative affairs office bode well for his success. But it will not be enough to have the best people giving the best advice in the White House and cabinet. It will ultimately depend on the president himself to show he can work with an independent, coequal branch made up of diverse personalities, interests, and ideologies—a branch that enjoys bipartisan unanimity on at least one principle: It is not about to abandon politics. Politics, after all, is simply a process of working through problems to build a consensus around mutually agreeable solutions—sometimes known as deliberative democracy.

If there is any conclusion to be drawn from recent history on the relative benefits of unified versus divided party government in the United States, it is this: The American system is capable of monumental accomplishments in times of crisis regardless of which party is in control of what lever of government, but the system can be just as incapable of doing anything when the people are not behind it—even with unified party control.

The American system is capable of monumental accomplishments in times of crisis regardless of which party is in control of what lever of government.

President Abraham Lincoln said as much when he observed, "With public sentiment, nothing can fail; without it, nothing can succeed." The success or failure of the Obama presidency will ultimately depend on the extent to which the people rally behind the plans and programs the new president and Congress are able to develop together as they work to address some of the most difficult problems this country has ever faced.

Critical Thinking

1. How does the system of checks and balances limit the ability of government to act?

2. What is unified party government? Which presidential administrations offer examples?

3. What two negative effects does unified party government have on Congress?

4. How does unified party control influence government's ability to get things done?

DONALD R. WOLFENSBERGER is director of the Congress Project at the Woodrow Wilson Center and author of *Congress and the People: Deliberative Democracy on Trial* (2000). His 28-year career as a staff member in the U.S. House of Representatives culminated in his position as chief of staff of the House Rules Committee.

Veto This!

When presidents veto a bill, they're exercising strength—or showing weakness. They usually win the override battles but sometimes lose the war for public approval.

CARL M. CANNON

The first presidential veto in American history was exercised, fittingly enough, by George Washington. He informed Congress in writing on April 5, 1792, that having "maturely considered the Act passed by the two Houses," he felt obligated to send it back on the grounds that it was unconstitutional. The legislation had to do with the number of citizens that each member of the House would represent. Having defeated the British on the field of battle—thereby giving the members of Congress their jobs to begin with—President Washington was accorded a high level of deference. No serious attempt to override the veto transpired, and Congress rewrote the measure to satisfy his objections.

Washington issued a single veto in his second term as well. This time, the dispute was on policy grounds, as the former general didn't cotton to the minutiae of a congressional plan for reorganizing the armed forces. He issued that veto on February 28, 1797; again, the veto stood. With these two actions, Washington initiated a tug-of-war between the executive and legislative branches of the federal government that persists to this day. The veto, a forgotten power during George W. Bush's first term, has now emerged as a prime battleground in the twilight months of his presidency.

"One thing that needs to be underscored is that because President Bush is a 'lame-duck' president, it doesn't mean that he is no longer powerful," said Chris Kelley, a political science professor at the University of Miami in Ohio. "The veto is a powerful weapon that the president simply must use from time to time."

Alexander Hamilton would have agreed. At the dawn of the Republic, Hamilton told his fellow Founders that the presidential veto (Latin for "I forbid") was "a qualified negative" that would serve as a brake on the passions of a popularly elected legislature. For five years, Bush did not avail himself of this authority, making him the only president except for John Quincy Adams to go an entire four-year term without vetoing anything that Congress sent him.

Was Bush practicing good government, or bad government? The answers to that question—and to the questions about Bush's

newfound fondness for the veto—are partly political, partly theoretical. The political portion of the question is the voters' to answer. It will be addressed on the 2008 campaign trail, where presidential and congressional candidates from both parties are parsing Bush's recent vetoes to boost their candidacies. The theoretical component has even more movable parts and is the continuation of an argument more than 200 years old.

The first U.S. president to use the prerogative to veto *major* legislation solely over policy objections was Andrew Jackson. He was also the first to see the veto's potential as a political tool: In 1832, Jackson vetoed the enabling legislation to extend the charter of the villified Second Bank of the United States. Although his economic reasoning was specious, his political antenna was flawless, and the 1832 bank veto helped to assure Jackson's re-election.

For the better part of two centuries, political scientists and constitutional scholars have debated the propriety of Jackson's willingness to use the veto as a political tool, even while the principle became the standard for all subsequent presidents. Two rival theories of what constitutes a good-government use of the veto emerged.

The first, in the words of Stephen Skowronek, a political science professor at Yale University, is that the Jackson veto precedent "made a mockery of the premier operating principle" of Jeffersonian democracy, that is, deference to people's representatives in Congress. Jackson's veto was an artifice, these critics have said over the years, that short-circuited the separation of powers and contributed to the rise of the "imperial presidency" so disfavored by the Founders. In substituting the whims of one person for the will of the people, the veto also—and inevitably—soured relations between the branches of government.

> **"The veto tilts the balance of power in Washington too far toward the status quo."**
>
> —Sanford Levinson,
> University of Texas professor

This was the precise complaint leveled against Bush last week when he vetoed a $35 billion, five-year expansion of the State Children's Health Insurance Program that passed both chambers of Congress with comfortable majorities and enjoyed bipartisan support.

"You [had] consensus across party and ideology, and a unity on the most important domestic issue, health care," Rep. Rahm Emanuel, D-Ill., said. "Except for one person."

But one person is all it takes—if that person is the president. "I think that this is probably the most inexplicable veto in the history of the country," Sen. Edward Kennedy, D-Mass., declared on the Senate floor. "It is incomprehensible: It is intolerable. It's unacceptable."

But accept it Congress must—unless Democrats can muster a two-thirds vote in each chamber to override. And that's where critics of the veto say that the system goes off the rails. "Put simply, the veto tilts the balance of power in Washington too far toward the status quo," says Sanford Levinson, professor of law and government at the University of Texas (Austin).

Levinson, author of a recent book, *Our Undemocratic Constitution: Where the Constitution Goes Wrong (and How We the People Can Correct It)*, asserts that anyone who thinks that judicial review of legislation passed by majorities has an autocratic tinge to it ought to be more worried about the presidential veto. He says that the Supreme Court has invalidated some 165 laws throughout U.S. history, while presidents have vetoed about 2,550 bills—only 106 of which Congress has managed to override. "If judicial activism is anti-democratic," he wrote recently, "then the presidential veto is, well, *very* anti-democratic."

There is, however, a second school of thought, represented by such scholars as Ronald C. Moe and Louis Fisher, who wrote about separation-of-powers issues for the Congressional Research Service. In this view, the presidential veto has a positive impact on the political process. For starters, the threat of a veto gives Congress an incentive to draw legislation more carefully, encouraging compromise. The veto can serve, as Alexander Hamilton suggested it might, as an additional brake against "improper laws" passed in the heat of the moment. "It establishes a salutary check upon the legislative body, calculated to guard the community against the effects of faction, precipitancy, or of any impulse unfriendly to the public good, which may happen to influence a majority of that body," Hamilton wrote.

Implicit in this view of checks and balances is a sophisticated notion: namely, that bad ideas, once signed into law, are more difficult to repeal than they were to enact. A contemporary illustration of Hamilton's fear may be the innocent sounding "Anti-Drug Abuse Act." Congress passed it hurriedly in 1986 without hearings, partially as a response to the cocaine-induced death of University of Maryland basketball star Len Bias. Coming as cheap crack, cocaine was turning urban streets into shooting galleries, the law prescribed far harsher sentences for possessing or dealing crack than it did for having powder cocaine.

That provision has put tens of thousands of young African-Americans in federal prison for far longer terms than white drug abusers, who tend to traffic in powder cocaine. President Reagan signed the law a week before the 1986 election. Eric Sterling, then a Democratic House aide who helped to draft the

bill, wistfully recalls wishing that Reagan had vetoed it. Sterling, who now heads the Criminal Justice Policy Foundation, has been trying for the better part of two decades to persuade Congress to repeal the 1986 statute that mandates harsh terms for low-level cocaine dealers. "The Framers would have offered this law as a perfect example of the proper use of the presidential veto," Sterling said. "The problem is that by virtue of [these laws'] popularity, they are the hardest vetoes to cast."

Who's in Charge?

Mirroring the ongoing philosophical discussion about the proper role of presidential vetoes, another conversation is taking place on a more practical political level: Are vetoes a sign of strength or weakness in a chief executive? Does it help a president to issue vetoes, or hurt him and his party? These, as Bush and his suddenly fractious Republicans are discovering during the current term of Congress, are not academic questions. Once again, there are two sides to the equation; and once again, it is clear that the dispute won't be settled in Bush's presidency.

Let's call the first viewpoint the Rodney King school of thought. Why *can't* we all get along? This argument holds that presidential vetoes are, almost by definition, a sign that the chief executive lacks power, leadership ability, and a large enough following to shape events. In other words, a president who has to veto has failed to persuade, can't compromise, can't get the White House's own legislation through Congress, and is unable to take the issue over the heads of Congress to the people.

"A strong president needs fewer vetoes because he's able to exercise sufficient control over the congressional agenda, whether through decisive influence over legislative formulation or judicious use of veto threats that make it unlikely bills the president would oppose would land on his desk," says Robert Spitzer, professor of political science at the State University of New York (Cortland).

Framed this way, Capitol Hill has more say-so in setting the veto-agenda than is generally acknowledged these days in Washington. In an influential 1978 book on the politics of the veto, political scientists Thomas Romer and Howard Rosenthal explored this point. The authors outlined a "monopoly agenda control model" in which Congress, not the president, determines the fate of veto threats. In their theory, the agenda-setter is the pivotal legislator on any given issue, who presents the White House with take-it-or-leave-it proposals. Thus, the president is essentially in a reactive, and therefore, subordinate, position. This is something of a postmodern (or, at least, post–Franklin Roosevelt) view, and it probably is not a coincidence that Romer and Rosenthal were doing their research when Gerald Ford was president.

Ford was a creature of the House, but as president he was also a captive of the huge Democratic majorities he inherited as voters in 1974 reacted against the Republican Party of Richard Nixon, Spiro Agnew, and Watergate. Despite serving as president for barely half a term, Ford has the distinction of tying for second place on the all-time list of presidential vetoes that were overridden by Congress. Ford, overridden 12 times, shares that dubious silver medal with President Truman, who recorded the lowest Gallup Poll job-approval rating in history.

The record-holder is Andrew Johnson, overridden 15 times, who was impeached by the House and nearly convicted in the Senate. The precipitating act of impeachment was Johnson's veto of a bill he believed—correctly, the Supreme Court later ruled—was unconstitutional.

"Many conventional presidency scholars argue that the use of a veto indicates a weak president, since the power of the presidency resides in his ability to bargain and persuade the Congress to go along with his policies," Kelley said. "Thus if he uses a veto, it means that his credibility with the Congress is low. Those who point to Ford as a failed president often will examine both his vetoes and the overrides."

Nolan McCarty, acting dean of the Woodrow Wilson School of Public and International Affairs at Princeton University, has described two other models for vetoes. In one, the White House and Congress have incomplete information about exactly what will precipitate a veto. Bush, for example, threatened to veto an expansion of the student loan program, but then didn't, perhaps leading wishful Democrats to believe that he would feel pressured to sign the SCHIP bill. The absence of a dominant

Presidents Usually Win

Congress is rarely able to muster the two-thirds majority of votes in both chambers to override a presidential veto. This list, based on a compilation by the Congressional Research Service, does not include pocket vetoes after Congress adjourned.

President	Vetoes	Overrides	Vetos that Stuck	Major Overrides
TRUMAN	180	12	Natural-gas deregulation 1950 Coastal tidelands 1946, 1952	Taft-Hartley labor relations 1947 Income-tax cuts 1947, 1948 McCarran Internal Security 1950 McCarran-Walter immigration quotas 1952
EISENHOWER	73	2	Natural gas 1956 Farm spending 1956, 1958 Housing programs 1959 Pollution control 1960	TVA spending 1959 Federal pay 1960
KENNEDY	12	0	Federal pensions 1961	
JOHNSON	16	0	Cotton quotas 1968	
NIXON	26	7	Minimum-wage increase 1973	Water Pollution Control 1972 War Powers Act 1973
FORD	48	12	Oil price controls 1975	Freedom of Information Act 1974
CARTER	13	2	Nuclear reactor 1977	Oil import fee 1980
REAGAN	39	9	Textile quotas 1988	South Africa sanctions 1986 Water projects 1987 Highway funding 1987
G.H.W. BUSH	29	1	Minimum-wage increase 1989 Job discrimination 1990 China trade status 1992 Family-medical leave 1990, 1992 Taxes 1992 Stem-cell research 1992 Campaign finance 1992	Cable TV 1992
CLINTON	36	2	Spending reductions 1995 Appropriations 1995 Bosnia arms embargo 1995 "Partial-birth" abortion 1996, 1997 Product liability 1996 Tax cuts 1999 Estate-tax repeal 2000	Line-item vetoes 1998 Securities litigation 1995
G.W. BUSH	4	0	Stem-cell research 2006, 2007 Iraq war limits 2007	

legislative actor is what leads to the impasse. "When there is such uncertainty," McCarty wrote, "vetoes may occur because the Legislature overestimates its ability to extract concessions from the president."

In the wake of Bush's SCHIP veto, perhaps the nation's capital finds itself in that fluid state of affairs—meaning that, eventually, compromise legislation will emerge. The president has left the door open, and Congress is home to a handful of moderate Republicans who hope that Bush and the Democrats will walk through that door together. Of course, there is another, less pleasant, place to be. McCarty describes this model as "Blame-Game Vetoes."

When one party accuses the other of making "war on children," it is a safe bet that partisan advantage, not meaningful negotiation, is at the frontal cortex of the party's collective brain. Not that the Democrats tried to hide it. "We're not going to compromise," Senate Majority Leader Harry Reid said flatly after Bush's recent veto. House Speaker Nancy Pelosi vowed that Democrats would try to override and to make the issue "a hard vote for Republicans." New Jersey's Democratic governor, Jon Corzine, said, "I hope we override the veto before we start worrying about compromise."

To produce legislation, the process usually needs to work the other way around. But this is the blame game. SCHIP "has got to be up there with motherhood and apple pie," Rep. Jim Cooper, D-Tenn., told the *Los Angeles Times,* apparently with a straight face. "This is Tiny Tim. And who is against Tiny Tim? The only person in all of literature was Ebenezer Scrooge."

So who is winning the blame game? The early signs were a thumbs-down for George W. Scrooge and a thumbs-up for the Democrats. Public opinion polls showed that the voters, egged on by Democrats and media editorialists, thought that Bush's veto was wrongheaded, if not heartless. Eventually, White House aides and a few Republicans joined the fray, raising various arguments to support Bush's position: Some of the "children" covered under this bill would be nearly 25 years of age; the earning power of some eligible families tops $80,000 a year; some people opting into the program already have private health insurance; the Democrats' plan would be funded with a regressive $1-a-pack tax on cigarettes—that kind of thing. There was truth (or some truth, anyway) to all of these assertions, but Bush did not make them in the days leading up to the veto. Speaking to reporters at the White House, Bush simply said he had "philosophical" differences with the Democrats.

That was code, pure and simple, intended for the ears of fiscal conservatives, who have grown disenchanted with the GOP leader who has run up huge budget deficits in each year of his presidency. Translated, Bush's words meant: "OK, OK, I'll quit spending tax dollars like a drunken sailor."

In this new spirit, Bush has threatened to veto 10 of 11 pending appropriations bills. Until now, nobody knew for sure whether he was serious. In his first term, Bush vetoed nothing. In year five of his presidency, despite threatening 133 vetoes, Bush issued a single one, on embryonic-stem-cell research. This year, he vetoed a similar stem-cell bill, along with a spending measure aimed at curbing escalation of the Iraq war. Now Bush has issued his fourth veto. Has he found his groove? Perhaps. But some believe that he waited too long.

"It's an hour too late," says Frank Luntz, the Republican communications guru who helped fashion the 1994 Contract with America. "And a dollar too short."

Situational Ethics

Until Democrats reclaimed Congress in the 2006 elections, the premium in Bushworld was indeed on getting along. Rodney King would have approved. In the first term, Nicholas Calio, then-White House director of legislative affairs, told *National Journal* that the two top Republicans in the House, Speaker Dennis Hastert and Majority Leader Tom DeLay, made it a point of pride to send no bill to 1600 Pennsylvania Avenue that would be vetoed. "It's a real principle with the speaker and DeLay," Calio said. John Feehery, Hastert's spokesman at the time, went further, asserting that his boss believed that to invite a presidential veto signaled "a breakdown in the system."

"We don't want to make political points with this president," Feehery added, "because we agree with him on almost everything." Congressional Republicans challenged Bush's veto threats only once, in 2002, on a campaign finance overhaul. Bush didn't like the bill, but he put his signature on it anyway, the overt evidence of his displeasure was that he didn't invite one of its principal authors, Sen. John McCain, R-Ariz., to the signing ceremony.

Another reason that Bush hasn't relied on the veto is that he routinely uses "signing statements" to assert that he will implement new legislation in ways that conform with his thinking and that of White House lawyers and policy makers. On other occasions, particularly as regards national security, this president hasn't even given that much deference to congressional intent: If White House lawyers deem a law, such as the statutes regarding the wiretapping of suspected foreign terrorists, to be technologically out-of-date, well, this administration just writes its own hall pass.

Thus, Bush's first term featured an odd combination of co-operating closely with Capitol Hill Republicans on some occasions and simply ignoring Congress on others. Along the way, Team Bush overlooked historic examples showing that sometimes a veto—along with a healthy dose of chutzpah—is just what it takes to make a president look strong. Truman, in his first term, lamented during several crippling national strikes that he lacked the executive authority to force trade union leaders to the bargaining table. Congress gave Truman that power in the Taft-Hartley Act. He promptly vetoed it, putting himself at long last in organized labor's good graces. Congress overrode the president's veto, and Truman happily used the power vested in him some dozen times. Moreover, he turned around and won re-election in 1948, with, yes, the help of labor. For a president, this is as good as it gets—veto nirvana.

Republicans were in charge of both ends of Pennsylvania Avenue during most of the first six years of Bush's presidency, so the chances for such showdowns were small. But Democrats ran the show when Franklin Roosevelt was president—and he vetoed 635 of their bills. According to presidential scholar William Leuchtenburg, Roosevelt would instruct White House aides to look for legislation that he could veto, "in order to remind Congress that it was being watched."

Alan Greenspan, who is old enough to remember FDR, believes that Bush—and the country—would have been well served if this president had done the same. "My biggest frustration remained the president's unwillingness to wield his veto against out-of-control spending," Greenspan wrote in his new book, *The Age of Turbulence: Adventures in a New World.* "Not exercising the veto power became a hallmark of the Bush presidency. . . . To my mind, Bush's collaborate-don't-confront approach was a major mistake."

Many movement conservatives couldn't agree more. They think that Bush's belated embrace of the veto might save the GOP's soul and give the Republican base a principle to be excited about. "The GOP needs to regain its brand on spending," says Grover Norquist, president of Americans for Tax Reform. "The Democrats are acting now in 2007 and 2008 as they did in 1993 and 1994: taxing, spending. And here the GOP can highlight its differences with vetoes and veto-upholding. It is a truly selfless act by Bush as he isn't running, but the GOP House and Senate guys are, and they need their brand back. This autumn's fight, which I hope to be long and drawn out and repetitive, will do for the GOP what they should have been doing over the past six years."

Other Republicans, most notably moderates who face tough re-election fights next year, are unnerved by Bush's newfound fiscal conservatism, and especially by his willingness to veto a children's health bill to prove it. "I believe this is an irresponsible use of the veto pen," said Sen. Gordon Smith, an Oregon Republican who faces a spirited challenge in 2008. "It's the White House that needs to give," added another Senate GOP centrist, Susan Collins of Maine.

The noises emanating from the White House don't give these worried Republicans much reassurance. "Good policy is good politics," said White House spokesman Tony Fratto last week. "If members stand on principle, they'll be just fine."

Principles can be in the eye of the beholder, however, especially in Washington, where situational ethics are routinely on display. Dan Mitchell of the libertarian Cato Institute points out that the money at stake in the health care initiative is small compared with the excess spending that Bush accepted when Republicans controlled Congress. "There certainly does seem to be a legitimate argument that the president only objects to new spending when Democrats are doing it," Mitchell said.

Bush might have more moral sway had he, back in 2002, vetoed a bipartisan and pork-laden $190 billion farm bill. Half a century ago, Dwight Eisenhower did just that. The Democrats pounced, thinking they had Ike right where they wanted him. "The veto of the farm bill," then-Senate Majority Leader Lyndon Johnson said, "can be described only as a crushing blow to the hopes and the legitimate desires of American agriculture." That was one description. Another was "fiscal restraint," something that Eisenhower had managed to make sexy—with his veto pen.

By the end of the 1959 Christmas recess, an unnamed White House aide was telling *Time* magazine, "When those congressmen come back in January, they're going to be so anxious to find something to cut that they'll cut their own wrists if necessary." On his way out of office, with high approval ratings and a federal budget nearly in balance, Eisenhower was *Time's* "Man of the Year."

Similar battle lines are drawn for the upcoming year, during which Democrats will try to hold their congressional majorities and recapture the White House. Will they succeed? They will if Sen. Hillary Rodham Clinton has anything to say about it. "With the stroke of a pen, President Bush has robbed nearly 4 million uninsured children of the chance for a healthy start in life and the health coverage they need but can't afford," the New York Democrat and 2008 presidential front-runner said after Bush's veto.

"This is vetoing the will of the American people," Clinton added. "I was proud to help create the Children's Health Insurance Program during the Clinton administration, which today provides health insurance for 6 million children."

Hillary Clinton was right about her role in SCHIP. The part of the story that she may be forgetting, however, is that her husband got traction as president after the Republicans took over Congress and he began wielding his veto pen—36 times before leaving office.

"Clinton's skillful and aggressive use of the veto was a hallmark of his domestic presidency after the Republicans gained control of Congress in 1994," wrote Charles Cameron, a political science professor at Princeton and the author of *Veto Bargaining: Presidents and the Politics of Negative Power.* "In some respects, he was more successful opposing Congress than he had been leading it, when the Democrats controlled the institution."

Reagan faced a House controlled by the opposition party and he, too, issued a spate of vetoes, 78 (half of them pocket vetoes). Congress overrode nine—matching Roosevelt's tally. The overrides didn't hurt either man's legacy. At least one of the 2008 presidential candidates has apparently taken this lesson to heart. Republican Mitt Romney, who as Massachusetts governor faced an overwhelmingly Democratic Legislature for four years, boasts of vetoing hundreds of appropriations while serving in Boston— and says he'd happily do it all over again in Washington.

"If I'm elected president, I'm going to cap nondefense discretionary spending at inflation minus 1 percent," he said recently. "And if Congress sends me a budget that exceeds that cap, I will veto that budget. And I know how to veto. I like vetoes."

Critical Thinking

1. Explain the perspective of those who believe the presidential power to veto legislation is unconstitutional. Do they see the veto as a political tool? Why do they believe that the ability to veto puts too much power in the hands of the president?

2. Explain the perspective of those who believe the presidential veto power has a positive impact on the political process. How does the veto, from this perspective, reinforce the concept of checks and balances?

3. How can a veto be viewed as a sign of presidential weakness? How can it be viewed as a sign of presidential strength?

4. Why are presidential vetoes difficult to override?

5. Compare President George W. Bush's use of the veto in his first term versus his second term. Why did his approach change?

ccannon@nationaljournal.com.

Dear Leader

The oil spill and the cult of the presidency.

JONATHAN CHAIT

Two years ago, the Cato Institute's Gene Healy wrote an insightful essay in *Reason* titled, "The Cult of the Presidency." Healy argued that the office of the president had assumed an almost supernatural place in American life. Not only had presidents assumed powers far beyond those originally intended—though I'd take exception to Healy's shrunken, nineteenth-century conception of the office's proper role—but the broader culture had also assigned it powers that go beyond the realm of politics itself. "The chief executive of the United States is no longer a mere constitutional officer charged with faithful execution of the laws," wrote Healy. "He is a soul nourisher, a hope giver, a living American talisman against hurricanes, terrorism, economic downturns, and spiritual malaise."

Healy could well have been writing about the curious reaction to President Obama's handling of the BP oil leak. Last week, Obama held a press conference putatively dedicated to explaining the state of the disaster and the government's response. The actual purpose of the event, as both the questioners and the questionee understood, was for Obama to perform his talismanic role.

Indeed, the assembled media judged the president's performance almost entirely in emotional terms. The initial reviews found him wanting. *New York Times* reporter Jeff Zeleny concluded, "[I]t remains an open question whether the measured tone that has become the soundtrack of Mr. Obama's presidency—a detached, calm, observational pitch—served to drive the point home that he is sufficiently enraged by the fury in the Gulf Coast." Maureen Dowd lambastes the president for having "willfully and inexplicably resisted fulfilling a signal part of his job: being a prism in moments of fear and pride, reflecting what Americans feel so they know he gets it."

The problem with this reaction is not that it is harsh. In a way, it is actually quite worshipful, in the literal sense of adopting the tone one takes toward a deity, albeit a deity one is currently questioning for his indifference. The assumption is that the primary variable here is not Obama's capacity to solve the problem but rather his interest in solving it. Yes, Obama said he wants to plug the hole. But did he *mean* it? We must know!

A similar assumption permeated the health care reform saga, which both the public and the news media thought of as a drama revolving around a single protagonist, the president. When health care seemed to be moving ahead in Congress, this reflected the brilliance of Obama's decision to allow Congress to take the lead, as opposed to Bill Clinton's presumed-fatal choice to craft a plan of his own. When it appeared stalled, the debate revolved around which tactical mistake on Obama's part could be to blame. Was he *too* deferential to Congress? Did he need to deliver another speech, and, if so, what kind? Or maybe he had spoken too often.

Nobody wanted to accept the reality that the veto point lay in the Senate, and that the primary mover was Nebraska Senator Ben Nelson, whom Obama could try to persuade but who would ultimately make up his own mind. If Obama made a concession to secure Nelson's support, disappointed liberals would rail at the president. It must have been that Obama didn't want, say, the public option badly enough. The scale of the disaster was too large for so small a character as Nelson to be its agent.

In the case of the BP disaster, the president's powers are assumed not only to surmount the separation of powers but even to extend to the limits of physics itself. The primary dynamic at work must be Obama's willpower.

To question the assumption of presidential omnipotence is not to absolve Obama of any responsibility. Some elements of the disaster clearly fall within the purview of executive action. Some critics have persuasively impugned the rapidity of Obama's efforts to mobilize containment of the spill. Others have, less persuasively, damned his failure to quickly reform the Minerals Management Service. (Reforming a dysfunctional culture takes time; consider Michelle Rhee's Battle of Stalingrad-esque struggle to remake D.C. public schools.)

But the cult of the presidency has made it impossible to differentiate between problems Obama can handle directly and those he can't. Obama has been bombarded with demands that he "take control" of plugging the leak through some unspecified rhetorical maneuver. Or, perhaps, that he just solve the problem himself. "I've been asked this week, 'Well, what does the president do to do a better job, you know, connecting on all this?'" says NBC's David Gregory, "You, you plug the leak, is what you do."

In reality, the federal government has no agency tasked with capping undersea oil leaks. All the necessary equipment, along with the expertise for operating it, resides with the private sector. Moreover, since BP will likely bear the full cost of the spill, it has every incentive to deploy its equipment as aggressively as possible. I have seen nobody even attempt to argue, in either practical or theoretical terms, that the government could do a better job of plugging the leak. The demand that Obama solve the problem is not an argument but an emotional state. To accept that Obama is not the man who will plug the hole or fail to do so would be like plunking down ten dollars to see *Superman* at the Cineplex only to watch Jimmy Olsen save the world.

Conservative critics have leapt upon the image of a hamstrung Obama to discredit the president and activist government. Both George Will and Charles Krauthammer recently cited Obama's 2008 speech promising that "the rise of the oceans [would begin] to slow." "Serves him right," snickered Will, who insists that the helplessness of government strikes at the core assumptions of "progressive politics." "[W]hen you anoint yourself King Canute, you mustn't be surprised when your subjects expect you to command the tides," gloats Krauthammer.

Of course, neither Obama nor liberals in general believe that government has limitless powers or responsibilities. Obama's promise to slow the rise of the oceans was not a claim of godlike powers. It was a specific promise to reduce carbon-dioxide emissions, one measurable effect of which is the rise of worldwide sea levels. This is a task well within the purview of government. The intellectual task of liberalism is not to make government responsible for everything. It is to rationally determine which things cannot be handled by the private sector. No less than the dogmatic anti-statism of the right, the cult of the presidency is an enemy of that task.

Critical Thinking

1. Explain the concept of the "Cult of the Presidency."
2. How has the prevailing view of the presidency affected President Barack Obama's handling of the Gulf oil spill in 2010?
3. Which elements of the Gulf oil spill can be addressed by the federal government? What items are more appropriately handled by the private sector?

The Obama Enigma

Disconnection from the Main Currents of American Life Turns Out to Be a Political Disadvantage

RAMESH PONNURU

"I serve as a blank screen on which people of vastly different political stripes project their own views," Barack Obama famously wrote in the prologue to *The Audacity of Hope*. He wrote as though this "blankness" were not part of a conscious strategy for winning the White House. It was the emptiness of his slogans—"we are the ones we've been waiting for"—that allowed liberals and moderates to consider him a soul mate. Being enigmatic also enabled him to be glamorous. Coolness and distance are not just an Obama strategy; they are also clearly integral to his personality. But they are a strategy.

That strategy has a flipside, which is that his opponents can project unattractive qualities on them. And oh have they tried. At the outer edges of our politics (and sanity) are those who affix to Obama an identity as a Muslim, or an Indonesian. At the beginning of his presidency, mainstream republicans were wary of attacking the president personally. But that reticence lasted only a few weeks. since then they have ventured to define him in several ways, all negative. He is weak and indecisive, they have said, especially during the drawn-out debate over his Afghanistan policy. He was acting like an "Ivy League professor," holding "seminars" instead of acting. At other times his opponents have said he is a machine politician: a practitioner of "the Chicago way." He is a radical. An elitist. A liar—as Rep. Joe Wilson shouted.

During the 2008 campaign, Karl Rove described him as someone who coasts on his charm rather than doing hard work. A Republican Web ad, similarly, portrayed him as a "celebrity." Since he got elected, republicans have labeled him "whiny" whenever he has blamed the nation's, or his own, troubles on the Bush administration, and "petulant" whenever he has attacked current Republicans. "Vain" and "arrogant" are also words they have attached to him.

Obama's sharpest mainstream critics have questioned his patriotism. When it comes to "identification with the nation and to all that binds its people together in pride and allegiance," *Wall Street Journal* columnist Dorothy Rabinowitz recently wrote, the president is deficient. "He is the alien in the White House." As oil has kept spilling into the Gulf of Mexico, even some of the president's fans have taken to faulting him for

showing too much aloofness and not enough emotion. They too believe that he is detached, even if they will not add "from his countrymen."

Not all of these critiques make sense, or hang together very well. Republicans might try to portray Obama as weak and indecisive toward the country's enemies and savage with his domestic opponents; but they are not going to convince the public that Obama the man is simultaneously ruthless and weak. A kind of elitism may well be inherent in his political philosophy, but the imputation of snobbery to our first black president, who was raised without a father, is inapt.

On the other hand, some of the charges stick. Obama is in some respects more liberal than previous Democratic presidents, and the evidence his defenders use to deny this fact consists chiefly of tactical retreats. Not fighting for single payer or a public option when Congress would not have passed either proves that he can count votes, not that he is a moderate. He is vain, even as successful politicians go: How many other politicians would say that they are better strategists than their strategist, better speechwriters than their speechwriter, etc.? He is thin-skinned: Has he ever responded to a criticism with self-deprecating humor, or grace? He regularly has an unpresidential air of being put upon. "Lying" is a strong term, but Obama also frequently says things that one would think he knows not to be true—such as that people who like their current health plans will be able to keep them under his reform.

Some of the critiques have clearly gotten to Obama. He told Matt Lauer that he spoke to experts about the oil spill so he would "know whose ass to kick." He was defending himself against the charge of being academic, unemotional, and passive. It was not, perhaps, the most persuasive thing this president has ever said. (At least he did not promise to create a new Department of Kick-Assery to be staffed by the best and brightest.)

The president was, of course, overcompensating. But he was also condescending. Perhaps all of the encomia to him for being uncommonly thoughtful have gone to his head. He assumes that the public will see the point of reason only if it is translated into terms of brute force.

Obama has long been considered an exceptionally talented politician, but he lacks some of the basic political skills one expects of the breed. He does not have an instinctive feel for the country's mood, and so he cannot find the right pitch—even, or especially, at moments of high national anxiety. President Clinton's reaction to the Oklahoma City bombing revived his presidency. This president, following the shootings at Fort Hood, proved incapable of rallying the country. His initial remarks were off-key, coming as they did after praise to some of his staffers and a "shout-out" to a distinguished member of the audience at a previously planned Tribal Nations Conference. Obama then allowed top officials to suggest that sacrificing "diversity" would be a greater tragedy than the massacre.

It can be said in Obama's defense that at a far more crucial moment, his predecessor delivered a more dismaying performance. President Bush's remarks on the evening of September 11 were the opposite of reassuring. But Bush righted himself within days at Ground Zero. It is hard to imagine this president grabbing the bullhorn.

In part, Obama's deficiency is a function of the inexperience that his opponents warned against during the 2008 campaign. Obama pledged to close Guantanamo Bay within a year of his inauguration. A more experienced leader might not have had any illusions about the progress from wish to reality. With more time on Capitol Hill, he might also have seen the dangers of letting the Democratic caucus set the legislative agenda. The president could have gotten a bipartisan stimulus if he had cut in big-spending Republicans—and who can doubt he would be in better shape now if he had?

But the deeper problem is Obama's disconnection from the major currents of American life. The country has been a commercial republic since its beginning; Obama has had almost no contact with business life. He also grew up in a much more left-wing milieu than any of his predecessors, and than the vast majority of Americans. During the campaign, he remarked that he was glad to be in Henry Wallace's home county. How many people his age think fondly of Wallace? (Reported *Politico*: "'I was amazed that he knew about Henry Wallace,' said Diane Weiland, the longtime director of the Henry A. Wallace Country Life Center, who was in the audience.")

Americans knew Barack Obama was to the left of most Americans when they elected him. They do not believe that he is a socialist. They do not think—at least yet—that he is untrustworthy. But some charges against leaders have a long fuse. Liberal charges that President Bush was a liar and a fool did not persuade Americans during his first term, but helped to poison his second. Americans may start to think that Obama is arrogant, and that he does not understand them. Those perceptions will be devastating if they also conclude that he's not up to the job.

Critical Thinking

1. What are some of the main Republican critiques of President Obama?
2. What are some of the political skills that Obama lacks, according to the author?
3. How has Obama's distant or disconnected nature affected his image?

When Congress Stops Wars
Partisan Politics and Presidential Power

WILLIAM G. HOWELL AND JON C. PEVEHOUSE

For most of George W. Bush's tenure, political observers have lambasted Congress for failing to fulfill its basic foreign policy obligations. Typical was the recent *Foreign Affairs* article by Norman Ornstein and Thomas Mann, "When Congress Checks Out," which offered a sweeping indictment of Congress' failure to monitor the president's execution of foreign wars and antiterrorist initiatives. Over the past six years, they concluded, Congressional oversight of the White House's foreign and national security policy "has virtually collapsed." Ornstein and Mann's characterization is hardly unique. Numerous constitutional-law scholars, political scientists, bureaucrats, and even members of Congress have, over the years, lamented the lack of legislative constraints on presidential war powers. But the dearth of Congressional oversight between 2000 and 2006 is nothing new. Contrary to what many critics believe, terrorist threats, an overly aggressive White House, and an impotent Democratic Party are not the sole explanations for Congressional inactivity over the past six years. Good old-fashioned partisan politics has been, and continues to be, at play.

It is often assumed that everyday politics *stops* at the water's edge and that legislators abandon their partisan identities during times of war in order to become faithful stewards of their constitutional obligations. But this received wisdom is almost always wrong. The illusion of Congressional wartime unity misconstrues the nature of legislative oversight and fails to capture the particular conditions under which members of Congress are likely to emerge as meaningful critics of any particular military venture.

The partisan composition of Congress has historically been the decisive factor in determining whether lawmakers will oppose or acquiesce in presidential calls for war. From Harry Truman to Bill Clinton, nearly every U.S. president has learned that members of Congress, and members of the opposition party in particular, are fully capable of interjecting their opinions about proposed and ongoing military ventures. When the opposition party holds a large number of seats or controls one or both chambers of Congress, members routinely challenge the president and step up oversight of foreign conflicts; when the legislative branch is dominated by the president's party, it generally goes along with the White House. Partisan unity, not institutional laziness, explains why the Bush administration's

Iraq policy received such a favorable hearing in Congress from 2000 to 2006.

The dramatic increase in Congressional oversight following the 2006 midterm elections is a case in point. Immediately after assuming control of Congress, House Democrats passed a resolution condemning a proposed "surge" of U.S. troops in Iraq and Senate Democrats debated a series of resolutions expressing varying degrees of outrage against the war in Iraq. The spring 2007 supplemental appropriations debate resulted in a House bill calling for a phased withdrawal (the president vetoed that bill, and the Senate then passed a bill accepting more war funding without withdrawal provisions). Democratic heads of committees in both chambers continue to launch hearings and investigations into the various mishaps, scandals, and tactical errors that have plagued the Iraq war. By all indications, if the government in Baghdad has not met certain benchmarks by September, the Democrats will push for binding legislation that further restricts the president's ability to sustain military operations in Iraq.

Neither Congress' prior languor nor its recent awakening should come as much of a surprise. When they choose to do so, members of Congress can exert a great deal of influence over the conduct of war. They can enact laws that dictate how long military campaigns may last, control the purse strings that determine how well they are funded, and dictate how appropriations may be spent. Moreover, they can call hearings and issue public pronouncements on foreign policy matters. These powers allow members to cut funding for ill-advised military ventures, set timetables for the withdrawal of troops, foreclose opportunities to expand a conflict into new regions, and establish reporting requirements. Through legislation, appropriations, hearings, and public appeals, members of Congress can substantially increase the political costs of military action—sometimes forcing presidents to withdraw sooner than they would like or even preventing any kind of military action whatsoever.

The Partisan Imperative

Critics have made a habit of equating legislative inactivity with Congress' abdication of its foreign policy obligations. Too often, the infrequency with which Congress enacts restrictive statutes is seen as prima facie evidence of the institution's failings. Sometimes it is. But one cannot gauge the health of the U.S. system of governance strictly on the basis of what Congress does—or does not do—in the immediate aftermath of presidential initiatives.

After all, when presidents anticipate Congressional resistance they will not be able to overcome, they often abandon the sword as their primary tool of diplomacy. More generally, when the White House knows that Congress will strike down key provisions of a policy initiative, it usually backs off. President Bush himself has relented, to varying degrees, during the struggle to create the Department of Homeland Security and during conflicts over the design of military tribunals and the prosecution of U.S. citizens as enemy combatants. Indeed, by most accounts, the administration recently forced the resignation of the chairman of the Joint Chiefs of Staff, General Peter Pace, so as to avoid a clash with Congress over his reappointment.

To assess the extent of Congressional influence on presidential war powers, it is not sufficient to count how many war authorizations are enacted or how often members deem it necessary to start the "war powers clock"—based on the War Powers Act requirement that the president obtain legislative approval within 60 days after any military deployment. Rather, one must examine the underlying partisan alignments across the branches of government and presidential efforts to anticipate and preempt Congressional recriminations.

During the past half century, partisan divisions have fundamentally defined the domestic politics of war. A variety of factors help explain why partisanship has so prominently defined the contours of interbranch struggles over foreign military deployments. To begin with, some members of Congress have electoral incentives to increase their oversight of wars when the opposing party controls the White House. If presidential approval ratings increase due to a "rally around the flag" effect in times of war, and if those high ratings only benefit the president's party in Congress, then the opposition party has an incentive to highlight any failures, missteps, or scandals that might arise in the course of a military venture.

After all, the making of U.S. foreign policy hinges on how U.S. national interests are defined and the means chosen to achieve them. This process is deeply, and unavoidably, political. Therefore, only in very particular circumstances—a direct attack on U.S. soil or on Americans abroad—have political parties temporarily united for the sake of protecting the national interest. Even then, partisan politics has flared as the toll of war has become evident. Issues of trust and access to information further fuel these partisan fires. In environments in which information is sparse, individuals with shared ideological or partisan affiliations find it easier to communicate with one another. The president possesses unparalleled intelligence about threats to national interests, and he is far more likely to share that information with members of his own political party than with political opponents. Whereas the commander in chief has an entire set of executive-branch agencies at his beck and call, Congress has relatively few sources of reliable classified information. Consequently, when a president claims that a foreign crisis warrants military intervention, members of his own party tend to trust

him more often than not, whereas members of the opposition party are predisposed to doubt and challenge such claims. In this regard, Congressional Democrats' constant interrogations of Bush administration officials represent just the latest round in an ongoing interparty struggle to control the machinery of war.

Congressional Influence and Its Limits

Historically, presidents emerging from midterm election defeats have been less likely to respond to foreign policy crises aggressively, and when they have ordered the use of force, they have taken much longer to do so. Our research shows that the White House's propensity to exercise military force steadily declines as members of the opposition party pick up seats in Congress. In fact, it is not even necessary for the control of Congress to switch parties; the loss of even a handful of seats can materially affect the probability that the nation will go to war.

The partisan composition of Congress also influences its willingness to launch formal oversight hearings. While criticizing members for their inactivity during the Bush administration, Ornstein and Mann make much of the well-established long-term decline in the number of hearings held on Capitol Hill. This steady decline, however, has not muted traditional partisan politics. According to Linda Fowler, of Dartmouth College, the presence or absence of unified government largely determines the frequency of Congressional hearings. Contrary to Ornstein and Mann's argument that "vigorous oversight was the norm until the end of the twentieth century," Fowler demonstrates that during the post–World War II era, when the same party controlled both Congress and the presidency, the number of hearings about military policy decreased, but when the opposition party controlled at least one chamber of Congress, hearings occurred with greater frequency. Likewise, Boston University's Douglas Kriner has shown that Congressional authorizations of war as well as legislative initiatives that establish timetables for the withdrawal of troops, cut funds, or otherwise curtail military operations critically depend on the partisan balance of power on Capitol Hill.

Still, it is important not to overstate the extent of Congressional influence. Even when Congress is most aggressive, the executive branch retains a tremendous amount of power when it comes to military matters. Modern presidents enjoy extraordinary advantages in times of war, not least of which the ability to act unilaterally on military matters and thereby place on Congress (and everyone else) the onus of coordinating a response. Once troops enter a region, members of Congress face the difficult choice of either cutting funds and then facing the charge of undermining the troops or keeping the public coffers open and thereby aiding a potentially ill-advised military operation.

On this score, Ornstein and Mann effectively illustrate Bush's efforts to expand his influence over the war in Iraq and the war on terrorism by refusing to disclose classified information, regularly circumventing the legislative process, and resisting even modest efforts at oversight. Similarly, they note that Republican Congressional majorities failed to take full advantage of their institution's formal powers to monitor and influence either the formulation or the implementation of foreign policy during the first six years of Bush's presidency. Ornstein and Mann, however, mistakenly attribute such lapses in Congressional oversight to a loss of an "institutional identity" that was ostensibly forged during a bygone era when "tough oversight of the executive was common, whether or not different parties controlled the White House and Congress" and when members' willingness to challenge presidents had less to do with partisan allegiances and more to do with a shared sense of institutional responsibility. In the modern era, foreign-policy making has rarely worked this way. On the contrary, partisan competition has contributed to nearly every foreign policy clash between Capitol Hill and the White House for the past six decades.

Divided We Stand

Shortly after World War II—the beginning of a period often mischaracterized as one of "Cold War consensus"—partisan wrangling over the direction of U.S. foreign policy returned to Washington, ending a brief period of wartime unity. By defining U.S. military involvement in Korea as a police action rather than a war, President Truman effectively freed himself from the constitutional requirements regarding war and established a precedent for all subsequent presidents to circumvent Congress when sending the military abroad. Although Truman's party narrowly controlled both chambers, Congress hounded him throughout the Korean War, driving his approval ratings down into the 20s and paving the way for a Republican electoral victory in 1952. Railing off a litany of complaints about the president's firing of General Douglas MacArthur and his meager progress toward ending the war, Senator Robert Taft, then a Republican presidential candidate, declared that "the greatest failure of foreign policy is an unnecessary war, and we have been involved in such a war now for more than a year. . . . As a matter of fact, every purpose of the war has now failed. We are exactly where we were three years ago, and where we could have stayed."

On the heels of the Korean War came yet another opportunity to use force in Asia, but facing a divided Congress, President Dwight Eisenhower was hesitant to get involved. French requests for assistance in Indochina initially fell on sympathetic ears in the Eisenhower administration, which listed Indochina as an area of strategic importance in its "new look" defense policy. However, in January 1954, when the French asked for a commitment of U.S. troops, Eisenhower balked. The president stated that he "could conceive of no greater tragedy than for the United States to become involved in an all-out war in Indochina." His reluctance derived in part from the anticipated fight with Congress that he knew would arise over such a war. Even after his decision to provide modest technical assistance to France, in the form of B-26 bombers and air force technicians, Congressional leaders demanded a personal meeting with the president to voice their disapproval. Soon afterward, Eisenhower promised to withdraw the air force personnel, replacing them with civilian contractors.

Eventually, the United States did become involved in a ground war in Asia, and it was that war that brought Congressional

opposition to the presidential use of force to a fever pitch. As the Vietnam War dragged on and casualties mounted, Congress and the public grew increasingly wary of the conflict and of the power delegated to the president in the 1964 Gulf of Tonkin resolution. In 1970, with upward of 350,000 U.S. troops in the field and the war spilling over into Cambodia, Congress formally repealed that resolution. And over the next several years, legislators enacted a series of appropriations bills intended to restrict the war's scope and duration. Then, in June 1973, after the Paris peace accords had been signed, Congress enacted a supplemental appropriations act that cut off all funding for additional military involvement in Southeast Asia, including in Cambodia, Laos, North Vietnam, and South Vietnam. Finally, when South Vietnam fell in 1975, Congress took the extraordinary step of formally forbidding U.S. troops from enforcing the Paris peace accords, despite the opposition of President Gerald Ford and Secretary of State Henry Kissinger.

Three years later, a Democratic Congress forbade the use of funds for a military action that was supported by the president—this time, the supply of covert aid to anticommunist forces in Angola. At the insistence of Senator Dick Clark (D-Iowa), the 1976 Defense Department appropriations act stipulated that no monies would be used "for any activities involving Angola other than intelligence gathering." Facing such staunch Congressional opposition, President Ford suspended military assistance to Angola, unhappily noting that the Democratic-controlled Congress had "lost its guts" with regard to foreign policy.

In just one instance, the case of Lebanon in 1983, did Congress formally start the 60-day clock of the 1973 War Powers Act. Most scholars who call Congress to task for failing to fulfill its constitutional responsibilities make much of the fact that in this case it ended up authorizing the use of force for a full 18 months, far longer than the 60 days automatically allowed under the act. However, critics often overlook the fact that Congress simultaneously forbade the president from unilaterally altering the scope, target, or mission of the U.S. troops participating in the multinational peacekeeping force. Furthermore, Congress asserted its right to terminate the venture at any time with a one-chamber majority vote or a joint resolution and established firm reporting requirements as the U.S. presence in Lebanon continued.

During the 1980s, no foreign policy issue dominated Congressional discussions more than aid to the contras in Nicaragua, rebel forces who sought to topple the leftist Sandinista regime. In 1984, a Democratic-controlled House enacted an appropriations bill that forbade President Ronald Reagan from supporting the contras. Reagan appeared undeterred. Rather than abandon the project, the administration instead diverted funds from Iranian arms sales to support the contras, establishing the basis for the most serious presidential scandal since Watergate. Absent Congressional opposition on this issue, Reagan may well have intervened directly, or at least directed greater, more transparent aid to the rebels fighting the Nicaraguan government.

Regardless of which party holds a majority of the seats in Congress, it is almost always the opposition party that creates the most trouble for a president intent on waging war. When, in the early 1990s, a UN humanitarian operation in Somalia devolved into urban warfare, filling nightly newscasts with scenes from Mogadishu, Congress swung into action. Despite previous declarations of public support for the president's actions, Congressional Republicans and some Democrats passed a Department of Defense appropriations act in November 1993 that simultaneously authorized the use of force to protect UN units and required that U.S. forces be withdrawn by March 31, 1994.

A few years later, a Republican-controlled Congress took similar steps to restrict the use of funds for a humanitarian crisis occurring in Kosovo. One month after the March 1999 NATO air strikes against Serbia, the House passed a bill forbidding the use of Defense Department funds to introduce U.S. ground troops into the conflict without Congressional authorization. When President Clinton requested funding for operations in the Balkans, Republicans in Congress (and some hawkish Democrats) seized on the opportunity to attach additional monies for unrelated defense programs, military personnel policies, aid to farmers, and hurricane relief and passed a supplemental appropriations bill that was considerably larger than the amount requested by the president. The mixed messages sent by the Republicans caught the attention of Clinton's Democratic allies. As House member Martin Frost (D-Tex.) noted, "I am at a loss to explain how the Republican Party can, on one hand, be so irresponsible as to abandon our troops in the midst of a military action to demonstrate its visceral hostility toward the commander in chief, and then, on the other, turn around and double his request for money for what they call 'Clinton's war.'" The 1999 debate is remarkably similar to the current wrangling over spending on Iraq.

Legislating Opinion

The voice of Congress (or lack thereof) has had a profound impact on the media coverage of the current war in Iraq, just as it has colored public perceptions of U.S. foreign policy in the past. Indeed, Congress' ability to influence executive-branch decision-making extends far beyond its legislative and budgetary powers. Cutting funds, starting the war powers clock, or forcing troop withdrawals are the most extreme options available to them. More frequently, members of Congress make appeals designed to influence both media coverage and public opinion of a president's war. For example, Congress' vehement criticism of Reagan's decision to reflag Kuwaiti tankers during the Iran-Iraq War led to reporting requirements for the administration. Similarly, the Clinton administration's threats to invade Haiti in 1994 were met with resistance by Republicans and a handful of skeptical Democrats in Congress, who took to the airwaves to force Clinton to continually justify placing U.S. troops in harm's way.

Such appeals resonate widely. Many studies have shown that the media regularly follow official debates about war in Washington, adjusting their coverage to the scope of the discussion among the nation's political elite. And among the elite, members of Congress—through their own independent initiatives and through journalists' propensity to follow them—stand out as the single most potent source of dissent against the president. The sheer number of press releases and direct feeds that members of Congress produce is nothing short of breathtaking. And through carefully staged hearings, debates,

and investigations, members deliberately shape the volume and content of the media's war coverage. The public posturing, turns of praise and condemnation, rapid-fire questioning, long-winded exhortations, pithy Shakespearean references, graphs, timelines, and pie charts that fill these highly scripted affairs are intended to focus media attention and thereby sway the national conversation surrounding questions of war and peace. Whether the media scrutinize every aspect of a proposed military venture or assume a more relaxed posture depends in part on Congress' willingness to take on the president.

Indeed, in the weeks preceding the October 2002 war authorization vote, the media paid a tremendous amount of attention to debates about Iraq inside the Beltway. Following the vote, however, coverage of Iraq dropped precipitously, despite continued domestic controversies, debates at the United Nations, continued efforts by the administration to rally public support, and grass-roots opposition to the war that featured large public protests. Congress helped set the agenda for public discussion, influencing both the volume and the tone of the coverage granted to an impending war, and Congress' silence after the authorization was paralleled by that of the press.

Crucially, Congressional influence over the media extended to public opinion as well. An analysis of local television broadcast data and national public-opinion surveys from the period reveals a strong relationship between the type of media coverage and public opinion regarding the war. Even when accounting for factors such as the ideological tendencies of a media market (since liberal markets tend to have liberal voters and liberal media, while conservative districts have the opposite), we found that the airing of more critical viewpoints led to greater public disapproval of the proposed war, and more positive viewpoints buoyed support for the war. As Congress speaks, it would seem, the media report, and the public listens.

As these cases illustrate, the United States has a Congress with considerably more agenda-setting power than most analysts presume and a less independent press corps than many would like. As the National Journal columnist William Powers observed during the fall of 2006, "Journalists like to think they are reporting just the facts, straight and unaffected by circumstance." On the contrary, he recognized, news is a product of the contemporary political environment, and the way stories are framed and spun has little to do with the facts. In Washington, the party that controls Congress also determines the volume and the tone of the coverage given to a president's war. Anticipating a Democratic Congressional sweep in November 2006, Powers correctly predicted that "if Bush suffers a major political setback, the media will feel freed up to tear into this war as they have never done before."

With the nation standing at the precipice of new wars, it is vital that the American public understand the nature and extent of Congress' war powers and its members' partisan motivations for exercising or forsaking them. President Bush retains extraordinary institutional advantages over Congress, but with the Democrats now in control of both houses, the political costs of pursuing new wars (whether against Iran, North Korea, or any other country) and prosecuting ongoing ones have increased significantly.

Congress will continue to challenge the president's interpretation of the national interest. Justifications for future deployments will encounter more scrutiny and require more evidence. Questions of appropriate strategy and implementation will surface more quickly with threats of Congressional hearings and investigations looming. Oversight hearings will proceed at a furious pace. Concerning Iraq, the Democrats will press the administration on a withdrawal timetable, hoping to use their agenda-setting power with the media to persuade enough Senate Republicans to defect and thereby secure the votes they need to close floor debate on the issue.

This fall, the Democrats will likely attempt to build even more momentum to end the war in Iraq, further limiting the president's menu of choices. This is not the first instance of heavy Congressional involvement in foreign affairs and war, nor will it be the last. This fact has been lost on too many political commentators convinced that some combination of an eroding political identity, 9/11, failures of leadership, and dwindling political will have made Congress irrelevant to deliberations about foreign policy.

On the contrary, the new Democratic-controlled Congress is conforming to a tried-and-true pattern of partisan competition between the executive and legislative branches that has characterized Washington politics for the last half century and shows no signs of abating. Reports of Congress' death have been greatly exaggerated.

Critical Thinking

1. In what ways is Congress able to influence the conduct and political costs of military action?

2. Why has partisanship defined the domestic politics of war?

3. What are some of the advantages the president is able to use to exert influence during wartime?

4. How did Congress's reactions to the Vietnam War illustrate opposition to the presidential use of force?

5. How does Congress's opposition or support of military action affect media and public perceptions of war?

WILLIAM G. HOWELL and **JON C. PEVEHOUSE** are Associate Professors at the Harris School of Public Policy at the University of Chicago and the authors of *While Dangers Gather: Congressional Checks on Presidential War Powers*.

From *Foreign Affairs*, vol. 86, no. 5, September/October 2007. Copyright © 2007 by Council on Foreign Relations. Reprinted by permission. www.ForeignAffairs.com

How to Get Our Democracy Back
There Will Be No Change Until We Change Congress

L AWRENCE L ESSIG

We should remember what it felt like one year ago, as the ability to recall it emotionally will pass and it is an emotional memory as much as anything else. It was a moment rare in a democracy's history. The feeling was palpable—to supporters and opponents alike—that something important had happened. America had elected, the young candidate promised, a transformational president. And wrapped in a campaign that had produced the biggest influx of new voters and small-dollar contributions in a generation, the claim seemed credible, almost intoxicating, and just in time.

Yet a year into the presidency of Barack Obama, it is already clear that this administration is an opportunity missed. Not be cause it is too conservative. Not because it is too liberal. But because it is too conventional. Obama has given up the rhetoric of his early campaign—a campaign that promised to "challenge the broken system in Washington" and to "fundamentally change the way Washington works." Indeed, "fundamental change" is no longer even a hint.

Instead, we are now seeing the consequences of a decision made at the most vulnerable point of Obama's campaign—just when it seemed that he might really have beaten the party's presumed nominee. For at that moment, Obama handed the architecture of his new administration over to a team that thought what America needed most was another Bill Clinton. A team chosen by the brother of one of DC's most powerful lobbyists, and a White House headed by the quintessential DC politician. A team that could envision nothing more than the ordinary politics of Washington—the kind of politics Obama had called "small." A team whose imagination—politically—is tiny.

These tiny minds—brilliant though they may be in the conventional game of DC—have given up what distinguished Obama's extraordinary campaign. Not the promise of health-care reform or global warming legislation—Hillary Clinton had embraced both of those ideas, and every other substantive proposal that Obama advanced. Instead, the passion that Obama inspired grew from the recognition that something fundamental had gone wrong in the way our government functions, and his commitment to reform it.

For Obama once spoke for the anger that has now boiled over in even the blue state Massachusetts—that our government is corrupt; that fundamental change is needed. As he told us, both parties had allowed "lobbyists and campaign contributions to rig the system." And "unless we're willing to challenge [that] broken system . . . nothing else is going to change." "The reason" Obama said he was "running for President [was] to challenge that system." For "if we're not willing to take up that fight, then real change—change that will make a lasting difference in the lives of ordinary Americans—will keep getting blocked by the defenders of the status quo."

This administration has not "taken up that fight." Instead, it has stepped down from the high ground the President occupied on January 20, 2009, and played a political game no different from the one George W. Bush played, or Bill Clinton before him. Obama has accepted the power of the "defenders of the status quo" and simply negotiated with them. "Audacity" fits nothing on the list of last year's activity, save the suggestion that this is the administration the candidate had promised.

> **'Audacity' fits nothing on the list of last year's activity, save the suggestion that this is the administration the candidate had promised.**

Maybe this was his plan all along. It was not what he said. And by ignoring what he promised, and by doing what he attacked ("too many times, after the election is over, and the confetti is swept away, all those promises fade from memory, and the lobbyists and the special interests move in"), Obama will leave the presidency, whether in 2013 or 2017, with Washington essentially intact and the movement he inspired betrayed.

That movement needs new leadership. On the right (the tea party) and the left (MoveOn and Bold Progressives), there is an unstoppable recognition that our government has failed. But both sides need to understand the source of its failure if either or, better, both together, are to respond.

At the center of our government lies a bankrupt institution: Congress. Not financially bankrupt, at least not yet, but politically bankrupt. *Bush v. Gore* notwithstanding, Americans' faith in the Supreme Court remains extraordinarily high—76 percent have a fair or great deal of "trust and confidence" in the Court. Their faith in the presidency is also high—61 percent.

But consistently and increasingly over the past decade, faith in Congress has collapsed—slowly, and then all at once. Today it is at a record low. Just 45 percent of Americans have "trust and confidence" in Congress; just 25 percent approve of how Congress is handling its job. A higher percentage of Americans likely supported the British Crown at the time of the Revolution than support our Congress today.

The source of America's cynicism is not hard to find. Americans despise the inauthentic. Gregory House, of the eponymous TV medical drama, is a hero not because he is nice (he isn't), but because he is true. Tiger Woods is a disappointment not because he is evil (he isn't), but because he proved false. We may want peace and prosperity, but most would settle for simple integrity. Yet the single attribute least attributed to Congress, at least in the minds of the vast majority of Americans, is just that: integrity. And this is because most believe our Congress is a simple pretense. That rather than being, as our framers promised, an institution "dependent on the People," the institution has developed a pathological dependence on campaign cash. The US Congress has become the Fundraising Congress. And it answers—as Republican and Democratic presidents alike have discovered—not to the People, and not even to the president, but increasingly to the relatively small mix of interests that fund the key races that determine which party will be in power.

This is corruption. Not the corruption of bribes, or of any other crime known to Title 18 of the US Code. Instead, it is a corruption of the faith Americans have in this core institution of our democracy. The vast majority of Americans believe money buys results in Congress (88 percent in a recent California poll). And whether that belief is true or not, the damage is the same. The democracy is feigned. A feigned democracy breeds cynicism. Cynicism leads to disengagement. Disengagement leaves the fox guarding the henhouse.

This corruption is not hidden. On the contrary, it is in plain sight, with its practices simply more and more brazen. Consider, for example, the story Robert Kaiser tells in his fantastic book *So Damn Much Money,* about Senator John Stennis, who served for forty-one years until his retirement in 1989. Stennis, no choirboy himself, was asked by a colleague to host a fundraiser for military contractors while he was chair of the Armed Services Committee. "Would that be proper?" Stennis asked. "I hold life and death over those companies. I don't think it would be proper for me to take money from them."

Is such a norm even imaginable in DC today? Compare Stennis with Max Baucus, who has gladly opened his campaign chest to $3.3 million in contributions from the healthcare and insurance industries since 2005, a time when he has controlled healthcare in the Senate. Or Senators Lieberman, Bayh and Nelson, who took millions from insurance and healthcare interests and then opposed the (in their states) popular public option for healthcare. Or any number of Blue Dog Democrats in the House who did the same, including, most prominently, Alabama's Mike Ross. Or Republican John Campbell, a California landlord who in 2008 received (as ethics reports indicate) between $600,000 and $6 million in rent from used car dealers, who successfully inserted an amendment into the Consumer Financial Protection Agency Act to exempt car dealers from financing rules to protect consumers. Or Democrats Melissa Bean and Walter Minnick, who took top-dollar contributions from the financial services sector and then opposed stronger oversight of financial regulations.

The list is endless; the practice open and notorious. Since the time of Rome, historians have taught that while corruption is a part of every society, the only truly dangerous corruption comes when the society has lost any sense of shame. Washington has lost its sense of shame.

As fundraising becomes the focus of Congress—as the parties force members to raise money for other members, as they reward the best fundraisers with lucrative committee assignments and leadership positions—the focus of Congressional "work" shifts. Like addicts constantly on the lookout for their next fix, members grow impatient with anything that doesn't promise the kick of a campaign contribution. The first job is meeting the fundraising target. Everything else seems cheap. Talk about policy becomes, as one Silicon Valley executive described it to me, "transactional." The perception, at least among industry staffers dealing with the Hill, is that one makes policy progress only if one can promise fundraising progress as well.

As the focus of Congressional work shifts toward fundraising, policy discussions are becoming increasingly 'transactional.'

This dance has in turn changed the character of Washington. As Kaiser explains, Joe Rothstein, an aide to former Senator Mike Gravel, said there was never a "period of pristine American politics untainted by money. . . . Money has been part of American politics forever, on occasion—in the Gilded Age or the Harding administration, for example—much more blatantly than recently." But "in recent decades 'the scale of it has just gotten way out of hand.' The money may have come in brown paper bags in earlier eras, but the politicians needed, and took, much less of it than they take through more formal channels today."

And not surprisingly, as powerful interests from across the nation increasingly invest in purchasing public policy rather than inventing a better mousetrap, wealth, and a certain class of people, shift to Washington. According to the 2000 Census, fourteen of the hundred richest counties were in the Washington area. In 2007, nine of the richest twenty were in the area. Again, Kaiser: "In earlier generations enterprising young men came to Washington looking for power and political adventure, often with ambitions to save or reform the country or the world. In the last fourth of the twentieth century such aspirations were supplanted by another familiar American yearning: to get rich."

Rich, indeed, they are, with the godfather of the lobbyist class, Gerald Cassidy, amassing more than $100 million from his lobbying business.

Members of Congress are insulted by charges like these. They insist that money has no such effect. Perhaps, they concede, it buys access. (As former Representative Romano Mazzoli put it, "People who contribute get the ear of the member and the ear of the staff. They have the access—and access is it.") But, the cash-seekers insist, it doesn't change anyone's mind. The souls of members are not corrupted by private funding. It is simply the way Americans go about raising the money necessary to elect our government.

But there are two independent and adequate responses to this weak rationalization for the corruption of the Fundraising Congress. First, whether or not this money has corrupted anyone's soul—that is, whether it has changed any vote or led any politician to bend one way or the other—there is no doubt that it leads the vast majority of Americans to believe that money buys results in Congress. Even if it doesn't, that's what Americans believe. Even if, that is, the money doesn't corrupt the soul of a single member of Congress, it corrupts the institution—by weakening faith in it, and hence weakening the willingness of citizens to participate in their government. Why waste your time engaging politically when it is ultimately money that buys results, at least if you're not one of those few souls with vast sums of it?

"But maybe," the apologist insists, "the problem is in what Americans believe. Maybe we should work hard to convince Americans that they're wrong. It's understandable that they believe money is corrupting Washington. But it isn't. The money is benign. It supports the positions members have already taken. It is simply how those positions find voice and support. It is just the American way."

Here a second and completely damning response walks onto the field: if money really doesn't affect results in Washington, then what could possibly explain the fundamental policy failures—relative to every comparable democracy across the world, whether liberal or conservative—of our government over the past decades? The choice (made by Democrats and Republicans alike) to leave unchecked a huge and crucially vulnerable segment of our economy, which threw the economy over a cliff when it tanked (as independent analysts again and again predicted it would). Or the choice to leave unchecked the spread of greenhouse gases. Or to leave unregulated the exploding use of antibiotics in our food supply—producing deadly strains of *E. coli.* Or the inability of the twenty years of "small government" Republican presidents in the past twenty-nine to reduce the size of government at all. Or . . . you fill in the blank. From the perspective of what the People want, or even the perspective of what the political parties say they want, the Fundraising Congress is misfiring in every dimension. That is either because Congress is filled with idiots or because Congress has a dependency on something other than principle or public policy sense. In my view, Congress is not filled with idiots.

The point is simple, if extraordinarily difficult for those of us proud of our traditions to accept: this democracy no longer works. Its central player has been captured. Corrupted. Controlled by an economy of influence disconnected from the democracy. Congress has developed a dependency foreign to the framers' design. Corporate campaign spending, now liberated by the Supreme Court, will only make that dependency worse. "A dependence" not, as the Federalist Papers celebrated it, "on the People" but a dependency upon interests that have conspired to produce a world in which policy gets sold.

No one, Republican or Democratic, who doesn't currently depend upon this system should accept it. No president, Republican or Democratic, who doesn't change this system could possibly hope for any substantive reform. For small-government Republicans, the existing system will always block progress. There will be no end to extensive and complicated taxation and regulation until this system changes (for the struggle over endless and complicated taxation and regulation is just a revenue opportunity for the Fundraising Congress). For reform-focused Democrats, the existing system will always block progress. There will be no change in fundamental aspects of the existing economy, however inefficient, from healthcare to energy to food production, until this political economy is changed (for the reward from the status quo to stop reform is always irresistible to the Fundraising Congress). In a single line: there will be no change until we change Congress.

That Congress is the core of the problem with American democracy today is a point increasingly agreed upon by a wide range of the commentators. But almost universally, these commentators obscure the source of the problem. Some see our troubles as tied to the arcane rules of the institution, particularly the Senate. Ezra Klein of the *Washington Post,* for example, has tied the failings of Congress to the filibuster and argues that the first step of fundamental reform has got to be to fix that. Tom Geoghegan made a related argument in these pages in August, and the argument appears again in this issue. (Of course, these pages were less eager to abolish the filibuster when the idea was floated by the Republicans in 2005, but put that aside.)

These arguments, however, miss a basic point. Filibuster rules simply set the price that interests must pay to dislodge reform. If the rules were different, the price would no doubt be higher. But a higher price wouldn't change the economy of influence. Indeed, as political scientists have long puzzled, special interests underinvest in Washington relative to the potential return. These interests could just as well afford to assure that fifty-one senators block reform as forty.

Others see the problem as tied to lobbyists—as if removing lobbyists from the mix of legislating (as if that constitutionally could be done) would be reform enough to assure that legislation was not corrupted.

But the problem in Washington is not lobbying. The problem is the role that lobbyists have come to play. As John Edwards used to say (when we used to quote what Edwards said), there's all the difference in the world between a lawyer making an argument to a jury and a lawyer handing out $100 bills to the jurors. That line is lost on the profession today. The profession would earn enormous credibility if it worked to restore it.

Finally, some believe the problem of Congress is tied to excessive partisanship. Members from an earlier era routinely point to the loss of a certain civility and common purpose. The game as played by both parties seems more about the parties than about the common good.

But it is this part of the current crisis that the dark soul in me admires most. There is a brilliance to how the current fraud is sustained. Everyone inside this game recognizes that if the public saw too clearly that the driving force in Washington is campaign cash, the public might actually do something to change that. So every issue gets reframed as if it were really a question touching some deep (or not so deep) ideological question. Drug companies fund members, for example, to stop reforms that might actually test whether "me too" drugs are worth the money they cost. But the reforms get stopped by being framed as debates about "death panels" or "denying doctor choice" rather than the simple argument of cost-effectiveness that motivates the original reform. A very effective campaign succeeds in obscuring the source of conflict over major issues of reform with the pretense that it is ideology rather than campaign cash that divides us.

Lobbying campaigns obscure the source of policy disputes with the pretense that it is ideology, not campaign cash, that divides us.

Each of these causes is a symptom of a more fundamental disease. That disease is improper dependency. Remove the dependency, and these symptoms become—if not perfectly then at least much more—benign.

As someone who has known Obama vaguely for almost twenty years—he was my colleague at the University of Chicago, and I supported and contributed to every one of his campaigns—I would have bet my career that he understood this. That's what he told us again and again in his campaign, not as colorfully as Edwards, but ultimately more convincingly. That's what distinguished him from Hillary Clinton. That's what Clinton, defender of the lobbyists, didn't get. It was "fundamentally chang[ing] the way Washington works" that was the essential change that would make change believable.

So if you had told me in 2008 that Obama expected to come to power and radically remake the American economy—as his plans to enact healthcare and a response to global warming alone obviously would—without first radically changing this corrupted machinery of government, I would not have believed it. Who could believe such a change possible, given the economy of influence that defines Washington now?

Yet a year into this administration, it is impossible to believe this kind of change is anywhere on the administration's radar, at least anymore. The need to reform Congress has left Obama's rhetoric. The race to dicker with Congress in the same way Congress always deals is now the plan. Symbolic limits on lobbyists within the administration, and calls for new disclosure limits for Congress are the sole tickets of "reform." (Even its

revolving-door policy left a Mack truck–wide gap at its core: members of the administration can't leave the government and lobby for the industries they regulated during the term of the administration. But the day after Obama leaves office? All bets are off.) Except for a vague promise in his State of the Union about overturning the Court's decision in *Citizens United v. Federal Election Commission* (as if that were reform enough), there is nothing in the current framework of the White House's plans that is anything more than the strategy of a kinder and gentler, albeit certainly more articulate, George W. Bush: buying reform at whatever price the Fundraising Congress demands. No doubt Obama will try to buy more reform than Bush did. But the terms will continue to be set by a Congress driven by a dependency that betrays democracy, and at a price that is not clear we can even afford.

Healthcare reform is a perfect example. The bill the Fundraising Congress has produced is miles from the reform that Obama promised ("Any plan I sign must include an insurance exchange . . . including a public option," July 19, 2009). Like the stimulus package, like the bank bailouts, it is larded with gifts to the most powerful fundraising interests—including a promise to drug companies to pay retail prices for wholesale purchases and a promise to the insurance companies to leave their effectively collusive (since exempt from anti-trust limitations) and extraordinarily inefficient system of insurance intact—and provides (relative to the promises) little to the supposed intended beneficiaries of the law: the uninsured. In this, it is the perfect complement to the only significant social legislation enacted by Bush, the prescription drug benefit: a small benefit to those who can't afford drugs, a big gift to those who make drugs and an astonishingly expensive price tag for the nation.

So how did Obama get to this sorry bill? The first step, we are told, was to sit down with representatives from the insurance and pharmaceutical industries to work out a deal. But why, the student of Obama's campaign might ask, were they the entities with whom to strike a deal? How many of the 69,498,516 votes received by Obama did they actually cast? "We have to change our politics," Obama said. Where is the change in this?

"People . . . watch," Obama told us in the campaign, "as every year, candidates offer up detailed healthcare plans with great fanfare and promise, only to see them crushed under the weight of Washington politics and drug and insurance industry lobbying once the campaign is over."

"This cannot," he said, "be one of those years."

It has been one of those years. And it will continue to be so long as presidents continue to give a free pass to the underlying corruption of our democracy: Congress.

There was a way Obama might have had this differently. It would have been risky, some might say audacious. And it would have required an imagination far beyond the conventional politics that now controls his administration.

No doubt, 2009 was going to be an extraordinarily difficult year. Our nation was a cancer patient hit by a bus on her way to begin chemotherapy. The first stages of reform thus had to be trauma care, at least to stabilize the patient until more fundamental treatment could begin.

But even then, there was an obvious way that Obama could have reserved the recognition of the need for this more fundamental reform by setting up the expectations of the nation forcefully and clearly. Building on the rhetoric at the core of his campaign, on January 20, 2009, Obama could have said:

> America has spoken. It has demanded a fundamental change in how Washington works, and in the government America delivers. I commit to America to work with Congress to produce that change. But if we fail, if Congress blocks the change that America has demanded—or more precisely, if Congress allows the special interests that control it to block the change that America has demanded—then it will be time to remake Congress. Not by throwing out the Democrats, or by throwing out the Republicans. But by throwing out both, to the extent that both continue to want to work in the old way. If this Congress fails to deliver change, then we will change Congress.

Had he framed his administration in these terms, then when what has happened has happened, Obama would be holding the means to bring about the obvious and critical transformation that our government requires: an end to the Fundraising Congress. The failure to deliver on the promises of the campaign would not be the failure of Obama to woo Republicans (the unwooable Victorians of our age). The failure would have been what America was already primed to believe: a failure of this corrupted institution to do its job. Once that failure was marked with a frame that Obama set, he would have been in the position to begin the extraordinarily difficult campaign to effect the real change that Congress needs.

Citizen-funded elections and constitutional reforms to ensure legislative integrity would make it difficult for money to buy results.

I am not saying this would have been easy. It wouldn't have. It would have been the most important constitutional struggle since the New Deal or the Civil War. It would have involved a fundamental remaking of the way Congress works. No one should minimize how hard that would have been. But if there was a President who could have done this, it was, in my view, Obama. No politician in almost a century has had the demonstrated capacity to inspire the imagination of a nation. He had us, all of us, and could have kept us had he kept the focus high.

Nor can one exaggerate the need for precisely this reform. We can't just putter along anymore. Our government is, as Paul Krugman put it, "ominously dysfunctional" just at a time when the world desperately needs at least competence. Global warming, pandemic disease, a crashing world economy: these are not problems we can leave to a litter of distracted souls. We are at one of those rare but critical moments when a nation must

remake itself, to restore its government to its high ideals and to the potential of its people. Think of the brilliance of almost any bit of the private sector—from Hollywood, to Silicon Valley, to MIT, to the arts in New York or Nashville—and imagine a government that reflected just a fraction of that excellence. We cannot afford any less anymore.

What would the reform the Congress needs be? At its core, a change that restores institutional integrity. A change that rekindles a reason for America to believe in the central institution of its democracy by removing the dependency that now defines the Fundraising Congress. Two changes would make that removal complete. Achieving just one would have made Obama the most important president in a hundred years.

That one—and first—would be to enact an idea proposed by a Republican (Teddy Roosevelt) a century ago: citizen-funded elections. America won't believe in Congress, and Congress won't deliver on reform, whether from the right or the left, until Congress is no longer dependent upon conservative-with-a-small-c interests—meaning those in the hire of the status quo, keen to protect the status quo against change. So long as the norms support a system in which members sell out for the purpose of raising funds to get re-elected, citizens will continue to believe that money buys results in Congress. So long as citizens believe that, it will.

Citizen-funded elections could come in a number of forms. The most likely is the current bill sponsored in the House by Democrat John Larson and Republican Walter Jones, in the Senate by Democrats Dick Durbin and Arlen Specter. That bill is a hybrid between traditional public funding and small-dollar donations. Under this Fair Elections Now Act (which, by the way, is just about the dumbest moniker for the statute possible, at least if the sponsors hope to avoid Supreme Court invalidation), candidates could opt in to a system that would give them, after clearing certain hurdles, substantial resources to run a campaign Candidates would also be free to raise as much money as they want in contributions maxed at $100 per citizen.

The only certain effect of this first change would be to make it difficult to believe that money buys any results in Congress. A second change would make that belief impossible: banning any member of Congress from working in any lobbying or consulting capacity in Washington for seven years after his or her term. Part of the economy of influence that corrupts our government today is that Capitol Hill has become, as Representative Jim Cooper put it, a "farm league for K Street." But K Street will lose interest after seven years, and fewer in Congress would think of their career the way my law students think about life after law school—six to eight years making around $180,000, and then doubling or tripling that as a partner, where "partnership" for members of Congress means a comfortable position on K Street.

Before the Supreme Court's decision in *Citizens United v. FEC,* I thought these changes alone would be enough at least to get reform started. But the clear signal of the Roberts Court is that any reform designed to muck about with whatever wealth wants is constitutionally suspect. And while it would take an enormous leap to rewrite constitutional law to make the Fair Elections Now Act unconstitutional, *Citizens United* demonstrates that the Court is in a jumping mood. And more ominously, the market for influence that that decision will produce may well overwhelm any positive effect that Fair Elections produces.

This fact has led some, including now me, to believe that reform needs people who can walk and chew gum at the same time. Without doubt, we need to push the Fair Elections Now Act. But we also need to begin the process to change the Constitution to assure that reform can survive the Roberts Court. That constitutional change should focus on the core underlying problem: institutional independence. The economy of influence that grips Washington has destroyed Congress's independence. Congress needs the power to restore it, by both funding elections to secure independence and protecting the context within which elections occur so that the public sees that integrity.

No amendment would come from this Congress, of course. But the framers left open a path to amendment that doesn't re quire the approval of Congress—a convention, which must be convened if two-thirds of the states apply for it. Interestingly, (politically) those applications need not agree on the purpose of the convention. Some might see the overturning of *Citizens United.* Others might want a balanced budget amendment. The only requirement is that two-thirds apply, and then begins the drama of an unscripted national convention to debate questions of fundamental law.

Many fear a convention, worrying that our democracy can't process constitutional innovation well. I don't share that fear, but in any case, any proposed amendment still needs thirty-eight states to ratify it. There are easily twelve solid blue states in America and twelve solid red states. No one should fear that change would be too easy.

No doubt constitutional amendments are politically impossible—just as wresting a republic from the grip of a monarchy, or abolishing slavery or segregation, or electing Ronald Reagan or Barack Obama was "politically impossible." But conventional minds are always wrong about pivot moments in a nation's history. Obama promised this was such a moment. The past year may prove that he let it slip from his hand.

For this, democracy pivots. It will either spin to restore integrity or it will spin further out of control. Whether it will is no longer a choice. Our only choice is how.

I magine an alcoholic. He may be losing his family, his job, and his liver. These are all serious problems. Indeed, they are among the worst problems anyone could face. But what we all understand about the dependency of alcoholism is that however awful these problems, the alcoholic cannot begin to solve them until he solves his first problem—alcoholism.

So too is it with our democracy. Whether on the left or the right, there is an endless list of critical problems that each side believes important. The Reagan right wants less government and a simpler tax system. The progressive left wants better healthcare and a stop to global warming. Each side views these issues as critical, either to the nation (the right) or to the globe (the left). But what both sides must come to see is that the reform of neither is possible until we solve our first problem first—the dependency of the Fundraising Congress.

This dependency will perpetually block reform of any kind, since reform is always a change in the status quo, and it is defense of the status quo that the current corruption has perfected. For again, as Obama said:

> If we're not willing to take up that fight, then real change— change that will make a lasting difference in the lives of ordinary Americans—will keep getting blocked by the de fenders of the status quo.

"Defenders of the status quo"—now including the souls that hijacked the movement Obama helped inspire.

Critical Thinking

1. In what ways does the author argue that Congress is corrupt?

2. How do campaign contributions from interest groups affect Congress?

3. How do outdated rules, lobbying, and partisanship impede the functioning of Congress?

4. What forms could citizen-funded elections take, and what effect would they have on Congress?

5. How would the author's suggestion of banning any member of Congress from working in lobbying or political consulting for seven years after the end of his or her term alter the influence of lobbying or special interest groups on Congress?

LAWRENCE LESSIG, a professor of law at Harvard Law School, is co-founder of the nonprofit Change Congress.

The Case for Congress

According to opinion polls, Congress is one of the least esteemed institutions in American life. While that should come as a shock, today it's taken for granted. What can't be taken for granted is the health of representative democracy amid this corrosive— and often unwarranted—distrust of its central institution.

LEE H. HAMILTON

Several years ago, I was watching the evening news on television when the anchorman announced the death of Wilbur Mills, the legendary former chairman of the House Ways and Means Committee. There was a lot the newscaster could have said. He might have recounted the central role Mills had played in creating Medicare. Or he might have talked about Mills's hand in shaping the Social Security system and in drafting the tax code. But he did not. Instead, he recalled how Mills's career collapsed after he was found early one morning with an Argentine stripper named Fanne Foxe. And then the anchorman moved on to the next story.

One of the perks of being chairman of an influential committee in Congress, as I was at the time, is that you can pick up the telephone and get through to a TV news anchor. Which I did. I chided the fellow for summing up Mills's career with a scandal. And much to my surprise, he apologized.

Americans of all stripes like to dwell on misbehavior by members of Congress. They look at the latest scandal and assume that they're seeing the *real* Congress. But they're not. They hear repeatedly in the media about missteps, but very little about the House leader who goes home on weekends to pastor his local church, or the senator who spends one day a month working in a local job to better understand the needs of constituents, or the many members who labor behind the scenes in a bipartisan way to reach the delicate compromises needed to make the system work.

I don't want to claim that all members are saints and that their behavior is always impeccable. Yet I basically agree with the assessment of historian David McCullough: "Congress, for all its faults, has not been the unbroken parade of clowns and thieves and posturing windbags so often portrayed. What should be spoken of more often, and more widely understood, are the great victories that have been won here, the decisions of courage and the visions achieved."

Probity in Congress is the rule rather than the exception, and it has increased over the years. When I arrived in Congress, members could accept lavish gifts from special interests, pocket campaign contributions in their Capitol offices, and convert their campaign contributions to personal use. And they were rarely punished for personal corruption. None of that would be tolerated now. Things still aren't perfect, but the ethical climate at the Capitol is well ahead of where it was a couple of decades ago. And, I might add, well ahead of the public's perception of it.

During my 34 years in the House of Representatives, I heard numerous criticisms of Congress. Many seemed to me perceptive; many others were far off the mark—such as when people thought that as a member of Congress I received a limousine and chauffeur, or didn't pay taxes, or was entitled to free medical care and Social Security coverage. When people are upset about Congress, their distress undermines public confidence in government and fosters cynicism and disengagement. In a representative democracy such as ours, what the American people think of the body that's supposed to reflect their views and interests as it frames the basic laws of the land is a matter of fundamental importance. I certainly do not think Congress is a perfect institution, and I have my own list of ways I think it could be improved. Yet often the public's view is based on misunderstanding or misinformation. Here are some of the other criticisms I've heard over the years:

Congress is run by lobbyists and special interests. Americans have differing views of lobbyists and special-interest groups. Some see them as playing an essential part in the democratic process. Others look at them with skepticism but allow them a legitimate role in developing policy. Most, however, see them as sinister forces exercising too much control over Congress, and the cynicism of this majority grew during the recent wave of corporate scandals, when it was revealed how extensively companies such as Enron and Arthur

Andersen had lobbied Congress. The suspicion that Congress is manipulated by powerful wheeler-dealers who put pressure on legislators and buy votes through extensive campaign contributions and other favors is not an unfounded concern, and it will not go away, no matter how fervently some might try to dismiss it.

That said, the popular view of lobbyists as nefarious fat cats smoking big cigars and handing out hundred-dollar bills behind closed doors is wrong. These days, lobbyists are usually principled people who recognize that their word is their bond. Lobbying is an enormous industry today, with billions of dollars riding on its outcomes. Special-interest groups will often spend millions of dollars on campaigns to influence a particular decision—through political contributions, grassroots lobbying efforts, television advocacy ads, and the like—because they know that they'll get a lot more back than they spend if a bill contains the language they want. They're very good at what they do, and the truth is, members of Congress can sometimes be swayed by them.

But the influence of lobbyists on the process is not as simple as it might at first appear. In the first place, "special interests" are not just the bad guys. If you're retired, or a homeowner, or use public transit or the airlines, or are concerned about religious freedom, many people in Washington are lobbying on your behalf. There are an estimated 25,000 interest groups in the capital, so you can be sure your views are somewhere represented. Advocacy groups help Congress understand how legislation affects their members, and they can help focus the public's attention on important issues. They do their part to amplify the flow of information that Thomas Jefferson called the "dialogue of democracy."

Of course, Congress often takes up controversial issues on which you'll find a broad spectrum of opinions. Public attention is strong, a host of special interests weigh in, and the views of both lobbyists and legislators are all over the map. In such circumstances, prospects are very small that any single interest group or lobbyist can disproportionately influence the results. There are simply too many of them involved for that to happen, and the process is too public. It's when things get quiet—when measures come up out of view of the public eye—that you have to be cautious. A small change in wording here, an innocuous line in a tax bill there, can allow specific groups to reap enormous benefits they might never have been granted under close public scrutiny.

The answer, it seems to me, is not to decry lobbying or lobbyists. Lobbying is a key element of the legislative process—part of the free speech guaranteed under the Constitution. At its heart, lobbying is simply people banding together to advance their interests, whether they're farmers or environmentalists or bankers. Indeed, belonging to an interest group—the Sierra Club, the AARP, the Chamber of Commerce—is one of the main ways Americans participate in public life these days.

When I was in Congress, I came to think of lobbyists as an important part of the *public discussion* of policy. I emphasize "public discussion" for a reason. Rather than trying to clamp down on lobbying, I believe we'd be better off ensuring that it happens in the open and is part of the broader policy debate. Our

challenge is not to end it, but to make sure that it's a balanced dialogue, and that those in power don't consistently listen to the voices of the wealthy and the powerful more intently than the voices of others. Several legislative proposals have been made over the years that would help, including campaign finance reform, tough restrictions on gifts to members of Congress, prohibiting travel for members and their staffs funded by groups with a direct interest in legislation, and effective disclosure of lobbyists' involvement in drafting legislation. But in the end, something else may be even more important than these proposals: steady and candid conversation between elected officials and the people they represent.

Members of Congress, I would argue, have a responsibility to listen to lobbyists. But members also have a responsibility to understand where these lobbyists are coming from, to sort through what they are saying, and then to make a judgment about what is in the best interests of their constituents and the nation as a whole.

Congress almost seems designed to promote total gridlock. People will often complain about a do-nothing Congress, and think that much of the fault lies in the basic design of the institution. When a single senator can hold up action on a popular measure, when 30 committees or subcommittees are all reviewing the same bill, when a proposal needs to move not just through both the House and the Senate but through their multilayered budget, authorization, and appropriations processes, and when floor procedures are so complex that even members who have served for several years can still be confused by them, how can you expect anything to get done? This feeling is magnified by the major changes American society has undergone in recent decades. The incredible increase in the speed of every facet of our lives has made many people feel that the slow, untidy, deliberate pace of Congress is not up to the demands of modern society.

It is not now, nor has it ever been, easy to move legislation through Congress. But there's actually a method to the madness. Basic roadblocks were built into the process for a reason. We live in a big, complicated country, difficult to govern, with enormous regional, ethnic, and economic differences. The process must allow time for responsiveness and deliberation, all the more so when many issues—taxation, health care, access to guns, abortion, and more—stir strong emotions and don't submit easily to compromise. Do we really want a speedy system in which laws are pushed through before a consensus develops? Do we want a system in which the views of the minority get trampled in a rush to action by the majority? Reforms can surely be made to improve the system, but the basic process of careful deliberation, negotiation, and compromise lies at the very heart of representative democracy. Ours is not a parliamentary system; the dawdling pace comes with the territory.

We misunderstand Congress's role if we demand that it be a model of efficiency and quick action. America's founders never intended it to be that. They clearly understood that one of the key roles of Congress is to slow down the process—to allow tempers to cool and to encourage careful deliberation, so that unwise or damaging laws do not pass in the heat of the moment and so that the views of those in the minority get a fair hearing. That basic vision still seems wise today. Proceeding carefully to develop consensus is arduous and exasperating work, but it's the only way to produce policies that reflect the varied perspectives of a remarkably diverse citizenry. People may complain about the process, but they benefit from its legislative speed bumps when they want their views heard, their interests protected, their rights safeguarded. I recognize that Congress sometimes gets bogged down needlessly. But the fundamental notion that the structure of Congress should contain road blocks and barriers to hasty or unfair action makes sense for our country and needs to be protected and preserved. In the words of former Speaker of the House Sam Rayburn, "One of the wisest things ever said was, 'Wait a minute.'"

There's too much money in politics. When people hear stories about all the fundraising that members of Congress must do today, they come to believe that Congress is a "bought" institution. I've often been told that in our system dollars speak louder than words, and access is bought and sold. By a 4 to 1 margin, Americans believe that elected officials are influenced more by pressures from campaign contributors than by what's in the best interests of the country. But in fact, the problem of money in politics has been with us for many years. It's become so much more serious in recent years because of the expense of television advertising. The biggest portion of my campaign budget in the last election I faced—$1 million, for a largely rural seat in southern Indiana—went for TV spots.

Having experienced it firsthand, I know all too well that the "money chase" has gotten out of hand. A lot of money from special interests is floating around the Capitol—far too much money—and we ignore the problem at our own peril. To be fair, many of the claims that special interests can buy influence in Congress are overstated. Though I would be the last to say that contributions have no impact on a voting record, it's important to recognize that most of the money comes from groups that already share a member's views on the issues, rather than from groups that are hoping to change a member's mind. In addition, many influences shape members' voting decisions—the most important of them being the wishes of their constituents. In the end, members know that if their votes aren't in line with what their constituents want, they won't be reelected. And *that,* rather than a campaign contribution, is what's foremost in their minds.

Still, it's an unusual member of Congress who can take thousands of dollars from a particular group and not be affected, which is why I've come to the view that the influence of money on the political process raises a threat to representative democracy. We need significant reform. We have a campaign finance system today that's gradually eroding the public's trust and confidence. It's a slow-motion crisis, but it is a crisis. It's not possible to enact a perfect, sweeping campaign finance bill today, and perhaps not anytime soon. Yet the worst abuses can be dealt with, one by one.

Critical Thinking

1. What are some of the things that members of Congress were permitted to do thirty years ago, which are no longer acceptable in today's ethical climate?

2. What is the role of special interest groups in Congress, according to this author?

3. What are the benefits of a slow-moving legislative process?

4. How can campaign finance reform address the influence of money in politics?

Lee H. Hamilton is director of the Wilson Center and director of the Center on Congress at Indiana University. He was U.S. representative from Indiana's Ninth District from 1965 to 1999, and served as chairman of the House Committee on International Relations, the Joint Economic Committee, and several other committees. This essay is adapted from his new book *How Congress Works and Why You Should Care,* published by Indiana University Press.

From *The Wilson Quarterly*, Spring 2004, pp. 12–17. Copyright © 2004 by Lee H. Hamilton. Reprinted by permission of Lee H. Hamilton and Woodrow Wilson International Center for Scholars.

The Case for Busting the Filibuster

It's time to abolish this undemocratic holdover from the days of slavery and segregation.

THOMAS GEOGHEGAN

This past spring, Senator Claire McCaskill wrote to me asking for $50 to help elect more Democrats, so we could have a filibuster-proof Senate. Now that Al Franken has finally been declared the sixtieth Democratic senator, her plea may seem moot. But even with Franken in office, we don't have a filibuster-proof Senate. To get to sixty on the Democratic side, we'll still have to cut deals with Democrats like Max Baucus, Ben Nelson and others who cat around as Blue Dogs from vote to vote. Whether or not Senator Arlen Specter is a Democrat, the real Democrats will still have to cut the same deals to get sixty votes.

> **Until we dump the filibuster, Obama's initiatives will strain for the needed sixty votes, allowing the GOP and Blue Dog Dems to stymie reform.**

Maybe we loyal Dems should start sending postcards like the following: "Dear Senator: Why do you keep asking for my money? You've already got the fifty-one votes you need to get rid of the filibuster rule." It's true—McCaskill and her colleagues could get rid of it tomorrow. Then we really would have a Democratic Senate, like our Democratic House.

She won't. The Democratic Senatorial Campaign Committee, which paid for her appeal, won't. They use the filibuster threat to hit us up for money. And as long as they do, you and I will keep on kicking in for a "filibuster-proof" Senate, which, with or without Franken, will never exist. Every Obama initiative will teeter around sixty, only the deal-cutting will go on deeper in the back rooms and be less transparent than before.

In the meantime, playing it straighter than Claude Rains, McCaskill and other Democrats tell us how shocked, yes, *shocked* they are that this deal-cutting is going on. May I quote her spring letter? "I'm writing to you today because President Obama's agenda is in serious jeopardy . . ."

It still is, as long as it takes sixty and not fifty-one votes to pass Obama's bills. But no, here's what she says: "Why?

Because Republicans in the Senate—the same ones who spent years kowtowing to George W. Bush—are *determined* to block each and every one of President Obama's initiatives."

But why is that a surprise, if there's a rule that lets forty-one senators block a bill? The surprise to people in other countries is that the Senate, already wildly malapportioned, with two senators from every state no matter how big or small the population, does not observe majority rule. Her next line:

"It's appalling really."

It sure is—the way she and other Democratic senators keep the filibuster in place. But let her go on:

"They're the ones who got us into this mess. Now they want to stand in the way of every positive thing the President tries to do to set things right. I'm sure it frustrates you as much as it does me."

Yes, Senator, it frustrates me. But Democratic senators who let this happen and then ask for my money frustrate me even more.

As a labor lawyer, I have seen the Senate filibuster kill labor law reform—kill the right to join a union, freely and fairly—in 1978 and 1994. And, no doubt, in 2010.

And in the end, all we get is a letter from Senator McCaskill asking for more money. Of course, I know there are all sorts of arguments made for the filibuster. For example: "But the filibuster is part of our country's history, and there's much to be said for respecting our history and tradition." Yes, well, slavery and segregation are also part of our history, and that's what the filibuster was used to defend. I'm all in favor of history and tradition, but I see no reason to go on cherishing either the filibuster or the Confederate flag.

Besides, that's not the filibuster we're dealing with. The post-1975 procedural filibuster is entirely unlike the old filibuster, the one Mr. Smith, as played by the unshaven Jimmy Stewart, stayed up all night to mount in his plea for honest government (though usually it was Senator Bullhorn defending Jim Crow). The *old* filibuster that you and I and Frank Capra and the Confederacy love so much was very rare, and now it's extinct. No one has stood up and read recipes for Campbell's Soup for decades. In 1975 Vice President

Nelson Rockefeller, in his role as president of the Senate, ruled that just fifty-one senators could vote to get rid of the filibuster entirely. A simple majority of liberals could now force change on a frightened old guard. But instead of dumping the filibuster once and for all, the liberals, unsure of their support, agreed to a "reformed" Rule 22. It was this reform that, by accident, turned the once-in-a-blue-moon filibuster into something that happens all the time. The idea was to reduce the votes needed to cut off debate from sixty-seven, which on the Hill is a big hill to climb, to just sixty. Liberals like Walter Mondale wanted to make it easier to push through civil rights and other progressive legislation. What's the harm in that?

The only problem is that, because the filibuster had rendered the chamber so laughable, with renegade members pulling all-nighters and blocking all the Senate's business, the "reformers" came up with a new procedural filibuster—the polite filibuster, the Bob Dole filibuster—to replace the cruder old-fashioned filibuster of Senate pirates like Strom Thurmond ("filibuster" comes from the Dutch word for freebooter, or pirate). The liberals of 1975 thought they could banish the dark Furies of American history, but they wound up spawning more demons than we'd ever seen before. Because the senators did not want to be laughed at by stand-up comedians, they ended their own stand-up acts with a rule that says, essentially:

"We aren't going to let the Senate pirates hold up business anymore. From now on, if those people want to filibuster, they can do it offstage. They can just file a motion that they want debate to continue on this measure indefinitely. We will then put the measure aside, and go back to it only if we get the sixty votes to cut off this not-really-happening debate."

In other words, the opposing senators don't have the stomach to stand up and read the chicken soup recipes. We call it the "procedural" filibuster, but what we really mean is the "pretend" filibuster.

But the procedural, or pretend, filibuster is an even worse form of piracy, an open invitation to senatorial predators to prey on neutral shipping, to which they might have given safe passage before. After all, why *not* "filibuster" if it's a freebie—if you don't actually have to stand up and talk in the chamber until you're not only half dead from exhaustion but have made yourself a laughingstock? That's what post-1975 senators began to do. In the 1960s, before the procedural filibuster, there were seven or fewer "old" filibusters in an entire term. In the most recent Senate term, there were 138.

At least with the old filibuster, we knew who was doing the filibustering. With the modern filibuster, senators can hold up bills without the public ever finding out their names. No one's accountable for obstructing. No senator runs the risk of looking like a fool. But while they're up there concealing one another's identity, the Republic is a shambles. And now, with a nominal sixty Democratic votes, the need for secrecy as to who has put everything on hold may be even greater than before.

"But just wait till 2010, when we get sixty-two or sixty-three Democrats." I'm sure that's what Senator McCaskill would tell me. "So come on, kick in." But Senator, where will they come from? They could come from bloody border states like yours (Missouri), or from deep inside the South. The problem with the filibuster is not so much that it puts Republicans in control but that it puts sena-

tors from conservative regions like the South, the border states and the Great Plains in control. The only true filibuster-proof Senate would be a majority that would be proof against those regions.

An astute book published in 2006, Thomas Schaller's *Whistling Past Dixie,* argued that to craft a presidential majority Democrats don't need the Southern vote. That may be true (although it turned out that Barack Obama made historic inroads in the South, winning three states there). But there is no way to whistle past Dixie when a non-Dixie presidential majority tries to get its program through the Senate. After 2010, we could have sixty-four Democrats in the Senate and still be in bad shape.

A filibuster-proof Senate, then, is a conceptual impossibility. Even with a hundred Democrats, a filibuster would still lock in a form of minority rule. Because among the Democrats there would arise two new subparties, with forty-one senators named "Baucus" blocking fifty-nine senators named "Brown."

Here's another argument for the filibuster: "If we get rid of it, we'll be powerless against the Republicans when they're in charge." That's why we need it, they say: we're waiting for the barbarians, for the nightmare of President Palin. People in the AFL-CIO tell me this even as the filibuster keeps the right to organize a union on ice and union membership keeps shrinking.

Or as a union general counsel said to me: "Everyone here in the DC office would be freaked out completely if we lost the filibuster. They think it's the only thing that saved us from Bush." Inside the Beltway, they all think it's the filibuster that saved those of us who read Paul Krugman from being shipped off to Guantánamo. Really, that's what many people on the left think. "If Bush ever came back, we'd need it."

Of course Bush, or a Bush equivalent, will come back—precisely because Obama and our side will be blocked by the filibuster. Obama is in peril until he gets the same constitutional power that FDR had, i.e., the right to pass a program with a simple majority (at least after Senator Huey Long finally ran out of words). But let's deal with the canard that the filibuster "saved" us from Bush. What's the evidence? Judicial nominations: that's the answer they give. Go ahead, name someone we blocked. Roberts? Alito? Of course there's Bork, whom we blocked in the 1980s. But we didn't block him with a filibuster.

Think seriously about whom we really stopped. Look, I'm all in favor of opposing atrocious right-wing nominations, and I admit that the filibuster, or at least the GOP's refusal to nuke it, did keep some appellate and district courts free of especially bad people. But I can tell you as a lawyer who does appellate work, who has to appear before these judges, it makes little difference to me if we lose the filibuster. All it means is that instead of a bad conservative, I end up with a *really* bad conservative. Either way, I still wind up losing.

I think I can say this on behalf of many liberal lawyers who appear before appellate courts: if we could give up the filibuster and get labor law reform or national health insurance, I'd put up with a slightly more disagreeable group of right-wing judges. We'll take the heat.

The fact is, as long as we have the filibuster, we ensure the discrediting of the Democratic Party and we're more likely, not less, to have a terrible bench.

Sure, sometimes liberal Democrats put the filibuster to good use when Republicans are in power. Sure, sometimes a liberal senator can use the filibuster to stop a piece of corporate piracy. It's impossible to prove that the filibuster *never* does any good. But the record is awfully thin. Look at all the financial deregulation that Senator Phil Gramm and leading Democrats like Larry Summers pushed through only a decade ago. The filibuster did not stop their effective repeal of the New Deal, but it would block the revival of it today.

On the other hand, Republicans and conservative Democrats use their filibusters on labor, health, the stimulus, everything. They can and will block all the change that Obama wanted us to believe in. And even when they lose, they win. For example, when we say that after a major rewriting of the stimulus package—a rewriting that seriously weakened the original bill—it "survived the filibuster," what we really mean is that it didn't.

But let's turn to the final objection: "No one in Washington cares about this. It's not on the agenda. It's a waste of time even to discuss it. What you're talking about is impossible."

What Washington insiders partly mean when they say this is, with a filibuster, any senator can stick up the Senate, and what senator is going to turn in his or her sidearm by giving up the right to demand sixty votes? That's why they're raising a million dollars a day. Otherwise, they'd be peacefully serving in the House. The right to filibuster is what makes each of them a small-town sheriff. That's why it would take massive marches in the streets to force them to give it up.

Indeed, it's hard to imagine how bloody the battle would be. The last time anything so traumatic happened on the Hill was in 1961, when the bigger procedural bar to majority rule was not in the Senate but the House. John Kennedy had just come in, and it was clear that his New Frontier program (we still didn't have Medicare) would go nowhere because of the power of the House Rules Committee chair, the now forgotten "Judge" Howard Smith. Kennedy had to enlist the Speaker of the House, Sam Rayburn, to break Smith's power to stop any bill he disliked from leaving House Rules. In the end, the battle to beat Smith probably killed Rayburn, who died later in the year.

It was an awful power struggle, and many were aghast that Kennedy had thrown away all his capital for this cause. But had he not done it, there probably would not have been a Civil Rights Bill, or certainly not the full-blown version of the Great Society that Lyndon Johnson pushed through after Kennedy's assassination. Imagine having to fight the battle for Medicare today. Without that war on Judge Smith, what we now call the "liberal hour" would not have come.

Nor will any "liberal hour" come in our time, until we bring the filibuster down. I know it seems hopeless. But so did knocking out slavery when the abolitionists first started, or segregation, when civil rights activists began their struggle against Jim Crow. It's a fair enough analogy, since the filibuster is one of the last remnants of racist politics in America: it was a parliamentary tactic used by the Calhounians to make extra certain slavery would stay around.

We should adopt the strategy of the antislavery movement, which in the early stages had three approaches:

1. The laying of petitions on the House. Forgive the archaic legal phrase: I mean petitions to Congress, both houses. In the era of John Quincy Adams—in case you missed the Steven Spielberg movie—there would be mass petitions, with Adams and others reading them on the House floor to the howls of the Southerners. Every group busted by a filibuster should lay on a petition. And start with the House, which is the only place it has a chance of being read.

2. Resolutions by the House, as a warm-up for the Senate. Such resolutions might read: "Resolved, that Congress has no authority to require supermajorities in any chamber except as authorized by the Constitution." Aren't House chairs tired of seeing their bills cast into black holes by senators whose names they never even know?

3. Evangelizing. The most effective tactic in the fight against slavery was the preaching of New England clergy against it. We can start in our battle against the filibuster by enlisting faculty at New England colleges to hold teach-ins. Teach the kids why "Yes, we can" can't happen with the current Senate rules.

By the way, the abolitionists knew the Senate was their enemy, just as it is our enemy today. Let's hope these tactics work for us in getting rid of this last vestige of slavery: Senate Rule 22. What's painful is that we have to cross some of our most sainted senators. But unless we decide to just give up on the Republic, there's no way out. To save the Obama presidency, we may have to fight our heroes.

Critical Thinking

1. How do the procedural filibusters of today differ from traditional filibusters?

2. How many senators' votes are needed to eliminate the filibuster? Why have senators not moved to eliminate the filibuster?

3. What are some of the arguments made in favor of retaining the filibuster?

4. How was the filibuster used in a racially motivated way by politicians in the pre-civil rights era? What strategies mirroring anti-slavery activists' tactics does the author recommend to those who wish to abolish the filibuster today?

THOMAS GEOGHEGAN, a lawyer in Chicago, is the author of *In America's Court: How a Civil Lawyer Who Likes to Settle Stumbled Into a Criminal Trial* and *Which Side Are You On? Trying to Be for Labor When It's Flat on Its Back* (both New Press).

Reprinted by permission from the August 31/September 7, 2009, issue of *The Nation*, pp. 18, 20–22. Copyright © 2009 by The Nation. For subscription information, call 1-800-333-8536. Portions of each week's Nation magazine can be accessed at www.thenation.com

Roberts versus Roberts
Just How Radical Is the Chief Justice?

JEFFREY ROSEN

Last month, the Supreme Court handed down its most polarizing decision since *Bush* v. *Gore*. The 5-4 ruling in *Citizens United* v. *Federal Election Commission* called into question decades of federal campaign finance law and Supreme Court precedents by finding that corporations have a First Amendment right to spend as much money as they want on election campaigns, as long as they don't consult the candidates. It was precisely the kind of divisive and unnecessarily sweeping opinion that Chief Justice John Roberts had once pledged to avoid.

In 2006, at the end of his first term on the Court, Roberts told me and others that he was concerned that his colleagues, in issuing 5-4 opinions divided along predictable lines, were acting more like law professors than members of a collegial court. His goal, he said, was to persuade his fellow justices to converge around narrow, unanimous opinions, as his greatest predecessor, John Marshall, had done. Roberts spoke about the need for justices to show humility when dealing with the First Amendment, adding that, unlike professors writing law review articles, judges should think more about their institutional role. "Yes, you may have another great idea about how to look at the First Amendment," he said, "but, if you don't need to share it to decide this case, then why are you doing it? And what are the consequences of that going to be?"

Since then, Roberts has presided over some narrow, unanimous (or nearly unanimous) rulings and some bitterly divisive ones. And so, it's been hard to tell how seriously he is taking his pledge to lead the Court toward less polarizing decisions. Then came *Citizens United,* by far the clearest test of Roberts's vision. There were any number of ways he could have persuaded his colleagues to rule narrowly; but Roberts rejected these options. He deputized Anthony Kennedy to write one of his characteristically grandiose decisions, challenging the president and Congress at a moment of financial crisis when the influence of money in politics—Louis Brandeis called it "our financial oligarchy"—is the most pressing question of the day. The result was a ruling so inflammatory that the president (appropriately) criticized it during his State of the Union address.

What all this says about the future of the Roberts Court is not encouraging. For the past few years, I've been giving Roberts the benefit of the doubt, hoping that he meant it when he talked about the importance of putting the bipartisan legitimacy of the Court above his own ideological agenda. But, while Roberts talked persuasively about conciliation, it now appears that he is unwilling to cede an inch to liberals in the most polarizing cases. If Roberts continues this approach, the Supreme Court may find itself on a collision course with the Obama administration—precipitating the first full-throttle confrontation between an economically progressive president and a narrow majority of conservative judicial activists since the New Deal.

The first indications that Roberts might not be as conciliatory as he promised came during his second term, which ended in 2007. During his first term, which his colleagues treated as something of a honeymoon, the Court had decided just 13 percent of cases by a 5-4 margin. But, in the next term, that percentage soared to 33 percent. (It would fluctuate up and down a bit over the next two years.) What's more, the 2007 term ended with unusually personal invective, as both liberal and conservative colleagues expressed frustration with Roberts. That year, during the Court's second encounter with the McCain–Feingold campaign finance law (which it would gut in *Citizens United*), Antonin Scalia accused Roberts of "faux judicial restraint," for chipping away at restrictions on corporate speech without overturning them cleanly. Meanwhile, the liberal justices seemed angry that Roberts was refusing to budge from rigid positions in divisive cases. "Of course, I got slightly exercised, and the way I show that is I write seventy-seven-page opinions," Justice Stephen Breyer told me in the summer of 2007, referring to his angry dissent from Roberts's 5-4 decision striking down affirmative action in public school assignments.

That same summer, I asked Justice John Paul Stevens whether Roberts would succeed in his goal of achieving narrow, unanimous opinions. "I don't think so," he replied. "I just think it takes nine people to do that. I think maybe the first few months we all leaned over backward to try to avoid writing separately." In other words, once his first term ended, Roberts faced a choice: In cases he cared intensely about, he could compromise his principles to reach common ground or he could stick to his guns and infuriate his opponents, who would feel they had been played for dupes. On virtually all of the most divisive constitutional topics, from affirmative action to partial-birth abortion, Roberts stuck to his guns.

There were some exceptions. Roberts managed to steer the Court toward narrow, often unanimous opinions in business cases, which now represent 40 percent of the Court's docket. (Though this didn't require him to significantly compromise his views, since most of these cases were decided in a pro-business direction.) And then, there was last term's voting-rights case, in which Roberts wrote an 8-1 decision rejecting a broad constitutional challenge to the Voting Rights Act and instead deciding the case on technical grounds. For those who wanted to believe that Roberts was a genuine conciliator, this was a powerful piece of evidence. Like others, I praised his performance in the case as an act of judicial statesmanship.

But, in retrospect, the ruling may have been less statesmanlike than it appeared. According to a source who was briefed on the deliberations in the case, Anthony Kennedy was initially ready to join Roberts and the other conservatives in issuing a sweeping 5-4 decision, striking down the Voting Rights Act on constitutional grounds. But the four liberal justices threatened to write a strong dissent that would have accused the majority of misconstruing landmark precedents about congressional power. What happened next is unclear, but the most likely possibilities are either that Kennedy got cold feet or that Roberts backed down. The Voting Rights Act survived, but what looked from the outside like an act of judicial statesmanship by Roberts may have in fact been a strategic retreat. Moreover, rather than following the principled alternative suggested by David Souter at the oral argument—holding that the people who were challenging the Voting Rights Act had no standing to bring the lawsuit—Roberts opted to rewrite the statute in a way that Congress never intended. That way, Roberts was still able to express his constitutional doubts about the law—as well as his doubts about landmark Supreme Court precedents from the civil rights era, which he mischaracterized and seemed ready to overrule.

The voting-rights case may help explain why Roberts didn't take a similarly conciliatory posture in *Citizens United.* After all, one was certainly available. Just as Roberts had implausibly but strategically held in the voting-rights case that Congress intended to let election districts bail out of federal supervision, he could have held—far more plausibly—in *Citizens United* that Congress never intended to regulate video-on-demand or groups with minimal corporate funding. As with the voting-rights case, judicial creativity could have been justified in the name of judicial restraint.

There is, of course, a charitable explanation for why Roberts took the conciliatory approach in one case but not the other: namely, that he felt the principles involved in *Citizens United* were somehow more important and therefore less amenable to compromise. As he told me in our 2006 interview, he has strong views that he, like his hero John Marshall, is not willing to bargain away. Marshall, Roberts said, "was not going to compromise his principles, and I don't think there's any example of his doing that in his jurisprudence."

But a less charitable explanation for the difference between the two cases is that Roberts didn't compromise on *Citizens*

United because, this time, he simply didn't have to. Kennedy was willing to write a sweeping opinion that mischaracterized the landmark precedent *Buckley* v. *Valeo* by suggesting that it was concerned only about quid pro quo corruption rather than less explicit forms of undue influence on the electoral system. (Congress had come to the opposite conclusion in extensive fact-finding that Kennedy ignored.) As Stevens pointed out in his powerful dissent, the opinion is aggressively activist in its willingness to twist and overturn precedents, strike down decades of federal law, and mischaracterize the original understanding of the First Amendment on the rights of corporations. "The only relevant thing that has changed" since the Court's first encounter with McCain–Feingold in 2003, Stevens wrote, "is the composition of this Court"—namely, the arrival of Roberts and Samuel Alito.

Some of Roberts's liberal colleagues have suggested that Roberts is a very nice man but that he doesn't listen to opposing arguments and can't be persuaded to change his mind in controversial cases. If so, he may have thought he could produce a unanimous court by convincing liberals to come around to his side, rather than by meeting them halfway. In the most revealing passage in his concurrence in *Citizens United,* he wrote that "we cannot embrace a narrow ground of decision simply because it is narrow; it must also be right." But the great practitioners of judicial restraint had a very different perspective. "A Constitution is not intended to embody a particular economic theory," Oliver Wendell Holmes wrote in his most famous dissent, in *Lochner* v. *New York.* "It is made for people of fundamentally differing views." Holmes always deferred to the president and Congress in the face of uncertainty. He would never have presumed that he knew the "right" answer in a case where people of good faith could plausibly disagree.

With Roberts apparently content to impose bold decisions on a divided nation on the basis of slim majorities, the question becomes: Is the Court now on the verge of repeating the error it made in the 1930s? Then, another 5-4 conservative majority precipitated a presidential backlash by striking down parts of FDR's New Deal. In January 1937, Roosevelt also criticized the Supreme Court's conservative activism in a State of the Union address. The following month, he introduced his court-packing plan. But, at the end of March—thanks to the famous "switch in time" by swing justice Owen Roberts, the Anthony Kennedy of his day—the Court retreated and began to uphold New Deal laws.

One lesson from the 1930s is that it takes only a handful of flamboyant acts of judicial activism for the Court to be tarred in the public imagination as partisan, even if the justices themselves think they are being moderate and judicious. Although vilified today for their conservative activism, both the Progressive and New Deal-era Courts had nuanced records, upholding more progressive laws than they struck down. As Barry Cushman of the University of Virginia notes, of the 20 cases involving maximum working hours that the Court decided during the Progressive era, there were only two in which the Court struck down the regulations. But those two are the ones that everyone remembers. And, during the New Deal era, Cushman adds, we remember the cases striking down the National Industrial Recovery Act and the first Agricultural Adjustment Act, forgetting that the Court upheld the centerpiece of FDR's monetary policy and, by a vote of 8-1, the Tennessee Valley Authority.

It's hard to imagine a full-scale assault by the Roberts Court on Obama's regulatory agenda because, with the exception of Clarence Thomas, the conservatives on today's Court tend to be pro-business conservatives, rather than libertarian conservatives, and are therefore unlikely to strike down government spending programs (like the bank bailouts and the Troubled Asset Relief Program) that help U.S. business. But it's not hard to imagine the four conservative horsemen, joined by the vacillating Kennedy, reversing other government actions that progressives care about. Later this term, for example, the Court may follow *Citizens United* with another activist decision, striking down the Public Company Accounting Oversight Board (nicknamed "Peek-a-Boo"), which was created to regulate accounting firm auditors in the wake of the Enron and Arthur Andersen scandals. If the Court strikes down Peek-a-Boo, even if the decision is narrow enough not to call into question the constitutionality of the Federal Reserve, it may provoke another sharp rejoinder from Obama that turns progressive rumbling against the Court into full-blown outrage.

It's impossible, at the moment, to tell whether the reaction to *Citizens United* will be the beginning of a torrential backlash or will fade into the ether. But John Roberts is now entering politically hazardous territory. Without being confident either way, I still hope that he has enough political savvy and historical perspective to recognize and avoid the shoals ahead. There's little doubt, however, that the success or failure of his tenure will turn on his ability to align his promises of restraint with the reality of his performance. Roberts may feel just as confident that he knows the "right" answer in cases like Peek-a-Boo as he did in *Citizens United*. But political backlashes are hard to predict, contested constitutional visions can't be successfully imposed by 5-4 majorities, and challenging the president and Congress on matters they care intensely about is a dangerous game. We've seen well-intentioned but unrestrained chief justices overplay their hands in the past—and it always ends badly for the Court.

Critical Thinking

1. What was Chief Justice Roberts' goal during his first term on the Supreme Court?

2. How has Roberts' approach to deciding cases changed since his first term?

3. What were the implications of the Supreme Court's decision in *Citizens United v. Federal Election Commission?*

4. How has the Roberts court begun to practice judicial activism? What lessons can be drawn from a similar period of conservative activism in the Supreme Court during the 1930s?

Court under Roberts Is Most Conservative in Decades

ADAM LIPTAK

Washington—When Chief Justice John G. Roberts Jr. and his colleagues on the Supreme Court left for their summer break at the end of June, they marked a milestone: the Roberts court had just completed its fifth term.

In those five years, the court not only moved to the right but also became the most conservative one in living memory, based on an analysis of four sets of political science data.

And for all the public debate about the confirmation of Elena Kagan or the addition last year of Justice Sonia Sotomayor, there is no reason to think they will make a difference in the court's ideological balance. Indeed, the data show that only one recent replacement altered its direction, that of Justice Samuel A. Alito Jr. for Justice Sandra Day O'Connor in 2006, pulling the court to the right.

There is no similar switch on the horizon. That means that Chief Justice Roberts, 55, is settling in for what is likely to be a very long tenure at the head of a court that seems to be entering a period of stability.

If the Roberts court continues on the course suggested by its first five years, it is likely to allow a greater role for religion in public life, to permit more participation by unions and corporations in elections and to elaborate further on the scope of the Second Amendment's right to bear arms. Abortion rights are likely to be curtailed, as are affirmative action and protections for people accused of crimes.

The recent shift to the right is modest. And the court's decisions have hardly been uniformly conservative. The justices have, for instance, limited the use of the death penalty and rejected broad claims of executive power in the government's efforts to combat terrorism.

But scholars who look at overall trends rather than individual decisions say that widely accepted political science data tell an unmistakable story about a notably conservative court.

Almost all judicial decisions, they say, can be assigned an ideological value. Those favoring, say, prosecutors and employers are said to be conservative, while those favoring criminal defendants and people claiming discrimination are said to be liberal.

Analyses of databases coding Supreme Court decisions and justices' votes along these lines, one going back to 1953 and another to 1937, show that the Roberts court has staked out territory to the right of the two conservative courts that immediately preceded it by four distinct measures:

In its first five years, the Roberts court issued conservative decisions 58 percent of the time. And in the term ending a year ago, the rate rose to 65 percent, the highest number in any year since at least 1953.

The courts led by Chief Justices Warren E. Burger, from 1969 to 1986, and William H. Rehnquist, from 1986 to 2005, issued conservative decisions at an almost indistinguishable rate—55 percent of the time.

That was a sharp break from the court led by Chief Justice Earl Warren, from 1953 to 1969, in what liberals consider the Supreme Court's golden age and conservatives portray as the height of inappropriate judicial meddling. That court issued conservative decisions 34 percent of the time.

Four of the six most conservative justices of the 44 who have sat on the court since 1937 are serving now: Chief Justice Roberts and Justices Alito, Antonin Scalia and, most conservative of all, Clarence Thomas. (The other two were Chief Justices Burger and Rehnquist.) Justice Anthony M. Kennedy, the swing justice on the current court, is in the top 10.

The Roberts court is finding laws unconstitutional and reversing precedent—two measures of activism—no more often than earlier courts. But the ideological direction of the court's activism has undergone a marked change toward conservative results.

Until she retired in 2006, Justice O'Connor was very often the court's swing vote, and in her later years she had drifted to the center-left. These days, Justice Kennedy has assumed that crucial role at the court's center, moving the court to the right.

Justice John Paul Stevens, who retired in June, had his own way of tallying the court's direction. In an interview in his chambers in April, he said that every one of the 11 justices who had joined the court since 1975, including himself, was more conservative than his or her predecessor, with the possible exceptions of Justices Sotomayor and Ruth Bader Ginsburg.

The numbers largely bear this out, though Chief Justice Roberts is slightly more liberal than his predecessor, Chief Justice Rehnquist, at least if all of Chief Justice Rehnquist's

33 years on the court, 14 of them as an associate justice, are considered. (In later years, some of his views softened.)

But Justice Stevens did not consider the question difficult. Asked if the replacement of Chief Justice Rehnquist by Chief Justice Roberts had moved the court to the right, he did not hesitate.

"Oh, yes," Justice Stevens said.

The Most Significant Change

"Gosh," Justice Sandra Day O'Connor said at a law school forum in January a few days after the Supreme Court undid one of her major achievements by reversing a decision on campaign spending limits. "I step away for a couple of years and there's no telling what's going to happen."

When Justice O'Connor announced her retirement in 2005, the membership of the Rehnquist court had been stable for 11 years, the second-longest stretch without a new justice in American history.

Since then, the pace of change has been dizzying, and several justices have said they found it disorienting. But in an analysis of the court's direction, some changes matter much more than others. Chief Justice Rehnquist died soon after Justice O'Connor announced that she was stepping down. He was replaced by Chief Justice Roberts, his former law clerk. Justice David H. Souter retired in 2009 and was succeeded by Justice Sotomayor. Justice Stevens followed Justice Souter this year, and he is likely to be succeeded by Elena Kagan.

But not one of those three replacements seems likely to affect the fundamental ideological alignment of the court. Chief Justice Rehnquist, a conservative, was replaced by a conservative. Justices Souter and Stevens, both liberals, have been or are likely to be succeeded by liberals.

Justices' views can shift over time. Even if they do not, a justice's place in the court's ideological spectrum can move as new justices arrive. And chief justices may be able to affect the overall direction of the court, notably by using the power to determine who writes the opinion for the court when they are in the majority. Chief Justice Roberts is certainly widely viewed as a canny tactician.

But only one change—Justice Alito's replacement of Justice O'Connor—really mattered. That move defines the Roberts court. "That's a real switch in terms of ideology and a switch in terms of outlook," said Lee Epstein, who teaches law and political science at Northwestern University and is a leading curator and analyst of empirical data about the Supreme Court.

The point is not that Justice Alito has turned out to be exceptionally conservative, though he has: he is the third-most conservative justice to serve on the court since 1937, behind only Justice Thomas and Chief Justice Rehnquist. It is that he replaced the more liberal justice who was at the ideological center of the court.

Though Chief Justice Roberts gets all the attention, Justice Alito may thus be the lasting triumph of the administration of President George W. Bush. He thrust Justice Kennedy to the court's center and has reshaped the future of American law.

It is easy to forget that Justice Alito was Mr. Bush's second choice. Had his first nominee, the apparently less conservative Harriet E. Miers, not withdrawn after a rebellion from Mr. Bush's conservative base, the nature of the Roberts court might have been entirely different.

By the end of her almost quarter-century on the court, Justice O'Connor was without question the justice who controlled the result in ideologically divided cases.

"On virtually all conceptual and empirical definitions, O'Connor is the court's center—the median, the key, the critical and the swing justice," Andrew D. Martin and two colleagues wrote in a study published in 2005 in The North Carolina Law Review shortly before Justice O'Connor's retirement.

With Justice Alito joining the court's more conservative wing, Justice Kennedy has now unambiguously taken on the role of the justice at the center of the court, and the ideological daylight between him and Justice O'Connor is a measure of the Roberts court's shift to the right.

Justice O'Connor, for her part, does not name names but has expressed misgivings about the direction of the court.

"If you think you've been helpful, and then it's dismantled, you think, 'Oh, dear,' " she said at William & Mary Law School in October in her usual crisp and no-nonsense fashion. "But life goes on. It's not always positive."

Justice O'Connor was one of the authors of McConnell v. Federal Election Commission, a 2003 decision that, among other things, upheld restrictions on campaign spending by businesses and unions. It was reversed on that point in the Citizens United decision.

Asked at the law school forum in January how she felt about the later decision, she responded obliquely. But there was no mistaking her meaning.

"If you want my legal opinion" about Citizens United, Justice O'Connor said, "you can go read" McConnell.

The Court without O'Connor

The shift resulting from Justice O'Connor's departure was more than ideological. She brought with her qualities that are no longer represented on the court. She was raised and educated in the West, and she served in all three branches of Arizona's government, including as a government lawyer, majority leader of the State Senate, an elected trial judge and, an appeals court judge.

Those experiences informed Justice O'Connor's sensitivity to states' rights and her frequent deference to political judgments. Her rulings were often pragmatic and narrow, and her critics said she engaged in split-the-difference jurisprudence.

Justice Alito's background is more limited than Justice O'Connor's—he worked in the Justice Department and then as a federal appeals court judge—and his rulings are often more muscular.

Since they never sat on the court together, trying to say how Justice O'Connor would have voted in the cases heard by Justice Alito generally involves extrapolation and speculation. In some, though, it seems plain that she would have voted differently from him.

Just weeks before she left the court, for instance, Justice O'Connor heard arguments in Hudson v. Michigan, a case about whether evidence should be suppressed because it was found after Detroit police officers stormed a home without announcing themselves.

"Is there no policy protecting the homeowner a little bit and the sanctity of the home from this immediate entry?" Justice O'Connor asked a government lawyer. David A. Moran, a lawyer for the defendant, Booker T. Hudson, said the questioning left him confident that he had Justice O'Connor's crucial vote.

Three months later, the court called for reargument, signaling a 4-to-4 deadlock after Justice O'Connor's departure. When the 5-to-4 decision was announced in June, the court not only ruled that violations of the knock-and-announce rule do not require the suppression of evidence, but also called into question the exclusionary rule itself.

The shift had taken place. Justice Alito was in the majority.

"My 5-4 loss in Hudson v. Michigan," Mr. Moran wrote in 2006 in Cato Supreme Court Review, "signals the end of the Fourth Amendment"—protecting against unreasonable searches—"as we know it."

The departure of Justice O'Connor very likely affected the outcomes in two other contentious areas: abortion and race.

In 2000, the court struck down a Nebraska law banning an abortion procedure by a vote of 5 to 4, with Justice O'Connor in the majority. Seven years later, the court upheld a similar federal law, the Partial-Birth Abortion Act, by the same vote.

"The key to the case was not in the difference in wording between the federal law and the Nebraska act," Erwin Chemerinsky wrote in 2007 in The Green Bag, a law journal. "It was Justice Alito having replaced Justice O'Connor."

In 2003, Justice O'Connor wrote the majority opinion in a 5-to-4 decision allowing public universities to take account of race in admissions decisions. And a month before her retirement in 2006, the court refused to hear a case challenging the use of race to achieve integration in public schools.

Almost as soon as she left, the court reversed course. A 2007 decision limited the use of race for such a purpose, also on a 5-to-4 vote.

There were, to be sure, issues on which Justice Kennedy was to the left of Justice O'Connor. In a 5-to-4 decision in 2005 overturning the juvenile death penalty, Justice Kennedy was in the majority and Justice O'Connor was not.

But changing swing justices in 2006 had an unmistakable effect across a broad range of cases. "O'Connor at the end was quite a bit more liberal than Kennedy is now," Professor Epstein said.

The numbers bear this out.

The Rehnquist court had trended left in its later years, issuing conservative rulings less than half the time in its last two years in divided cases, a phenomenon not seen since 1981. The first term of the Roberts court was a sharp jolt to the right. It issued conservative rulings in 71 percent of divided cases, the highest rate in any year since the beginning of the Warren court in 1953.

Judging by the Numbers

Chief Justice Roberts has not served nearly as long as his three most recent predecessors. The court he leads has been in flux. But five years of data are now available, and they point almost uniformly in one direction: to the right.

Scholars quarrel about some of the methodological choices made by political scientists who assign a conservative or liberal label to Supreme Court decisions and the votes of individual justices. But most of those arguments are at the margins, and the measures are generally accepted in the political science literature.

The leading database, created by Harold J. Spaeth with the support of the National Science Foundation about 20 years ago, has served as the basis for a great deal of empirical research on the contemporary Supreme Court and its members. In the database, votes favoring criminal defendants, unions, people claiming discrimination or violation of their civil rights are, for instance, said to be liberal. Decisions striking down economic regulations and favoring prosecutors, employers, and the government are said to be conservative.

About 1 percent of cases have no ideological valence, as in a boundary dispute between two states. And some concern multiple issues or contain ideological cross-currents.

But while it is easy to identify the occasional case for which ideological coding makes no sense, the vast majority fit pretty well. They also tend to align with the votes of the justices usually said to be liberal or conservative.

Still, such coding is a blunt instrument. It does not take account of the precedential and other constraints that are in play or how much a decision moves the law in a conservative or liberal direction. The mix of cases has changed over time. And the database treats every decision, monumental or trivial, as a single unit.

"It's crazy to count each case as one," said Frank B. Cross, a law and business professor at the University of Texas. "But the problem of counting each case as one is reduced by the fact that the less-important ones tend to be unanimous."

Some judges find the entire enterprise offensive.

"Supreme Court justices do not acknowledge that any of their decisions are influenced by ideology rather than by neutral legal analysis," William M. Landes, an economist at the University of Chicago, and Richard A. Posner, a federal appeals court judge, wrote last year in The Journal of Legal Analysis. But if that were true, they continued, knowing the political party of the president who appointed a given justice would tell you nothing about how the justice was likely to vote in ideologically charged cases.

In fact, the correlation between the political party of appointing presidents and the ideological direction of the rulings of the judges they appoint is quite strong.

Here, too, there are exceptions. Justices Stevens and Souter were appointed by Republican presidents and ended up voting with the court's liberal wing. But they are gone. If Ms. Kagan wins Senate confirmation, all of the justices on the court may be expected to align themselves across the ideological spectrum in sync with the party of the president who appointed them.

The proposition that the Roberts court is to the right of even the quite conservative courts that preceded it thus seems fairly well established. But it is subject to qualifications.

First, the rightward shift is modest.

Second, the data do not take popular attitudes into account. While the court is quite conservative by historical standards, it is less so by contemporary ones. Public opinion polls suggest that about 30 percent of Americans think the current court is too liberal, and almost half think it is about right.

On given legal issues, too, the court's decisions are often closely aligned with or more liberal than public opinion, according to studies collected in 2008 in "Public Opinion and Constitutional Controversy" (Oxford University Press).

The public is largely in sync with the court, for instance, in its attitude toward abortion—in favor of a right to abortion but sympathetic to many restrictions on that right.

"Solid majorities want the court to uphold Roe v. Wade and are in favor of abortion rights in the abstract," one of the studies concluded. "However, equally substantial majorities favor procedural and other restrictions, including waiting periods, parental consent, spousal notification, and bans on 'partial birth' abortion."

Similarly, the public is roughly aligned with the court in questioning affirmative action plans that use numerical standards or preferences while approving those that allow race to be considered in less definitive ways.

The Roberts court has not yet decided a major religion case, but the public has not always approved of earlier rulings in this area. For instance, another study in the 2008 book found that "public opinion has remained solidly against the court's landmark decisions declaring school prayer unconstitutional."

In some ways, the Roberts court is more cautious than earlier ones. The Rehnquist court struck down about 120 laws, or about six a year, according to an analysis by Professor Epstein. The Roberts court, which on average hears fewer cases than the Rehnquist court did, has struck down fewer laws—15 in its first five years, or three a year.

It is the ideological direction of the decisions that has changed. When the Rehnquist court struck down laws, it reached a liberal result more than 70 percent of the time. The Roberts court has tilted strongly in the opposite direction, reaching a conservative result 60 percent of the time.

The Rehnquist court overruled 45 precedents over 19 years. Sixty percent of those decisions reached a conservative result. The Roberts court overruled eight precedents in its first five years, a slightly lower annual rate. All but one reached a conservative result.

Critical Thinking

1. Why did the appointment of Justice Samuel Alito have a significant impact on the composition of the Supreme Court?

2. How do the Roberts court's decisions striking down laws or reversing precedent differ from those of previous courts?

3. Describe the roles of Justice O'Connor and Justice Kennedy as the court's "swing votes." How have these two justices differed in their approach to the role?

4. How does the political party of a president nominating a Supreme Court justice predict the ideological nature of the justice's decisions while seated on the court?

5. If the Roberts court continues along its current ideological trajectory, what types of decisions and outcomes are likely in the future?

Marking Time
Why Government Is Too Slow

BRUCE BERKOWITZ

I n recent years we have been witness to a portentous competition between two determined but dissimilar rivals on the international scene. In one corner we have al-Qaeda, founded in the early 1990s, the transnational Islamic terrorist organization led by Osama bin Laden. In the other corner, we have the government of the United States of America, established in 1787, at present the most powerful state on the planet. The key question defining this competition is this: Who has the more agile organization? Al-Qaeda, in planning and executing a terrorist attack, or the United States, in planning, developing and executing the measures to stop one?

Let's look at the record. Sometime during the spring of 1999, Khalid Sheikh Mohamed visited bin Laden in Afghanistan and asked if al-Qaeda would fund what came to be called the "planes operation"—the plan for suicide attacks using commercial airliners. (Mohamed had been mulling the plot since at least 1993, when he discussed it with his nephew, Ramzi Yousef, one of the terrorists behind the first World Trade Center bombing and the attempted Philippine-based effort to bring down a dozen U.S. airliners over the Pacific in 1995.) Bin Laden agreed, and by the summer of 1999 he had selected as team leaders four al-Qaeda members—Khalid al-Mihdhar, Nawaf al-Hazmi, Tawfiq bin Attash (also known as "Khallad") and Abu Bara al-Yemen.

These four team leaders entered the United States in early 2000 and started taking flying lessons that summer. The so-called "muscle" hijackers, the 15 terrorists tasked with overpowering the crews on the targeted flights, began arriving in April 2001 and spent the summer preparing for the September 11 attack. So from the point in time that a government contracting official would call "authority to proceed" to completion, the operation took approximately 27 months.

Now let's track the U.S. response. U.S. officials began debating options for preventing future terrorist attacks immediately following the September 11 strike. Congress took a year to debate the statute establishing the Department of Homeland Security. George W. Bush, who originally opposed creating a new department, changed his mind and signed the bill into law on November 25, 2002. A joint House-Senate committee finished the first investigation of intelligence leading up to the attack in December 2002. The 9/11 Commission issued its report on July 22, 2004, recommending among other things the establishment of a Director of National Intelligence and a new National Counterterrorism Center. President Bush established the NCTC by Executive Order on August 27, 2004.

Adoption of the Intelligence Reform and Terrorism Prevention Act, which embodied most of the Commission's other proposals, took another three months. The measures it authorized—including the creation of a Director of National Intelligence—lay fallow until a second commission, investigating intelligence prior to the war in Iraq, issued its own report four months later. The new Director was sworn in on April 21, 2005. Total response time, charitably defined: about 44 months, and implementation continues today.

Obviously, planning an attack and adjusting defenses to prevent a subsequent attack are not comparable tasks. Still, it is hard to avoid concluding that organizations like al-Qaeda are inherently nimbler than governments, especially large and highly bureaucratized governments like ours. As things stand now, terrorists can size up a situation, make decisions and act faster than we can. In military terms, they are "inside our decision cycle."

Recall July 7, 2005, for example, when terrorists bombed three London Underground trains and a double-decker city bus, killing 52 commuters. The four bombs exploded within a minute of each other, an operationally and technically challenging feat that is a hallmark of al-Qaeda attacks. A "martyrdom video" proclaiming allegiance to al-Qaeda and taped months earlier by one of the bombers, Muhammad Sidique Khan, soon surfaced on al-Jazeera. Khan apparently made the video during a visit to Pakistan, and investigators concluded that an earlier trip to Pakistan in July 2003 also had something to do with the attack. If so, then the planning of the London attack required two years, possibly less.

Organizations like al-Qaeda are inherently nimbler than governments, especially large ones like ours.

Again, it may seem unfair to compare a government bureaucracy, American or British, with a network of loosely organized, small terrorist cells. But unfairness is the point: Terrorists will *always* make the conflict between us as "unfair" as possible, avoiding our strengths and exploiting our vulnerabilities however they can. So will insurgency leaders and rogue dictators, who also happen to be surreptitious WMD proliferators; narco-traffickers and money launderers, who aid terrorists either wittingly or inadvertently. The U.S. government and similarly arrayed allies will simply lose battle after battle if our adversaries absorb information, make decisions, change tactics and act faster than we can.

Reading the 9/11 Commission Report one cannot help but be struck by how often simple delay and chronic slowness led to disaster on September 11. President Clinton told the Commission that he had asked for military options to get rid of bin Laden in late 1999. But General Hugh Shelton, Chairman of the Joint Chiefs of Staff, was reluctant to provide them. Secretary of Defense William Cohen thought the President was speaking only hypothetically. The one person who could have given a direct order to cut through the resistance and ambiguity, President Clinton himself, did not do so. He thought that raising his temper wouldn't accomplish anything, so he allowed himself to be slow-rolled, and the issue went essentially unaddressed.

The problem wasn't just at the top, however. Down below in the bureaucracy, things were just as bad—case in point, the Predator. The now-famous robotic aircraft was originally built for battlefield reconnaissance and was later modified to carry missiles. The U.S. Air Force had flown Predators in the Balkans since 1996, but Afghanistan was trickier. The aircraft had a limited range and thus needed a remote base and data uplinks to get the information back to Washington. It took until July 2000 to work out these details, and two more months to deploy the Predator over Afghanistan.

Predator operators thought they spotted bin Laden in September 2000, but U.S. officials disagreed over rules of engagement. National Security Advisor Samuel Berger wanted greater confidence in bin Laden's location before approving a strike, and he worried about civilian casualties. At the same time, Air Force leaders were reluctant to carry out what looked to them, not unreasonably, like a covert operation, and the CIA was reluctant to undertake a direct combat operation—or to violate the Executive Order prohibiting assassination.

These disagreements dragged into 2001 as the Bush Administration took office. Then President Bush put everything on hold while National Security Advisor Condoleezza Rice directed a comprehensive plan to eliminate al-Qaeda. George Tenet, the Director of Central Intelligence, deferred the legal over whether the CIA could take part in an attack until the Administration had prepared its new strategy. So it went, until the clock ran out and the terrorists killed nearly 3,000 people.

Or take the inability of the Immigration and Naturalization Service (INS), as it existed on September 11, 2001, to track the whereabouts of known terror suspects and to report relevant information about their attempts to enter the country to other Federal agencies. The INS failed to meet its homeland security responsibilities partly because Congress systematically underfunded it. But even worse, the INS had failed to disentangle its different functions; keeping some people out of the country while letting others in. Meanwhile, everyone—the White House, Congress, the bureaucracy—failed to agree on a solution that both dealt with illegal immigration while also allowing entry to laborers essential to the American economy. The security problem flowing from this failure is obvious: As long as underfunded bureaucrats are unable to regulate the enormous flow of illegal immigrants seeking work, they will never be able to detect and track the few truly dangerous people trying to enter the country.

Of course, the story of the run-up to 9/11 is an oft-told one. Yet almost everyone seems to miss the core problem from which all others followed: There was always time for another meeting, another study, another round of coordination. Virtually no one was worrying about the clock—about whether *time itself mattered*. It's not that every concern raised didn't have some legitimate rationale (at least within the legal-bureaucratic culture that characterizes the U.S. government). It's the fact that, while we were working out legal issues, al-Qaeda was developing and executing its plan.

This same problem surfaced again a year later. Just about everyone agrees now that the United States was unprepared for the insurgency in Iraq, but most overlook that someone else was also unprepared: the insurgents. U.S. analysts who interviewed captured Iraqi officials and military officers for the Defense Department have concluded that Iraqi leaders had not prepared a "stay-behind" or "rope-a-dope" strategy. They had never planned to forfeit the conventional war in order to win a guerrilla war later on. Iraqi military leaders believed they would lose the war and just wanted to get it over with quickly. Saddam Hussein's security services and core Ba'ath Party operatives kept the lid on the various sects, tribes and ethnic groups so that they could not plan a guerrilla war either. The result was that *no one* was prepared for an insurgency. The United States, its coalition partners, Ba'athis who had escaped capture, tribal leaders, religious authorities, foreign fighters—everyone was starting from scratch. So when Saddam's statue came down in Firdos Square on April 9, 2003, the question that mattered most was who could organize and execute faster, the would-be insurgents or the U.S. government?

Alas, we were left in the starting blocks. The insurgents organized much faster than U.S. officials could recognize and respond. We were playing catch-up from the beginning, which is another way of saying we were losing.

Things would perhaps not be so bad if the war on al-Qaeda and the war in Iraq were exceptional. In truth, the problem is pervasive and getting worse. "Organizational agility" sounds abstract, but it really boils down to specific questions: How long does it take to deliver a critical weapon or information system? How fast can an agency bring new people on board? How fast can it change its mix of people if it needs to? In short, *how fast can government agencies act—and is this fast enough to stay ahead of the competition?*

The U.S. government is not always woefully slow. The response to the December 2004 Southeast Asian tsunami, for example, was admirably quick and reasonably effective under the circumstances. So was the relief mission that the United States effectively led following the massive earthquake that rocked northern Pakistan in October 2005. However, these few exceptions aside, the U.S. government has become an increasingly ponderous beast, unable to act quickly or even to understand how its various parts fit together to act at all.

Once, When We Were Fast

It was not always so. After the surprise attack at Pearl Harbor, one of the most heavily damaged ships was the battleship USS *West Virginia*. Most of its port side had been blown away. The ship sank rapidly, but on an even keel on the bottom of the harbor. The Navy needed every 16-inch gun it could muster, so Navy leaders decided to repair the ship. It was not easy, but the USS *West Virginia* steamed into Puget Sound in April 1943 to be refitted and modernized. It rejoined the fleet in June 1944, thirty months after it was sunk, took part in several operations and was present for the surrender ceremonies in Tokyo Bay in September 1945. By comparison, after al-Qaeda agents in Yemen damaged the USS *Cole* far less severely with a single improvised bomb in October 2000, it took 16 months to retrieve the still-floating destroyer and complete repairs in Pascagoula, Mississippi. The ship did not then leave its home port in Norfolk, Virginia, for its first deployment until November 2003—37 months later.

World War II offers many examples like the recovery of the *West Virginia* in which organizations worked with remarkable alacrity. Take the effort to build the first atomic bomb. Albert Einstein wrote to Franklin D. Roosevelt on August 2, 1939, alerting him to the possibilities of nuclear weapons. He met with FDR about a month later, which led Roosevelt to establish the Uranium Committee to research military applications of nuclear fission. Vannevar Bush, Roosevelt's science adviser, persuaded the President to accelerate the project in October 1941, as war with Germany and Japan seemed likely. On September 14, 1942, Brigadier General Leslie Groves was appointed director of the new Manhattan Project, marking the formal start of the project to build the atomic bomb. The Trinity test, the world's first nuclear explosion, took place on July 16, 1945, and Hiroshima was bombed on August 6, less than a month later. The entire effort, costing $21 billion in today's dollars, developed three different means of producing fissile material, two bomb designs and three devices.

Or consider the Office of Strategic Services, the predecessor of today's CIA. President Roosevelt appointed William Donovan as his "Coordinator of Information" in July 1941, and the OSS was itself established in June 1942. Harry Truman disbanded it in September 1945. In other words, the entire history of the OSS— what many consider the Golden Age of American intelligence— spanned just 37 months. In that short time it recruited, trained and deployed a workforce of about 13,000 people. William Casey, directing OSS espionage in Europe, stood up his entire network in about 18 months. By comparison, after 9/11 Tenet said on

several occasions that it would require five years to rebuild the CIA's clandestine service.

Or recall the war in the Pacific. The Battle of the Coral Sea was fought in May 1942, the Battle of Midway a month later. Within six months of Pearl Harbor, the U.S. Navy had destroyed five Japanese carriers, along with most of Japan's naval aircraft and aviators. It has taken us longer just to get organized for the so-called War on Terror (to the extent that we *are* organized for it) than it did to fight and win World War II.

Delivering the Product

Everything else today is moving faster, thanks to jet airliners, interstate highways, the computer and the Internet. But government, including the parts responsible for national security, is moving slower, and it's getting worse.

Everyone knows, for example, that weapons have been getting more expensive per unit, but few realize that it now also takes much longer to get a weapon into the hands of the warfighter. In the early 1940s, it took 25 months to get a new fighter like the P-47 Thunderbolt into action from the time the government signed a contract for a prototype. In the late 1940s, this delay had grown to about 43 months for an early jet fighter like the F-86 Sabre. By the 1960s, the F-4 Phantom required 66 months, and its 1970s replacement, the F-15 Eagle, 82 months. The latest fighter to enter service, the F-22 Raptor, traces its development to a prototype built under a contract signed in October 1986. The prototype first flew in September 1990, and the production model entered service in December 2005—a total of 230 months, or about 19 years. Put another way, that comes to slightly longer than the typical career of an officer in the U.S. Air Force. (The new F-35 Lighting II, which will replace the F-16, is slated to require "just" 15 years from signing the contract for the prototype to when it enters service. We'll see.)

One might think the problem with jet aircraft is a result of the growing technical complexity of modern fighter aircraft, but that argument does not hold up. No rule says that the more complex a technology is, the longer it takes to deliver. Government aircraft of *all* kinds take longer to develop, and longer than their commercial counterparts. Compare a military transport, like the C-17 Globemaster III with the new Boeing 787 Dreamliner. The C-17 required 12 years to enter service, while the 787—more complex than the C-17 in many respects—will take just four. And the 787, for example, will require a little *less* time to develop than its predecessor from the early 1990s, the 777.[1]

The problem holds for most weapons other than airplanes, too—ships, tanks, electronic systems and so on. Threats are changing much faster than we can develop the means to counter them. This is why some officials occasionally say we have to anticipate requirements further into the future. But that's simply unrealistic. When you try to forecast two decades ahead because your weapon takes twenty years to develop, it isn't analysis: it's fortune telling.

The ever-slowing pace of government appears in other ways, as well. Simply getting a presidential administration into place is a stellar example. According a 2005 National Academy of Sciences study, every Administration since Kennedy's has taken longer than its predecessor to fill the top 500 jobs in government. In the 1960s it took just under three months; today it is three times as long. A new administration isn't up and running until almost a year after the election that put it in office. How can a team possibly win the Big Game if half the players don't show up until the end of the first quarter?

That is more or less what happened in 2001 as al-Qaeda was preparing 9/11. The Bush Administration's Cabinet Secretaries were confirmed and ready to go when the new President was sworn in on January 20, 2001, but that was about it. The Administration didn't nominate Paul Wolfowitz to be Deputy Secretary of Defense until February 5, and he had to wait until March 2 to be confirmed and sworn in. Wolfowitz's wait was comparatively short; most positions took longer to fill. Richard Armitage, nominated for Deputy Secretary of State, waited until March 23, 2001. Six months passed before the top Defense Department leadership was in place. Douglas Feith, the Under Secretary of Defense for Policy—as in "policy for combating terrorists"—was *last* to be sworn in, in July 2001.

What is so depressing about the National Academy of Science study is that the problem just keeps getting worse. If top officials have to wait two or three months at the beginning of an administration, candidates for positions at the assistant secretary level in the middle of a term can often wait six months or more. Further down the food chain, bringing on new staff is paced largely by how long it takes to obtain a security clearance. For civil servants, this can take almost a year, for government contractors, the average is about 450 days.

Why?

What explains this bureaucratic torpor? In part, government is slowing down because more people insist on getting involved. Ever more congressional committees, lobbyists and oversight organizations vie to get their prerogatives enacted in a law, regulation or procedure. As the participants multiply, workloads expand and everything slows down.

At another level, it's because there is more obligatory paperwork to handle—financial disclosure in the case of officials, cost justification in the case of contracts, quality assurance documentation in the case of hardware. At yet another level, it's because all organizations have standard procedures that never seem to get shorter or more flexible; quite the reverse. New procedures are almost always cumulative, accreting in ever thicker layers of bureaucratic hoariness. Indeed, we may be seeing a classic case of "organizational aging," a phenomenon perhaps first defined by economist Anthony Downs back in 1967.

In his classic book, *Inside Bureaucracy,* Downs observed that when organizations are first established, they have few rules, written or unwritten, and because new organizations tend to be small, they have a flat, short chain of command with little hierarchy. As time goes by, alas, organizations add personnel. Since managers can oversee only a limited number of people, they develop a reporting hierarchy, which adds to the time and difficulty of making a decision. More members are in a position to say "no," and the joint probability of "yes" diminishes. This translates into the well-known bureaucratic adage, "Where

there's a will, there's a won't." The fact that people expect promotion to positions with greater responsibility (and pay) also encourages the establishment of more management slots with the selective power to say "no," or just to kibbitz. Either way, the process takes more time.

Also, as organizations mature, they develop dogma—sometimes written, sometimes simply part of the organization's culture. This, of course, is exactly what bureaucracies are supposed to do: simplify decisions and improve efficiency by adopting rules. This is fine, until the rules become cumbersome or no longer appropriate to the situation—which is exactly what is happening today.

But the most insidious problem of all is that as organizations mature their character changes. New organizations with few rules offer lots of challenge and risk, so they tend to attract risk-takers who want to make their own rules. Mature organizations with well-defined rules and missions, on the other hand, attract the "Organization Man"—the sort who wants to plug himself in and carry out tasks as set forth in an official, approved job description.

This is why it is somewhere between ironic and pointless to hear critics complain that this or that long-established government organization needs to become less risk-averse and more innovative. Inevitably, they are speaking to people who, by self-selection, are where they are *precisely because they are risk-averse.* They *like* the way things are; they would not otherwise have joined the organization and stayed with it. Organization Men are no less patriotic, dedicated or capable than risk-takers; they're just temperamentally opposite.

If we are serious about gaining agility, we will clearly have to break some china. Improving agility means more than just rearranging boxes on an organization chart, though that is mostly what we have tried to do. There have been countless studies on how to streamline contracting, speed up background investigations, shorten the process of nominating and confirming appointees, and so on. None of these recommendations will ever amount to anything unless we find a way to produce a new mix of people who can develop new ways of doing things, and attract the kinds of recruits who thrive on doing just that.

It's easy to get lost in the day-to-day specifics of why it takes so long to get anything done in the American national security community today. It is far more important to recognize that the underlying theme connecting all the sources of our sloth is that we are trying to balance risk with speed, and there is rarely a champion for speed. The risks that concern people take many forms—that some group will be underrepresented in a decision, that a design or work task will be flawed, that a secret will be compromised, that someone will cheat the government, that an official will have a conflict of interest. Whatever the specifics, we lose agility every time we manage risk by adding a step to reduce the probability of something bad happening. Rarely does anyone with responsibility, opportunity or power say that we should accept more risks so that we can act faster.

It is easy to argue for doing something to avoid some hypothetical bad thing happening. It is much harder to argue that one can take so many precautions against some kinds of risk that other kinds of risk actually increase due to an organization's diminished capacity to act in a timely fashion. The real question is, or ought to be, how much speed do we want to sacrifice in order to reduce certain kinds of risk? There is no single, objective answer to such a question, but without advocates and mechanisms for greater speed, we will be protected against risk so well that arguably our most dangerous adversaries will beat us every time.

Examples of Speed and Success

Lest we be *too* pessimistic, there are cases—including a few fairly recent ones—in which government organizations moved out smartly on national security missions. These cases show us what we need to do if we want organizations to move fast. Consider, for example:

- *The U-2 aircraft:* In the 1950s, the United States needed a higher-flying airplane to take pictures of Soviet military facilities. The CIA gave Lockheed authority to proceed in December 1954; the aircraft flew its first reconnaissance mission over the Soviet Union in July 1956. Total time required: 18 months.
- *The Explorer 1 satellite:* Desperate to match the Soviet Sputnik I launched in October 1957, the Defense Department authorized the Army Ballistic Missile Agency to prepare a satellite for launch on November 8, 1957. Werner von Braun's team launched it three months later, on January 31, 1958.
- *The GBU-28:* At the start of Operation Desert Storm in 1991, the Air Force discovered it did not have a bomb that could penetrate Iraq's deepest underground shelters. To pack enough kinetic energy, the bomb had to be long, streamlined and heavy. The Air Force Research Laboratory took surplus gun barrels from eight-inch howitzers as a casing, filled them with explosive, bolted an existing laser guidance system to the front end, and— after assigning it an official Air Force designation— delivered a bomb in 27 days.
- *JAWBREAKER:* President Bush asked for options to respond to the September 11 attacks. The CIA presented its plan two days later to use Northern Alliance forces as a surrogate army. CIA units, called "JAWBREAKER," arrived in weeks, and Kabul was taken on November 14, 2001.

These programs are all related to national security, but they are as different from one another as one can imagine. One is an aircraft development program, one a space research mission, one a weapon system and one a covert paramilitary operation. The Army, Air Force and CIA are all represented. Two were in wartime, two in peacetime. Yet they share some common features, the most important of which seems to be that someone was willing to bend rules and take responsibility for getting things done. This is a logical—even a *necessary*—condition for speed.

Every organization has a "natural" maximum speed defined by its standard procedures, which are designed to reduce risk. Some are formal, others implicit. Together they establish the organization's operations—who has to confer with whom, who can approve, what materials have to be prepared and so on. Organizations usually operate well below this optimum speed, but in principle one could analyze any organization and then assess whether it can act faster than its competitors. It is hard to measure maximum speed precisely, but it is easy to identify most of the "hard points" that constitute it, like the one official or office lying in the critical path of workflow. Conversely, when government organizations have moved faster than their normal maximum speeds, it's almost always because someone either bent the rules or managed to evade them. Consider the cases cited above.

In developing the U-2, the CIA avoided the constraining pace of the annual Federal budget cycle by using its special authority to spend money without a specific appropriation—the first time the CIA had used that authority to develop a major system like an aircraft. The CIA also wasn't bound to Defense Department regulations, so rather than use the arduous military acquisition and contractor selection process, the CIA simply chose Lockheed.

Lockheed's famous "Skunk Works," in turn, shortened or eliminated many steps a military contractor would usually take. For example, by having all its people working in one location, an engineer could ask metal workers to adjust the design on the spot with a conversation rather than a meeting, and follow up with documentation later. This would violate normal Defense Department acquisition regulations.

The Army also broke rules in building the Explorer 1 satellite—specifically, the rule saying that the Army wasn't supposed to build satellites. The Defense Department and White House had given the Navy that mission. Major General John Medaris, the Army Ballistic Missile Agency director, "went out on a limb," as he put it, and set aside hardware that later gave the Army the ability to get off a quick shot after the Soviets launched Sputnik.

The U-2 and Explorer 1 also had something in common: They "stole" a lot of technology from other programs, using them in ways that no one had originally intended but that sped up the process. The U-2's design was in many ways just like that of the F-104 Starfighter that Lockheed had designed earlier for the Air Force, but with longer wings and a lot of weight cut out. The rocket that launched Explorer 1 was based on an Army Redstone ballistic missile, which, in turn, was an updated V-2 that the Army's German engineers had developed during World War II.

In the case of the GBU-28, the Air Force Development Test Center team compressed a development program that would ordinarily have taken two years into less than two weeks by taking engineering shortcuts and a more liberal approach to safety. For example, it tested the aerodynamics and ballistics of the weapon with a single drop, rather than the usual thirty.

Note that it required an individual with the *authority* and *inclination* to make the decision on how to interpret a contract or a standard. If a person could not legally give approval, the organization would not have followed his direction. If a person had not been willing to use his authority (and, in the process, accept responsibility), nothing would have happened, either— which brings us to JAWBREAKER.

CIA officers like Gary Schroen, who first went into Afghanistan to prepare the operation immediately after 9/11, had largely acted on their own initiative in the 1990s when they kept up personal contacts with Northern Alliance figures like Ahmed Shah Masoud. After the Soviets were defeated in the U.S. supported guerrilla war from 1980 to 1989, the CIA had turned its interest elsewhere. Schroen's contacts and experience in the region greased the re-establishment of the relationship when the United States decided to retaliate against al-Qaeda and the Taliban.

After the fighting started, the CIA was fortunate to have officers on hand with admitted inclinations for focusing more on results than procedures. Gary Berntsen, who took command of JAWBREAKER as the fighting began, once described himself as a "bad kid" from Long Island who graduated second from the bottom in his high school. Once in the CIA, he bragged about his "grab-'em-by-the-collar" approach.

As Admiral Ernest King supposedly said about wartime, "When they get in trouble, they send for the sons of bitches." If you don't have SOBs on staff and a way to get them to the front line, organizations will plod along at their routine pace. True, if everyone broke the rules all the time, there would be no rules. But one of the keys to a fast organization that can beat its opponent to the punch is almost always a willingness to break the rules. This is nothing new. It was said often in the 19th century that Paris sent officials into the French countryside not to enforce rules, but to decide judiciously when and how to ignore them.

How to Get Faster

If we want more speed and agility, some lessons are clear. We must: Make sure U.S. national security organizations have a legal mechanism for bending or breaking existing rules; make sure they have the means for having such rule-benders at hand; make sure these rule-benders exercise influence; and make sure they don't get out of control. (Even unofficially designated rule-benders need *some* clear lines of accountability.)

We need to allow responsible senior officials to put the government in overdrive when it's really important.

Basically, we need to allow responsible senior officials to put the government into overdrive when it's really important. With the possible exception of the operating forces of the military and their counterparts in the intelligence community, even top officials lack this ability today. This encourages other kinds of risks: workarounds. Cabinet secretaries who need to get decisions fast and begin operations expeditiously know that they cannot entrust such matters to the standing bureaucracy. But workarounds and shortcuts spite the institutional memory of an organization and court disaster from ignorance. Iran-Contra is a good example of a workaround gone wrong. The only way to avoid such dangers is to make the responsible bureaucracies faster only when they really need to be fast.

There is always a tension between orthodoxy and innovation, and between direct command and checks and balances. There is no sure-fire way to ensure the best mix. But we don't seem to be close now, or even trying to get closer. Ultimately, our willingness to balance different sorts of risk must be a political decision, in which voters can turn incumbents out and try something else if they are dissatisfied. But if we don't at least have the foundation for rule-bending, they will never get that choice.

What then, should we do? First, to build agility into the key parts of the U.S. government, Congress will clearly have to cooperate. That's the system; that's the Constitution. It is therefore folly for any administration to try to steamroll the legislators—as the then-popular Bush Administration did from about 2002 to 2004, such as when it shunted aside congressional concerns that the Iraq insurgency was gaining steam rather than entering its "last throes," or that U.S. forces did not have the resources to deal with the worsening situation. Accepting these concerns and criticisms quickly would have both improved the situation and solidified support for the effort by getting Congress' "buy in" on the record.

Second, we should consider establishing a small number of powerful "bottleneck breakers" in the Executive Office of the President. Senior experienced officials could be designated by the White House, formally or informally. The important thing is that officials down the line know that these bottleneck breakers are acting at the behest of the president to make sure his policies are carried out. Unlike the too-familiar "czars" that have been given responsibility for drug enforcement, energy conservation and, most recently, the war in Iraq, these officials would know how, and be given the authority, to work quickly and quietly with the Office of Management and Budget. It would take only a few examples of a sequestered budget line, a dismissed appointee or a transferred senior executive to give these bottleneck-breaker envoys the implicit power they require. The very existence of such EOP envoys, and the only occasional demonstration of their authority, would work wonders with hidebound, risk-averse bureaucrats.

Other measures that would counter the natural tendency of bureaucracies to slow down come readily to mind:

- Requiring senior civil service executives to periodically do a tour in a different Executive Branch department. This would make them more familiar with conditions in other departments, so they could anticipate what might slow down an action. It would also build social networks that could help clear these impediments.
- Create an "up or out" system of promotion for senior executives resembling the approach used in the military to create a dynamic that keeps the bureaucracy from getting too settled.

- Adopt a mandatory, congressionally approved, periodic de-layering of bureaucracies.
- Increase the number of Schedule C appointments to give new administrations a better ability to rattle cages. We need not repeal the Pendleton Act completely, but the trend in most sectors of the economy is toward "at will" employment. As an employee rises higher in the organization, it should be easier to move or remove him or her.

One could think of other measures in the same vein, and some have. The point, however, is that if we do not do *something* to increase the speed of government, we will be sure to fall behind future events, get beaten to the punch, and lose ground to our most ruthless competitors. Given the stakes in today's world, that is a loss we cannot afford.

Note

1. Also consider today's automobiles, which are much more complex than earlier models. Like jet fighters, cars today go faster and handle better. They can also locate their current position and tell you how to reach your destination—all while meeting ever-tougher safety and emissions standards. Yet the time required to develop a car and get it into the showroom *is*

getting shorter all the time. Toyota is best at about two years, and it is trying to cut this time to 12 months. Ford and GM are trying to keep up, but still take one to two years longer than Toyota—one reason they have been taking a beating in the market.

Critical Thinking

1. Why are actors like terrorist organizations often more agile than governments?
2. What is organizational agility? What are some of the specific questions that factor into organizational agility?
3. What are several World War II-era examples of U.S. government nimbleness? How does government performance in today's war on terror compare unfavorably?
4. What are some of the reasons why government bureaucracy has become so slow?
5. Name some recent examples of U.S. government agility and success. What, according to the author, can be done to improve the speed and dexterity of the U.S. government?

BRUCE BERKOWITZ is a research fellow at the Heaver Institution at Stanford University. He was Director of Forecasting and Evaluation at the Department of Defense from 2004–05.

From *The American Interest*, September/October 2007, pp. 59–70. Copyright © 2007 by American Interest. Reprinted by permission.

Legislation Is Just the Start

The new financial reform law is a good reminder of how much takes place in Washington after a bill gets signed. In the nation's capital, says former Congressman Lee Hamilton, "legislation is just the start."

LEE HAMILTON

You might imagine, now that President Obama has signed the massive financial reform package into law, that the issue is behind us. Hardly. In a way, the President's signature was just the starter's pistol.

This is because, despite its length—over 2000 pages—and the many months of negotiations that went into crafting it, the financial overhaul measure leaves countless issues to be resolved later by federal regulators and the lobbyists who will try to influence their decisions. It is a textbook example of the limits inherent in a legislative product, and of the manner in which Congress relies on a mix of concrete action and ambiguous ball-punting to cobble together a majority.

The law undoubtedly changes the nation's financial landscape. It creates a new Bureau of Financial Consumer Protection; strengthens regulation of financial holding companies; regulates derivatives; places new limits—the so-called "Volcker Rule"—on the amount of money a bank can invest in hedge funds and private equity funds; buttresses the Securities and Exchange Commission; and tries to discourage excessive risk-taking.

It is also filled with the sorts of compromises the legislative process demands. The "Volcker Rule" was written off, watered down, and then somewhat re-strengthened on its way to passage. The consumer protection agency was initially to be a standalone regulator, but then was placed within the Federal Reserve in order to calm some concerns. The language on derivatives went through a complex series of balance-seeking negotiations between those who wanted highly restrictive regulation and those who opposed it.

The result is a grand and sweeping law that nonetheless leaves many issues unresolved and much room for interpretation in the future. When you have such ambiguities in new statutes—as is frequently the case—it amounts to an invitation to further struggle on the part of the bureaucrats who must give shape and form to the ideas contained in the measure, and the lobbyists whose clients have much at stake in the results.

According to an analysis by the U.S. Chamber of Commerce, the measure calls for 350 rules to be formulated, 47 studies to be conducted—which is Congress' way of signaling action on an issue without actually making any decisions—and 74 reports. The creation of new entities—the consumer protection agency, a board of regulators to assess risk in the financial system—also will engender much executive-branch maneuvering and back-and-forth with Congress as they're set up and staffed.

Moreover, lobbyists don't stop work when a law is passed; in some ways, that's when their work truly begins, as they strive to build relationships with the regulators who will oversee their industry and try to influence the regulations that will soon enough begin to flow from various executive-branch agencies.

The difference, of course, is that for all its faults, Congress is a relatively transparent and accountable institution. What takes place in regulators' offices is far less visible. As the activity surrounding financial reform now passes beyond public view, political considerations will become less important but the stakes will grow higher. Out of the public's eye, the special interests' influence will grow, and arguments about how to interpret the language contained in the law will blossom—and, inevitably, spill over into the courts. For years to come, there will be enormous demand for lawyers capable either of making sense out of ambiguous legislative language, or of making the strongest possible arguments in favor of interpretations that just happen to favor their clients.

Yet in the end, it's the executive branch that benefits most from what Congress has done. The entire measure is a significant gift of power to federal agencies and financial regulators, who now have to make decisions about how they intend to wield their power. You can already see how significant their role will be in the early maneuvering over who might head the new Bureau of Consumer Financial Protection: each possible appointee, who must be approved by the Senate, would approach the job differently, and in the weeks following the bill's passage the nuances of their approaches were probably the hottest single topic of debate over breakfast, lunch and dinner tables in Washington.

It is important to remember, in the end, that the authority to act is not the same as acting. That is why, while Congress made some important decisions in the process of crafting its bill, the true import of the financial reform package will only reveal itself gradually. There is an old saying in Washington that "nothing is ever decided for good there." For legislation, that's certainly true.

Critical Thinking

1. How does the 2010 financial reform law signed by President Obama change the nation's financial landscape?

2. What were some of the compromises contained in the financial reform legislation?

3. What are some of the actions required by the financial reform package? How are these actions accomplished once a law like this one is passed?

LEE HAMILTON is Director of the Center on Congress at Indiana University. He was a member of the U.S. House of Representatives for 34 years.

Teaching a Hippo to Dance

The most brilliant policies will fail if government does not attract talented people and free them to do their best work.

AMY WILKINSON

Four years ago, I left Silicon Valley to accept a presidential appointment as a White House fellow. After undergoing months of interviews and obtaining a top-secret security clearance, I moved to Washington, D.C., to join a class of 12 nonpartisan White House fellows and to work in the Office of the U.S. Trade Representative. After my fellowship ended I stayed on, caught up in the challenging work of improving the nation's trade policies. My old business-school friends and my colleagues at the consulting firm McKinsey & Company were perplexed. Why would anyone want to serve in the federal government, the epitome of everything that is slow, bureaucratic, and opaque?

There, in a nutshell, is a major problem confronting American government in the 21st century: how to attract talented young people—not just to the prestigious jobs that bring you face to face with a cabinet secretary or the president but to the line jobs that exist across the civil service. It is not just a recruiting challenge. Government will only attract the people it needs when it refashions itself so that public servants can serve the public effectively.

The federal government deserves more credit than it gets, but it is still a slow-moving behemoth. To reinvigorate our federal system and attract fresh talent, we must transform our aged, hierarchical institutions into modern networks of scale and impact. In effect, we must teach a hippopotamus to dance.

Like government, hippos are enormous, weighed down by a heavy mid section and designed with disproportionately big mouth and teeth. Stubby legs, a natural system of checks and balances, support their tremendous bulk. They are powerful, yet slow to change. When perturbed, hippos can move quickly—as the federal government did in passing the $700 billion bailout in just two weeks. Yet usually they plod along, preferring to slumber in murky waters.

In today's networked world, our hippo must dance in sync with private-sector and nonprofit partners. Keeping pace will require a more engaged federal workforce, realignment of out-of-date incentives, and an ability to meet the expectations of modern workers. To succeed, government must get the people piece right.

There are some bright lights in government leadership, and some of the brightest are at the local level. In San Francisco, Mayor Gavin Newsom, a former wine and restaurant entrepreneur, has forged alliances with businesses in housing and other fields, established a 24-hour hotline to promote accountability in city services, and pushed forward on such controversial initiatives as universal health care. In Newark, New Jersey, Mayor Cory Booker has partnered with the Bill & Melinda Gates Foundation and other foundations to jump-start the city's dysfunctional public school system with a $19 million charter school initiative. He has embraced new technologies such as ShotSpotter, an acoustic surveillance system that detects gunshots in seconds, to control crime. "I always say that the biggest problem in America is not a problem of material poverty," Booker said in an interview. "It's a poverty of imagination. It's a poverty of innovation. It's a poverty of action."

Often, what many regard as the very nature of government—its notoriously multilayered bureaucracy—stifles needed innovation and initiative. The average memo originating in a State Department bureau requires between two and 10 sign-offs and five to eight approvals through the chain of command before it reaches the secretary. Beyond whatever sense of public mission individuals bring to their work, there is often little incentive to excel. As one Foreign Service officer I spoke to joked, "At the end of the year I go to the GS schedule, reference my rank and years of service, and poof, there's my promotion cycle and salary."

The high-caliber employees that government does manage to attract are often driven out of public service. Many of the strongest junior people leave government frustrated by mid-level management that is ineffective but will never be fired. Retaining star talent requires replacing our current seniority-based system with merit-based promotions. A close colleague, who distinguished himself while working with Colin Powell, recently left the Foreign Service, discouraged by the bureaucratic mindset. When he was nominated for a fast-track promotion, human resources denied the advancement, stating that there were "already qualified people at that grade level." He is now a partner in an advisory firm.

Today's young professionals expect adaptable work schedules, state-of-the-art technology, and a measure of autonomy. Most of all, we are looking for work that allows us to have an impact. Speed and flexibility define our lives. If we have a question, we Google it. We Skype friends in Poland and instant-message colleagues in Shanghai. These changes have their parallels in organizational life. In the private sector, "flash teams" assemble to tackle specific challenges, disband, and reconfigure as situations evolve. Large companies such as Best Buy allow people at all levels throughout the company to participate electronically and in person in efforts to solve problems. The symbolic apex of this new world may be the professional temp agencies that attract large numbers of workers in high-skills fields, from accounting to graphic design, because these people prefer short assignments and constant change.

In the search for people with talent and ideas, the new field of social entrepreneurship provides stiff competition for government. Rather than work their way up in government or large corporations, many civic-minded leaders in their twenties and thirties now launch nonprofit or business ventures to address social injustices, using business partnerships, grants, and donations.

"Our generation is saying we need private innovation and private initiative to solve big, public problems," Jacqueline Novogratz explained when we met in her New York office. She is the founder and CEO of Acumen Fund, a nonprofit equivalent of a venture capital firm that backs private-sector and nonprofit enterprises that help the poor. "I think that it's a parallel with when John F. Kennedy said we want the best and brightest in government. Today, we want the best and brightest in this field of social enterprise." Bill Drayton, father of the social entrepreneurship movement and founder of a similar organization called Ashoka, told me, "We're in the business of 'everyone a change maker.'" Ashoka has supported some 2,000 social entrepreneurs around the world in launching social start-ups to address ills ranging from domestic violence to water pollution. Half of them, Drayton says, are able to bring about changes in national policy within five years.

The United States is the world's most innovative nation, yet our government is out of sync with today's realities. With more than 2.6 million employees, the federal government is the nation's largest employer. As I can attest after seven years in the corporate world, business does not always escape the problems of bureaucracy. Just ask General Motors, Ford, and Chrysler. But big corporations learn to be nimble in order to compete against agile, new entrants. Government is what is called, in the business world, an incumbent player; it is blind to competition. Change must come from within, beginning at the top. As New York mayor Michael Bloomberg explained, "Part of the government's problem is that it never delegates. In the White House, for example, they control everything."

The antiquated condition of our national government today would have troubled the Founding Fathers.

The antiquated condition of our national government would have troubled the Founding Fathers, who were political entrepreneurs and the creators of revolutionary new public institutions. It is true that they did not design American government to be fast. Our system of checks and balances, along with the diffusion of power among local, state, and federal authorities, is designed to inhibit rapid change. Yet if the Founders were wary of overweening government, they hardly favored *ineffective* government.

Technology offers one route to breaking down barriers and improving productivity. Before the development of Web 2.0 technologies, for example, it would have taken many months to gather information across stovepiped government agencies. Last year, when the Office of Management and Budget needed to compile a database of congressional budgetary earmarks, government personnel were able to bypass normal bureaucratic channels by using a wiki that allowed people from all over the government to report directly on a shared website. They did the job in just 10 weeks, turning up 13,496 earmarks.

Government is clearly in need of such new ideas, but the culture of public institutions is risk averse. Gilman Louie, former CEO of In-Q-Tel, a nonprofit corporation created by the Central Intelligence Agency to promote defense technologies, put the problem in graphic terms when I interviewed him: "The most surprising thing was that if terrorists rolled a hand grenade down the middle of a room, all our CIA employees would jump out of their seats and throw their bodies on it to protect everyone else. They would all give up their lives for one another and their country. However, if someone ran into the room and said, 'I need someone to make a decision, but if it's the wrong one it will be the end of your career, but I need an answer now,' all of them would run toward the door." The problem with public institutions is that the consequence of failure means that there is no reward for risk taking and thus no innovation. Government agencies must change to say that it is all right to fail, just not catastrophically. To do this, they need to evaluate employees not on the success or failure of any particular decision, but on the overall outcome of their performance.

United States Government Policy and Supporting Positions, commonly known as the "Plum Book," lists more than 7,000 available jobs in the new administration. Many of these positions are reserved for cabinet secretaries and other officials to hire their own personal staffs. Barack Obama will award about 3,000 positions, from White House chief of staff to principal deputy under secretary of defense for policy.

There is no shortage of job seekers, but the cumbersome appointment process deters many talented people, and the incoming administration has set up even more hurdles. Prospective Obama appointees are presented with a seven-page questionnaire about their personal and professional lives. They must append copies of all resumés and biographical statements from the past 10 years, list gifts worth more than $50 that they and their spouse have received from anyone other than close friends or relatives, and divulge their and immediate family members' affiliations with Fannie Mae, Freddie Mac, or any other institution receiving government bailout funds. Applicants are also expected to disclose their "Internet presence," including e-mails, Facebook pages, blog posts, and aliases used to communicate online.

Once past the screening, these prospective federal appointees enter a labyrinth of forms, investigations, and intrusive personal and financial disclosures. The process is embarrassing and confusing, and often requires that they seek outside expert advice to process forms and financial information—which applicants pay for out of their own pockets. Senate confirmation proceedings for cabinet secretaries start in January, but subcabinet and Schedule C appointees, the folks who do the nuts-and-bolts work, can wait many months. Only 30 percent of George W. Bush's national security appointees were in place on 9/11, eight months after he took office.

The career civil service faces an even greater challenge. Last year, the Partnership for Public Service estimated that nearly 530,000 personnel—a third of the federal government's workforce—will retire by 2012. "Help wanted" should become Washington's byword if these jobs—many of them critical senior positions—are to be filled by first-rate people. Yet Donna Shalala, the former secretary of health and human services and current president of the University of Miami, said recently at the Woodrow Wilson Center that government recruiters don't even come to her campus: "Kids in Miami are interested in government but have no information about how to apply."

Indeed, a recent Gallup poll found that 60 percent of those under age 30 have never been asked to consider a job in government. Thirty-three percent would give such a request a great deal of consideration if asked by their parents, and 29 percent if asked by the newly elected president. The first challenge government must overcome is ignorance about government opportunities. The nonprofit Teach for America, by contrast, is beating out consulting firms and banks to recruit college graduates. Last year, 25,000 individuals applied to Teach for America and more than 3,700 started teaching in the nation's toughest inner-city schools.

Government must get into the headhunting business. At business schools the pitch could be, *You want to manage complexity and lead a team? Great. We've got big budgets and complex problems. Which would you like to tackle first, health care or Social Security reform?* At law schools, recruiters could ask, *Are you good at negotiating contentious issues and analyzing contradictory information? Perfect. When can you start?* Let's offer undergraduates career tracks that let them quickly rotate through assignments at State, Energy, Defense, and other agencies.

During the recent election campaign, President Obama vowed to "transform Washington" and "make government cool again." And why not? Why shouldn't public service be highly esteemed? Americans rally to support exceptional athletes who compete in the Olympic Games. We applaud extraordinary scientists who work to cure cancer and superior military forces that defend our homeland. We want the best Hollywood talent to entertain us and super computer geeks to invent the next Google. But when it comes to government service we set our sights low.

Last year's election turned ordinary citizens into activists who not only donated money and canvassed door to door in unprecedented numbers but used new media to blog, organize campaign events, and form networks. The question now is how our 44th president will harness civic engagement to govern more effectively. Millions of Americans are waiting by their BlackBerries, iPhones, and laptops to find out.

Critical Thinking

1. Why do many talented government employees leave public service?
2. What lessons can be drawn from the private sector to improve government bureaucracy?
3. How can technology improve government performance and productivity?
4. How could a recruiting strategy help government attract new talent?

AMY WILKINSON, a public-policy scholar at the Woodrow Wilson Center, is writing a book about the next generation of leadership.

From *The Wilson Quarterly,* Winter 2009, pp. 59–62. Copyright © 2009 by Amy Wilkinson. Reprinted by permission of Amy Wilkinson and Woodrow Wilson International Center for Scholars.

UNIT 3

Process of American Politics

Unit Selections

Learning Outcomes

After reading this unit you should be able to:

- Identify different institutions, processes, and groups that are generally thought to serve as links between American citizens and their government.

- Identify and analyze recent changes in the American party system and assess the likely effects of those changes on the practice of American democracy.

- Outline alleged shortcomings in the way American elections are conducted and assess whether they impair the practice of democracy in the United States to any significant extent.

- Cite important points about American interest groups that appear in this unit and assess whether they work to the advantage or detriment of American democracy.

- Identify and analyze recent changes in media that relate to the way that the American political system functions, and decide whether each of the changes you have cited is likely to improve or harm the practice of American democracy.

- Compare and contrast the challenges that contemporary newspapers are facing, the rise of the Internet, and the popularity of partisan media outlets such as Fox News and MSNBC. Determine which of these phenomena will have the most significant long-term effects on the way the American political system functions.

- Summarize the role that money plays in the practice of American democracy and assess the extent it plays a harmful role. If you conclude that money does play a harmful role, recommend what steps should be taken to remedy the situation. If you conclude that money's role in American democracy is not harmful, defend that position.

Student Website

www.mhhe.com/cls

According to many political scientists, what distinguishes more democratic political systems from less democratic ones is the degree of control that citizens exercise over government. This unit focuses on institutions, groups, and processes that can serve as links between Americans and their government.

The first three sections address parties, elections, voters, interest groups, and the role of money in campaigns and governing. Recent changes in these areas may affect American politics for decades to come, and these changes are the major focus of many of the readings in these sections. The fourth section addresses media in the American political system, the role(s) that they play, and how they are changing.

One noteworthy development in the past few decades has been growing polarization between the two major parties. Republican and Democratic members of Congress have both become more likely to toe their party's line in opposition to the other party, with partisan voting increasingly becoming the norm on Capitol Hill. Some decry this increase in partisanship, while others think that sharper and more consistent policy differences between Democrat and Republican officeholders will make elections more consequential.

Incumbents' advantages in winning re-election to both the House of Representatives and the Senate have also grown in recent years, so much so, that despite Americans' dissatisfaction with President Bush and his Republican supporters in Congress, most observers emphasized how difficult it would be for Democrats to regain majority control of the House and Senate in the 2006 congressional elections. But Democrats *did* win control of both houses that year, illustrating what many consider to be a good example of American democracy at work. In the 2008 elections, of course, led by presidential candidate Barack Obama, Democrats won an even larger majority of seats in each house of Congress. Regardless of these results, incumbency advantages—including the way House districts are drawn, name recognition, and easier access to campaign contributions—are likely to remain a concern for those who would like to reform the democratic process in the United States.

Besides, the way House district lines are drawn and incumbents' other built-in advantages, American elections suffer from all sorts of other shortcomings. Many of these problems became apparent during the controversy over the outcome of the 2000 presidential election, and reform measures were enacted both in Congress and in many states. Despite some improvements in the way elections are conducted in the American political system, many aspects of U.S. election mechanics still seem inferior to election mechanics in many other western democracies.

Campaign financing became a major concern after the 1972 presidential election. Major campaign finance reform laws passed in 1974 and 2002 (the latter is the so-called McCain-Feingold Act) have been aimed at regulating the influence of campaign contributions in the electoral process, but they have met, at best, with only partial success. The history of these and other major campaign finance laws is intertwined with a handful of Supreme Court decisions that have ruled parts of the laws as unconstitutional. In its controversial 5-4 ruling in *Citizens United v. Federal Election Commission* in January 2010,

© The McGraw-Hill Companies, Inc./Christopher Kerrigan, photographer

the Supreme Court voided one key element in the McCain-Feinstein Act that was aimed at restricting corporate spending in campaigns.

As recent bribery and corruption scandals make clear, the fundamental challenge of how to reconcile free speech, the freedom of an individual to spend money as he or she wishes, the costs of campaigns, and the fairness of elections remain. In the summer of 2007, Barack Obama publicly pledged to accept public financing—and the accompanying condition that a candidate who accepts public financing can spend only the sum provided by the government if he became his party's nominee. A year later, Obama changed his mind, and became the first and only presidential general election candidate to decline public financing since it became available beginning with the 1976 election. Obama made this decision because he was advised that he could raise more than three times as much money from supporters as the sum provided through public financing, and the advice he received was correct. Democratic candidate Obama *did* raise and spend more than three times as much money as his general election opponent, Republican John McCain, who accepted public financing and the accompanying spending limit. A noteworthy irony is that most Democrats have been stronger proponents of campaign finance regulation and public financing than most Republicans, notwithstanding John McCain's long-standing leadership in reform efforts.

This unit also treats the roles of interest groups in the American political process and their impact on what government can and cannot do. While "gridlock" is a term usually applied to a situation that some observers think results from "divided government," in which neither major party controls the presidency and both houses of Congress, it seems that gridlock—and perhaps favoritism in policymaking—may also result from the interaction of interest groups and various government policymakers. The weakness of parties in the United States, compared to parties in other Western democracies, is almost certainly responsible for the unusually strong place of interest groups in the American political system. In turn, one can wonder whether the current era of stronger, more disciplined parties in government will eventually contribute to the weakening of interest groups.

Selections in the fourth section address how media—old and new shape political communication and political behavior in the American political system. Television and radio news broadcasts and newspapers are not merely passive transmitters of information. They inevitably shape—or distort—what they report to their audiences, and greatly affect the behavior of people and organizations in politics. Television talk shows, radio talk-back shows, and thirty-minute "infomercials" have entered the political landscape with considerable effect. In 2004, televised attack ads paid for by so-called 527 committees targeted both presidential candidates and seemed to affect voters' views. In 2008, Barack Obama's campaign perfected some of the Internet fund-raising techniques pioneered by Republican candidate John McCain in 2000 and Democratic candidate Howard Dean in 2004, who unsuccessfully sought the Democratic party's presidential nomination. Obama's remarkable run for the presidency included his vanquishing and outspending Democratic rival Hillary Clinton, who herself raised and spent more money on her nomination campaign than any candidate in history, *except* Obama. Then, as mentioned above, Obama outspent John McCain by a more than three-to-one margin in the general election campaign.

As already suggested, one key to Obama's extraordinary fundraising prowess in 2007–2008 was the Internet, the medium that has revolutionized many aspects of American life. In addition to facilitating fundraising, the Internet played another role in the 2008 campaign by hosting political YouTube segments that played to large segments of the population, including some who tended to avoid traditional news media outlets. Finally, as selections in the fourth section of this unit show, online news reports and commentaries are threatening the very existence of traditional hard-copy newspapers.

Internet References

The Gallup Organization
www.gallup.com
The Henry L. Stimson Center
www.stimson.org
Influence at Work
www.influenceatwork.com
LSU Department of Political Science Resources
www.lsu.edu/politicalscience
NationalJournal.com
http://nationaljournal.com
Poynter Online
www.poynter.org
RAND
www.rand.org
Real Clear Politics
www.realclearpolitics.com

The 'Enduring Majority'—Again

No, the Democrats will not be in power forever . . .

JAY COST

After the Democrats' triumphs in two consecutive elections, left-wing pundits have returned to an old meme: The party's majority will be enduring. In a report published by the Center for American Progress, liberal author Ruy Teixeira boldly proclaimed: "A new progressive America has emerged with a new demography, a new geography, and a new agenda. . . . All this adds up to big change that is reshaping our country in a fundamentally progressive direction. . . . These trends will continue." Other liberals—most notably John Judis of *The New Republic* and Alan Abramowitz of Emory University—have similarly argued that Obama's election ushered in a new, enduring Democratic majority.

This essay will rebut some of the claims made by advocates of this idea. It will also offer a broader perspective on how to understand the 2008 election, and what it means for the Republican party and conservatives in the future.

What makes this task difficult is that it's hard to nail down exactly what the phrase "enduring Democratic majority" is supposed to mean. Which "progressive" policies will be passed? How much control over the government will Democrats have? For how long they will have it? Just how enduring will it be? These questions are typically left unanswered. Recently Judis commented to the *Huffington Post*: "The only circumstances that could bring back the Republicans is Obama's failure to stem the recession." This, of course, would make it indistinguishable from just about every majority in the country's history.

If this sounds like an unfalsifiable hypothesis to you, you're not alone. Judis and Teixeira floated a version of the same argument in their book *The Emerging Democratic Majority* in 2002, just a few months before the Republicans regained control of the Senate and increased their majority in the House. After the 2006 midterm election, they resurrected their thesis in an article for *The American Prospect* titled "Back to the Future" and subtitled "The re-emergence of the emerging Democratic majority." To explain away the years of GOP dominance, they invented a new psychological concept—"de-arrangement." What this means, they explained, is that

the focus on the war on terror not only distracted erstwhile Democrats and independents but appeared to transform, or de-arrange, their political worldview. They temporarily became more sympathetic to a whole range of conservative assumptions and approaches.

This is a textbook case of special pleading. If creating an *ad hoc* concept out of whole cloth is the only way to salvage a theory, it's time to find a new theory. The concept is not particularly helpful to them, either. After all, couldn't conservatives explain away 2006 and especially 2008 with "dearrangement"? Perhaps our cool, ultra-liberal president bewitched true Republicans with his post-partisan campaign gibberish, and these voters will soon see the error of their ways.

Ultimately, engaging with the advocates of the "enduring Democratic majority" hypothesis is like punching sand. The rules of the game are set up so that the majority is considered enduring even if a recession terminates it or it is interrupted by years of Republican governance. In other words: Heads they win, tails you lose.

It is fairly easy to get away with this kind of unrigorous thinking when you are preaching to the liberal choir. However, this argument has found its way into conservative circles, usually among pundits who blame the party's decline on a lack of attention to their favorite issue. That's misguided, because while the party has been in tough spots before, it has bounced back pretty quickly. Every time the party has suffered a setback, like 1992, it was not long before a comeback, like 1994. Even after Franklin Roosevelt swept the Democrats into office in the 1932 elections, and extended Democratic gains in 1934 and 1936, Republicans came bouncing back in 1938, returning to Capitol Hill with enough numbers to block New Deal legislation with the first of many bipartisan conservative coalitions.

Nevertheless, I sense that many conservatives think the current period in the wilderness will actually last 40 years. This feeling of dread is not a huge surprise, given the attention the "enduring Democratic majority" hypothesis has received from the iron triangle of the mainstream media, the Democratic party, and left-wing interest groups. What follows should help conservatives see that there is a lot more sizzle than steak to this idea.

As we go through the details, it's important to keep the big picture in mind. Analysts like to talk about the movement of this or that group in the last election, but the context is of crucial importance. Voters cast their ballots last fall amid an economy that was shrinking at a 6.3 percent annual rate. This was a dramatic contraction, precipitated by a financial calamity that had struck just weeks before. Additionally, President Bush's job approval had fallen to less than 30 percent due to largely non-ideological concerns like his handling of Iraq and Hurricane Katrina. That's an unwinnable environment for any party. When you're losing, you're losing. Nothing in the data looks particularly good, but this does not mean the data are always going to look bad. The course of politics is not a straight line, and liberal analysts are simply wrong to assume that subsequent elections will look like the previous one.

One point often cited by proponents of the enduring-majority hypothesis is the voting preference of young Americans. There is no doubt that President Obama scored a huge victory among young voters, winning 66 percent of those under 30. Proponents think this group of voters will be important to the party's continuing success.

Perhaps—but this is the same argument we might have heard in 1972, when George McGovern lost the popular vote by 23 points but won voters aged 18 to 24 by a point. In 1976, now aged 22 to 28, this cohort voted for Jimmy Carter roughly in line with the whole country. They went slightly for Ronald Reagan in 1980, and in 1984 and 1988 the GOP had a breakthrough, as they voted for Reagan and then for George H. W. Bush at the same rate as the whole country. By 2008, these voters—most of them now in their late 50s—went for Obama by a point. Given that the whole country voted for Obama by 7 points, we'd have to conclude that they now have a Republican tilt. In other words, though this cohort of voters looked quite Democratic when they were young, the GOP won them over later, when the political pendulum swung its way again.

Past performance is no guarantee of future results. Young voters age, their lives change, and so can their politics.

It's like your financial analyst's disclaimer: Past performance is no guarantee of future results. As young voters age, their lives change, and so can their politics. One big source of change is marriage. Typically, committed conservatives vote Republican and committed liberals vote Democratic, regardless of marital status. But for moderates and the non-ideological, marriage makes a big difference. In 2000 and 2004, George W. Bush did better than Al Gore and John Kerry among moderate voters of nearly all ages if they were married. The big question for the future, which advocates of the enduring-majority view cannot yet answer, is: Will young, unmarried voters follow the older cohorts and trend to the GOP after they marry, or will they stay with the Democrats? None of this is meant to minimize the significance of Obama's accomplishment in bringing young voters to his side, or the work that conservatives will have to do to win over the so-called Millennial Generation. The point is that one cannot simply extrapolate from the 2008 results.

Then there are the "professionals." This is the rather tendentious term typically applied to anybody with a graduate degree.

The idea here is that these voters—driving hybrids, shopping at co-ops, hyphenating their last names, and so on—are more sympathetic to progressive views, and are solid Democrats.

Indeed they are. But so what? First of all, the fraction of "professionals" has held fairly constant since 1988, making up 16 to 18 percent of the electorate. They have consistently voted 3 to 7 more points Democratic than the rest of the nation. Given their relatively small size, they have not been decisive. They have not stopped the GOP from winning three of the last six presidential elections, or holding the House of Representatives for twelve years in a row.

It's hard to argue that there's been much of a shift along educational lines. Of all college-educated voters who voted for one of the two major parties, Obama won 53 percent. Ditto non-college voters. In 1992, Bill Clinton performed about the same across education groups, after factoring out the Perot vote: He won 53 percent of college grads and 55 percent of non-college grads. So in 16 years, not much has changed.

Those who expect an enduring Democratic majority also make much of the fact that, in a few decades, the United States will be a minority-majority nation, with whites making up less than half the population. Whether or not this is true, I can say that they tend to overstate the consequences of the underlying trend.

Let's start with black voters. There is no doubt Obama performed very well with them. Typically, the GOP wins about 10 percent of the black vote. In 2008, John McCain won just 4 percent. Obama also brought an unprecedented number of black Americans to the polls. Last year, blacks actually constituted a larger share of the electorate than they do of the population as a whole.

The critical question, as yet unanswerable, is whether these numbers can be sustained. Is this a "personal" vote for Obama, or the beginning of a new trend? It is too soon to say. Nevertheless, we can say that the GOP's performance with blacks has been horrible. George W. Bush won only 26 percent of self-identified *conservative* blacks in 2004. In other words, black Americans who are ideologically sympathetic to the GOP still vote heavily Democratic. The Republicans need to work on this. Minimally, they should strive to make black conservatives comfortable voting for the conservative party.

Hispanics are another matter, though you can't tell that to most advocates of the enduring-majority hypothesis. In a recent article, Abramowitz—arguing that demographic trends will favor the Democrats for decades—allocated white conservatives to the GOP and white liberals to the Democrats, and predicted that white moderates would be swing voters. He then allocated *all* ethnic and racial minorities to the Democrats. This must have come as a shock to the 3.67 million Hispanics who voted for McCain last year. They are a testament to the fact that Hispanic voters cannot be viewed through the same lens as black voters. In fact, they have recently behaved more like white voters, breaking for the party that is closer to their ideology. George W. Bush won 69 percent of Hispanic conservatives and 41 percent of Hispanic moderates in 2004. He did better than any previous Republican by winning about 40 percent of all Hispanics.

Hispanics swung against McCain in 2008, but the Arizona senator still won the same share as George H. W. Bush did in 1988, even though the latter ran in a much more favorable political climate. Additionally, McCain did better than Gerald Ford in 1976 and Bob Dole in 1996. In other words, Hispanics have slowly become more Republican in recent cycles. To place them in the Democratic column so confidently is to ignore this, as well as Bush's breakthrough in 2004. But maybe these deviations can be chalked up to de-arrangement, too.

Nevertheless, conservatives must make outreach to Hispanics a priority—especially if they want to win states such as Nevada, Colorado, and New Mexico. Even though Bush did better with Hispanic conservatives than with black conservatives, too many still "defected" to Kerry. Obama probably won many more Hispanic conservatives, so there is a lot of work to be done. Abramowitz and other Democrats might be content to overlook Bush's performance among Hispanics, but conservatives should not overlook Obama's.

Finally, any discussion about the burgeoning minority vote favoring the Democrats must acknowledge that the GOP has done better with white voters in recent decades. No Democrat has won a majority of whites since Lyndon Johnson in 1964, although Jimmy Carter came close in 1976. Bill Clinton nearly won a plurality in 1992 and 1996. Yet Al Gore lost the white vote to George W. Bush by twelve points in 2000, and Bush improved among whites in 2004, winning 58 percent despite a tough war in Iraq and weak job growth after the 2001 recession. This was about the same share his father pulled in 1988, though the elder Bush had the benefit of running on years of peace and job-creating prosperity.

John McCain won 55 percent of the white vote, the largest share ever to go to a losing presidential candidate, even though President Bush was hugely unpopular and the country was plummeting into a deep recession. Part of McCain's success with whites was probably due to hesitation among some to vote for a black candidate; just as Obama may have won some votes because of his race, he may have lost others. Still, the 2008 result fits with a trend we have seen for 40 years. Whereas Carter and Clinton won Arkansas, Kentucky, Louisiana, Tennessee, and West Virginia thanks to strong showings among white voters, those voters have since flocked to the Republican party, pushing these states out of reach for the Democrats, even in years that favor their party as heavily as 2008 did.

The migration of whites to the GOP has helped counter the advantage the Democrats might otherwise have enjoyed from demographic changes.

This migration of whites to the GOP has helped counter the advantage the Democrats might otherwise have enjoyed from demographic changes. The net effect of all this has been imperceptible to date. Compare the election of 2008 with the last time the Democrats took the White House, in 1992. That year,

the Democrats nominated a fresh-faced, 40-something governor promising change amid a weak economy and an unpopular incumbent named Bush. He won 53.5 percent of the two-party vote and 370 Electoral College votes. In 2008, they nominated a fresh-faced, 40-something senator promising change amid a weak economy and an unpopular incumbent named Bush. He won 53.7 percent of the two-party vote and 365 Electoral College votes.

Ultimately, the increasing share of non-whites in the population might tip the scales to the Democrats, as proponents of the enduring-majority hypothesis suggest. But that claim rests on the assumption that the GOP will not match their gains with equal improvements among whites and Hispanics. In other words, those partial to the "enduring Democratic majority" hypothesis are arguing *for* the continuation of some recent trends but *against* the continuation of others.

The comparison between 1992 and 2008 is instructive. From a certain perspective, they are extremely similar: a weak economy, an unpopular incumbent, and so on. The top-line numbers look identical—but underneath them are dramatically different voting coalitions. What conclusions can we draw from this?

First, voting coalitions are in flux. This is the principal reason to question the "enduring Democratic majority" hypothesis—it rests on the false assumption that the parties' electorates are static. Voting coalitions change because the parties work to change them. In 2000 Governor Bush surveyed President Clinton's voting coalition and realized that it was vulnerable in several spots. He exploited those vulnerabilities in his race against Clinton's vice president, Al Gore. Eight years later, Senator Obama found weaknesses in Bush's coalition that he could exploit in his race against Senator McCain. This process is not unique. Each successful challenger finds marginal voters on the other side who can be persuaded to switch. The fact that Obama did this does not mean that the 200-year process is somehow at an end. It means that it is continuing.

This is precisely what we should expect from two broad-based political parties whose objective is to acquire power in our diverse republic: The losers will adapt to the new environment, and the winners will have trouble keeping their voters in the fold. Governing coalitions are stitched together around limited, common goals, and as politicians achieve those goals the coalitions unravel. How was it, for instance, that high earners voted Democratic in 2008? One reason was the GOP's 1980s cuts in tax rates. Those tax cuts have long since come to be taken for granted, removing an issue for the party and thus making it a victim of its own success.

Defeating the party of an unpopular incumbent is the easy part. The hard part is governing to the satisfaction of a majority coalition—which the Democrats have not yet done. Holding his coalition together could be real trouble for Obama. It remains to be seen whether the people who voted for him can be united around some positive goals, or whether they simply voted against Bush and the recession. Candidate Obama was adept at obfuscation during the campaign, trying hard to be all things to

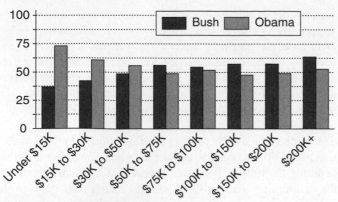

Bush 2004 and Obama 2008 share of vote by income group.
Source: National exit polls.

all people, but you can't do that when you're actually running the government; you have to decide who wins and who loses.

Michael Barone has noted that Obama has a top-bottom voting coalition, which could be unstable. The accompanying chart makes that clear.

The core of Bush's support came from middle earners, with a tilt toward the upper end. Obama's electorate, on the other hand, samples heavily from the poles. This presents an obvious policy problem. The president is promising large increases in government benefits, which will go mostly to lower-income voters. How to pay for it? Heavy tax increases on high earners will damage him among his upper-income voters. If he raises taxes too many times, the wealthy suburbs around Philadelphia and D.C. will suddenly start trending red again. So what to do? It seems the president's solution is $1 trillion budget deficits

from here to eternity. Will the middle tolerate that? Those who earn between $50,000 and $100,000 per year were not terribly partial to Obama last November—and their incomes are such that they are already sacrificing important goals as they balance their family budgets. How will they react when they see Obama abandoning the last pretenses of fiscal discipline?

In the final analysis, I'd suggest that the "enduring Democratic majority" theory consists of a few good ideas surrounded by a lot of wind. The liberals who offer it are honest and well intentioned, but their enthusiasm has gotten the best of them. Their thesis appears to be impervious to falsifying evidence. Its empirical claims are overstated and offered without appropriate context. It fails to take into account American electoral history, in particular how and why the parties have shared power over time and why we can expect that to continue into the future. Conservatives should focus on finding a way back to the majority, and ignore those who say it can't be done.

Critical Thinking

1. What is the "enduring Democratic majority" hypothesis?
2. How might changing U.S. demographics affect the liberal-conservative balance?
3. How changing voting coalitions put the "enduring majority" hypothesis into question?
4. What are the main problems with the "enduring Democratic majority" theory, according to the author?

MR. JAY COST writes the HorseRaceBlog for RealClearPolitics.com.

Polarized Pols versus Moderate Voters?

STUART TAYLOR JR

What explains the ever-more-bitter ideological polarization that roils our politics today? Is it a reflection of an ever-more-bitterly polarized public? Or are most Americans relatively moderate and thus poorly represented by their immoderate political parties and elected representatives?

These questions have been the subject of lively debate among political scientists in recent years. Now comes Morris Fiorina, a scholar at Stanford University and the Hoover Institution, with a new book announcing its thesis in the title: *Disconnect: The Breakdown of Representation in American Politics.*

Fiorina is the leading exponent of the view that the public is no less moderate and no more polarized than in the past, and thus is ill-served by fervently liberal and conservative elected representatives and political activists.

The Fiorina book will not end the debate about what he has called "the myth"—and other political scientists insist is the reality—of a deeply polarized electorate. But the author does cite new evidence that our elected representatives cleave more dramatically to the left and right ends of the political spectrum than those they purport to represent. He also helps illuminate the causes of the undoubted polarization of political elites over the past generation while adding some insights, such as why many self-described conservative voters are less conservative than you might think.

Some fundamental points are undisputed. So close to unanimity have Republicans been in opposing President Obama's major domestic initiatives that "one would have to look as far back as the 1890s to find party-line voting so sharp on the most salient legislative issues of the day," as Pietro Nivola of the Brookings Institution observed in a recent paper. So internally homogeneous have the political parties become that almost every Republican in Congress is to the right of almost every Democrat. More important, perhaps, the vast majority of Republicans are so far to the right of the vast majority of Democrats in Congress that the moderates who once played a critical role in brokering compromises have virtually disappeared.

And the congressional culture of the 1950s and early 1960s, "where Democrats and Republicans generally treated each other with civility during working hours—and many drank, played poker, and golfed together after hours—is long gone," Fiorina writes.

The disagreements among political scientists focus on whether, as Fiorina argues, the vast majority of voters "appear to be little changed in their moderate orientation from those citizens of a generation ago."

That's the premise of his thesis that in America today, there is a disconnect between an unrepresentative political class and the citizenry it intends to represent, with "a relatively moderate electorate" forced to choose between "relatively extreme candidates."

A new book portrays "a relatively moderate electorate" forced to choose between "relatively extreme candidates."

Fiorina rests his arguments largely on surveys, including the following.

- The percentage of Republican delegates to nominating conventions who identified themselves as "very conservative" has risen from about 12 percent to more than 30 percent since 1972, and the percentage of "very liberal" Democratic delegates has grown from about 8 percent to nearly 20 percent. By contrast, surveys of the general public show little change in "very conservative" and "very liberal" percentages.

- Surveys of voters' views on a range of major issues show "a nonideological public moving rightward on some issues, leftward on others, and not moving much at all on still others" between the 1984 and 2004 elections.

- The incendiary issues—including abortion, gay marriage, and gun control—that command so much political energy and media attention fall far down the list when voters are asked what they think are the most important issues facing the country. Meanwhile, despite all the talk of a culture war, Republicans as well as Democrats have become more accepting of homosexuality in general.

- Members of the public express much more ambivalence on divisive issues than do members of the political class. Indeed, Fiorina writes, most voters "may not want a clear choice between a constitutional prohibition of abortion and abortion on demand . . . between launching wars of choice and ignoring developing threats."

- "Americans are even less ideological than their self-characterizations would suggest," Fiorina adds. He notes that when voters are questioned about specific issues, only one-fifth of those who call themselves conservatives take right-of-center positions on both economic and social issues—while fully one-third "do not actually have conservative policy views" on *either* economic or social issues. (By contrast, 62 percent of self-identified liberals take liberal positions on both economic and social issues.)

The surprising number of not-really-conservative self-described conservatives also casts doubt on the importance of the long-standing preference for "conservative" over "liberal" in voter self-identifications—40 percent to 20 percent in a recent Gallup Poll. Apparently, Fiorina suggests, many Americans whose actual views are not very conservative "hear or see the latest liberal silliness and figure, 'If that's liberal, I must be a conservative.' "

Other political scientists, including Alan Abramowitz of Emory University, have written detailed rebuttals of Fiorina's vision of the electorate.

Nivola said in an interview, "The nation's political parties are polarized from top to bottom." In a recent paper, he cited polls showing that the gaps between the liberal leanings of most Democratic citizens and the conservative leanings of most Republicans in today's world are large indeed: 76 percent of Democrats versus only 31 percent of Republicans thought that the government should guarantee health insurance for all Americans; 62 percent of Republicans versus only 25 percent of Democrats opposed the Obama administration's efforts to help financial institutions from failing; 59 percent of Democrats versus only 36 percent of Republicans thought that we should be willing to pay higher prices to protect the environment; and 66 percent of Republicans versus only 33 percent of Democrats thought that the U.S. must win the war in Afghanistan.

Nivola and others also cite data suggesting that red states have gotten redder and blue states bluer in recent decades, both in the lopsidedness of their votes for Republican and Democratic candidates and in other measures such as church attendance and attitudes toward abortion, gun control, and other social issues.

To some extent the critiques of Fiorina's arguments are over matters of degree. "No knowledgeable observer doubts that the American public is less divided than the political agitators and vocal elective office-seekers who claim to represent it," Nivola and William Galston, also of Brookings, concede in their introduction to a 2006 book of essays titled *Red and Blue Nation.* And more than one-third of Americans call themselves independents and eschew identification with either party.

"The number of deeply committed ideologues in America, though difficult to measure precisely, probably isn't much larger today than at earlier points in our history, which is to say minuscule," my *National Journal* colleague Ronald Brownstein wrote in his 2007 book, *The Second Civil War.* "What's unusual now is that the *political system* is more polarized than the country. Rather than reducing the level of conflict, Washington increases it."

The decline of patronage jobs and other material rewards as a major motivation for political engagement, the increasing importance of party primaries dominated by the most-intense partisans, and the displacement of smoke-filled rooms by "power to the

people" activism, Fiorina writes, "had the unanticipated and perverse effect of making American politics less representative." The reason was that "political power and influence were transferred to political activists who were not like most people," and who were less interested in representing the views of constituents than in imposing their ideological "view of a better world on the rest of society."

Demographic changes also drove the polarization of the political parties. These changes included the migration of blacks to the North; the growth and Republicanization of the Sun Belt; the political mobilization of conservative evangelicals; the rise of suburbs; the fading of broad-based associations such as Rotary and Kiwanis clubs as points of contact between representatives and their constituents; and the replacement of these clubs by advocacy groups for causes such as peace, race, environmentalism, feminism, abortion, and gun control plus their conservative counterparts.

And in a "disturbing feedback loop," Fiorina says, those who are most open-minded often withdraw from politics for fear of introducing "conflicts into their relationships with others in their work and social circles."

One result is that politicians focus more on ideology and the demands of their party base than on solving problems. Another is that "disinformation and even outright lies become common as dissenting voices in each party leave or are silenced." All this "makes voters less likely to trust government."

Fiorina is not optimistic that institutional reforms can improve problems so deeply rooted in demographic change. But he does hope that social changes now at work—especially the fading force of the divisive convulsions of the 1960s—might depolarize our politics somewhat.

The fading force of the divisive convulsions of the 1960s might depolarize our politics somewhat.

Meanwhile, it would be nice if more politicians and activists would heed the wisdom of one of our greatest judges, Learned Hand: "The spirit of liberty is the spirit which is not too sure that it is right."

Critical Thinking

1. Why is the U.S. political system more polarized than the voting public?
2. How does extreme liberal-versus-conservative political ideology make government less representative of the American people?
3. How might changing social views and norms affect the polarization of political views in the U.S.?

The Tea Party Paradox

The country has indeed moved right. Yet it's not clear whether this is happening in a way that helps Republicans in the long run.

JONATHAN RAUCH

The polls are weeks from opening, yet the meaning of the 2010 midterm election results is already in dispute. Already, Republicans are crowing about their resurgence. Already, Democrats are saying, "Not so fast."

Peter Wehner, an astute analyst with the Ethics and Public Policy Center and a former official of the George W. Bush administration, points to opinion polls showing that a growing percentage of Americans regard the Democrats as too liberal. "What's happening, in other words, is that an increasing number of Americans are becoming more conservative," he blogged recently. "This is more fallout from the Age of Obama. Mr. Obama is, for the GOP, the gift that keeps on giving."

Wrong, replies Ruy Teixeira, a Democratic-leaning political analyst and a senior fellow with the liberal Center for American Progress. "It's not Obama that's the gift that keeps on giving, it's the economy that's the gift that keeps on giving," he said in a recent interview. "I think it's a judgment on how things are going in the country. I don't think it's a judgment to take the country in a conservative direction."

Oddly, both analyses may be correct. The country has indeed moved to the right in the past few years. Yet it's not clear whether this is happening in a way that helps Republicans.

A close look at recent polling data—mostly from the Pew Research Center for the People and the Press, whose help this writer gratefully acknowledges—reveals a peculiarity. Call it the Tea Party Paradox. The very forces that are leading to the Republican surge in 2010 may also create a painful dilemma for the GOP thereafter. The reason lies with an emerging phenomenon of which the tea party movement is just a leading indicator: the rise of "debranded" Republicans.

Begin at Wehner's beginning, with an important fact about which he is right.

According to polling by the Gallup Organization, the universe of Americans who identify themselves as liberal has stayed pretty constant since 1997, at about 20 percent. Over the course of the past few years, however, self-identified moderates have declined in number by about 5 percentage points; meanwhile, since 2008, self-identified conservatives have ticked up by about that much. That's the Obama effect, or at least, perhaps more accurately, the Obama-era effect. Pew's polls show the same trend, albeit less pronounced.

But here's the problem for Republicans: As this Pew chart shows, the rising tide of conservatism has not increased the Republicans' market share. Over the past decade or so, the country has grown more conservative but less Republican.

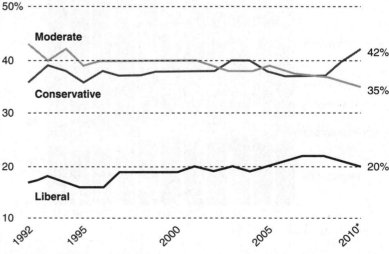

Conservatism Is on the Rise ... How would you describe your political views?

*As of June.

Source: Gallup

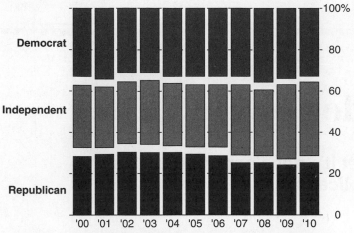

... but Republican Partisanship Is Stagnant Party identification

Source: Pew Research Center

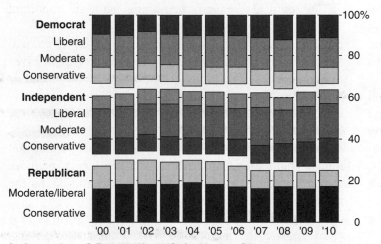

Independent Conservatives Gain Market Share

Source: Pew Research Center

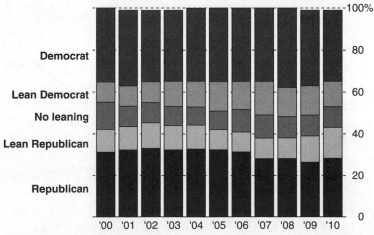

Republicans' Brand in Decline*

* Registered voters.

Source: Pew Research Center

Why? Pew's eight-category breakdown of the public by both party and ideology suggests the answer.

Independents' market share has increased at the expense of Republicans'. And, since about 2006, the leading growth category has been *conservative* independents.

These are "Republican-leaners"—independents who look, sound, and generally vote much as Republicans do, but who reject the party label. According to Pew, early in the 2000s, the electorate contained one Republican-leaner for every three Republicans; by 2010, the ratio was one for every two. Indeed, among registered voters, debranded Republicans have been the only growth category in the past few years, Pew's data show.

What's up with these right-wing refugees from Republicanism? Pew's data allow us to compare these voters with partisans and other independents, first in 1997 (or in one case, 1995), when Newt Gingrich's Republican Revolution was playing out, and again earlier this year.

The six questions in the left-hand chart on the facing page focus on the government's size and mission—core concerns of the tea party movement, and also, as the survey results suggest, of debranded Republicans as a group. On the question of whether the government gives short shrift to the middle class, partisans and independent-leaners have all moved in the direction of disenchantment. But on the five other questions, which ask, in various ways, about the size and scope of government, a different and distinctive pattern emerges.

First, the lines spread out—and they spread to the right. From 1997 to 2010, opinion among Democrats and Democratic-leaners changed only a little, and not in a consistent direction. Non-leaning independents grew a notch more conservative. Republicans and Republican-leaners, however, grew *much* more conservative.

The result is a wider range of opinion, and with it greater polarization, driven largely by conservatives' movement away from the center. None of those findings will surprise anyone who has followed the public discourse, which has been marked by an increase in anti-government stridency, sometimes radicalism, on the right.

A second trend is also noticeable. Far from being wishy-washy, in 1997 Republican-leaning independents were about as skeptical of government as were Republicans. In 2010, they became, if anything, even more conservative. Today, your average Republican-leaning independent is at least as anti-government as your average Republican. Why? Probably because self-identified Republicans include moderates and even a sprinkling of liberals.

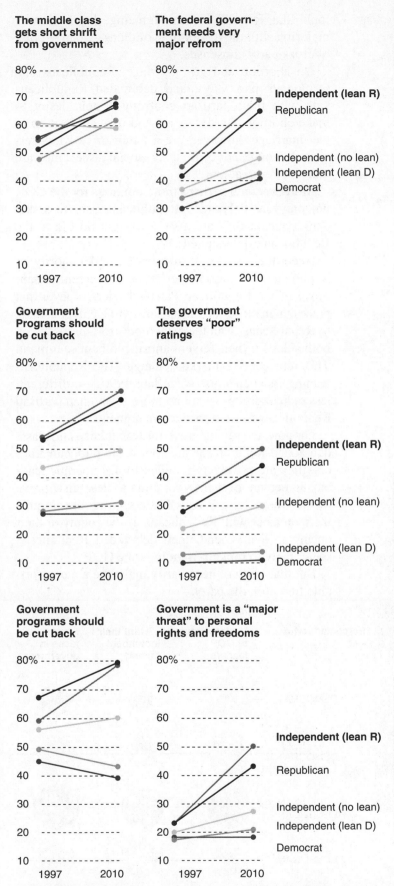

The middle class gets short shrift from government

The federal government needs very major reform

Independent (lean R)
Republican

Independent (no lean)
Independent (lean D)
Democrat

Government Programs should be cut back

The government deserves "poor" ratings

Independent (lean R)
Republican

Independent (no lean)

Independent (lean D)
Democrat

Government programs should be cut back

Government is a "major threat" to personal rights and freedoms

Independent (lean R)

Republican

Independent (no lean)
Independent (lean D)

Democrat

Debranded Republicans Are Fiercely Anti-Government Percent agreeing that . . .

Source: Pew Research Center

Republican-leaners seem to be less diverse ideologically. They look like not just Republicans in exile; they look like *conservative* Republicans in exile. The seepage of Republican debranding has been from the right edge of the party.

One effect has been to change the complexion of the independent electorate. The chart below shows where independents fell relative to Democratic and Republican partisans on 11 "values indexes" measured by Pew—first in 2007, then again in 2009. (The center line is halfway between the partisan camps.)

In a span of only two years, independents went from leaning solidly Democratic on most issues to being scattered toward the middle and often leaning Republican. That was a significant rightward swerve.

But not on all issues. In the chart, issues are ranked by how far independents have moved toward the GOP. The larger rightward trend, toward the top of the list, is on economic and regulatory issues, such as government responsiveness, the size of the social safety net, and attitudes toward business and opportunity. On social issues and security, independents show little or no rightward movement. "Scope of government," which finds independents standing pat while partisans swapped places and flew apart (probably because of the switch in party control of the White House), is an exception to an otherwise definite pattern: Independents are looking not so much more conservative as more libertarian.

What appears to be happening is that debranded Republicans are more economically than socially conservative. True, many of them may be both, but the issues that motivate them are primarily economic. Their flight from the Republican Party is pulling the average ideology of independents in a libertarian direction, a trend amplified by a milder tendency of non-leaning independents to move in the same direction.

This is not to say that debranded Republicans are social liberals, or that they are likely to break with the GOP over social issues. The charts from Pew data, suggest that it's a question of degree, at least on four hot-button cultural issues.

On whether illegal immigrants should be able to obtain U.S. citizenship—provided they undergo background checks, pay fines, and have jobs—Republican-leaners look similar to partisan Republicans. Contrary to stereotype, a majority of Republican-leaners and Republicans agree with an even larger majority of Democrats in *favoring* conditional citizenship. Republican-leaners likewise

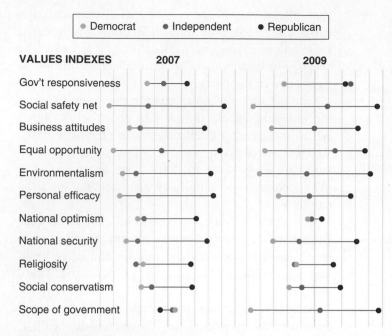

Democrat   Independent   Republican

VALUES INDEXES   2007   2009

- Gov't responsiveness
- Social safety net
- Business attitudes
- Equal opportunity
- Environmentalism
- Personal efficacy
- National optimism
- National security
- Religiosity
- Social conservatism
- Scope of government

Independents Have Veered Right

Source: Pew Research Center

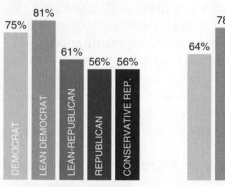

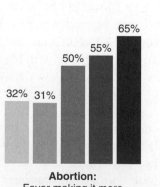

Immigration: Favor citizenship for illegals if they undergo background checks, pay fines, and have jobs (6/10)

75% DEMOCRAT
81% LEAN DEMOCRAT
61% LEAN-REPUBLICAN
56% REPUBLICAN
56% CONSERVATIVE REP.

Evolution: Humans have evolved over time (5/09)

64%
78%
56%
54%
51%

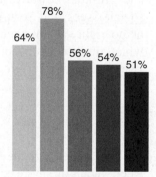

Abortion: Favor making it more difficult for a woman to get (8/09)

32%
31%
50%
55%
65%

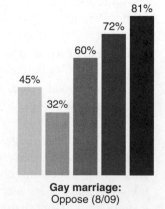

Gay marriage: Oppose (8/09)

45%
32%
60%
72%
81%

Debranded Republicans Are Less Socially Conservative

Source: Pew Research Center

look like Republicans in agreeing, by a slender majority, with the theory of evolution—again, a point of cross-party consensus.

On abortion and gay marriage, Republicans and Democrats part ways, and debranded Republicans side with their partisan confreres. Their desire to make abortions harder to get and their opposition to gay marriage, however, are a notch or two less fervent. Although not centrists on social issues, they are neither fire-breathers.

Moreover, and perhaps more ominous for the GOP, not only are debranded Republicans cool to social conservatism, they are also downright hostile to the Republican establishment.

According to Pew's surveys, a solid majority of Republican-leaning independents, 55 percent, disapprove of the Republican Party's leaders, a level that places them closer on the spectrum to Democrats than to Republicans. And they stand out from partisans on both sides for their fervent anti-incumbent sentiment. This represents a marked change: The Republican-leaning independents of the late 1990s—a different, less radical group—were no more likely than partisan Republicans to want to evict incumbents.

For now, the saving grace for Republicans is this: If debranded Republicans are sour on Republican leaders, they are positively repelled by Democratic leaders. 84 percent of them, according to Pew, disapprove of the Democratic Party's leaders, a figure that puts them on a par with Republicans. If the enemy of their enemy is their friend, then debranded Republicans seem likely to remain friendly to the GOP.

But that will not necessarily make them a comfortable fit within the party.

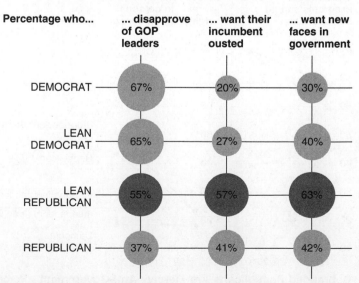

Percentage who...	... disapprove of GOP leaders	... want their incumbent ousted	... want new faces in government
DEMOCRAT	67%	20%	30%
LEAN DEMOCRAT	65%	27%	40%
LEAN REPUBLICAN	55%	57%	63%
REPUBLICAN	37%	41%	42%

Republican-Leaners Dislike Republican Leaders

Source: Pew Research Center

A pollster isolated in a prison cell for the past five years, with access to polling data but no other news, would have had no trouble spotting the breaking away of Republican-leaning independents, and she probably would have identified it as the most curious and potentially consequential change in the country's partisan structure. When, on release from isolation, she learned about the tea party's emergence, she would not have been surprised at all—except, perhaps, to wonder why it took so long. Indeed, if the tea party movement had not arisen, something else a lot like it probably would have.

So who wins from the rise of debranded Republicans? In the short-term, almost certainly the GOP. In 2010, debranded Republicans will be voting against Democrats, and at high rates: Like Republicans, three-fourths of them tell Pew they are "absolutely certain" to vote, a figure that puts their enthusiasm 10 percentage points ahead of Democrats'.

"This is an incredibly mobilized group of people right now," says Michael Dimock, Pew's associate director for research. "There's no question they're going to vote Republican." At least in 2010, debranded Republicans look like a reliable segment of the GOP coalition.

Beyond that, however, the picture becomes murkier. Debranded Republicans may present the GOP with an unpleasant strategic dilemma.

The party is already well to the right of the country's center. Here is another version of a chart you saw earlier, this time omitting independents to emphasize the ideological mix among partisans.

In 2010, the Democratic Party is a coalition of liberals, conservatives, and moderates, with moderates making up the largest share. The GOP, however, has become, for all practical purposes, a conservative party, with conservatives outnumbering combined moderates and liberals by better than 2-to-1.

Republicans' problem is that core conservative constituencies—particularly white working-class and Christian voters—are shrinking as a share of the electorate. Core center-left constituencies—minorities, left-leaning women, professionals, and socially liberal Millennial Generation voters—are growing. The demographic trends appear to require Republicans to expand beyond their conservative base just to keep from losing ground.

But debranded Republicans, unlike ordinary partisans, demand purity in exchange for their votes. They want to move the party to the right, at least on economic issues, and as of now they appear to be succeeding. "The evidence is that the Republican Party is shifting in their direction," Dimock says. "You've seen their effect in the primaries already."

Debranded Republicans have shown convincingly that they are willing to split the party and overthrow Republican incumbents they deem insufficiently conservative. But if, in doing so, they drive moderates away, they isolate the party.

In Washington, Republican moderates are scarce and isolated already. True, both parties' leaderships have seen the ideological extremes gain at the expense of the center. In his new book, The Disappearing Center: Engaged Citizens, Polarization, and American Democracy, Emory University political scientist Alan Abramowitz uses a standardized left–right vote-scoring scale (the so-called DW-NOMINATE scale) to compare the ideological makeup of the House in the 95th Congress (1977–78) with that of the House in the 108th (2003–04). The center is indeed thinning out.

Notice, though, how much more pronounced the trend is among Republicans than Democrats. Between the late

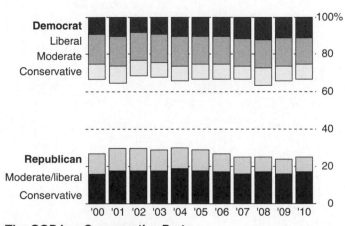

The GOP Is a Conservative Party

Source: Pew Research Center

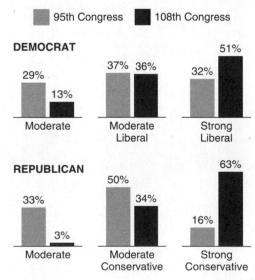

The House Veers Left and Especially Right

Source: Alan Abramowitz, *The Disappearing Center*

1970s and today, "strong conservatives" quadrupled their share of the Republican caucus and changed from being half as common as moderates to outnumbering them by an astonishing 20-to-1. Even without debranded Republicans to consider, this is not a party well positioned to reach out to the middle.

"If Republicans do well in this election—and they will do well—the tea party people are going to be right out front claiming credit for everything good that happened," Teixeira says. "That means they're going to define Republicans even more than they're defining them today, and that will make it very hard for Republicans to do what they have to do as they move into the 2012 cycle, which is move to the center. How do the Republicans do that when they've unleashed all these furies? It's very difficult."

Over the next couple of years, Obama and congressional Democrats could help Republicans escape their dilemma by pulling to the left and thus driving the center of the country to the right—far enough right to let the GOP build a winning coalition of libertarian independents, Republican partisans, and disaffected moderates.

If, however, Obama and the Democrats begin to look serious about controlling spending and deficits, if the economy recovers, and if bailouts fade into the past, the Republicans may find themselves with an unpleasant choice: Lose by embracing debranded Republicans, or lose by abandoning them—but lose either way.

Critical Thinking

1. What are "debranded" Republicans?

2. As a group, how do debranded Republicans view social and economic issues? How have they changed the general composition of independent voters?

3. How will debranded Republicans impact Republican Party election results in the short term and in the long-term?

4. What effect has the increasingly conservative nature of the Republican and Republican-leaning electorate had on Republican leadership and ideology?

America Observed

Why foreign election observers would rate the United States near the bottom.

ROBERT A. PASTOR

Few noticed, but in the year 2000, Mexico and the United States traded places. After nearly two centuries of election fraud, Mexico's presidential election was praised universally by its political parties and international observers as free, fair, and professional. Four months later, after two centuries as a model democracy, the U.S. election was panned as an embarrassing fiasco, reeking with pregnant chads, purged registration lists, butterfly ballots, and a Supreme Court that preempted a recount.

Ashamed, the U.S. Congress in 2002 passed the Help America Vote Act (HAVA), our first federal legislation on election administration. But two years later, on November 2, more than 200,000 voters from all 50 states phoned the advocacy organization Common Cause with a plethora of complaints. The 2004 election was not as close as 2000, but it was no better—and, in some ways, worse. This was partly because the only two elements of HAVA implemented for 2004 were provisional ballots and ID requirements, and both created more problems than they solved. HAVA focused more on eliminating punch-card machines than on the central cause of the electoral problem, dysfunctional decentralization. Instead of a single election for president, 13,000 counties and municipalities conduct elections with different ballots, standards, and machines. This accounts for most of the problems.

On the eve of November's election, only one-third of the electorate, according to a *New York Times* poll, said that they had a lot of confidence that their votes would be counted properly, and 29 percent said they were very or somewhat concerned that they would encounter problems at the polls. This explains why 13 members of Congress asked the United Nations to send election observers. The deep suspicion that each party's operatives had of the other's motives reminded me of Nicaragua's polarized election in 1990, and of other poor nations holding their first free elections.

Ranking America's Elections

The pro-democracy group Freedom House counts 117 electoral democracies in the world as of 2004. Many are new and fragile. The U.S. government has poured more money into helping other countries become democracies than it has into its own election system. At least we've gotten our money's worth. By and large, elections are conducted better abroad than at home. Several teams of international observers—including one that I led—watched this

U.S. election. Here is a summary of how the United States did in 10 different categories, and what we should do to raise our ranking.

1. Who's in Charge? Stalin is reported to have said that the secret to a successful election is not the voter but the vote counter. There are three models for administering elections. Canada, Spain, Afghanistan, and most emerging democracies have nonpartisan national election commissions. A second model is to have the political parties "share" responsibility. We use that model to supervise campaign finance (the Federal Election Commission), but that tends to lead either to stalemates or to collusions against the public's interest. The third, most primitive model is when the incumbent government puts itself in charge. Only 18 percent of the democracies do it this way, including the United States, which usually grants responsibility to a highly partisan secretary of state, like Katherine Harris (formerly) in Florida or Kenneth Blackwell in Ohio.

2. Registration and Identification of Voters. The United States registers about 55 percent of its eligible voters, as compared with more than 95 percent in Canada and Mexico. To ensure the accuracy of its list, Mexico conducted 36 audits between 1994 and 2000. In contrast, the United States has thousands of separate lists, many of which are wildly inaccurate. Provisional ballots were needed only because the lists are so bad. Under HAVA, all states by 2006 must create computer-based, interactive statewide lists—a major step forward that will work only if everyone agrees not to move out of state. That is why most democracies, including most of Europe, have nationwide lists and ask voters to identify themselves. Oddly, few U.S. states require proof of *citizenship*—which is, after all, what the election is supposed to be about. If ID cards threaten democracy, why does almost every democracy except us require them, and why are their elections conducted better than ours?

3. Poll Workers and Sites. Dedicated people work at our polling stations often for 14 hours on election day. Polling sites are always overcrowded at the start of the day. McDonald's hires more workers for its lunchtime shifts, but a similar idea has not yet occurred to our election officials. Poll workers are exhausted by the time they begin the delicate task of counting the votes and making sure the total corresponds to the number who signed in, and, as a result, there are discrepancies. When I asked about the qualifications for selecting a poll worker, one county official told me, "We'll take anyone with a pulse."

Mexico views the job as a civic responsibility like jury duty, and citizens are chosen randomly and trained. This encourages all citizens to learn and participate in the process.

4. Voting Technologies. Like any computers, electronic machines break down, and they lose votes. Canada does not have this problem because it uses paper ballots, still the most reliable technology. Brazil's electronic system has many safeguards and has gained the trust of its voters. If we use electronic machines, they need paper-verifiable ballots.

5. Uniform Standards for Ballots, Voting, Disputes. The Supreme Court called for equal protection of voters' rights, but to achieve this, standards need to be uniform. In America, each jurisdiction does it differently. Most countries don't have this problem because they have a single election commission and law to decide the validity of ballots.

6. Uncompetitive Districts. In 2004, only three incumbent members of Congress—outside of House Majority Leader Tom DeLay's gerrymandered state of Texas—were defeated. Even the Communist Party of China has difficulty winning as many elections. This is because state legislatures, using advanced computer technologies, can now draw district boundaries in a way that virtually guarantees safe seats. Canada has a nonpartisan system for drawing districts. This still favors incumbents, as 83 percent won in 2004, but that compares with 99 percent in the United States. Proportional representation systems are even more competitive.

7. Campaign Finance and Access to the Media. The United States spent little to conduct elections last November, but almost $4 billion to promote and defeat candidates. More than $1.6 billion was spent on TV ads in 2004. The Institute for Democracy and Electoral Assistance in Stockholm reported that 63 percent of democracies provided free access to the media, thus eliminating one of the major reasons for raising money. Most limit campaign contributions, as the United States does, but one-fourth also limit campaign expenditures, which the Supreme Court feared would undermine our democracy. In fact, the opposite is closer to the truth: Political equality *requires* building barriers between money and the ballot box.

8. Civic Education. During the 1990s, the federal government spent $232 million on civic education abroad and none at home. As a result, 97 percent of South Africans said they had been affected by voter education. Only 6 percent of Americans, according to a Gallup Poll in 2000, knew the name of the speaker of the House, while 66 percent could identify the host of *Who Wants to Be a Millionaire?* Almost every country in the world does a better job educating citizens on how to vote.

9. The Franchise. The Electoral College was a progressive innovation in the 18th century; today, it's mainly dictatorships like communist China that use an indirect system to choose their highest leader.

10. International Observers. We demand that all new democracies grant unhindered access to polling sites for international observers, but only one of our 50 states (Missouri) does that. The Organization for Security and Cooperation in Europe, a 55-state organization of which the United States is a member, was invited by Secretary of State Colin Powell to observe the U.S. elections, yet its representatives were permitted to visit only a few "designated sites." Any developing country that restricted observers to a few Potemkin polling sites as the United States did would be roundly condemned by the State Department and the world.

On all 10 dimensions of election administration, the United States scores near the bottom of electoral democracies. There are three reasons for this. First, we have been sloppy and have not insisted that our voting machines be as free from error as our washing machines. We lack a simple procedure most democracies have: a log book at each precinct to register every problem encountered during the day and to allow observers to witness and verify complaints.

McDonald's hires extra workers at lunchtime, but this has not yet occurred to our election officials. Poll workers are exhausted by the time they start counting votes.

Second, we lack uniform standards, and that is because we have devolved authority to the lowest, poorest level of government. It's time for states to retrieve their authority from the counties, and it's time for Congress to insist on national standards.

Third, we have stopped asking what we can learn from our democratic friends, and we have not accepted the rules we impose on others. This has communicated arrogance abroad and left our institutions weak.

The results can be seen most clearly in our bizarre approach to Iraq's election. Washington, you may recall, tried to export the Iowa-caucus model though it violates the first principle of free elections, a secret ballot. An Iraqi ayatollah rejected that and also insisted on the importance of direct elections (meaning no Electoral College). Should we be surprised that the Iraqi Election Commission chose to visit Mexico instead of the United States to learn how to conduct elections?

Critical Thinking

1. What is the central cause of the United States' electoral problem?
2. What are the three models used for administering elections in a democracy? What are the drawbacks of the model used by the United States?
3. What are the advantages of a nationwide election system?
4. Why does the United States perform poorly in administering elections?

ROBERT A. PASTOR is director of the Center for Democracy and Election Management and a professor at American University. At the Carter Center from 1986–2000, he organized election-observation missions to about 30 countries, including the United States.

From *The American Prospect,* vol. 16, no. 1, January 4, 2005, pp. A2–A3. Copyright © 2005. Reprinted with permission from Robert A. Pastor and The American Prospect, Washington, DC. All rights reserved. www.prospect.org

Six Myths about Campaign Money

The Supreme Court's ruling in *Citizens United* has spawned arguments that oversimplify money's real role in politics.

ELIZA NEWLIN CARNEY

When the Supreme Court decided in January to toss out the decades-old ban on direct corporate and union campaign spending, U.S. politics changed overnight. In *Citizens United v. Federal Election Commission,* the high court ruled 5–4 that unions and corporations could spend money from their vast treasuries on campaigns. The decision applies to for-profit and nonprofit corporations alike, scrambling the deck for political players of all stripes.

The ruling also intensified the never-ending political money wars: Democrats have fought in vain to push through a broad new disclosure bill, and Republicans have renewed their systematic legal assault on the remaining campaign finance laws. The Court, in a deregulatory mood, appears eager to dismantle the rules still further. At the same time, voters are unusually engaged in the campaign finance debate.

It's a critical turning point in the world of election law, but advocates fighting over free speech versus corruption remain as polarized as ever. Both sides trot out arguments that oversimplify money's real role in politics and make it harder to identify solutions and common ground. Each of the following six myths contains a grain of truth but papers over important nuances. Inevitably, regulating democracy is messy and complicated. The solution rarely can be reduced to a sound bite; there often is no silver bullet.

Corporate Money Will Now Overwhelm Elections

President Obama has been among those sounding the alarm that corporations, in the wake of *Citizens United,* will swamp campaigns with private money.

"This ruling opens the floodgates for an unlimited amount of special-interest money into our democracy," Obama declared in his weekly radio address shortly after the ruling. "It gives the special-interest lobbyists new leverage to spend millions on advertising to persuade elected officials to vote their way, or to punish those who don't."

Reform advocates toss around big numbers and dire warnings. They point to ExxonMobil's $85 billion in profits in 2008 and note that if the company spent just 10 percent of that on politics, the outlay would be $8.5 billion. That's three times more than the combined spending of the Obama and McCain presidential campaigns and every single House and Senate candidate in that election.

So far, however, no such corporate spending tsunami has materialized. If anything, labor unions have jumped in more quickly to exploit the new rules, dumping millions of dollars into Arkansas's Democratic Senate primary and other high-profile races this year. One reason may be that, unlike corporate executives, union leaders don't risk offending shareholders and customers if they openly bankroll candidates.

Actually, neither unions nor corporations will shift vast new resources into campaigns, some political scientists argue. The reason? These players could spend any of their money on politics, through issue advertising, even before the *Citizens United* ruling. Their one constraint was that they had to avoid explicit campaign messages, such as "vote for" or "vote against." The high court's ruling will make such issue advocacy less common because corporate and labor leaders are free to pay for unvarnished campaign endorsements and attacks.

"I don't think you're suddenly going to find 1 percent of corporate gross expenditures moving into politics, largely because there were so many ways to spend that money before," says Michael J. Malbin, executive director of the nonpartisan Campaign Finance Institute. Even before the ruling, about half of the states permitted direct corporate and union campaign expenditures—yet that money didn't appear to overwhelm state races.

To be sure, corporate campaign spending often flies below the radar, in both state and federal elections. Corporations tend to funnel their money through trade associations and front groups, making it hard to trace. New business- and GOP-friendly groups have cropped up, pledging to spend tens of millions of dollars in the coming election. Moreover, it's still early: Most big spending doesn't surface until the last two months before Election Day. And the post-*Citizens United* landscape is so uncertain that its real impact may not be felt until 2012, some experts predict.

Still, ominous talk of exponential campaign spending hikes is starting to look overstated. In the short term, at least, the ruling may do more to change the nature of political spending than its volume.

The *Citizens United* Ruling Won't Change Much

In the absence of an obvious corporate money surge, some analysts have downplayed the *Citizens United* ruling's importance, arguing that it does little to alter the political playing field.

"In a lot of ways, this decision is more marginal than cataclysmic in terms of what it will do to the campaign finance system," election lawyer Joseph Sandler, the former Democratic National Committee counsel and a member of Sandler Reiff & Young, maintained in a conference call the day the Court ruled. The decision's fans have tended to pooh-pooh the public reaction as so much hysteria and hyperbole.

But, in fact, the ruling has sweeping, long-term ramifications, election-law experts and even some conservatives say. Although spikes in corporate and union spending have yet to materialize, the decision signals a turnabout on the Supreme Court and a seismic shift in constitutional and campaign finance law.

That's because the Court's action sets legal precedents that threaten other long-standing pillars of the campaign finance regime, from disclosure rules to party spending curbs, the foreign-money ban, and even contribution limits. *Citizens United* is but one of dozens of campaign finance challenges that conservatives have brought and continue to bring before the high court, emboldened by its deregulatory tilt under Chief Justice John Roberts.

Some of these challenges have fallen short. In *Doe v. Reed,* the Court in June tossed out a suit brought by conservative activist James Bopp Jr. challenging state disclosure rules for voters who sign ballot petitions. Also in June, the Court turned back a Bopp-led challenge to the federal ban on soft (unregulated) money. In *Republican National Committee v. Federal Election Commission,* Bopp had argued that the RNC should be free to collect soft money for independent spending that's not coordinated with candidates.

Still, the high court all but invited further challenges that may succeed down the road. It concluded, for example, that if Bopp could show that petition signers had been harassed, the disclosure rules may, in fact, violate the Constitution. *RNC v. FEC* may also be back. That case was an "as-applied challenge," limited to specific circumstances. But the Court left the door open to a broader, facial attack on the soft-money rules.

"I have little doubt that if a facial challenge is brought to the soft-money provisions, the justices will be ready to hear it," says Richard L. Hasen, a professor at Loyola Law School in Los Angeles.

Most important, the high court's *Citizens United* opinion articulates a new, unusually narrow view of what constitutes corruption. The majority abandoned the position, upheld in previous Supreme Court cases, that campaign finance limits may be justified on the grounds that big money gives its donors "undue influence" or "access."

"The fact that speakers may have influence over or access to elected officials does not mean that these officials are corrupt," the majority opinion states, explaining that only quid pro quo corruption may be regulated. If access and ingratiation are not corruption, Hasen notes that places contribution limits, among other regulations, in serious jeopardy.

"It's a very narrow definition of corruption that is going to have, I predict, a range of very negative consequences across the campaign finance spectrum," he says. The upshot: After several decades of straddling the fence on political money but largely upholding regulations, the high court has shifted sharply in favor of free speech. Over time, disclosure and public financing may be the only regulations that this Court finds constitutional.

Congress Is More Corrupt than Ever

Given the public's disgust with government these days, it should come as no surprise that most voters think that Washington lawmakers are in the pocket of special interests.

In one poll, nearly 80 percent of respondents told a bipartisan team of researchers earlier this year that members of Congress are controlled by the groups that help fund their political campaigns. By contrast, fewer than 20 percent said that lawmakers "listen more to the voters." Such attitudes cut across the political spectrum, according to pollsters at Greenberg Quinlan Rosner Research (D) and McKinnon Media (R), which conducted the survey.

Yet leading political scientists have found the exact opposite; they've hunted in vain for proof of a correlation between money and votes over a period of decades. In study after study, "the evidence is scant to nonexistent" that political action committee contributions affect roll-call votes, says Stephen Ansolabehere, a professor of government at Harvard University.

Ansolabehere says he began his academic career convinced that campaign contributions "are an important leverage point for corporations and interest groups." But after reviewing some 80 political science analyses spanning several decades, from the 1970s through about 2005, he admits that he was forced to reconsider. The vast majority of studies, he says, conclude that "the probability of success of a bill was unaffected by total contributions."

What really sways lawmakers, the studies suggest, are constituents and party affiliation. "Constituent need trumps all," Ansolabehere says. "And party is also very important. So once you factor in parties and constituents, there is just not much room there for contributors and interest groups to have much influence."

True, reform advocates—and many lawmakers—say that such ivory-tower analyses don't square with real life inside the Beltway. Direct PAC contributions, which these academic studies target, represent only a small slice of the political money pie. Independent campaign expenditures and largely unregulated issue ads play a growing role, as do "bundled" contributions that lobbyists round up to curry favor with candidates.

Policy-making, of course, goes way beyond simple roll-call votes. Millions in corporate profits can ride on whether a bill is postponed, amended, or even scuttled—decisions that take place at the margins and behind closed doors, and leave no trace.

One political scientist who thinks that these academics are "out of their minds" is Rep. Mike Quigley, D-Ill., elected on the heels of the scandal that ousted Gov. Rod Blagojevich, D-Ill., now awaiting a verdict in his corruption trial. Quigley has a master's degree in public policy from the University of Chicago, but he takes issue with his fellow academics.

"I don't need that degree to help me understand the connection between money and policy decisions," he says. "It's very hard to prove an actual quid pro quo. Although some [politicians] are stupid and go over the top, most are careful." Quigley adds that he has heard his House colleagues wonder aloud how their votes will affect PAC contributions: "Members think about their constituencies, of course. But they're also thinking about the PACs."

Even so, reflexive public cynicism overlooks new rules and attitudes since the Watergate era, when donors carried around briefcases stuffed with cash. Lawmakers now face contribution limits and reporting rules; the soft-money ban enacted in 2002; and the stricter ethics and lobbying rules imposed in 2007 after the Jack Abramoff lobbying scandal.

The atmosphere has changed, too. Ethics-compliance teams and seminars are de rigueur at lobby shops and on Capitol Hill, and the Internet has made it easier for follow-the-money watchdog groups, reporters, bloggers, tweeters, and even average citizens to connect the dots.

"I think the people up on the Hill are bending over backwards to make sure they don't even approach the lines that have been set by the Honest Leadership and Open Government Act and the Senate ethics rules," said William J. McGinley, a partner at Patton Boggs who specializes in political law. "And I think the culture has changed quite a bit."

There is no shortage of controversies, of course—witness the recent Office of Congressional Ethics investigation into more than half a dozen lawmakers who collected donations from Wall Street donors within 48 hours of the House vote on financial services legislation. Still, popular caricatures of a widely corrupt Congress tar all lawmakers with the same brush even as politicians arguably face more-exacting rules, expectations, and public scrutiny than ever.

Money Equals Speech

If money were really speech, as conservatives like to argue, then virtually all election laws would be unconstitutional.

That is not the case—at least not yet.

Certainly, the First Amendment exhorts that "Congress shall make no law . . . abridging the freedom of speech, or of the press." In their systematic legal challenge to virtually the entire campaign finance regime, free-speech champions invariably quote this mandate. In its *Citizens United* ruling, the Supreme Court acknowledges that political speech "is central to the meaning and purpose of the First Amendment."

But even this deregulatory high court has not gone so far as to conclude that all election rules violate the Constitution. Contribution limits, for one, are a constitutional means "to ensure against the reality or appearance of corruption," the *Citizens United* majority found. The Court also left other key rules, including the soft-money ban and the disclosure laws, firmly in place.

In equating money with speech, conservatives cast political contributions in a rosy light. More campaign spending is invariably better, they insist, because donations underwrite ads and communications that enrich the public dialogue. Given how much corporations spend on commercial products such as potato chips, foes of regulation argue, U.S. elections actually cost remarkably little.

"This case will lead to more spending in political elections," enthused former FEC Chairman Bradley Smith, a professor at Capital University Law School and the chairman of the Center for Competitive Politics, shortly after the *Citizens United* ruling. "We expect to see more speech. We think that's a good thing."

But even if blatant corruption is not rampant on Capitol Hill, as many voters presume, private money potentially distorts policy-making—if for no other reason than that lawmakers must devote so much time to begging for it. American democracy, after all, is not fast-food advertising.

"If large concentrations of wealth can move easily and freely, and increasingly without transparency, through the political system, it's bound to have some influence on the nature of those decisions," says Thomas Mann, a senior fellow in governance studies at the Brookings Institution. "It doesn't have to be a quid pro quo to harm the political system."

Over time, the Supreme Court's logic in *Citizens United* may, in fact, lead it to dismantle all but a few core regulations, as some scholars predict. But we're not there yet. In the meantime, limiting campaign cash remains constitutional, and unfettered private money cannot be genuinely equated with freedom of speech.

Disclosure Is the Silver Bullet

In throwing out the longtime corporate and union spending bans, Associate Justice Anthony Kennedy assured that disclosure laws would safeguard against abuses.

"With the advent of the Internet, prompt disclosure of expenditures can provide shareholders and citizens with the information needed to hold corporations and elected officials accountable for their positions and supporters," Kennedy wrote for the majority in *Citizens United*.

Yet Kennedy's idealized vision of transparency is at odds with the real world of politics, many scholars argue. For one thing, no law requires corporations to tell shareholders whether they're spending treasury money on elections, points out Monica Youn, counsel to the democracy program at New York University School of Law's Brennan Center for Justice.

"Justice Kennedy's decision assumed a background of disclosure laws that simply didn't exist," she says. "When corporate spending does occur, it tends to be covert and to be very hard to track."

Indeed, disclosure rules are particularly spotty when it comes to independent campaign expenditures. Unlike PACs that donate directly to politicians, which must exhaustively report every penny that comes in and goes out of their coffers, groups that spend money independently of candidates need not tell much about their funding sources.

Such independent spenders must report only the money explicitly *earmarked* for an ad. That means that overhead costs paid for by a corporation or a union might never see the light of day. Money transfers between committees also routinely obscure funding sources. For their part, nonprofit advocacy groups, which are increasingly a magnet for political money, face virtually no reporting requirements.

These loopholes prompted Sen. Charles Schumer, D-N.Y., and Rep. Chris Van Hollen, D-Md., to write a broad disclosure bill in response to *Citizens United.* The measure would block big spenders from hiding behind shadowy groups with patriotic names, the lawmakers said, by forcing those running campaign ads to report their top donors and appear in on-air disclaimers.

But the bill died by filibuster in the Senate last month after winning approval in the House. Controversial provisions involving government contractors and foreign-owned corporations hurt the so-called Disclose Act—Democracy Is Strengthened by Casting Light on Spending in Elections. Republicans assailed it as pro-union, and critics blasted a last-minute exemption for the National Rifle Association and other big national groups.

The Disclose Act's real problem, however, was that it imposed elaborate reporting rules not only on unions and corporations but also on all incorporated groups—including advocacy and nonprofit organizations on the Left and Right. It's one thing, it turns out, to require politicians and political parties to publicly report their activities; it's another to ask grassroots groups to do the same.

This helps explain why Republicans, having argued for decades that disclosure is the solution to regulating political money, have reversed course. If anything, conservatives are pushing for less transparency, not more, in a series of legal and regulatory challenges. Disclosure is under fire, says Richard Briffault, a Columbia University law professor, in part because it is taking center stage as one of the few remaining campaign finance restrictions that this Supreme Court appears likely to uphold.

"Disclosure has many values," Briffault says. "But we are becoming more aware of the down sides of disclosure, and we may need to focus more carefully on what we need to know."

It would be nice if disclosure could offer up a clean, popular solution to the campaign finance mess. But like so many facets of election law, disclosure is turning out to be incomplete, complex, and controversial.

Public Financing Will Never Happen

It's true that public financing fixes in their current form will probably not win approval in this Congress, or even the next.

But the mantra that public financing will *never* pass overlooks some important recent developments.

- An innovative model for public financing that would provide multiple matching funds to reward candidates for collecting small, low-dollar donations has the potential to resuscitate the debate and bridge partisan divides.

- Advocates are better funded and organized than ever. A pair of good-government groups has pledged to spend $5 million this year and as much as $15 million over the next 18 months on a high-profile lobbying and advertising campaign to promote the Fair Elections Now Act to publicly fund congressional candidates. The House version of this bill has 159 co-sponsors, and 30 more will soon sign on, its backers say.

- Voters are unusually angry about political money. Anti-Washington sentiment; the *Citizens United* ruling; and high-profile lobbying wars over health care, Wall Street, and climate-change legislation have all thrust special-interest money into the public eye. Voters overwhelmingly object to the *Citizens United* decision, and a majority of them support the Fair Elections Now Act, recent polls show.

Outside the Beltway, "people seem much unhappier with the system than I can recall," observes former FEC Chairman Trevor Potter, president of the nonpartisan Campaign Legal Center. "And I think that inevitably pushes public funding, and new forms of the match, to the forefront."

Public financing faces big hurdles, of course. A Republican takeover of one or both chambers on Capitol Hill this fall will kick the can farther down the road. Recession and unemployment may make it harder to convince voters that lawmakers deserve what critics call taxpayer-financed campaigns.

Half a dozen states offer public financing to statewide and legislative candidates, but even these efforts are under fire. Recent lawsuits, including one heading for the Supreme Court, challenge state rescue funds that give more money to publicly financed candidates who face deep-pocketed opponents. If these suits prevail, fewer candidates may want to participate in the system.

The Achilles' heel of both the presidential and the state public financing models is that they impose spending caps on candidates who opt into the system. That makes the money unappealing and explains why presidential candidates, including Obama, have abandoned public financing.

This problem, however, is easy to fix: Simply drop the spending caps. Leading political scientists argue that it's time to adopt a "floors-not-ceilings" approach that matches small donations without limiting spending. Such a model appeals to some conservatives and may move to the fore if the high court continues to roll back existing rules.

"There's donor fatigue, there's candidate fatigue, and there's lobbyist fatigue," says ex-Rep. Bob Edgar, D-Pa., the president of Common Cause, which has teamed with Public Campaign to push for public financing. The two groups just launched their first wave of TV ads. It may be a quixotic quest, but slowly, over time, public financing may gain traction.

Critical Thinking

1. Why might a large increase in corporate spending on elections not necessarily occur after the *Citizens United* case? What are other possible long-term ramifications of the decision?

2. What consequences will the Supreme Court's narrow definition of corruption in the *Citizens United* case have on campaign financing?

3. What do academic analyses conclude about the effect of political action committee contributions on Congressional votes? What do those who disagree with these studies argue about?

4. Why is disclosure not necessarily the answer to fears of corporate influence on elections after the *Citizens United* case?

5. Explain the factors indicating that public financing of elections is still a possibility.

The American Presidential Nomination Process: The Beginnings of a New Era

BRUCE STINEBRICKNER

L et me start with two points that provide essential context for considering significant changes occurring in the American presidential nomination process today. First, in every presidential election since 1860 (that is, in the last 37 presidential elections) either the Democratic or Republican candidate has won and become president of the United States. Thus, the presidential nomination process serves to identify the *only* two individuals who ultimately have a chance to become president of the United States. Second, since the introduction of presidential primaries in the early twentieth century, the American people have played a much bigger role in the American presidential nomination process than their counterparts in any comparable nomination process in the world.

These two points testify to the importance and uniqueness of the American presidential nomination process. But the process by which major party candidates for president are nominated has not remained static since the introduction of presidential primaries early in the twentieth century, much less since the time of President George Washington. The presidential nominating process has sometimes changed suddenly on account of deliberate and focused reform efforts, and sometimes at a more measured and evolutionary pace.

I begin this article with an overview of the history of the presidential nomination process in the United States, identifying four distinct eras and laying the groundwork for the suggestion that we are entering or about to enter a *fifth* era in the way major party presidential nominees are chosen. Second, from the vantage point of November 2007, I identify the major changes that have arrived—or are arriving—on the scene, tracing their origins back to 2004 or 2000 as needed. Third, by assessing the likely consequences of these changes, I make the case that they represent more than minor revisions or routine evolution of the presidential nomination process. Instead, I argue that a sea change—a major transformation—in the process seems to be at hand.

Four Eras in the Presidential Nomination Process
The First Era: The Congressional Caucus Era (ca. 1800–1828)

Revolutionary War hero George Washington became the first president of the United States, serving two terms in office after having been elected unanimously by the Electoral College in 1788 and again in 1792. After Washington retired, party caucuses in Congress (that is, meetings of all the members of Congress who identified with each party) assumed the function of nominating presidential candidates. In six consecutive presidential elections from 1800 through 1828, every successful candidate had first been nominated by his party's congressional caucus. This first era in the presidential nominating process—the Congressional Caucus era—came to an end in 1831–1832, when parties began to hold national nominating conventions to choose their presidential candidates.

The end of the Congressional Caucus era—which some pejoratively called the "King Caucus" era—is significant. Had members of Congress continued to control the presidential nomination process, a key distinction between the American system of government and the parliamentary system of government would probably not have emerged. At the heart of parliamentary systems such as those in Great Britain, Australia, Japan, Italy, and India lies the relationship between candidates for prime minister (and prime ministers) and members of the lower house of parliament. As these systems have come to operate today, a party's members in parliament choose their leader, and that leader becomes the party's candidate for prime minister. Voters play a decisive role in selecting the prime minister by choosing between the parties, their policy positions, and their prime ministerial candidates in general elections. The end of the Congressional Caucus era in the United States severed the direct link between Congress and presidential nominations. In turn, the relationships between Congress and American presidential candidates, on the one hand, and parliaments and prime ministerial candidates in parliamentary democracies, on the other, developed in fundamentally different ways.[1]

The Second Era: National Conventions of Party Regulars or Activists (ca. 1831–1908)

By ending the direct and controlling role of members of Congress in choosing their parties' presidential candidates, the introduction of national nominating conventions in 1831–1832 marked the beginning of the second era in the history of the nominating process. From 1831 to the early twentieth century, delegates to national nominating conventions were individuals active in party organization affairs at the state and local levels. Party officeholders such as state and county party chairs as well as other party regulars became delegates. The national conventions were gatherings of party organization people—that is, party leaders and other party activists—from all the states, with each state party sending a number of delegates roughly proportional to the population of that state in comparison with other states.

In the twentieth century, two significant changes in the methods for selecting delegates to the parties' quadrennial national conventions gave birth to the third and fourth eras in the history of the presidential nomination process.

The Third Era: The "Mixed System" for Choosing Delegates to National Conventions (ca. 1912–1968)

In the early twentieth century, state governments introduced what has been called "the most radical of all the party reforms adopted in the whole course of American history"—the direct primary.[2] Accompanying the introduction of direct primaries for such offices as member of the United States House of Representatives, governor, state legislator, and mayor, was the introduction of presidential primaries by a number of states. A key objective was to reform, revitalize, and enhance American democracy.

Presidential primaries to choose delegates to national nominating conventions were used by twelve states in 1912. From 1916 through 1968, between thirteen and twenty states used presidential primaries, with roughly 35% to 45% of delegates (a minority, but a significant minority nevertheless) to the national conventions typically being chosen in primaries.[3] Because the remaining delegates were party organization activists, this era in the history of the presidential nominating process has been called the "mixed system."

Although reformers had managed, for the first time, to introduce mass popular involvement in choosing a sizable proportion of delegates to national conventions, their efforts did not result in all delegates being selected by voters in primaries. Even this "mixed system," however, introduced mass involvement in the process for nominating presidential candidates to an unprecedented extent and to a degree unrivalled in

the nomination process for any other nation's highest elected government office.

In practice, since no candidate of either party's nomination was likely to win every delegate chosen in presidential primaries and, until 1936, Democratic convention rules required a successful candidate to win two-thirds of the delegates' votes, major party nominees during the "mixed system" era typically had to gain substantial support among those delegates coming from states that did not hold presidential primaries. Even so, "inside" and "outside" strategies for winning a party's nomination were possible. A candidate could concentrate on gaining support directly from the party organization regulars who would be attending the relevant national convention, an "inside" strategy illustrated by Hubert Humphrey's successful 1968 candidacy for the Democratic presidential nomination. Alternatively, a candidate could emphasize the primaries and seek to show sufficient electoral appeal in primary states to convince party leaders and the rest of the delegates to support his candidacy. Candidate Dwight Eisenhower used an "outside" strategy in winning the Republican presidential nomination in 1952, and candidate John F. Kennedy did likewise in winning the Democratic nomination in 1960.

The last year of the "mixed system" era, 1968, was a tumultuous and violent year in American politics. Opponents of the Vietnam War supported the anti-war candidacies of Senators Eugene McCarthy and Robert Kennedy for the Democratic presidential nomination. Kennedy was assassinated in June 1968 and, even though McCarthy or Kennedy had won virtually all the presidential primaries while taking strong anti-war positions, the "mixed system" left McCarthy with substantially less than a majority of delegates at the 1968 Democratic convention in Chicago. Adopting an "inside" strategy in seeking the Democratic party's presidential nomination that year, Vice President Hubert Humphrey did not oppose American involvement in the war being waged by his patron, President Lyndon Johnson, and did not compete in a single presidential primary. Yet Humphrey was duly nominated as his party's presidential candidate. The selection of Humphrey marked the end of the "mixed system" that had made his nomination possible.

The Fourth Era: The Plebiscitary Model for Choosing Delegates to the National Convention (1972–present)

Anti-war opponents of Hubert Humphrey waged vigorous protests in the streets of Chicago outside the 1968 Democratic convention and were violently subdued by Chicago police under the direction of Mayor Richard Daley, a Democrat and a leading supporter of Hubert Humphrey's nomination. As a consolation prize of sorts, the convention voted to establish a reform commission, which came to be known as the McGovern-Fraser Commission, reflecting the names of the two Democratic members of Congress—Senator George McGovern and Congressman Donald Fraser—who, in succession, chaired the commission.

The Commission's charge was to look for ways to make the selection of delegates to future Democratic conventions more transparent and democratic.

The McGovern-Fraser Commission uncovered and reported many interesting—some might say scandalous—points about how delegates were selected in various states and made recommendations about how to reform the system. The recommendations went into effect in 1972 and served to democratize the selection of delegates to the national conventions. (Even though the Commission was a Democratic party body, implementation of its recommendations affected the presidential nomination process for both major parties.) Presidential primaries were used to select a clear majority of delegates to national conventions. Those states not using primaries were required to open their party-run delegate selection procedures to all registered voters identifying with either party. These procedures became known as the "caucus/convention" alternative to presidential primaries, an alternative that Iowa, among other states, adopted. In effect, the McGovern-Fraser reforms completed the work of the early twentieth-century reformers, and a new era in the nominating process—the Plebiscitary Model—began in 1972, four years after the "mixed system" had led to the tumultuous and violence-marred nomination of Democrat Hubert Humphrey in Chicago. The name for this new era emphasizes the newly dominant role that the mass electorate could play in the reformed presidential nomination process, since "plebiscitarian" comes from the Latin word "plebs," which refers to the "common people."

A Closer Look at the Operation of the Plebiscitary Model

My central contention in this article is that changes in the functioning of the presidential nomination process in the first decade of the twenty-first century have been so significant that they signal or foreshadow the pending arrival of a new era, the *fifth*, in the history of the presidential nomination process. A brief examination of selected characteristics of the process in operation under the Plebiscitary Model will provide essential background for subsequently considering the major and noteworthy changes that are becoming apparent in 2007–2008.

My earlier discussion of the "mixed system" (ca. 1912–1968) and the "plebiscitary model" (1972–present) addressed changes in how delegates to national conventions were selected in the states. The "mixed system" began when a sizable minority of states introduced presidential primaries to select delegates to the national convention, thus opening the presidential nomination process to the public to an extent that was unique among the world's democracies. The "plebiscitary model" reformed the "mixed system" in ways that led a majority of states to adopt presidential primaries and required the remaining states to make their party-based caucus/convention systems accessible to all registered voters identifying with the relevant party.

Timing and Scheduling

By the 1950s, New Hampshire had established the "first-in-the-nation" status of its quadrennial presidential primary. Two decades later, Iowa successfully laid claim to scheduling its precinct caucuses, the initial stage of its caucus-convention system that operated over several months, shortly before the New Hampshire primary *and* before any other state started its delegate selection process. This Iowa-New Hampshire sequence has begun the delegate selection processes of the fifty states in every presidential election year since 1972. Candidates, news media, campaign contributors, pollsters, political activists, and the attentive public have all paid disproportionate attention to campaign activities and outcomes in these two states.

The sequence of other states' delegate selection processes has been more variable than the Iowa-first/New Hampshire-second part of the schedule, but a noteworthy phenomenon called "Super Tuesday" emerged in the 1980s. "Super Tuesday" came to refer to a Tuesday in March a few weeks after the New Hampshire primary on which a number of states (initially, mostly Southern states) scheduled their presidential primaries or caucuses. One initial objective was to increase the impact of "moderate" Southern states in the selection of the Democratic presidential nominee. With the introduction of Super Tuesday and ensuing variations in which states participated in Super Tuesday in a given presidential election year, the idea of more deliberately self-conscious and self-serving scheduling seemed to catch on. Some states (like California) that had traditionally held their delegate selection processes "late" (that is, in April, May, or June) began to schedule their selection processes earlier. These movements contributed to a phenomenon called "frontloading," which refers to crowding more and more state delegate selection processes into the months of January, February, and March, rather than having them spread out over the traditional February-through-June period.

After the Plebiscitary Model took hold in 1972, the sequence of delegate selection processes in the states seems to have become more visibly contentious among the states, the bunching of a number of states' primaries and caucuses on a single day became more prevalent (not only on "Super Tuesday," but on other single dates as well), and more delegate selection contests were "front-loaded" to the January-March period, while fewer occurred in April through June.

The "Invisible Primary"

Besides the acceptance of an Iowa–New Hampshire–Super Tuesday sequence in states' delegate selection processes, other expectations about broader matters of timing and scheduling in the presidential nomination process also developed. In the 1970s an observer coined the term "invisible primary" to refer to the activities of candidates and relevant others in the year or so *before* delegate selection processes began in Iowa and New Hampshire early in a presidential election year.[4] The "invisible primary" was, of course, not an actual presidential primary; that is, it was *not* an election run by a state government in which registered voters choose delegates to a national nominating convention. *Nor* was it "invisible." But the term, especially the word "invisible," is helpful in understanding how the presidential nomination process has been changing in the early twenty-first century.

The term "invisible primary" conveyed the largely unnoticed—at least by the general public and to some extent news media—activities in which would-be presidential candidates engaged in the years before presidential general elections.

Would-be candidates met with party leaders, high-ranking government officials, potential campaign contributors, and the like to gain support for their possible candidacy. But typically the would-be candidates did not openly declare their candidacies until late in the year preceding a presidential general election, and media attention was sporadic and not particularly intense. To the average American, these activities were all but "invisible." Even so, the "invisible primary" was hardly irrelevant to the outcome of the presidential nomination process that culminated in the selection of the parties' presidential candidates. The resulting campaign experience, fund-raising, and endorsements, not to mention media commentators' impressions and evaluations, presumably influenced candidates' prospects when the actual state-by-state delegate selection processes began.

Campaign Financing

In 1974, in the aftermath of the Watergate scandal associated with President Richard Nixon and his 1972 re-election campaign, Congress passed the Federal Election Campaign Act, initiating a system of campaign finance regulation that continues in its broad outlines to this day. Subsequent court decisions, legislation (most notably, the Bipartisan Campaign Reform Act of 2002, otherwise known as the McCain-Feingold Act), and administrative regulations (issued mostly by the Federal Election Commission, a six-member government body established by the 1974 Act) have left a tangled and complicated set of rules that apply to the financing of campaigns for presidential nominations.

Campaigns for a presidential nomination became subject to a host of reporting and accounting requirements. The amount that individuals could contribute to a single candidate's campaign was limited, and the government provided "matching" funds to candidates if they met certain conditions in their initial fundraising and agreed to accept limits on their state-by-state and overall campaign spending. The system of matching funds was designed to prevent candidates or would-be candidates who lacked reasonably widespread support in a number of states from receiving government subsidies for their campaigns. To become eligible for matching funds, a candidate had to raise $5000 in contributions of $250 or less in each of twenty states. Thereafter, contributions of up to $250 were matched by an equal amount of government funding. These matching provisions were unique to campaigns for presidential nominations and applied to neither presidential general election nor congressional campaigns. And, to repeat for the sake of emphasis, a candidate's acceptance of matching funds brought restrictions, specifically an overall spending limit for the candidate's nomination campaign and a limit on the amount that s/he could spend in each state (based on each state's population).[5]

The era of the Plebiscitary Model began in 1972, but the matching provisions of the Federal Election Campaign Act of 1974 did not take effect until the 1976 presidential nomination contests. Approximately fifty "serious" candidates sought the Democratic and Republican presidential nominations between 1976 and 1992, and only one—Republican John Connally in 1980, who won only one delegate—did not accept matching funds while campaigning for the presidential nomination.[6] In 1996, the issue of matching funds became significant when a very wealthy but relatively unknown candidate seeking the Republican presidential nomination, Steve Forbes, followed in Connally's footsteps and declined matching funds. In contrast, Republican Bob Dole, the well-known frontrunner for his party's nomination, accepted matching funds and their accompanying spending limits. Forbes poured millions of his own dollars into television advertising, which made Dole spend millions of dollars in response. Dole eventually and somewhat easily prevailed over Forbes and other contenders, but, by late March, 1996, he had spent almost all that he was legally allowed to spend until he was formally nominated by his party's national convention during the summer of 1996. This situation, many observers have noted, left him a sitting duck for several months of effective television advertising launched by the incumbent president, Bill Clinton, who had been unopposed for his party's renomination in 1996. In turn, Dole, who could not buy ads to respond to Clinton's barrage until the summer, fell hopelessly behind his formidable Democratic opponent before being officially nominated.[7]

Recent Changes in the Presidential Nomination Process

Three noteworthy recent changes in the presidential nomination process involve timing and scheduling, campaign financing, and interaction between the two: (1) an earlier start to campaigning and other candidate activities, (2) the introduction of "Super Duper Tuesday" in 2008, and (3) what has been termed the "collapse" of the system of matching funds in the financing of campaigns for the presidential nomination.[8] The first and third changes are not attributable solely to the 2007–2008 nominating cycle; both have their origins in earlier years, most particularly in the 2000 and 2004 contests. The second change, the introduction of "Super Duper Tuesday," stems more specifically from the 2007–08 nominating cycle. What I have termed a *sea change* in the process for nominating presidential candidates has been emerging during at least the two most recent presidential election cycles, while the extent and durability of the changes have become significantly more apparent during the on-going 2007–08 cycle.

An Earlier Start

One change in timing is straightforward and has been much reported: Candidates' serious and visible campaigning for presidential nominations was well under way by the beginning of 2007, a full calendar year before delegate selection processes were scheduled to begin early in the presidential election year of 2008. All sorts of activities associated with candidates' attempts to win their parties' nominations have been occurring earlier than in preceding nomination cycles.

Some candidates seeking to be elected president in 2008 declared their candidacies in late 2006. For example, former two-term Iowa governor Tom Vilsack, more than a political nonentity but less than a putative front-runner in the Democratic party's 2008 presidential nomination competition, announced his candidacy in November 2006 and officially withdrew on 23 February 2007. On the other hand, former Senator Fred

Thompson, whose name surfaced as a potentially formidable candidate for the Republican presidential nomination in the first half of 2007, delayed formal announcement of his candidacy until early September. Commentators wondered why he had waited so long to announce and whether it was too late. Major Democratic contenders John Edwards, Barack Obama, and Hillary Clinton, and major Republican contenders Mitt Romney, Rudy Giuliani, and John McCain all announced their candidacies before March 2007.[9]

Nationally televised debates among Republican and Democratic candidates were in full swing during the first half of 2007. By the summer of 2007, a half-dozen debates among Republican candidates and another half-dozen among Democratic candidates had been aired, with a similar number scheduled to occur in the second half of the year. Six to nine candidates participated in each of these events, which varied in sponsorship (from television stations to labor unions to Howard University) and format (from a single moderator to CNN's YouTube-based venture).

Finally, news media provided extensive coverage of nomination campaigns and the like during the period that used to be called the "invisible primary." Candidates' debate performances, poll results, policy positions, campaign fund-raising efforts, and other "horse race" aspects of the campaign were reported, and systematic comparisons of candidates' proposals on issues such as the Iraq war and health care reform were occasionally provided. In the summer of 2007, *The New York Times* conducted interviews with voters across the United States and reported that they were unusually engaged by the early campaigning as well as "flinching at the onslaught of this early politicking."[10]

The Collapse of the System of Matching Funds

In 2000, Republican candidate George W. Bush was the first presidential nominee of either major party who had not accepted matching funds during his campaign for his party's nomination. In 2003, two leading candidates for the Democratic nomination, Howard Dean and John Kerry, followed Bush's lead of four years earlier and opted out of matching funds. The 1996 predicament of Republican Bob Dole that resulted from his acceptance of matching funds and the accompanying spending limits doubtless influenced later decisions by candidates Bush, Dean, and Kerry. By the start of the 2007–2008 presidential nomination cycle, no major contender for either party's nomination was expected to accept matching funds, although eventually Democrat John Edwards decided to do so. By 2007, the path that Republican nominee Bush had taken in 2000 had become the norm for all but one major candidate. In turn, the system of spending limits that depend on candidates' acceptance of matching funds has been undermined and, in effect, probably ended, at least among major candidates.

Several additional observations about the end of the "old" system of presidential nomination financing are in order. In the absence of spending limits that would have accompanied acceptance of matching funds, fund-raising for 2007–08 presidential nomination campaigns grew enormously. Hillary Clinton's 2007 first quarter total of 26 million dollars and fellow Democrat candidate Barack Obama's close second of 25.6 million can be contrasted with 7.4 million, the total for candidate John Edwards, the leading Democratic fund-raiser in the first quarter of 2003, and 8.9 million, Democratic candidate Al Gore's total in the first quarter of 1999.

The maximum that a candidate could receive in matching funds in the 2007–08 nomination cycle was approximately 21 million dollars. When almost all of the front-running candidates of both parties opted out of the matching system, they were concluding that that amount of partial public funding was not a sufficient reason to accept matching funds. More valuable than 21 million dollars of public funding was the freedom not to abide by the spending limits that accompanied the acceptance of matching funds. Through the end of the third quarter of 2007, Clinton had raised 90.6 million dollars and Obama 80.3 million, while the two candidates who were leading the Republican field in fund-raising, Mitt Romney and Rudy Giuliani, had raised 62.8 million and 45.8 million dollars, respectively.[11]

The demise of the "matching" system for financing campaigns for the presidential nomination cannot be attributed solely to the 2007–08 presidential nomination cycle. Foreshadowed by the predicament in which Republican candidate Bob Dole found himself in March 1996, the "collapse" of the matching system is an early twenty-first century phenomenon that culminated in 2007–08.

The Money Primary

Amidst earlier declarations of candidacy (and, sometimes, withdrawals), earlier and numerous televised debates, earlier extensive media coverage, and the collapse of the system of matching funds, a new term was coined to replace "invisible primary" as a name for the early period of the presidential nomination process—the "money primary." Federal Election Commission (FEC) regulations require quarterly reports of candidates' fund-raising activities in the years preceding presidential general elections (and monthly reports in presidential election years). As 31 March 2007 approached, journalists anticipated the required candidate filings and what they would show in fund-raising prowess and contributors' support. News media reported and analyzed candidates' first-quarter filings with the FEC against a background of different fund-raising expectations for different candidates. On the Democratic side, Barack Obama was judged to have performed especially well, raising 25.6 million dollars, just a little less than front-runner Hillary Clinton and substantially more than John Edward's 14 million. On the Republican side, candidate John McCain fell short of fund-raising expectations and prospects for his candidacy were discounted accordingly, while competitor Mitt Romney's stock rose on account of his first quarter fund-raising total of 20.7 million dollars, six million more than the amount raised by the second-place finisher at that stage of the Republican money primary, Rudy Giuliani.[12]

Through all the changes, news media retained their prominent role as assessors of the nominating competition. Years earlier, when the term *invisible primary* applied, news media had been dubbed the "Great Mentioner" because of their role in identifying candidacies that should be taken seriously. For a candidate not to be mentioned by journalists was like being afflicted with a politically terminal illness. In 2007, news media assessments continued to help the attentive public gauge the on-going horse race among candidates. Poll results—both national polls and polls in the early caucus and primary states of Iowa, New Hampshire, and South Carolina—and the results of the quarterly "money primaries" were combined with other information and intuitions to make assessments of who was winning, who was gaining or losing ground, and the like. What seemed new in 2007 was the extent of early candidate activity, including the plethora of televised debates in the first half of the year and especially the salience of the "money primary." Campaigns for the two major parties' presidential nominations seemed to be in full swing early in 2007, nearly two years before the November 2008 general election and a year before the states' delegate selection processes were set to begin in Iowa in January 2008.

Super Duper Tuesday and Related Matters

What should probably, because of the earlier start to full-scale campaigning, be called the *2007–2008* presidential nomination process also brought noteworthy change in the clustering of delegate selection processes in the states. During the 1988 presidential nominating process, sixteen mostly Southern states scheduled their delegate selection processes on a single day in early March that was called "Super Tuesday." Such clustering of many states' primaries and caucuses on a single day continued to occur in subsequent years and "Super Tuesday" became a quadrennial event. In 2004, a second, smaller clustering of states on a single Tuesday in March after Super Tuesday was dubbed "mini-Tuesday."

Prior to 2008, the sequence of delegate selection processes in the states during the era of the Plebiscitary Model typically had the following pattern: Iowa; New Hampshire; and, fairly soon thereafter, "Super Tuesday," which grew beyond its original Southern focus to include more non-Southern states. Super Tuesday was sometimes decisive—and sometimes not—in determining eventual presidential nominees, and outcomes in Iowa and especially New Hampshire continued to play disproportionately influential roles.

The phenomenon of Super Tuesday, coupled with a general tendency in the direction of more and more "frontloading," led in 2008 to what was variously dubbed "Super Duper Tuesday," "Tsunami Tuesday," and even "Unofficial National Primary Day." By mid-2007, at least twenty states that together accounted for more than 50% of the delegates to each national convention had scheduled their delegate selection processes for 5 February 2008, a short time after Iowa, New Hampshire, Nevada, and South Carolina were scheduled to hold their delegate selection processes.

As of this writing in November, 2007, the significance of Super Duper Tuesday remains to be seen, but the outcomes of twenty-odd states' delegate selection processes on that day may well be decisive. In other words, 5 February 2008 may become

the functional equivalent of a national presidential primary in which, as a consequence of voters casting ballots in at least twenty states *on a single day,* the presidential nominees of both major parties will be determined.

The idea of holding a succession of regional primaries (for example, four of them, each including a contiguous bloc of states in which approximately one-fourth of the population of the United States lives) or a single national primary is not new. Both ideas have been advocated as possible reforms to the presidential nomination process, often with an eye to reducing or eliminating the disproportionate impact of Iowa and New Hampshire. The creation of "Super Duper Tuesday" on 5 February 2008 resulted from decisions by individual states and small groups of states to hold their delegate selection processes on that date, rather than from any single, coordinated reform effort. As the magnitude and implications of "Super Duper Tuesday" came into focus, California, New York, and Florida, among other states, began to re-think the scheduling of *their* 2008 delegate selection processes.

The outline of the Florida story, as of this writing (November, 2007), bears reporting. In May, 2007, the Florida legislature scheduled its presidential primaries for 29 January 2008. Doing so violated both major parties' rule that only Iowa, New Hampshire, Nevada, and South Carolina could hold delegate selection processes before 5 February 2008. In August 2007, the Democratic national party decided that any Florida delegates elected before 5 February 2008 would not be seated at the 2008 Democratic national convention. In late September, the Florida Democratic Party announced its continuing support for holding the Florida presidential primaries on the forbidden 29 January date.[13] The final outcome of this controversy remains to be seen, but one reporter suggested that it might eventually result in the end of Iowa's and New Hampshire's traditional primacy in the presidential nomination calendar.[14]

A Sea Change and a New Era

I have pointed to three recent and significant changes in the presidential nomination process: (1) earlier sustained and public campaigning by candidates, so that public declarations of candidacies and serious campaigning are well underway two years before a presidential general election, (2) the establishment of what may function as an "unofficial national primary" early in February 2008, which reflects the convergence or perhaps even culmination of two earlier trends: (i) increased "frontloading" of the states' delegate selection processes and (ii) growing inclination of states to schedule their delegate selection processes on a single day a few weeks after Iowa and New Hampshire in an attempt to reduce the disproportionate influence of those two states in the outcome of the presidential nomination process, and (3) the demise of the system of matching funds that had anchored the regulation of presidential nomination campaign financing since the passage of the Federal Election Campaign Act in 1974.

What are the implications of these changes? Why might they matter? A simple answer is that these changes will likely affect the sort of individuals who are likely to be nominated and perhaps those who are likely to run. More specifically, the new era, whose beginnings have, in my view, become clearly visible in the 2007–08 cycle, will give the "dark horse," the underdog, the relatively little-known presidential aspirant, less chance to be nominated.

"Dark horses" emerged frequently enough during the "mixed system" era (1912–1968) to make them a staple of political lore. Sometimes such candidates emerged after an unexpectedly strong showing in important primaries, sometimes after party bosses and delegates at a deadlocked convention turned their backs on the two or three leading contenders and sought a "new face" whom supporters of the leading contenders could accept.

Under the Plebiscitary Model, the dramatic increase in the number of delegates chosen by the mass electorate meant that the outcome of early delegate selection processes, especially in Iowa and New Hampshire, led to successful nominations of Democratic dark horse candidates George McGovern and Jimmy Carter in 1972 and 1976, respectively. Little known Democrat Bill Clinton's nomination in 1992 was also a largely unexpected outcome. Yet each won their party's nomination by successfully navigating the sequence of states' delegate selection processes that operated under the Plebiscitary Model. Carter's first-place finish among candidates in Iowa in 1976 ("undecided" was Iowans' first choice), followed by his win in the New Hampshire primary, put the relatively unknown former governor of Georgia on track to be nominated. McGovern's 1972 and Clinton's 1992 successful quests to be nominated followed roughly similar scripts.

Why does the current sea change in the presidential nomination process threaten such dark horse candidacies? Let me begin with the existence of "Super Duper Tuesday," which may function *almost* as a national primary in 2008. So-called retail politics can work in small states such as Iowa and New Hampshire. The little known candidate can, by dint of arduous campaigning, impress attentive Iowa and New Hampshire voters by shaking hands, attending small meetings in people's homes, knocking on doors, and the like. It has been said (almost surely apocryphally) that an Iowa or New Hampshire voter does not take a presidential nomination candidate seriously until the voter has shaken the candidate's hand at least twice! In such a "retail politics" environment, the advantages of initial name recognition, endorsements from leading national political figures, money, and even campaign organization are less important than in the "wholesale politics" required by big state primaries or multiple-state primaries held on a single day. To the extent that "Super Duper Tuesday" approximates a national primary and the wholesale politics that that would entail, the chances of a dark horse or little-known candidate are lessened. Perhaps, as some observers have suggested, the Iowa-New Hampshire-Nevada-South Carolina-Super Duper Tuesday sequence in 2008 will not result in 5 February 2008 functioning as a national presidential primary. Perhaps it will. Regardless, Super Duper Tuesday seems to constitute movement in the direction of a national primary (or at least a series of regional primaries, which would also require wholesale politics), with such a development working to undermine dark horse candidacies.

The collapse of the system of matching funds also seems to disadvantage dark horse or underdog candidacies. Well-known front-runners typically can raise more money than less well-known underdogs. Even so, the matching system worked to narrow the gap between the campaign resources of front-runners and those of underdogs.

The third change in the presidential nomination process that I have identified—the earlier start of full-scale campaigning and resulting news media attention—might on first glance seem to enhance the chances of potential dark horse candidates. The longer the campaigning, it would seem, the more likely an underdog could out-perform better known opponents and overcome their greater resources both over the long haul and in the face of simultaneous contests in a large number of states on "Super Duper Tuesday." In addition, the argument might continue, if such an underdog performed well in the early going, the resource gap between him/her and his/her better known opponents would likely be lessened.

The counter-argument would run in an opposite direction. The superior resources of the front-running candidates and the earlier start to the campaign make it all the more unlikely that an underdog can win. The front-running candidates have more time during which to effectively spend their resources on TV ads and the like, and more time for their larger and better-financed on-the-ground organizations to produce effects. Moreover, news media identification of the top tier of candidates, based partly on the results of the money primary, has longer to sink in with the mass public and, perhaps, become the received wisdom. Finally, the earlier start to serious campaigning means that an underfinanced, underdog candidate needs to compete that much longer against better known, better financed candidates without the prospect of a headline-grabbing victory or at least an unexpectedly strong showing in Iowa or New Hampshire. Instead, the demoralizing effects of the well-publicized money primary undermine underdogs' credibility, often to the point of no return.

As should be clear, I am less certain about the effects of the lengthened nomination campaign season on dark horse candidacies than I am about the effects of an "unofficial national primary" and the demise of the system of matching funds. But, taken as a whole, recent changes in the nomination process that, in my judgment, constitute—or, at the very least, foreshadow—a sea change seem destined to undermine underdog candidacies.

Before closing, let me do one more brief round of "so what?" analysis. Suppose one wanted to change the operation of the Plebiscitary Model to eliminate virtually any chance of underdog candidates such as George McGovern (1972), Jimmy Carter (1976), and, in the 2007–08 cycle, Democrats Tom Vilsack and Chris Dodd and Republicans Tommy Thompson and Sam Brownback, four seasoned politicians with relevant government experience, but little name recognition among the public. To accomplish such an objective, one might introduce the recent changes in the presidential nomination process identified in this article. The latest sea change in the presidential nomination process may relate especially to the sorts of qualities major party presidential nominees need to have. If widespread name recognition and celebrity status—both of which, to be sure, can result from high profile experience in government, a point that sometimes is overlooked—and/or moneyed connections sufficient to raise vast sums of contributions are to be essential characteristics for a presidential nominee, then the nomination process is moving in an accommodating direction.

Perhaps the fifth era in the history of the presidential nomination process will come to be known as "the post-dark horse era," "the celebrity candidate era," "the national (or regional) primary era," or even "the era after the demise of Iowa's and New Hampshire's primacy." Whatever the new era comes to be called and whatever exact shape it takes, please do not say that no one told you it was coming.

Notes

1. The overview of the history of the American presidential nomination process presented here and continued below draws substantially from Bruce Stinebrickner, "The Presidential Nominating Process: Past and Present," *World Review* 19, No. 4 (October 1980), pp. 78–102.

2. The quotation comes from Austin Ranney, as quoted in Stinebrickner, p. 80. Austin Ranney, *Curing the Mischiefs of Faction: Party Reform in America* (Berkeley, California: University of California Press, 1975), p. 121.

3. For a table displaying exact numbers of states using presidential primaries for every presidential election year between 1912 and 2004, see "Table 3-1 Votes Cast and Delegates Selected in Presidential Primaries, 1912–2004," in *Presidential Elections, 1789–2004* (Washington, D.C.: CQ Press, 2005), p. 104.

4. See Arthur T. Hadley, *The Invisible Primary* (Englewood Cliffs, NJ: Prentice Hall, 1976).

5. For more details, see David B. Magleby and William G. Mayer, "Presidential Nomination Finance in the Post-BCRA Era," in William G. Mayer, ed., *The Making of the Presidential Candidates 2008* (Lanham, Maryland: Rowman and Littlefield, 2008), pp. 141–168. The summary of the matching provisions given here is drawn largely from pp. 142–143.

6. Magleby and Mayer, p. 144.

7. This Forbes-Dole-Clinton account is taken largely from Magleby and Mayer, pp. 149–152.

8. Magleby and Mayer use the subtitle "The *Collapse* of the Matching Fund Program" on p. 149 of their chapter (emphasis added). Martin Frost, former member of the U.S. House of Representatives and former chairman of the Democratic Congressional Campaign Committee, observed early in 2007 that it would not be a surprise if the matching system for presidential nomination process financing "simply disappears" after the 2007–08 cycle. "Federal Financing of Presidential

Campaigns May Be History," FoxNews.com, 8 January 2007: 23 September 2007, <http://www.foxnews.com>.

9. Announcements signaling a candidacy for a party's 2008 presidential nomination often occurred at more than a single point in time. Several candidates made a combination of announcements, presumably to increase the increments of media attention that such announcements were expected to produce. A single candidate's announcements in 2007 might include the following: that s/he was going to make an "important announcement" in a few days, that s/he was going to begin "exploring" whether to become a candidate (or that s/he was forming an "exploratory committee" to "test the waters"), that s/he had "decided" to become a candidate, and that s/he was "formally" declaring his or her candidacy.

10. Adam Nagourney. "Voters Excited Over '08 Race; Tired of It, Too." *The New York Times*, 9 July 2007, A1.

11. Federal Election Commission: 29 November 2007, http://www.fec.gov/finance/disclosure/srssea.shtml/.

12. "First Quarter 2007 FEC Filings," *Washington Post:* 30 September 2007 <http://projects.washingtonpost.com/2008-presidential-candidates/finance/2007/q1/>.

13. Abby Goodnough, "Florida Democrats Affirm an Early Primary," *The New York Times,* 24 September 2007, A12.

14. "World News", ABC, WRTV, Indianapolis, 24 September 2007, correspondent Jake Tapper: "Democrats are convinced that this is the beginning of the end of the Iowa-New Hampshire monopoly."

Critical Thinking

1. How did Congressional caucuses once nominate presidential candidates?

2. Why were direct primaries introduced? What was their effect on the presidential nomination process?

3. What is the Plebiscitary Model for nominations? What alternative to direct primaries does it include?

4. What are the three most significant and recent changes to the presidential nomination process?

5. What are the implications of the collapse of the matching funds system for presidential candidates?

6. What is a "dark horse" candidate? Why does the current transformative change in the presidential nomination process threaten "dark horses"?

I want to thank Luke Beasley, Allison Clem, Annie Glausser, Christina Guzik, Kelsey Kauffman, David Parker, Amy Robinson, and Randall Smith for their helpful comments on an earlier draft of this article. I also want to thank Luke Beasley for his work in locating presidential candidates' announcement dates for the four most recent presidential elections.

Don't Call Them Lobbyists

The Obama Administration aimed to reduce the power of K Street, but Washington's influence brokers have proved adept at adapting their tactics to the shifting landscape.

THEO FRANCIS AND STEVE LEVINE

Despite the rhetoric of the past 18 months, few in the nation's capital really believed the Beltway lobbyist would disappear overnight just because a new President vowed to change business-as-usual in Washington and Congress heightened scrutiny. Yes, lobbyists now must heed stringent new disclosure rules; the gift-giving and golf outings have largely vanished. But the influence game rolls on in Obama's Washington.

That isn't to say, of course, that nothing has changed. The Democrats have set in motion a landslide of potentially transformative legislation: an overhaul of the U.S. health-care system; a sweeping energy and climate-change bill; new regulations to rein in the financial markets; and more. "There are a lot of challenges for business," says Steve Elmendorf, a longtime aide to former House Democratic Leader Dick Gephardt who now runs his own lobbying firm. "When there are challenges, they hire help."

Elmendorf says businesses are hiring lobbyists to help with "a lot of challenges."

With so much legislation and so many new rules, many K Streeters are adjusting their playbooks. One lobbyist says that where a client once hired two firms—one Republican, one Democrat—it now may hire five, including specialists for each house of Congress and at least one big-picture strategist. Twitter, Facebook, and sophisticated Web sites have become de rigueur tools of influence. And lobbyists are looking to cooperate more often with lawmakers—or at least appear to be doing so—rather than simply training their guns on bills they deem hostile.

At a time when lobbying is under assault, the most effective practitioner is sometimes someone who technically isn't a lobbyist. The rules say lobbyists must register with the feds if they call or visit lawmakers, staff, or key Administration officials to influence policy at least twice in a quarter—and also spend at least 20% of their time for any given client on "lobbying-related" activities. Registering as a lobbyist nowadays is "like walking around with a scarlet letter," says a lobbying-law specialist. That helps explain why more lobbyists are deregistering and setting up shop as arm's-length strategists. These people don't contact lawmakers or Administration officials on behalf of clients, but instead offer an insider's insight into which lawmakers are likely to be most receptive to what arguments and how procedural battles could play out. Such advice is in demand as companies and business groups sort out how to tackle multiple issues at once. "There's more of a premium on strategic thinking now," says John Jonas, a registered lobbyist who established the health-care practice at lobbying powerhouse Patton Boggs.

Thomas A. Daschle, the former Senate majority leader, now serves as a "special policy adviser" and strategist at Alston & Bird, focusing in part on health care and financial services. He never registered as a lobbyist. Former Bush Administration counselor Ed Gillespie, a lobbyist for most of the past decade, opted not to reregister this year. Instead he has started Ed Gillespie Strategies, offering companies "strategic planning," "message development," and "crisis management." He declined to comment for this story. Daschle says he doesn't lobby directly but lends others insight into legislative terrain and the tendencies of lawmakers he knows well.

Sometimes these "strategic" lobbyists suggest that their clients do the schmoozing themselves, as meeting with a company CEO is often more palatable to lawmakers than lunching with lobbyists. The Managed Funds Assn., which represents hedge funds, has stepped up its fly-ins. The National Association of Manufacturers recently brought in more than 300 executives. 3M is also among those sending executives more often, says John Woodworth, who oversees the company's supply chain. "It sends more of a message if you're willing to spend your time," Woodworth says.

Lobbyists are increasingly taking the fight to the people—or, at least, to their own people. This month the American Farmland Trust, a relatively small farm lobby focused on conservation,

Lobbying's Big Spenders

Percentage change in lobbying expenditures by top U.S. organizations, first-half 2008 vs. first-half 2009

Company/organization	Increase
American Wind Energy Assn.	403%
Dow Chemical	119
ConocoPhillips	108
CVS/Caremark	108
Chevron	104

Data: Center for Responsive Politics

plans to mobilize its 30,000 members to urge Farm Belt senators to support the cap-and-trade bill. Using articles in trade publications, talk-radio appearances, Twitter, and Facebook, the group aims to win the backing of rural-state senators, some of whom are concerned about how the measure would affect fuel costs as well as electricity prices in states heavily dependent on coal power.

Bipac, the country's oldest business lobby, says interest in grassroots campaigns has picked up sharply of late. "To the degree this town becomes more difficult for lobbyists to have face time with policymakers, there's going to have to be another way for them to make their message known," says President and CEO Gregory S. Casey. Murphy Oil, an El Dorado (Ark.) oil and gas company, has affixed tear-off leaflets to its gas pumps. The leaflets warn that the "current legislative proposals could cause gas prices to increase at least 60%" and direct customers to a Web site operated with Bipac's help. The site offers arguments against the cap-and-trade bill—and Casey says half its visitors click to e-mail lawmakers on the issue.

Tried-and-true tactics still work, of course. In late June, power industry lobbyists managed to get a last-minute amendment slapping tariffs on steel and other carbon-intensive imports into climate-change legislation. But the K Street crowd is less likely now to try killing legislation outright. "The smart strategy is getting taken care of, or getting [lawmakers] to go in a different direction," says Jonas, the Patton Boggs lobbyist. By signing on to White House health-reform efforts, he says, the pharmaceutical industry transformed itself "from Public Enemy No. 1 to the tolerated in-law." One by one, other health-care organizations have followed suit. Appearing cooperative is the new name of the game.

"There's a fair amount of rhetoric around things that all of us think are important, like climate change, health care, the economy. The actual content is completely different than what most of us are hearing. Most of this is generating incredible deficits for our children; most of it is happening much too quickly in the wrong ways. On fiscal stimulus, on climate change, on health care, we don't like what's happening. It's not just against the oil industry. It's doesn't make sense for America."
—James Hackett, CEO, Anadarko Petroleum

"I would say Obama's health-care reform is making more progress than a lot of people would have predicted. We're on the verge of a bill coming out of the House that's clearly going to happen. Nobody seems to have walked away from the table yet. Well, some have walked away from the table. But there's still a lot of people working."
—Jeffrey B. Kindler, CEO, Pfizer

"For the near-term crisis, the Treasury and Federal Reserve actions have been very good. We were staring into the abyss. The possibility of Armageddon was there. [Yet] the stimulus package they put through, which was crucial to the turnaround, is failing. It is embarrassing when China does a stimulus package more effectively than we can, and we are a free enterprise system."
—Mike Jackson, CEO, AutoNation

CEO reporting was organized and led by chief of correspondents Joseph Weber and Los Angeles correspondent Chris Palmeri. Other contributors: Michael Arndt, Amy Barrett, Matthew Boyle, Peter Burrows, Nanette Byrnes, Kerry Capell, John Carey, Tania Chen, Roger Crockett, Cliff Edwards, Peter Elstrom, Dean Foust, Ron Grover, Burt Helm, Arik Hesseldahl, Rob Hof, David Kiley, Jena McGregor, Arlene Weintraub, Lauren Young.

Critical Thinking

1. Outline some of the disclosure and operating rules that lobbyists must abide by.
2. Why are many Washington lobbyists now operating as advisors or strategists who do not conduct direct lobbying activities?
3. How do the tactics of "strategists" differ from those of lobbyists? What similar services do they provide?

With Jane Sasseen, Elise Craig, and Keith Epstein in Washington.

From *Bloomberg BusinessWeek*, August 10, 2009, pp. 43–44. Copyright © 2009 by Bloomberg BusinessWeek. Reprinted by permission of Bloomberg LP.

Born Fighting

RONALD BROWNSTEIN

Apart from his political skills, two forces above all have propelled Barack Obama in his once-improbable quest for the presidency.

One is on vivid display this week: a wave of dissatisfaction with the country's direction that has created a visceral demand for change. That wave has reached towering heights amid the financial crisis roiling Wall Street and consuming Washington. No other candidate has drawn more power than Obama has from that desire to shift course.

With much less fanfare, this week also marked a milestone in the evolution of the second force that has lifted Obama: the rise of the Internet as a political tool of unparalleled power for organizing a vast activist and donor base.

Ten years ago this week, Wes Boyd and Joan Blades, two California-based software developers (their company created the "Flying Toaster" screensaver), posted an online petition opposing the drive by congressional Republicans to impeach President Clinton. The one-sentence petition urged Congress instead to censure Clinton and "move on." Within days the couple had collected hundreds of thousands of names. Thus was formed MoveOn.org, the first true 21st-century political organization.

Born fighting, MoveOn has become the point of the spear for the Democratic Left through eight years of combat with President Bush over issues from Iraq to Social Security. No group has been more influential, innovative, or controversial in devising the Internet-based organizing strategies that are precipitating the new age of mass political participation symbolized by Obama's immense network of contributors and volunteers. "In the evolution of this, they were there at the very beginning," says veteran Democratic strategist Joe Trippi.

MoveOn's political impact must be measured on two levels: message and mechanics. The group's techniques draw praise in both parties. Boyd and Blades, and later Eli Pariser, a young organizer who has become MoveOn's leading force, recognized that the Internet created unprecedented opportunities for organizing. Traditionally, causes and candidates faced daunting expenses in trying to find like-minded people through advertising, direct mail, or canvassing. But the Internet reversed the equation: Once MoveOn established itself at the forefront of liberal activism, millions of people who shared its views found it at little (or no) cost to the group.

"Our observation was: Whenever we fight, we get stronger."

—Wes Boyd, MoveOn.org founder

Indeed, MoveOn quickly discovered that the more fights it pursued, the more names it collected—and the more it increased its capacity to undertake new campaigns. "There's this old model of political capital: Every time you fight, you are spending something," Boyd says. "Our observation was: Whenever we fight, we get stronger."

Fueled by this dynamic, MoveOn routinely generates levels of activity almost unimaginable not long ago. Since 1998, it has raised $120 million; it mobilized 70,000 volunteers for its get-out-the-vote effort in 2004, and might triple that number this year. It now stands at 4.2 million members, after adding 1 million, mostly through social-networking sites, this year.

The purposes to which MoveOn applies these vast resources are more debatable. The group has become a favored target for Republicans and a source of anxiety for some Democratic centrists, who worry that it points the party too far left. On domestic issues, it fits within the Democratic mainstream. But on national security, it defines the party's left flank. MoveOn resisted military action not only in Iraq but also in Afghanistan. And on both foreign and domestic concerns, it often frames issues in terms so polarizing that it risks alienating all but the most committed believers. The group's lowest moment came in 2007 when it bought a newspaper ad disparaging Gen. David Petraeus, the U.S. commander in Iraq, as "General Betray Us" on the grounds that he would attempt to mislead Congress about the war. Petraeus's brilliant subsequent progress in stabilizing

Iraq has only magnified the unseemliness of that accusation. "I wouldn't have done the headline the exact same way," Pariser now concedes.

Still, as candidates and groups in both parties adapt its strategies for online organizing, MoveOn can justly claim a central role in igniting the surge in grassroots activism that is transforming American politics. "Regardless of your political convictions, you have to feel like this is a very healthy thing for democracy," Pariser says. MoveOn's causes may divide, but Democrats and even many Republicans are increasingly uniting around the bottom-up vision of political change that these ardent activists have helped to revive.

Critical Thinking

1. On what two levels has MoveOn.org had the greatest political impact?
2. Why is MoveOn.org a target for Republicans and cause of concern among centrist Democrats?
3. How has MoveOn.org changed political activism?

Why They Lobby

WINTER CASEY

Thank You for Smoking, the 2005 film based on a novel by Christopher Buckley, follows the life of Nick Naylor, a chief spokesman for Big Tobacco with questionable morals, who makes his living defending the rights of smokers and cigarette-makers and then must deal with how his young son, Joey, views him. Naylor may have been a fictitious character, but Washington has its share of lobbyists arguing for the interests of industries with a perceived darker side.

The cynical response in Washington is that career decisions and political give-and-take revolve around money: Greenbacks triumph over ethics. There is little argument from lobbyists that their profession's financial rewards have an undeniable allure. But those who represent socially sensitive industries such as tobacco and alcohol have a lot more to say about why, out of all the potential job opportunities, they chose and often "love" what they do.

Representing "sin" industries, such as tobacco, alcohol, or gambling, can provide a challenge like no other.

For some, the job is a result of personal history or connections. For others, lobbying on behalf of a difficult industry provides a challenge like no other. They all make it a point to note that the First Amendment sanctions lobbying: "the right of the people . . . to petition the government for a redress of grievances."

Tobacco

In the film, Naylor works for the Academy of Tobacco Studies, which Buckley based on the Tobacco Institute, the industry's former trade association. Andrew Zausner, a partner at the firm Dickstein Shapiro (which occupies some of the Tobacco Institute's old space), is a registered lobbyist for Lorillard Tobacco, the Cigar Association of America, and Swisher International. He has been working on behalf of tobacco clients for nearly 30 years, ever since he fell into the industry when he was a partner at a New York City law firm that represented Pinkerton Tobacco.

Zausner feeds off the challenge of lobbying for tobacco interests. "The more unpopular the client, the better you have to be as a lobbyist," he declares. "Believing in your client's position

makes you a more forceful advocate." Although Zausner doesn't want his children to use tobacco, he notes that the "product has been continuously used in the United States before the United States existed" and says that the industry has a legitimate point of view and a constitutional right to express it.

Beau Schuyler lobbies for UST Public Affairs, a subsidiary of the holding company that owns U.S. Smokeless Tobacco and Ste. Michelle Wine Estates. A former congressional aide to two Democratic House members from his native state of North Carolina—in the heart of tobacco country—Schuyler says that the "opportunity to work internally at one of the oldest continually listed companies on the New York Stock Exchange was just too good to pass up."

Gambling

James Reeder, a lobbyist at Patton Boggs, has spent about half his time over the past decade representing the gambling industry. He insists he didn't seek out this niche, adding, "I tell my grandchildren that gambling is a bad habit . . . and to go fishing."

Shortly after Reeder joined Patton Boggs, a client named Showboat called the firm looking for someone who knew about Louisiana because the company was interested in building a casino there. Reeder happened to be from the Pelican State and was put on the case. He reasoned that Louisiana has always been a home to illegal gambling, and "if the culture of the state supports the industry, [the state] might as well make it legal and reap the benefits and get more tax money." Reeder eventually lobbied in about 17 states to get legislation passed to allow casinos—then mostly on riverboats.

"Whenever you take on one of these vices like booze or gambling and you just pass a law to say it is illegal," Reeder says, "you end up like in Prohibition, when the mob took over the liquor business."

Reeder excelled at lobbying for the gambling industry even though he avoids games of chance. "I don't gamble, because I am not a good card player," he says. "My friends would die laughing because I would go to offices to talk to clients on gambling and I would never go into a casino." If a lawmaker was morally opposed to gambling, Reeder wouldn't argue with him, he says.

John Pappas began working for the industry as a consultant for the Poker Players Alliance while at Dittus Communications. Then the alliance asked him to open its own Washington office.

Pappas calls poker a game of skill that has a rich history in America. He grew up playing cards with family members and friends, and noted during an interview that he would be playing poker with 20 lawmakers that evening at a charity tournament. "Responsibility in all aspects of life is paramount," he says.

Firearms

Richard Feldman's book, *Ricochet: Confessions of a Gun Lobbyist,* has been gaining the former National Rifle Association employee some attention recently. Feldman says that the gun control issue, like most, is not black and white. Working for the NRA, he says, "was the best job I ever had." The "huge power" he was able to wield "in the middle of major political battles" was more attractive to him at the time than the money he earned.

Feldman says he would sometimes play hardball but "didn't hit below the belt" in his pursuit of the gun industry's objectives. "Lobbying an issue that you have some special passion on (guns) is like waking up every day already having consumed a triple espresso," he said in an e-mail to *National Journal.* "On the other hand, if you can empathize with your client's position regardless of the issue, one can be a more convincing advocate, which I've always viewed as the more critical aspect of truly effective lobbying.

John Velleco ran his own painting company before he took a job in 1993 as an intern at the Gun Owners of America. Today, he is director of federal affairs for the 350,000-member group. "Most people, no matter what side of any particular issue they're on, don't always have the time to sort through what's happening in the D.C. sausage factory, so they depend on groups like GOA to keep them informed," he says. "Politicians may not like it, but my job is not to represent the views of the Congress to the people, but the views of American gun owners to the Congress."

Video Games

Because many video games contain a fair share of gunplay and other violence, Entertainment Software Association President Michael Gallagher has had to address complaints that playing violent games causes psychological harm such as increased aggression.

His group lobbies against "efforts to regulate the content of entertainment media in any form, including proposals to criminalize the sale of certain video games to minors; create uniform, government-sanctioned entertainment rating systems; or regulate the marketing practices of industry."

Gallagher, a former assistant Commerce secretary for communications and information in the Bush administration, calls video games a great form of family entertainment. The titles are responsibly rated, he says, and the gaming consoles have easy-to-use parental controls.

"I have been playing video games all my life," Gallagher says, including with his children. He contends that his industry "leads all forms of media when it comes to disclosure on what's in the game" and says that it works with retailers to "make sure minors can't buy games that are inappropriate for them."

Alcohol

Lobbyists who work for the beer, wine, and spirits industries have to deal with a host of negative images, among them drunk-driving accidents, underage drinking, and the effects of alcohol on health.

Lobbyists say their work is protected by the First Amendment—the right to "petition the government for a redress of grievances."

Mike Johnson, a lobbyist for the National Beer Wholesalers Association, acknowledges that alcohol is a "socially sensitive product" and says that is why the industry operates under strict government guidelines.

"I am blessed. I get to represent some great family-owned and -operated businesses that are very active in their communities and provide some really great jobs," Johnson says. "I am completely comfortable one day having a conversation with my son about who I work for, because I can tell him what a great job that beer distributors do in ensuring a safe marketplace and in protecting consumers from a lot of the problems we see with alcohol in other places in the world."

Craig Wolf, president of the Wine & Spirits Wholesalers, calls alcohol a "great social lubricant" that "creates great environments." Wolf got involved in wine-industry issues when he was counsel for the Senate Judiciary Committee. As his job there was ending, Wolf was offered the post of general counsel at the association; he took over as president in 2006.

"The key to advocating for a socially sensitive product is doing business responsibility," Wolf says. "We spend more time and resources [on the issue of] responsible consumption of alcohol then all other issues combined."

Distilled Spirits Council President Peter Cressy says, "I was interviewed for this position precisely because the Distilled Council wanted to continue and increase its very serious approach to fighting underage drinking." As chancellor of the University of Massachusetts (Dartmouth), Cressy says, he was active in "fighting binge drinking on campuses." The opportunity to join the council, which has lobbyists in 40 states, gave him the chance to have a national audience, he says. After nine years with the council, Cressy notes, he "has not been disappointed."

Snack Foods

Nicholas Pyle stands at the policy divide where junk food meets America's bulging waistlines. "I love my job," says Pyle, a lobbyist for McKee Foods, the makers of Little Debbie, America's leading snack-cake brand.

Many of the brand's affordable treats contain a dose of sugar, along with corn syrup, partially hydrogenated oil, bleached flour, and artificial flavor. Little Debbie "has been the target of a number of folks out there who want to paint people as a victim of the foods they eat," says Pyle, who is also president of the Independent Bakers Association. Little Debbie is a "wonderful food, great product, wholesome," with a wonderful image, he says. Pyle explains that he and his children enjoy the snacks.

"The big question of obesity is all about personal responsibility and people balancing [snacking] with a healthy and active lifestyle," Pyle insists. He contends that McKee, a family-owned business, doesn't target children in its marketing. "We market to the decision makers in the household," he says, adding that the company doesn't advertise on Saturday morning cartoon shows.

Snack Food Association President and CEO Jim McCarthy says that lobbying is one of his many duties as head of the organization. "Our belief is that all foods fit into the diet," McCarthy says, and "we don't like the term 'junk food.'" Products made by his segment of the industry—which include potato chips, party mix, corn snacks, snack cakes, and cookies—all contain natural ingredients such as vegetables, nuts, and fruit, he says.

The industry has developed healthier products over the years, McCarthy says, but at "certain times consumers haven't bought these products." He attributes the obesity problem to a lack of exercise and shortcomings in educating people about the need for a balanced diet.

Challenging Stereotypes

No matter what industry they represent, lobbyists interviewed for this article said that a good practitioner of their profession knows all sides of an issue, enabling lawmakers and their staffs to make the best-informed decision. "The system weeds out the bad actors, and the honest folks are the most successful and the longest-lasting," one lobbyist says.

Although many of the lobbyists acknowledge some familiar situations in *Thank You for Smoking,* they insist that the stereotypes are not altogether fair. "I think people don't understand the importance of lobbying to the system. If I don't explain what we do and I am not here to explain it to people, Congress will make uninformed decisions without understanding the consequences to the industry," a former liquor lobbyist says.

"Everyone draws the line in the sand about what they will or will not work on," says Don Goldberg, who leads the crisis communications practice at Qorvis Communications and was a key player on President Clinton's damage-response team. "The line is not set in stone.

"If you don't believe the points you are arguing are the best argument for your client and also that it's truthful, then you shouldn't be in this business," Goldberg continues. "I strongly believe in the First Amendment, [but] I don't believe the First Amendment is the reason to take on clients. The reason to take on clients is, they have a good story to tell and they are honest and reputable organizations."

But James Thurber, director of the Center for Congressional and Presidential Studies at American University, says that at the end of the day, money is a good explanation for why many lobbyists end up in their positions. This is especially true when it comes to tobacco, which was the leading preventable cause of disease and death in the United States in 2007, according to the Centers for Disease Control and Prevention.

For consumers, the message that lobbyists appear to be sending is that the individual is responsible for making the right choices in life. Yet the profusion of advertising, marketing ploys, political rhetoric, and seemingly conflicting studies can be bewildering. And although the financial incentive is ever-present, lobbyists believe they fill a fundamental role in society and deserve some relief from the negative stereotypes.

Critical Thinking

1. What are some of the reasons why lobbyists represent socially sensitive industries?
2. What role does financial compensation play in lobbyists' choice of career path?
3. How do lobbyists fulfill a fundamental role in society?

Tea Minus Zero

The tea party menace will not go quietly.

JOHN B. JUDIS

Liberals have responded to the Tea Party movement by reaching a comforting conclusion that there is no *way* these guys can possibly be for real. The movement has variously been described as a "front group for the Republican party" and a "media creation"; Paul Krugman has called Tea Party rallies "AstroTurf (fake grass roots) events, manufactured by the usual suspects."

I can understand why liberals would want to dismiss the Tea Party movement as an inauthentic phenomenon; it would certainly be welcome news if it were. The sentiments on display at Tea Party rallies go beyond run-of-the-mill anti-tax, anti-spending conservatism and into territory that rightly strikes liberals as truly disturbing. Among the signs I saw at an April 15 protest in Washington: **"If it sounds like Marx and acts like Stalin it must be Obama," "Stop Obama's brownshirt infiltraitors,"** and **"Obama bin lyin"** which was accompanied by an illustration of the president looking like a monkey.

But the Tea Party movement is not inauthentic, and—contrary to the impression its rallies give off—it isn't a fringe faction either. It is a genuine popular movement, one that has managed to unite a number of ideological strains from U.S. history—some recent, some older. These strains can be described as many things, but they cannot be dismissed as passing phenomena. Much as liberals would like to believe otherwise, there is good reason to think the Tea Party movement could exercise considerable influence over our politics in the coming years.

The movement essentially began on February 19, 2009, when CNBC commentator Rick Santelli, speaking from the floor of the Chicago Mercantile Exchange, let loose against the Obama administration's plan to help homeowners who could no longer pay their mortgages. "This is America!" Santelli exclaimed. "How many of you people want to pay for your neighbors' mortgage that has an extra bathroom and can't pay their bills?" Santelli called for a "Chicago Tea Party" to protest the administration's plan.

Santelli's appeal was answered by a small group of bloggers, policy wonks, and Washington politicos who were primarily drawn from the libertarian wing of the conservative movement.

They included John O'Hara from the Illinois Policy Institute (who has written a history of the movement, titled *A New American Tea Party*); Brendan Steinhauser of FreedomWorks, a Washington lobbying group run by former Representative Dick Armey; and blogger Michael Patrick Leahy, a founder of Top Conservatives on Twitter. The initial round of Tea Party protests took place at the end of February in over 30 cities. There were more protests in April, and, by the time of the massive September 12 protest last year, the Tea Party movement had officially arrived as a political force.

Like many American movements, the Tea Parties are not tightly organized from above. They are a network of local groups and national ones (Tea Party Patriots, Tea Party Express, Tea Party Nation), Washington lobbies and quasi-think tanks (FreedomWorks, Americans for Prosperity), bloggers, and talk-show hosts. There are no national membership lists, but extensive polls done by Quinnipiac, The Winston Group, and *Economist*/YouGov suggest that the movement commands the active allegiance of between 13 percent and 15 percent of the electorate. That is a formidable number, and, judging from other polls that ask whether someone has a "favorable" view of the Tea Parties, the movement gets a sympathetic hearing from as much as 40 percent of the electorate.

Tea Partiers' favorite politician is undoubtedly Sarah Palin—according to the *Economist*/YouGov poll, 71 percent of Tea Partiers think Palin "is more qualified to be president than Barack Obama" (and another 15 percent are "not sure")—but, more than anyone else, the movement takes its cues from Glenn Beck. Unlike fellow talkers Rush Limbaugh and Sean Hannity, Beck has never been a conventional Republican; he calls himself a conservative rather than a member of the GOP. While Limbaugh has attempted to soft-pedal his personal failings, the baby-faced Beck makes his into a story of redemption. He is, in his own words, an "average, everyday person." You need to have followed Beck's conspiratorial meanderings to understand what preoccupies many members of the Tea Party movement. At the Washington demonstration in April, for instance, there were people holding signs attacking Frances Fox Piven and Richard Cloward, two 1960s-era Columbia University sociologists who, Beck claims, were the brains behind both the community group ACORN and Obama's attempt to destroy capitalism by bankrupting the government through national health care reform.

In the last year, the movement's focus has shifted from demonstrations to elections. Currently, Tea Party groups are backing Republican Senate candidates in Kentucky, Utah, and Florida, while trying to knock off Democratic Senators Harry Reid in Nevada and Arlen Specter in Pennsylvania. In some places, Tea Party organizations have begun to displace the state GOP. Last month, Action is Brewing, the northern Nevada Tea Party affiliate, hosted a televised debate for the Republican gubernatorial and senatorial candidates. In addition, numerous candidates are running for Congress as Tea Party supporters.

The Tea Parties are the descendants of a number of conservative insurgencies from the past two generations: the anti-tax rebellion of the late '70s, the Moral Majority and Christian Coalition of the '80s and '90s, and Pat Buchanan's presidential runs. Like the Tea Partiers I saw in Washington—and the picture of the Tea Partiers put forward by the Winston and Quinnipiac polls—these movements have been almost entirely white, disproportionately middle-aged or older, and more male than female (though parts of the Christian right are an exception on this count). A majority of their adherents generally are not college-educated, with incomes in the middle range—attributes that also closely match the Tea Party movement's demographic profile. (A misleading picture of Tea Partiers as college-educated and affluent came from a *New York Times*/CBS poll of people who merely "support," but don't necessarily have anything to do with, the Tea Party movement. The other polls surveyed people who say they are "part of" the movement.)

Sociologists who have studied these earlier movements describe their followers as coming from the "marginal segments of the middle class." That's a sociological, but also a political, fact. These men and women look uneasily upward at corporate CEOs and investment bankers, and downward at low-wage service workers and laborers, many of whom are minorities. And their political outlook is defined by whether they primarily blame those below or above for the social and economic anxieties they feel. In the late nineteenth and early twentieth century, the marginal middle class was the breeding ground for left-wing attacks against Wall Street. For the last half-century, it has nourished right-wing complaints about blacks, illegal immigrants, and the poor.

It isn't just demography that the Tea Parties have in common with recent conservative movements; it's also politics. To be sure, some of the original Tea Party organizers were young libertarians, many of whom, like Brendan Steinhauser, voted for Ron Paul in 2008 and have rediscovered Ayn Rand's ethic of rational selfishness. They remain part of the movement—one sign I saw at the Washington rally read, **"we are john galt,"** referring to the hero of *Atlas Shrugged*—but, as the movement has grown, its adherents have become more conventionally conservative. As Grover Norquist likes to point out, what distinguishes one conservative group from another is not their

members' overall views, but what "moves" them to demonstrate or to vote. The Christian right, for instance, went to the barricades over abortion and gay marriage, yet most members also hold conservative economic views. Likewise, the Tea Partiers have been moved to action by economic issues, but they share the outlook of social conservatives. According to the *Economist*/YouGov poll, 74 percent of Tea Party members think abortion is "murder," and 81 percent are against gay marriage. Sixty-three percent are in favor of public school students learning that "the Book of Genesis in the Bible explains how God created the world"; 62 percent think that "the only way to Heaven is through Jesus Christ." These beliefs are on display at rallies: In Washington, one demonstrator in clerical garb held a sign saying, **"God Hates Taxes."** Moreover, aside from the followers of Ron Paul, Tea Party members also share the post-September 11 national security views of the GOP. When Tea Partiers were asked to name the "most important issue" to them, terrorism came in third out of ten, behind only the economy and the budget deficit.

If you look at the people who are running as pro–Tea Party candidates, you discover that some of them have simply graduated from one stage of the conservative movement to another. Jason Meade, who is running for Congress in Ohio, was just out of school, working in his father's business and playing music, when he "returned to the church and left the music world behind." Now 38, he sees his participation in Tea Party politics as a continuation of his 12 subsequent years in ministry school. "I decided to try and minister in a new way; by trying to be involved in the protection of the freedoms and liberty that God has given us and that have been woven into the fabric of our country," he wrote on his website. Jason Sager, 36, who is running in a Republican congressional primary northeast of Tampa, got into conservative politics in the wake of September 11. A Navy veteran, he joined a group called Protest Warrior that staged counter-demonstrations at antiwar rallies, and he was a volunteer in George W. Bush's 2004 campaign. After Obama's election, he got involved with Glenn Beck's 912 Project and, then, with the local Tea Parties.

But the Tea Parties' roots in U.S. history go back much further than the conservative movements of recent decades. The Tea Parties are defined by three general ideas that have played a key role in US politics since the country's early days the first is an obsession with decline. This idea, which traces back to the outlook of New England Puritans during the seventeenth century, consists of a belief that a golden age occurred some time ago; that we are now in a period of severe social, economic, or moral decay; that evil forces and individuals are the cause of this situation; that the goal of politics is to restore the earlier period; and that the key to doing so is heeding a special text that can serve as a guidebook for the journey backward. (The main difference between the far right and far left is that the left locates the golden age in the future.) The Puritans were trying to reproduce the circumstances of early Christianity in New England, using the Bible as their guiding text. Their enemies were Catholics and the Church of

England, who they believed had corrupted the religion. For the Tea Partiers, the golden age is the time of the Founders, and adherence to the Constitution is the means to restore this period in the face of challenges from secular humanism, radical Islam, and especially socialism.

Beck has been instrumental in sacralizing the Constitution. He has touted the works of the late W. Cleon Skousen, a John Birch Society defender who projected his ultraconservative views back onto the Founding Fathers. In *The 5000 Year Leap,* which has been reissued with a foreword by Beck, Skousen claimed that the Founders "warned against the 'welfare state'" and against "the drift toward the collectivist left."

In Arizona, Tea Party members hand out copies of the Constitution at political meetings the way a missionary group might hand out Bibles. The San Antonio Tea Party group has demanded that politicians sign a "contract with the Constitution." In speeches, Tea Partiers cite articles and amendments from the Constitution the same way that clerics cite Biblical verses. Speaking at the Lakeland Tea Party rally on tax day, Jason Sager said, "You are now able to see the most pressing issue that faces our nation and our society. Do you know what that issue is? We are now witnessing the fundamental breakdown of the republican form of government that we are guaranteed in Article Four, Section Four of our Constitution." In typical fashion, Sager did not go on to explain what Article Four, Section Four was. (You can look it up. I had to.)

Just as the Puritans believed Catholics and the Church of England were undermining Christianity, the Tea Partiers have fixated on nefarious individuals and groups—Saul Alinsky, **acorn,** and, of course, Obama himself—who they believe are destroying the country. (According to the *Economist*/YouGov poll, 52 percent of Tea Party members think **acorn** stole the 2008 election from John McCain; another 24 percent are still not sure.) "America has let thieves into her home," writes Beck, "and that nagging in your gut is a final warning that our country is about to be stolen." Their determination to locate the threat outside the United States accounts for their emphasis on Obama being a socialist, Marxist, communist, or even fascist—all of which are foreign faiths—rather than what he is: a conventional American liberal. It also helps explain the repeated references to Obama's African father. And it explains why some Tea Partiers continue to believe, in the face of incontrovertible evidence, that Obama was born outside the United States. The *Economist*/YouGov poll found that 34 percent of Tea Party members think he was not born in the United States, and another 34 percent are not sure.

But how could a movement that cultivates such crazy, conspiratorial views be regarded favorably by as much as 40 percent of the electorate? That is where the Tea Party movement's second link to early U.S. history comes in. The Tea Partiers may share the Puritans' fear of decline, but it is what they share with Thomas Jefferson that has far broader appeal: a staunch anti-statism. What began as a sentiment of the left—a rejection of state monopolies—became, after the industrial revolution and the rise of the labor movement, a weapon against progressive reforms. The basic idea—that government is a "necessary evil"—has retained its power, and, when the

economy has faltered, Americans have been quick to blame Washington, perhaps even before they looked at Wall Street or big corporations. It happened in the late '70s under Jimmy Carter and in the early '90s under George H.W. Bush; and it has happened again during Obama's first 18 months in office. According to a Pew poll, the percentage of Americans "angry" with government has risen from 10 percent in February 2000 to 21 percent today, while another 56 percent are "frustrated" with government.

Of course, during Franklin Roosevelt's first term, most voters didn't blame the incumbent administration for the Great Depression. Roosevelt was able to deflect blame for the depression back onto the Hoover administration and the "economic royalists" of Wall Street and corporate America. But Roosevelt took office at the nadir of the Great Depression, and his policies achieved dramatic improvements in unemployment and economic growth during his first term. Obama took office barely four months after the financial crisis visibly hit, and he has had to preside over growing unemployment.

Simmering economic frustration also accounts for the final historical strain that defines the Tea Parties: They are part of a tradition of producerism that dates to Andrew Jackson. Jacksonian Democrats believed that workers should enjoy the fruits of what they produce and not have to share them with the merchants and bankers who didn't actually create anything. The Populists of the late nineteenth century invoked this ethic in denouncing the Eastern bankers who held their farms hostage. Producerism also underlay Roosevelt's broadsides against economic royalists and Bill Clinton's promise to give priority to those who "work hard and play by the rules."

During the 1970s, conservatives began invoking producerism to justify their attacks on the welfare state, and it was at the core of the conservative tax revolt. While the Jacksonians and Populists had largely directed their anger upward, conservatives directed their ire at the people below who were beneficiaries of state programs—from the "welfare queens" of the ghetto to the "illegal aliens" of the barrio. Like the attack against "big government," this conservative producerism has most deeply resonated during economic downturns. And the Tea Parties have clearly built their movement around it.

Producerism was at the heart of Santelli's rant against government forcing the responsible middle class to subsidize those who bought homes they couldn't afford. In his history of the Tea Party movement, O'Hara described an America divided between "moochers, big and small, corporate and individual, trampling over themselves with their hands out demanding endless bailouts" and "disgusted, hardworking citizens getting sick of being played for chumps and punished for practicing personal responsibility." The same theme recurs in the Tea Partiers' rejection of liberal legislation. Beck dismissed Obama's health care reform plan as "good old socialism . . . raping the pocketbooks of the rich to give to the poor." Speaking to cheers at the April 15 rally in Washington, Armey denounced the progressive income tax in the same terms. "I can't steal your money and give it to this guy," he declared. "Therefore, I shouldn't use the power of the state to steal your money and give it to this guy."

The Tea Parties are not managed by the Republican National Committee, and they are not really a wing of the GOP. It is telling that Beck devoted his February speech at the Conservative Political Action Conference to bashing Republicans—and that, in a survey of 50 Tea Party leaders, the Sam Adams Alliance found that 28 percent identify themselves as Independents and 11 percent as Tea Party members rather than Republicans. Still, the Tea Partiers' political objective is clearly to push the GOP to the right. They agitated last summer for a Republican party-line vote against health care reform and are now arguing that states have a constitutional right to refuse to comply with it. They have been calling the offices of Republican senators to demand that they oppose a bipartisan compromise on financial regulatory reform. In South Carolina, they have attacked Senator Lindsey Graham, who is also a favorite Beck target, for backing a cap-and-trade bill. The Arizona Tea Party pressured Governor Jan Brewer to sign the now-infamous bill targeting illegal immigrants. And Tea Party Nation has issued a "Red Alert" to prevent Congress from adopting "amnesty" legislation.

If the GOP wins back at least one house of Congress in November, the Tea Parties will be able to claim victory and demand a say in Republican congressional policies. That could lead to a replay of the Newt Gingrich Congress of 1995–1996, from which the country was lucky to escape relatively unscathed. But, beyond this, it's hard to say what will become of the movement. If the economy improves in a significant way next year, it is likely to fade. That is what happened to the tax revolt, which peaked from 1978 to 1982 and then subsided. But if the economy limps along—say, in the manner of Japan over the last 15 years—then the Tea Parties will likely remain strong, and may even become a bigger force in U.S. politics than they are now.

For all of its similarities to previous insurgencies, the Tea Party movement differs in one key respect from the most prominent conservative movement of recent years, the Christian right: The Tea Parties do not have the same built-in impediments to growth. The Christian right looked like it was going to expand in the early '90s, but it ran up against the limit of its politics, which were grounded ultimately in an esoteric theology and a network of churches. If it strayed too far from the implications of that theology, it risked splitting its membership. But, if it articulated it—as Pat Robertson and others did at various inopportune moments—then it risked alienating the bulk of Americans. The Tea Parties do not have the same problem. They have their own crazy conspiracy theories, but even the wackiest Tea Partiers wouldn't demand that a candidate seeking their endorsement agree that **acorn** fixed the election or that Obama is foreign-born. And their core appeal on government and spending will continue to resonate as long as the economy sputters. None of this is what liberals want to hear, but we might as well face reality: The Tea Party movement—firmly grounded in a number of durable U.S. political traditions and well-positioned for a time of economic uncertainty—could be around for a while.

Critical Thinking

1. What factors suggest that the Tea Party will continue to be influential in American politics?
2. Identify the three main ideas that define the Tea Party movement.
3. What is the ultimate political aim of the Tea Party? What implications does it have for the Republican Party's agenda?
4. In what key way does today's Tea Party movement differ from the conservative Christian right movement of recent years?

The Revolution Will Not Be Published

Why we must shift our attention from "save newspapers" to "save society."

CLAY SHIRKY

In 1993 the Knight-Ridder newspaper chain began investigating piracy of Dave Barry's popular column, which was published by the *Miami Herald* and syndicated widely. In the course of tracking down the sources of unlicensed distribution, they found many things, including the copying of his column on usenet; a 2,000-person mailing list also reading pirated versions; and a teenager in the Midwest who was doing some of the copying himself, because he loved Barry's work so much he wanted everybody to be able to read it.

One of the people I was hanging around with online back then was Gordy Thompson, who managed Internet services at the *New York Times.* I remember Thompson saying something like, *When a 14-year-old kid can blow up your business in his spare time, not because he hates you but because he loves you, then you got a problem.*

I think about that conversation a lot these days.

The problem newspapers face isn't that they didn't see the Internet coming. They not only saw it miles off, they figured out early on that they needed a plan to deal with it, and during the early '90s they came up with not just one scheme but several.

One was to partner with companies like America Online, a fast-growing subscription service that was less chaotic than the open Internet. Another approach was to educate the public about the behaviors required of them by copyright law. New payment models such as micropayments were proposed. Alternatively, newspapers could pursue the profit margins enjoyed by radio and TV, if they became purely ad-supported. Still another plan was to convince tech firms to make their hardware and software less capable of sharing, or to partner with the businesses running data networks to achieve the same goal. Then there was the nuclear option: educate the public about copyright law and sue those who break it, making an example of them.

In all this conversation, there was one scenario that was widely regarded as unthinkable: that the ability to share content wouldn't shrink, it would grow.

Walled-off content would prove unpopular. Digital advertising would reduce inefficiencies, and therefore profits. Dislike of micropayments would prevent widespread use. People would resist being educated to act against their own desires. Old habits of advertisers and readers would not transfer online. Even

ferocious litigation would be inadequate to constrain massive, sustained law-breaking.

Revolutions create a curious inversion of perception. In ordinary times, people who describe the world around them are seen as pragmatists, while those who imagine fabulous alternative futures are viewed as radicals. The last couple of decades haven't been ordinary, however. Inside the papers, the pragmatists were the ones simply looking out the window and noticing that the real world was increasingly resembling the unthinkable scenario. These people were treated as if they were barking mad. Meanwhile, the people envisioning micropayments and lawsuits, visions unsupported by reality, were regarded not as charlatans but as saviors.

When reality is labeled unthinkable, it creates a kind of sickness in an industry. Leadership becomes faith-based, while employees who have the temerity to disagree are herded into Innovation Departments, where they can be ignored enmasse. This shunting aside of the realists in favor of the fabulists has different effects on different industries at different times. One of the effects on newspapers is that many of their most passionate defenders are unable, even now, to plan for a world in which the industry they knew is visibly going away.

The curious thing about the various plans hatched in the '90s is that they were, at base, all the same plan. The details differed, but the core assumption behind all imagined outcomes was that the organizational form of the newspaper, as a general-purpose vehicle for publishing a variety of news and opinion, was basically sound, and only needed a digital facelift. As a result, the conversation has degenerated into enthusiastic grasping at straws, pursued by skeptical responses.

"The *Wall Street Journal* has a paywall, so we can too!" (Financial information is one of the few kinds of information whose recipients don't want to share.) "Micropayments work for iTunes, so they will work for us!" (Micropayments work only where the provider can avoid competitive business models.) "The *New York Times* should charge for content!" (They've tried, with qPass and later TimesSelect.) "*Cook's Illustrated* and

Consumer Reports are doing fine on subscriptions!" (Those publications forgo ad revenues; users are paying not just for content but for unimpeachability.)

Round and round this goes, with the people committed to saving newspapers demanding to know "If the old model is broken, what will work in its place?" To which the answer is: Nothing. There is no general model with which newspapers can replace the one the Internet just broke.

With the old economics destroyed, organizational forms perfected for print production have to be replaced with structures optimized for digital data. It makes increasingly less sense even to talk about a publishing industry, because the core problem it solves—the difficulty, complexity, and expense of making something available to the public—has stopped being a problem.

Elizabeth Eisenstein's magisterial treatment of Gutenberg's invention, *The Printing Press as an Agent of Change,* first published in 1979, opens with a recounting of her research into the early history of the printing press. She was able to find many descriptions of life in the early 1400s, the era before movable type. Literacy was limited, the Catholic Church was the pan-European political force, Mass was in Latin, and the average book was the Bible. She was also able to find endless descriptions of life in the late 1500s, after Gutenberg's invention had started to spread. Literacy was on the rise, as were books written in contemporary languages, Copernicus had published his epochal work on astronomy, and Martin Luther's use of the press to reform the Church was upending both religious and political stability.

What Eisenstein focused on, however, was not a description of what the world looked like before and after the spread of print—that's child's play, and all too typical in most historical texts on the subject. She chose instead to analyze how we got from one era to the next.

It was, as it turns out, chaotic. When the Bible was translated into local languages some people saw it as an educational boon, others as the work of the devil. Erotic novels appeared, prompting the same sort of response. Copies of Aristotle and Galen circulated widely, but direct encounter with the relevant texts revealed that the two sources clashed, tarnishing faith in the Ancients. As novelty spread, old institutions seemed exhausted while new ones seemed untrustworthy; as a result, people almost literally didn't know what to think. If you can't trust Aristotle, who can you trust?

Only in retrospect were experiments undertaken during the wrenching transition to print revealed to be turning points. Aldus Manutius, a Venetian printer and publisher, invented the smaller octavo volume. What seemed like a minor change—take a book and shrink it—was in retrospect a key innovation in the democratization of the printed word. As books became cheaper, more portable, and therefore more desirable, they expanded the market for all publishers, heightening the value of literacy still further.

That is what real revolutions are like. The old stuff gets broken faster than the new stuff is put in its place. The importance of any given experiment isn't apparent at the moment it appears; big changes stall, small changes spread. Ancient social bargains, once disrupted, can be neither mended nor quickly replaced, since any such bargain takes decades to solidify.

And so it is today. When people demand to know how we are going to replace newspapers, they are really demanding to be told that we are not living through a revolution. They are demanding to be told that old systems won't break before new systems are in place. They are demanding to be told that ancient social bargains aren't in peril, that core institutions will be spared, that new methods of spreading information will improve previous practice rather than upending it. They are demanding to be lied to.

There are fewer and fewer people who can convincingly tell such a lie.

If you want to know why newspapers are in such trouble, the most salient fact is this: Printing presses are terrifically expensive to set up and to run. This bit of economics, normal since Gutenberg, limits competition while creating positive returns to scale for the press owner, a happy pair of economic effects that feed on each other.

In a notional town with two perfectly balanced newspapers, one paper would eventually generate some small advantage—a breaking story, a key interview—at which point both advertisers and readers would come to prefer it, however slightly. That paper would in turn find it easier to capture the next dollar of advertising, at lower expense, than the competition. This would increase its dominance, which would further deepen those preferences, repeat chorus.

For a long time, longer than anyone in the newspaper business has been alive, in fact, print journalism has been intertwined with these economics. The expense of printing created an environment where Wal-Mart was willing to subsidize the Baghdad bureau. This wasn't because of any deep link between advertising and reporting, nor was it about any real desire on the part of Wal-Mart to have its marketing budget go to international correspondents. It was just an accident. Advertisers had little choice other than to have their money used that way, since they didn't really have any other vehicle for display ads.

The competition-deflecting effects of printing cost got destroyed by the Internet, where everyone pays for the infrastructure, and then everyone gets to use it. And when Wal-Mart, and the local Maytag dealer, and the law firm hiring a secretary, and that kid down the block selling his bike, were all able to use that infrastructure to get out of their old relationship with the publisher, they did. They'd never really signed up to fund the Baghdad bureau anyway.

Newspaper people argue that their labor benefits society as a whole. This is true. But "you're gonna miss us when we're gone" has never been much of a business model.

People in the newspaper business often note that their labor benefits society as a whole. This is true, but irrelevant to the problem at hand; "you're gonna miss us when we're gone" has never been much of a business model.

It's true that the print media do much of society's heavy journalistic lifting, from teasing out every angle of a huge story to the grind of attending the city council meeting, in case something happens. This coverage is beneficial even for people who aren't newspaper readers, because the work of print journalists is used by everyone from politicians to district attorneys to talk radio hosts to bloggers.

So who will cover that city council meeting when the newspaper reporter on that beat loses her job?

I don't know. Nobody knows. The Internet turns 40 this fall. Public access is less than half that age. Web use, as a normal part of life for a majority of the developed world, is less than half *that* age. We just got here. Even the revolutionaries can't predict what will happen.

Imagine, in 1996, asking some Net-savvy soul to expound on the potential of craigslist, then just a year old and not yet incorporated. The answer you'd almost certainly have gotten would be extrapolation: "Mailing lists can be powerful tools," "Social effects are intertwining with digital networks," etc. What no one would have told you, could have told you, was what actually happened: Craiglist became a critical piece of infrastructure. Not the idea of craigslist, or the business model, or even the software driving it. Craigslist itself spread to cover hundreds of cities and has become a part of public consciousness about what is now possible. Only in retrospect are experiments revealed to be turning points.

Society doesn't need newspapers. What we need is journalism. For a century, the imperatives to strengthen journalism and to strengthen newspapers have been so tightly bound together as to be indistinguishable. That's been a fine accident, but when that accident stops, as it is stopping before our eyes, we're going to need lots of other ways to strengthen journalism.

When we shift our attention from "save newspapers" to "save society," the imperative changes from "preserve current institutions" to "do whatever works"—and what works today isn't the same as what used to work.

We don't know who the Aldus Manutius of the current age is. It could be Craig Newmark, or Caterina Fake. It could be Martin Nisenholtz, or Emily Bell. It could be some 19-year-old kid few of us have heard of, working on something we won't recognize as vital until a decade hence. Any experiment, though, designed to provide new models for journalism is going to be an improvement over hiding from the real, especially in a year when, for many papers, the unthinkable future is already in the past.

For the next few decades, journalism will be made up of overlapping special cases. Many of these models will rely on amateurs as researchers and writers. Many of these models will rely on sponsorship or grants or endowments instead of revenues. Many of these models will rely on excitable 14-year-olds distributing the results. Many of these models will fail. No one experiment is going to replace what we are now losing with the demise of news on paper, but over time, the collection of new experiments that do work might give us the journalism we need.

Critical Thinking

1. How have the public's access to and attitudes toward accessing online news content manifested in the past decade? How does this behavior differ from those in the industry that were planned for?

2. Why has the concept of a publishing industry become outmoded in the internet age?

3. What is the primary reason traditional newspapers are at risk?

4. What are the societal benefits of traditional print news coverage? How might these benefits continue in the new era of online journalism?

CLAY SHIRKY, an adjunct professor at New York University's graduate program in interactive telecommunications, has written extensively about the Internet since 1996. His essays on the online experience have been featured in publications such as the *New York Times, Wired,* and *Harvard Business Review.* His critically acclaimed book *Here Comes Everybody: The Power of Organizing Without Organizations* was published by Penguin in 2008. Excerpted from a post on the author's website (March 13, 2009); www.shirky.com.

Build the Wall

Most readers won't pay for news, but if we move quickly, maybe enough of them will. One man's bold blueprint.

DAVID SIMON

To all of the bystanders reading this, pardon us. The true audience for this essay narrows necessarily to a pair of notables who have it in their power to save high-end journalism—two newspaper executives who can rescue an imploding industry and thereby achieve an essential civic good for the nation. It's down to them. The rest of the print journalism world is in slash-and-burn mode, cutting product and then wondering why the product won't sell, rushing to give away what remains online and wondering further why that content is held by advertisers to be valueless. The mode is full-bore panic.

And yet these two individuals, representing as they do the two fundamental institutions that sit astride the profession, still have a card to play, and here's a shard of good news: it's the only card that ever really mattered. Arthur Sulzberger Jr. and Katharine Weymouth, publishers of *The New York Times* and *The Washington Post,* are at the helms of two organizations trying to find some separate peace with the digital revolution, though both papers have largely failed to do so, damaging their own still-formidable institutions and, on a deeper level, eviscerating more vulnerable regional newspapers and newspapering as whole. Yet incredibly, they delay, even though every day of inertia means another two dozen reporters somewhere are shown the door by a newspaper chain, or another foreign bureau closes, or another once-precise and competent newsroom decides it will make do without a trained city editor, an ombudsman, or a fully staffed copy desk.

This then, is for Mr. Sulzberger and Ms. Weymouth:

Content matters. And you must find a way, in the brave new world of digitization, to make people pay for that content. If you do this, you still have a product and there is still an industry, a calling, and a career known as professional journalism. If you do not find a way to make people pay for your product, then you are—if you choose to remain in this line of work—delusional.

I know that content wants to be free on the Internet. I know that the horse was long ago shown the barn door and that, belatedly, the idea of creating a new revenue stream from online subscriptions seems daunting and dangerous. I know that commentary—the froth and foam of print journalism—sells itself cheaply and well on thousands of blogs. I know that the relationships between newspapers and online aggregators—not to mention The Associated Press and Reuters—will have to be revisited and revised. True, all true.

Most of all, I know that here you are being individually asked to consider taking a bold, risk-laden stand for content—that antitrust considerations prohibit the *Times* and the *Post,* not to mention Rupert Murdoch or the other owners, from talking this through and acting in concert. Would that every U.S. newspaper publisher could meet in a bathroom somewhere and talk bluntly for fifteen minutes, this would be a hell of a lot easier. And yes, I know that if one of you should try to go behind the paywall while the other's content remains free, then, yes, you would be destroyed. All that is apparent.

But also apparent is the fact that absent a radical revisiting of the dynamic between newspapering and the Internet, there will be little cohesive, professional, first-generation journalism at the state and local level, as your national newspapers continue to retrench and regional papers are destroyed outright.

You must act. Together. On a specific date in the near future—let's say September 1 for the sheer immediacy of it—both news organizations must inform readers that their websites will be free to subscribers only, and that while subscription fees can be a fraction of the price of having wood pulp flung on doorsteps, it is nonetheless a requirement for acquiring the contents of the news organizations that spend millions to properly acquire, edit, and present that work.

No half-measures, either. No TimesSelect program that charges for a handful of items and offers the rest for free, no limited availability of certain teaser articles, no bartering with aggregators for a few more crumbs of revenue through microbilling or pennies-on-the-dollar fees. Either you believe that what The *New York Times* and *The Washington Post* bring to the table every day has value, or you don't.

You must both also individually inform the wire-service consortiums that unless they limit membership to publications, online or off, that provide content only through paid subscriptions, you intend to withdraw immediately from those consortiums. Then, for good measure, you might each make a voluntary donation—let's say $10 million—to a newspaper trade group to establish a legal fund to pursue violations of copyright, either by online aggregators or large-scale blogs, much in the way other industries based on intellectual property have fought to preserve their products.

And when the Justice Department lawyers arrive, briefcases in hand, to ask why America's two national newspapers did these things in concert—resulting in a sea change within newspapering as one regional newspaper after another followed suit in pursuit of fresh, lifesaving revenue—you can answer directly: We never talked. Not a word. We read some rant in the *Columbia Journalism Review* that made the paywall argument. Blame the messenger.

Truth is, a halting movement toward the creation of an online subscription model already exists; at this writing, internal discussions at both the *Times* and the *Post* are ongoing, according to sources at both papers. And one small, furtive, and cautious meeting of newspaper executives took place in Chicago in May to explore the general idea of charging for online distribution of news. As for Rupert Murdoch, his rethought decision not to freely offer *The Wall Street Journal* online speaks volumes, as do his recent trial balloons about considering an online subscription model for less unique publications. Where the *Times* and the *Post* lead, Murdoch and, ultimately, every desperate and starving newspaper chain will simply follow. Why? Because the need to create a new revenue stream from the twenty-first century's information-delivery model is, belatedly, apparent to many in the industry. But no one can act if the *Times* and the *Post* do not; the unique content of even a functional regional newspaper—state and municipal news, local sports and culture—is insufficient to demand that readers pay online. But add to that the national and international coverage from the national papers that would no longer be available on the Internet for free but could be provided through participation in the news services of the *Times* and the *Post* and, finally, there is a mix of journalism that justifies a subscription fee.

Time is the enemy, however, and the wariness and caution with which the *Times* and the *Post* approach the issue reveal not only how slow industry leaders have been to accurately assess the realities, but how vulnerable one national newspaper is to the other. Should the *Times* go behind a pay curtain while the Post remains free, or vice versa, the result would be a short-term but real benefit to the newspaper that fails to act, and fiscal bleeding for the newspaper attempting to demand recompense for work that is elsewhere being provided free of charge. Neither the *Times* nor the *Post* can do this alone.

Will it work? Is there enough demand for old-line, high-end journalism in the age of new media? Will readers pay for what they have already accepted as free? And can industry leaders claw their way back in time to the fateful point when they mistook the Internet as a mere advertising opportunity for their product?

Perhaps, though the risks are not spread equally. Given the savage cutting that has been under way at regional, chain-owned newspapers over the last decade or more, it may be too late for some metro dailies; they may no longer have enough legitimate, unique content to compel their readership to pay. But for the *Times* and the *Post*—entities that are still providing the lion's share of journalism's national, international, and cultural relevance—their reach has never been greater.

The proof is that while online aggregation and free newspaper websites have combined to batter paid print circulation figures, more people are reading the product of America's newspapers than ever before. Certainly more of them are reading the *Times* (nearly 20 million average unique visitors monthly) and the *Post* (more than 10 million monthly unique visitors), though they are doing it online and not paying for the privilege. And tellingly, the *Times*—its product still unmatched in print or online by other mainstream publications or anything that new media has yet offered—has transformed its print circulation into a profit center for the first time in years, merely by jacking up the price, with newsstand prices rising in June to $2 and up to $6 on Sunday.

Clearly, the product still moves. But to what purpose, when more and more readers rightly identify the immediate digitized version as superior, yet pay nothing for that version, and online advertising simply doesn't deliver enough revenue? If the only way to read the *Times* is to buy the *Times,* online or off, then readers who clearly retain a desire for that product will reach for their wallets. And those comfortable acquiring their news at a keyboard will be happy to pay much less than they do for home delivery.

No doubt some mavens of new media who have read this far have spittle in the corners of their mouths at the thought of the dying, tail-dragging dinosaurs of mainstream journalism resurrecting themselves by making the grand tool of the revolution—the Internet—less free. There is no going backward, they will declare, affronted by the idea that a victory already claimed can even be questioned. The newspaper is all but dead, they will insist. Long live the citizen journalist.

Not so fast. While their resentment and frustration with newspapers—given the industry's reduced editorial ambitions—are justified, their reasoning and conclusions are not. A little history:

For the first thirty years of its existence as America's primary entertainment medium, television was—after the initial purchase of the set itself—provided at no cost to viewers, instead subsidized by lucrative ad revenues. The notion of Americans in 1975 being asked to pay a monthly bill for their television consumption would have seemed farcical. Yet in the ensuing thirty years, we have become a nation that shells out $60, $70, or $120 in monthly cable fees; indeed, whole vistas of programming exist free of advertising revenue, subsidized entirely by subscriptions.

How did this happen?

Again, content is all. The move to the pay-cable model was preceded by an expansive effort to create additional programming to justify the upgrade from network fare to multichannel packaging. In the beginning, some of that new content amounted to little more than feature-film purchases, additional sports, and twenty-four-hour news and weather. But ultimately, the quantitative increase in programming was accompanied by a qualitative improvement in television fare. You paid more, you got more: HBO, Showtime, Cinemax, and, ultimately, a string of niche channels catering to specific audiences and interests. One can critique American TV however ruthlessly one wishes, but the industry is doing something right. More channels, more programming, more revenue—indeed, a revenue stream where none had existed.

By contrast, we have American newspapering, an industry that a quarter century ago was—pound for pound—as lucrative as television, with Wall Street commanding profit margins of 25 and 30 percent. As with television, circulation was accepted as a loss leader, strongly subsidized so that the money it cost to deliver content was more than made up by advertising dollars.

But unlike television, in which industry leaders were constantly reinvesting profits in research and development, where a new technology like cable reception would be contemplated for all its potential and opportunity, the newspapering world was content to send its treasure to Wall Street, appeasing analysts and big-ticket shareholders. There was no reinvestment in programming, no intelligent contemplation of new and transformational circulation models, no thought beyond maximized short-term profit.

Incredibly, and in direct contrast to the growth of television, the remaining monopoly newspapers in American cities—roped together in unwieldy chains and run by men and women who had, by and large, been reared in boardrooms rather than newsrooms—spent the last of their profitable days *cutting* product, scaling back news holes, shedding veteran reporters, and reducing the scope of coverage. Hiring freezes and buyouts were ongoing in the early and mid-1990s, all of this happening amid the unspoken assumptions that the advertising base was everything, that content didn't really matter, that news was the stuff troweled into the columns next to the display ads, that there was more profit producing a half-assed, mediocre paper than a good one.

In the 1970s, American auto manufacturing was complicit in its own marginalization through exactly the same mindset: Why not churn out Pacers and Gremlins and Vegas, providing cheap, shoddy vehicles that would be rapidly replaced with newer cheap, shoddy vehicles? What would captive American consumers do? Buy a car from Japan? Germany? South Korea?

Well, yes, as it turns out. But the analogy doesn't quite capture the extraordinary incompetence exhibited by the newspaper industry. After all, a Toyota is a good car and all that was required for Detroit to begin its agonizing decline was for consumers to be offered a legitimate choice.

In the newspaper industry, however, the fledgling efforts of new media to replicate the scope, competence, and consistency of a healthy daily paper have so far yielded little in the way of genuine competition. A blog here, a citizen journalist there, a news website getting under way in places where the newspaper is diminished—some of it is quite good, but none of it so far begins to achieve consistently what a vibrant newspaper, staffed with competent, paid beat reporters and editors, once offered. New-media entities are not yet able to truly cover—day after day—the society, culture, and politics of cities, states, and nations. And until new models emerge that are capable of

paying reporters and editors to do such work—in effect becoming online newspapers with all the gravitas this implies—they are not going to get us anywhere close to professional journalism's potential.

Detroit lost to a better, new product; newspapers, to the vague suggestion of one.

Beyond Mr. Sulzberger and Ms. Weymouth—and yes, get cracking, you two; September comes fast—there is, in retrospect, a certain wonderment that so many otherwise smart people in newspapering could have so mistaken the Internet and its implications. A lot has been written on this phenomenon and more will follow, but three factors are worth noting—if only because of their relevance to the online subscription model that is clearly required:

First, there is the familiar industrial dynamic in which leaders raised in one world are taken aback to find they have underestimated the power of an emerging paradigm.

When I left my newsroom in 1995, the Internet was a mere whisper, but even five years later, as its potential was becoming a consideration in every other aspect of American life, those in command of *The Baltimore Sun* were explaining the value of their free website in these terms: this is advertising for the newspaper. Young readers will see what we do by "surfing the Web" and finding our site, and they will read some, and then settle down and buy the newspaper.

Looking back, it sounds comical. Absent the buyouts and layoffs and lost coverage of essential issues, it would be buggy-whip-maker funny. But as it stands, the misapprehension of men and women who spent their lives believing in the primacy of newsprint is as tragic as the strategists who built battleships even after Billy Mitchell used air power to bomb one to the ocean floor in 1921. Regardless, it was industry-wide in newsrooms. On the business side, they were a little busy hurling profits at Wall Street to pay much attention.

Second, the industry leaders on both the business and editorial sides came of age in an environment in which circulation had long been a loss leader, when newspapers never charged readers what it actually cost to get the product to their doorstep. Advertising, not content, was all.

This specific dynamic maximized everyone's blindness to the real possibilities of a subscription model. Every reader who can be induced to accept an online subscription to a newspaper—at even a half or a third the price of doorstep delivery—represents the beginning of a new and quite profitable revenue stream.

For example, if *The Baltimore Sun*'s product isn't available in any other fashion than through subscription—online or off—and if there is no profit to be had in delivering the paper product to homes at existing rates, then by all means, jack up those rates—raise hard-copy prices and drive as many readers as possible online, where you charge less, but at a distinct profit.

Yes, you would lose readers. But consider: 10 percent of the existing 210,000 *Baltimore Sun* readers, for example, who pay a subscription rate less than half the price of home delivery, or roughly $10, would represent about $2.5 million a year. Absent the cost of trucks, gas, paper, and presses, money like that represents the beginnings of a solid revenue stream. In the same fashion, the first handful of subscribers to HBO watched bad movies and boxing, but as the revenue grew, it paid for original programming and, ultimately, a vast expansion of product. First, someone had to dream it. At newspapers, no one did. Newspaper dreams of the last fifty years involved luscious department-store display ads and fat classified sections—visions that can no longer be.

Last, and perhaps most disastrous, the rot began at the bottom and it didn't reach the highest rungs of the profession until far too much damage had been done.

As early as the mid-1980s, the civic indifference and contempt of product inherent in chain ownership was apparent in many smaller American markets. While this was discussed in some circles, usually as a matter of mild rumination, little was done by the industry to address a dynamic by which men in Los Angeles or Chicago or New York, at the behest of Wall Street, determined what sort of journalism would be practiced in Baltimore, Denver, Hartford, or Dallas. If you happened to labor at a newspaper that was ceding its editorial ambition to the price-per-share, it may have been agony, but if you were at the *Times,* the *Post, The Wall Street Journal,* or the *Los Angeles Times,* you were insulated. As the Internet arrived, profit margins were challenged and buyouts began at even the largest, most viable monopoly papers in regional markets. But only when the disease reached their own newsrooms did it really matter to the big papers.

Last year at *The Washington Post,* the paper's first major buyout arrived at about the time of its six Pulitzer victories. The day the prizes were announced, newsroom staffers publicly predicted that such winning journalism would likely not be replicated at the *Post* in an era of cutbacks. This, they moaned, might be the newspaper's last great prize haul. But of course the buyout of one hundred reporters at the *Post,* while painful and damaging, represented a bit more than a 10 percent reduction in force. At that point, the loss of the same number of reporters at *The Baltimore Sun* would have been a 30 percent reduction. The *Sun,* at this point, has had about eight rounds of buyouts and layoffs, beginning well before the arrival of the Internet, dropping the editorial staff from 500 to 160. Given that kind of carnage, there was no need for the *Post* to have any prize-based worries. In the end, the *Times,* the *Post,* and the *Journal* will be taking up more seats at the Pulitzer luncheon, not fewer. With whom, after all, do they think they are still competing?

The cancer devouring journalism began somewhere below the knee, and by the time the disease reached the self-satisfied brain of the Washington and New York newsrooms, the prognosis was far worse. Or to employ another historical metaphor: when they came for the Gannett papers, I said nothing, because I was not at a Gannett paper.

For the industry, it is later than it should be; where a transition to online pay models would once have been easier with a healthy product, now the odds for some papers are long. But given the timeline, here are a few possible outcomes, if the *Times* and the *Post* go ahead and build that wall.

First scenario: The *Times* and the *Post* survive, their revenue streams balanced by still-considerable print advertising, the bump in the price of home delivery and newsstand sales, and, finally, a new influx of cheap yet profitable online subscriptions.

And reassured that they can risk going behind the paywall without local readers getting free national, international, and cultural reporting from the national papers, and having seen that the paid-content formula can work, most metro dailies will follow suit. As they do, they re-emphasize that which makes them unique: local coverage, local culture, local voices—coupled with wire-service offerings from the national papers otherwise available only through paid sites.

In our scenario, metro papers re-emphasize that which makes them unique: local coverage, local culture, local voices.

Some of the chain dailies may well make the mistake of taking the fresh revenue and rushing it back to Wall Street. We need to worry that although readers, like television viewers, might be convinced to pay online for a strong, unique product, there is little in the last twenty years to suggest that newspaper chains would reinvest to create such a product. For those papers, it's likely that a thin online subscriber base will reflect the hollowness of their product.

But in our scenario, others do reinvest in their newsrooms, hiring back some of the talent lost. Coverage expands, becomes more local, even neighborhood-based, which in turn leads to more online subscriptions, as well as additional online advertising lured by those subscribers.

Second scenario: In those cities where regional papers collapse, the vacuum creates an opportunity for new, online subscription-based news organizations that cover state and local issues, sports, and finance, generating enough revenue to maintain a slim—but paid—metro desk. Again, given the absence of circulation costs, such an outcome becomes, by conservative estimates, entirely possible.

Here is a back-of-the-envelope plan. In a metro region the size of Baltimore, where 300,000 once subscribed to a healthy newspaper, imagine an initial market penetration of a tenth of that—30,000 paid subscribers (in a metro region of more than 2.5 million), who are willing to pay $10 per month. This is less than half their previous *Sun* home-delivery rate for the only product in town that covers local politics, local culture, local sports, and financial news—using paid reporters and paid editors to produce a consistent, professional product.

That's $300,000 a month in revenue, or $3.6 million a year, with zero printing or circulation costs. Moreover, that total doesn't include whatever money online advertising might generate. Advertisers—considering a *paid* circulation base rather than meaningless Web hits—might be willing to once again pay a meaningful rate.

Round it up to $4 million in total revenue, then knock off a half million in operating and promotional costs. At $100,000 a position for editors and reporters, that's a metro desk of some thirty-five paid souls, enough to provide significant coverage of a city and its suburbs. If the reporters are on $50,000 contracts and benefits are not initially included, it's a newsroom of seventy—larger than the *Sun*'s metro staff in the nineties.

And if that online-only, paid-subscription daily were a locally-run *nonprofit,* with every increase in subscriptions going to fund additional coverage, well, what more does professional journalism require to survive at the state and local level?

Third scenario: Except for one in which professional journalism doesn't endure in any form, this is the worst of all worlds. The *Times* and the *Post* survive because their coverage is unique and essential. But the regional dailies, too eviscerated to offer a credible local product, cannot entice enough online subscriptions to make do. They wither and die. And further, new online news ventures are stillborn because both national papers become exactly that—national.

Imagine major American cities without daily newspapers, and further imagine the *Times* or the *Post* employing just enough local journalists in regional markets to produce zoned editions—*The New York Times* with, say, a ten-person St. Louis bureau, giving readers two or three pages of metro, sports, and local business coverage. Or a *Washington Post* edition for the Baltimore region, using a dozen ex-*Sun* staffers to create a thin but viable product, where once a comprehensive metro daily once stood.

The joke then would be on the Justice Department lawyers as well. The longer it takes for the newspaper industry to get its act together, the more likely it is that regional dailies will be too weak and hollow to step through the online-subscription portal. Even

localized Internet startups—the fledgling, digitized versions of professional newsrooms—will find themselves competing with, or bought out by, national monoliths. More monopoly, not less, for as long as we continue to fret the antitrust issues.

But all of this is, of course, academic. Because at this moment, Mr. Sulzberger and Ms. Weymouth have yet to turn that last card. Until they find the will and the courage to do so, no scenario other than the slow strangulation of paid, professional journalism applies. Meanwhile, we dare to dream of a viable, online future for American newsrooms.

Critical Thinking

1. Why is paid content necessary to the future of the newspaper industry?
2. Why have paid subscription models for online publications largely failed?
3. What lessons can the newspaper industry draw from the evolution of the broadcast television industry?
4. Explain the three main reasons why industry insiders have failed to understand the implications of internet-based news delivery.
5. If the *New York Times* and the *Washington Post* convert to paid content models, what three possible scenarios might occur, according to the author's predictions?

DAVID SIMON is a writer, author, and television producer. He is the creator of HBO's *The Corner, Generation Kill,* and *The Wire.* From 1982 to 1995, he was a reporter at *The Baltimore Sun.*

A See-Through Society

How the Web is opening up our democracy.

MICAH L. SIFRY

It may be a while before the people who run the U.S. House of Representatives' Web service forget the week of September 29, 2008. That's when the enormous public interest in the financial bailout legislation, coupled with unprecedented numbers of e-mails to House members, effectively crashed www.house.gov. On Tuesday of that week, a day after the House voted down the first version of the bailout bill, House administrators had to limit the number of incoming e-mails processed by the site's "Write Your Representative" function. Demand for the text of the legislation was so intense that third-party sites that track Congress were also swamped. GovTrack.us, a private site that produces a user-friendly guide to congressional legislation, had to shut down. Its owner, Josh Tauberer, posted a message reading, "So many people are searching for the economic relief bill that GovTrack can't handle it. Take a break and come back later when the world cools off."

Once people did get their eyes on the bill's text, they tore into it with zeal. Nearly a thousand comments were posted between September 22 and October 5 on PublicMarkup.org, a site that enables the public to examine and debate the text of proposed legislation set up by the Sunlight Foundation, an advocacy group for government transparency (full disclosure: I am a senior technology adviser to Sunlight). Meanwhile, thousands of bloggers zeroed in on the many earmarks in the bill, such as the infamous reduction in taxes for wooden-arrow manufacturers. Others focused on members who voted for the bill, analyzing their campaign contributors and arguing that Wall Street donations influenced their vote.

The explosion of public engagement online around the bailout bill signals something profound: the beginning of a new age of political transparency. As more people go online to find, create, and share vital political information with one another; as the cost of creating, combining, storing, and sharing information drops toward zero; and as the tools for analyzing data and connecting people become more powerful and easier to use, politics and governance alike are inexorably becoming more open.

We are heading toward a world in which one-click universal disclosure, real-time reporting by both professionals and amateurs, dazzling data visualizations that tell compelling new stories, and the people's ability to watch their government from below (what the French call *sousveillance*) are becoming commonplace. Despite the detour of the Bush years, citizens will have more opportunity at all levels of government to take an active part in understanding and participating in the democratic decisions that affect their lives.

Log On, Speak Out

The low-cost, high-speed, always-on Internet is changing the ecology of how people consume and create political information. The Pew Internet & American Life Project estimates that roughly 75 percent of all American adults, or about 168 million people, go online or use e-mail at least occasionally. A digital divide still haunts the United States, but among Americans aged eighteen to forty-nine, that online proportion is closer to 90 percent. Television remains by far the dominant political information source, but in October 2008, a third of Americans said their main provider of political information was the Internet—more than triple the number from four years earlier, according to another Pew study. Nearly half of eighteen-to-twenty-nine-year-olds said the Internet was their main source of political info.

Meanwhile, we're poised for a revolution in participation, not just in consumption, thanks to the Web. People talk, share, and talk back online. According to yet another study by Pew, this one in December 2007, one in five U.S. adults who use the Internet reported sharing something online that they created themselves; one in three say they've posted a comment or rated something online.

People are eager for access to information, and public officials who try to stand in the way will discover that the Internet responds to information suppression by routing around the problem. Consider the story of a site you've never seen, ChicagoWorksForYou.com. In June 2005, a team of Web developers working for the city of Chicago began developing a site that would take the fifty-five different kinds of service requests that flow into the city's 311 database—items like pothole repairs, tree-trimming, garbage-can placement, building permits, and restaurant inspections—and enable users to search by address and "map what's happening in your neighborhood" The idea was to showcase city services at the local level.

ChicagoWorks was finished in January 2006, with the support of Mayor Richard Daley's office. But it also needed to be reviewed by the city's aldermen and, according to a source who worked on the project, "they were very impressed with its functionality, but they were shocked at the possibility that it would go public." Elections were coming up, and even if the site showed 90 percent of potholes being filled within thirty days, the powers-that-be didn't want the public to know about the last 10 percent. ChicagoWorksForYou.com was shelved.

But the idea of a site that brings together information about city services in Chicago is alive and kicking. If you go to Every-Block.com, launched in January 2008, and click on the Chicago link, you can drill down to any ward, neighborhood, or block and discover everything from the latest restaurant-inspection reports and building permits to recent crime reports and street closures. It's all on a Google Map, and if you want to subscribe to updates about a particular location and type of report, the site kicks out custom RSS feeds. Says Daniel O'Neil, one of Every Block's data mavens, "Crime and restaurant inspections are our hottest topics: Will I be killed today and will I vomit today?"

EveryBlock exists thanks to a generous grant from the Knight News Challenge, but its work, which covers eleven cities, including New York, San Francisco, and Washington, D.C., offers a glimpse of the future of ubiquitous and hyperlocal information. EveryBlock's team collects most of its data by scraping public sites and spreadsheets and turning it into understandable information that can be easily displayed and manipulated online.

It may not be long before residents of the cities covered by EveryBlock decide to contribute their own user-generated data to flesh out the picture that city officials might prefer to hide. EveryBlock founder Adrian Holovaty tells me that his team is figuring out ways for users to connect directly to each other through the site. Forums that allowed people to congregate online by neighborhood or interest would enable EveryBlock users to become their cities' watchdogs. If city agencies still won't say how many potholes are left unfilled after thirty days, people could share and track that information themselves.

Such a joint effort is no stretch to young people who have grown up online. Consider just a couple of examples: since 1999, RateMyTeachers.com and RateMyProfessors.com have collected more than sixteen million user-generated ratings on more than two million teachers and professors. The two sites get anywhere from half a million to a million unique visitors a month. Yelp.com, a user-generated review service, says its members have written more than four million local reviews since its founding in 2004. As the younger generation settles down and starts raising families, there's every reason to expect that its members will carry these habits of networking and sharing information into tracking more serious quality-of-life issues, as well as politics.

Cities Lead the Way

Recognizing this trend, some public officials are plunging in. In his "State of the City" speech in January 2008, New York Mayor Mike Bloomberg promised to "roll out the mother of

---

A Sunshine Timeline

1966

FOIA passes. Without the votes to sustain his threatened veto, and with Bill Moyers, his press secretary, urging him on, LBJ signs the bill. But he nixes a press release announcing the new law, and forgoes a signing ceremony, the only time in his tenure he did so. (Ironic footnote: Donald Rumsfeld co-sponsored the bill.)

---

all accountability tools." It is called Citywide Performance Reporting, and Bloomberg promised it would put "a wealth of data at people's fingertips—fire response times, noise complaints, trees planted by the Parks Department, you name it. More than five hundred different measurements from forty-five city agencies." Bloomberg, whose wealth was built on the financial-information company he built, says he likes to think of the service as a"Bloomberg terminal for city government—except that it's free."

Bloomberg's vision is only partly fulfilled so far. A visitor to the city's site (nyc.gov) would have a hard time finding the "Bloomberg terminal for city government" because it's tucked several layers down On the Mayor's Office of Operations page, with no pointers from the home page.

Still, the amount of data it provides is impressive. You can learn that the number of families with children entering the city shelter system is up 31 percent over last year, and that the city considers this a sign of declining performance by the system. Or you can discover that the median time the city department of consumer affairs took to process a complaint was twenty-two business days, and that that is considered positive! Another related tool, called NYC*SCOUT, allows anyone to see where recent service requests have been made, and with a little bit of effort you can make comparisons between different community districts. New York's monitoring tools still leave much to be desired, however, because they withhold the raw data—specific addresses and dates-of-service requests—that are the bones of these reports. This means the city is still resisting fully sharing the public's data with the public.

Compare that to the approach of the District of Columbia. Since 2006, all the raw data it has collected on government operations, education, health care, crime, and dozens of other topics has been available for free to the public via 260 live data feeds. The city's CapStat online service also allows anyone to track the performance of individual agencies, monitor neighborhood services and quality-of-life issues, and make suggestions for improvement. Vivek Kundra, D.C.'s innovative chief technology officer, calls this "building the digital public square." In mid-October, he announced an "Apps for Democracy" contest that offered $20,000 in cash prizes for outside developers and designers of websites and tools that made use of the city's data catalog.

In just a few weeks, Kundra received nearly fifty finished Web applications. The winners included:

- iLive.at, a site that shows with one click all the local information around one address, including the closest places to go shopping, buy gas, or mail a letter; the locations of recently reported crimes; and the demographic makeup of the neighborhood;
- Where's My Money, DC?—a tool that meshes with Facebook and enables users to look up and discuss all city expenditures above $2,500; and
- Stumble Safely, an online guide to the best bars and safe paths on which to stumble home after a night out.

The lesson of the "Apps for Democracy" contest is simple: a critical mass of citizens with the skills and the appetite to engage with public agencies stands ready to co-create a new kind of government transparency. Under traditional government procurement practices, it would have taken Kundra months just to post a "request for proposals" and get responses. Finished sites would have taken months, even years, for big government contractors to complete. The cost for fifty working websites would have been in the millions. Not so when you give the public robust data resources and the freedom to innovate that is inherent to today's Web.

The Whole Picture

So, how will the Web ultimately alter the nature of political transparency? Four major trends are developing.

First, the day is not far off when it will be possible to see, at a glance, the most significant ways an individual, lobbyist, corporation, or interest group is trying to influence the government. Here's how Ellen Miller, executive director of the Sunlight Foundation and a longtime proponent of open government, sees the future of transparency online: "If I search for Exxon, I want one-click disclosure," she says. "I want to see who its PAC is giving money to, who its executives and employees are supporting, at the state and federal levels; who does its lobbying, whom they're meeting with and what they're lobbying on; whether it's employing former government officials, or vice versa, if any of its ex-employees are in government; whether any of those people have flown on the company's jets. And then I also want to know what contracts, grants, or earmarks the company has gotten and whether they were competitively bid."

She continues: "If I look up a senator, I want an up-to-date list of his campaign contributors—not one that is months out of date because the Senate still files those reports on paper. I want to see his public calendar of meetings. I want to know what earmarks he's sponsored and obtained. I want to know whether he is connected to a private charity that people might be funneling money to. I want to see an up-to-date list of his financial assets, along with all the more mundane things, like a list of bills he's sponsored, votes he's taken, and public statements he's made. And I want it all reported and available online in a timely fashion."

This vision isn't all that far away. In the last three years, thanks in large measure to support from Sunlight, OMB Watch (a nonprofit advocacy organization that focuses on budget issues, regulatory policy, and access to government) created

A Sunshine Timeline

1986

In the wake of India's Bhopal disaster, the Emergency Planning and Community Right-to-Know Act mandates development of national and local systems to respond to leaks of dangerous chemicals. Included is the requirement, for the first time, that computerized regulatory information be made public.

FedSpending.org, a searchable online database of all government contracts and spending. The Center for Responsive Politics (OpenSecrets.org), meanwhile, has developed searchable databases of current lobbying reports, personal financial disclosure statements of members of Congress, sponsored travel, and employment records of nearly ten thousand people who have moved through the revolving door between government and lobbying. Taxpayers for Common Sense (Taxpayer.net) is putting the finishing touches on a complete online database of 2008 earmarks.

The National Institute on Money in State Politics, headed by Ed Bender, is filling in the picture at the state level, aiming to give the public "as complete a picture as possible of its elected leaders and their actions, and offer information that helps the public understand those actions," he says. "This would start with the candidates running for offices, their biographies and their donors, and would follow them into the statehouses to their committee assignments and relationships with lobbyists, and finally to the legislation that they sponsor and vote for, and who benefits from those actions."

The incoming Obama administration, meanwhile, has expressed a commitment to expanding government transparency, promising as part of its "ethics agenda" platform (change.gov/agenda/ethics_agenda) to create a "centralized Internet database of lobbying reports, ethics records, and campaign-finance filings in a searchable, sortable, and downloadable format," as well as a "'contracts and influence' database that will disclose how much federal contractors spend on lobbying, and what contracts they are getting and how well they complete them."

To insure that all citizens can access such a database, we can hope that Obama pushes universal Internet access as part of his investment in infrastructure. As Andrew Rasiej and I argued in *Politico* in December, "Just as we recognized with the Universal Service Act in the 1930s that we had to take steps to ensure everyone access to the phone network, we need to do the same today with affordable access to high-speed Internet. Everything else flows from this. Otherwise, we risk leaving half our population behind and worsening inequality rather than reducing it."

3-D Journalism

A second trend propelling us toward a greater degree of political transparency is data visualization. The tools for converting boring lists and lines of numbers into beautiful, compelling images get more powerful every day, enabling a new kind of 3-D journalism: dynamic and data-driven. And in many cases, news consumers can manipulate the resulting image or chart, drilling into its layers of information to follow their own interests. My favorite examples include:

- The Huffington Post's Fundrace, which mapped campaign contributions to the 2008 presidential candidates by name and address, enabling anyone to see whom their neighbors might be giving to;
- The *New York Times*'s debate analyzer, which converted each candidate debate into an interactive chart showing word counts and speaking time, and enabled readers to search for key words or fast forward; and
- The Sunlight Foundation and Taxpayers for Common Sense's Earmarks Watch Map (earmarkwatch.org/mapped), which layered the thousands of earmarks in the fiscal 2008 defense-appropriations bill over a map of the country allowing a viewer to zero in on specific sites and see how the Pentagon scatters money in practically every corner of the U.S.

The use of such tools is engendering a collective understanding of, as Paul Simon once sang, the way we look to us all. As news consumers grow used to seeing people like CNN'S John King use a highly interactive map of the United States to explain local voting returns, demand for these kinds of visualizations will only grow.

Little Brother Is Watching, Too

The third trend fueling the expansion of political transparency is *sousveillance,* or watching from below. It can be done by random people, armed with little more than a camera-equipped cell phone, who happen to be in the right place at the right time. Or it can be done by widely dispersed individuals acting in concert to ferret out a vital piece of information or trend, what has been called "distributed journalism." In effect, Big Brother is being watched by millions of Little Brothers.

For example, back in August, San Francisco Mayor Gavin Newsom was having coffee at a Starbucks in Malibu when he was spotted by a blogger who took a couple of photos and posted them online. The blogger noted that Newsom was "talking campaign strategy" with someone, but didn't know who. The pictures came to the attention of *San Francisco Chronicle* reporter Carla Marinucci, who identified that person as political consultant Garry South. Soon political bloggers were having a field day, pointing out that the liberal mayor was meeting with one of the more conservative Democratic consultants around. This is *sousveillance* at its simplest.

The citizen-journalism project "Off the Bus," which ultimately attracted thousands of volunteer reporters who posted their work on The Huffington Post during the 2008 election, was *sousveillance* en masse. Much of their work was too opinionated or first-person oriented to really break news, but Mayhill Fowler's reporting of Barack Obama's offhand remarks at a San Francisco fundraiser about "bitter" blue-collar workers

A Sunshine Timeline

2003
World Bank begins supporting FOI-related conditions in agreements with some developing countries, but stops short of making right-to-know laws mandatory. According to Privacy International, today roughly eighty-one governments worldwide have some form of FOI law.

at least briefly changed the course of the campaign. And there are numerous examples of bloggers and their readers acting in concert to expose some hidden fact. The coalition of bloggers known as the "Porkbusters" were at the center of an effort to expose which senator had put a secret hold on a bill creating a federal database of government spending, co-sponsored by none other than Barack Obama and Tom Coburn. Porkbusters asked their readers to call their senators, and by this reporting process, discovered that Senator Ted Stevens of Alaska was the culprit. Soon thereafter, he released his hold. Likewise, Josh Marshall has frequently asked readers of Talking Points Memo to help him spot local stories that might be part of a larger pattern. It was this technique that helped him piece together the story of the firings of U.S. Attorneys around the country, for which he won the Polk Award.

The World's A-Twitter

The final trend that is changing the nature of transparency is the rise of what some call the World Live Web. Using everything from mobile phones that can stream video live online to simple text message postings to the micro-blogging service Twitter, people are contributing to a real-time patter of information about what is going on around them. Much of what results is little more than noise, but increasingly sophisticated and simple-to-use filtering tools can turn some of it into information of value.

For example, in just a matter of weeks before the November election in the U.S., a group of volunteer bloggers and Web developers loosely affiliated with the blog I edit, techPresident.com, built a monitoring project called Twitter Vote Report. Voters were encouraged to use Twitter, as well as other tools like iPhones, to post reports on the quality of their voting experience. Nearly twelve thousand reports flowed in, and the result was a real-time picture of election-day complications and wait times that a number of journalistic organizations, including NPR, PBS, and several newspapers, relied on for their reporting.

Nothing to Hide

The question for our leaders, as we head into a world where bottom-up, user-generated transparency is becoming more of a reality, is whether they will embrace this change and show that they have nothing to hide. Will they actively share all that is relevant to their government service with the people who, after all, pay their salaries? Will they trust the public to understand the complexities of that information, instead of treating them like children who can't handle the truth?

The question for citizens is, Will we use this new access to information to create a more open and deliberative democracy?

The question for citizens, meanwhile, is, Will we use this new access to information to create a more open and deliberative democracy? Or will citizens just use the Web to play "gotcha" games with politicians, damaging the discourse instead of uplifting it?

"People tend not to trust what is hidden" write the authors of the November 2008 report by a collection of openness advocates entitled "Moving Toward a 21st Century Right-to-Know Agenda." "Transparency is a powerful tool to demonstrate to the public that the government is spending our money wisely, that politicians are not in the pocket of lobbyists and special-interest groups, that government is operating in an accountable manner, and that decisions are made to ensure the safety and protection of all Americans." In the end, transparency breeds trust. Or rather, transparency enables leaders to earn our trust. In the near future, they may have to, because more and more of us are watching.

Critical Thinking

1. How has the internet fundamentally changed the way people access and share information?

2. Describe how the cities of New York and Washington, DC took different approaches to sharing information online with the public. Which city is more transparent? What are the benefits or drawbacks of each model?

3. What are the four major trends in the internet's influence on political transparency?

4. Why should universal internet access be included in a federal infrastructure investment plan, according to the author?

MICAH L. SIFRY is co-founder of the Personal Democracy Forum, an annual conference on how technology is changing politics; editor of its group blog techPresident.com; and a senior technology adviser to the Sunlight Foundation.

Governing in the Age of Fox News

The polarization of the American media has deep historical roots—the republic came into being amidst a vigorous partisan press. But the splintering of public attention and the intensification of ideological journalism—In particular, the rise of Fox News—have created unique challenges for President Obama. Is it possible to have partisan media that retain professional standards of reporting?

PAUL STARR

The fight between the Obama White House and Fox News may look like a replay of previous presidential conflicts with the media. After all, antagonism between presidents and elements of the press is a fine American tradition. But the Fox News phenomenon is different, and its development reflects a deeper change in the public itself that presents a new challenge for presidential leadership.

What was once an expansive mass public has lost some of its old breadth and, at its core, become more intense and combative. A growing percentage of people, especially among the young, no longer regularly follow the news in any medium, while those who remain the most attentive and engaged tend to be sharply polarized along ideological lines. On both ends of the political spectrum, people interested in politics increasingly view national leadership through the prism of the partisan media that dominate cable news, talk radio, and the blogosphere.

Before cable and the Internet, the way for a president to reach the national public was through national media that sought to appeal to audiences spanning the partisan divide. The major newspapers, wire services, and broadcast networks controlled the flow of news from Washington and the president's access to the channels of persuasion, yet they operated more or less according to the standards of professional journalism, and the White House could exercise plenty of leverage in its media relations by selectively leaking news and granting exclusive interviews. So despite sometimes antagonistic relations with the press, presidents were able to use it to reach abroad and relatively coherent national public.

But now that the old behemoths of the news are in decline, the unified public they assembled is fading too. Neither the broadcast networks nor the newspapers have the reach they once did, raising concerns about whether the press will be able to serve its classic function as a watchdog over government. That problem also has a flip side. Precisely because the press is often critical of political leaders, it provides them legitimacy when it validates the grounds for their decisions. A press that is widely trusted by the public for its independence and integrity is also a resource for building consensus. Thus when the public

sorts itself according to hostile, ideologically separate media—when the world of Walter Cronkite gives way to the world of Glenn Beck and Keith Olbermann—political leadership loses a consensus-building partner. This is the problem that faces Barack Obama. It is not, however, an unprecedented one.

To most Americans, at least until recently, it had long seemed a settled matter that the media should have no relationship with political parties—but that has not been the norm throughout American history, much less in other countries. In many democracies, newspapers and other media have developed in parallel with political parties (sometimes directly financed and controlled by them), while elsewhere the media have been independent, with no partisan connection. The prevailing model for how American presidents interact with the media has gone through three historical stages. As a young republic (and to a large extent even after the Civil War), the nation had partisan newspapers; the second stage, stretching across the 20th century, was characterized by powerful, independent media outlets that kept their distance from the parties; and in the third stage, we now have a hybrid system that combines elements of the first two.

The founding period in American history created a new and richly supportive environment for the press. Britain and other European states, seeing popular newspapers as a political threat, had limited what they could say and imposed heavy taxes to raise their costs and reduce their circulation. America's Founders, in contrast, believed that the circulation of news and political debate could help preserve their fragile republic. So besides guaranteeing the press its freedom, they excluded it from taxation and subsidized its development by setting cheap postal rates for mailing newspapers to subscribers. The government thereby underwrote the costs of a national news network without regulating its content. Public officials also subsidized specific newspapers they favored, by awarding generous contracts for government printing and paying fees for official notices. Together with subscription and advertising income, the postal and printing subsidies provided the financial basis for a development of the press so rapid that by 1835, the United States, even though it was still almost entirely rural, probably had the highest per capita newspaper circulation in the world.

Under many regimes, government subsidies have made the press politically subservient. But in the United States, the postal subsidies benefited all newspapers without limitation based on viewpoint—and newspapers did clearly express their ideological stances. And because of the separation of powers and the federal system, printing subsidies from different branches and levels of government went to newspapers from different parties. In fact, rather than solidifying incumbent power, the early environment of the press paved the way for two insurgent presidential candidates, Thomas Jefferson in 1800 and Andrew Jackson in 1828.

Jefferson's Democratic-Republicans were the first party to exploit the press environment established by the Founders, and they did so despite adversity. In 1798, during an undeclared war with France, President John Adams's Federalists enacted the infamous Sedition Act, making it a crime to publish "false, scandalous, and malicious writing" about the president (though not about the vice president, who at the time was none other than Jefferson himself, the leader of the opposition). The Adams administration used the act to prosecute leading Jeffersonian editors and close down their papers—but the Jeffersonians more than offset those losses by establishing dozens of new papers in the run-up to the election of 1800. In the process, they demonstrated that the press could serve as a lever for overturning power in the United States.

Political parties at this time were only loose coalitions of leaders; they had no ongoing organization except their newspapers, and in practice, the parties and their newspapers were almost indistinguishable. Local editors were key party organizers, and local party leaders often met in the newspaper office. According to some historians, this partisan press belonged to the "dark ages" of American journalism. But it played a central role in mobilizing political participation and creating a vibrant democracy. And at no time was that more the case than in 1828, when Jackson's supporters built a network of Democratic papers across the country, and voting turnout increased sharply.

Once in office, Jackson established the practice (which lasted until 1860) of having a quasi-official paper that spoke directly for the president and received federal patronage. Still, the press continued to be highly competitive, and the presidential newspaper did not become a stable monopoly. In the 32 years following Jackson's election, 11 different papers in Washington served as presidential organs, and by the 1860s they were so outstripped in circulation by advertising-supported metropolitan dailies that a separate paper representing the president had become obsolete. Beginning with Lincoln, presidents communicated with the public through commercially financed newspapers, though many of these continued to have strong partisan identities.

The rise of the mass press inaugurated a long, second era in presidential communication, spanning most of the 20th century, when national leaders had to adapt to new realities, including the growing role of reporters as independent interpreters of the news and the development of media with national reach. In the late 19th century, presidents literally kept journalists at a distance (reporters had to wait outside the White House gates for news from officials coming and going). Presidents also did not represent themselves, nor were they seen, as the central actors in the nation's politics. Only at the turn of the century, as "congressional government" gave way to a stronger executive, did presidents begin to cultivate the press and make themselves more visible by seizing the opportunities for public persuasion and influence that mass communications provided.

If Jefferson and Jackson were the two breakthrough presidents in the era of the partisan press, the two Roosevelts were their counterparts as presidential innovators in the mass media of the 20th century. Although the shift began under his predecessor, William McKinley, Theodore Roosevelt brought reporters into the White House on a more regular basis, providing them for the first time with a press room. He also projected his influence more widely, giving more speeches than earlier presidents had and making the most of his office as a "bully pulpit." With his charm and energy, Roosevelt infused the presidency with qualities that have served as a model for leadership through the media ever since.

Natural gifts were also critical to Franklin Roosevelt's success. The first Roosevelt, a Republican, had had the advantage of dealing with a press that was predominantly Republican in its sympathies. FDR, however, as a Democrat, was convinced that he needed to circumvent hostile Republican newspaper publishers to reach the public directly. Radio gave him that power. Unlike Herbert Hoover, Roosevelt spoke in a conversational style in his "fireside chats," creating the sense among his listeners that he was talking directly to them in their living rooms.

The advent of television highlighted the personality and performative abilities of the president even more than had radio. What the fireside chat was for FDR, the televised news conference was for John F Kennedy—an opportunity to show off personal qualities to maximum advantage. In the era of the captive mass public, from the 1950s through the '70s—when people had access to only a few TV channels, and the three national networks had a 90 percent share of the audience—the president had command of the airwaves, and the narrative of the evening news typically cast him as the dominant actor in the nation's daily political drama.

For a time, this seemed to be the permanent structure of the news and national politics in the age of electronic media. In retrospect, it was the peaking of the unified national public, the moment just before cable TV and the Internet began breaking it up, bringing the media to another historic turning point.

From the founding era to the late 20th century, the news in America enjoyed an expanding public. In the 1800s, postal policies and advances in printing technology cut the price of the printed word and, together with wider access to education, enabled more Americans to read newspapers and become civically literate. In the 20th century, radio, newsreels at the movies, and television extended the reach of the news even farther.

It was only reasonable to assume, then, that the digital revolution would repeat the same pattern, and in some respects it has; online news is plentiful and (mostly) free. But a basic rule of communication is that abundance brings scarcity: an abundance of media creates a scarcity of attention. So although journalists and politicians have new ways to reach the public, the public has acquired even more ways to ignore them. Politics and other news are at our fingertips, but a lot of us don't want to go there. Between 1998 and 2008, according to surveys by the Pew Research Center, the number of Americans who say they don't get the news in any medium on an average day rose from 14 percent to 19 percent—and from 25 percent to 34 percent among 18-to-24-year-olds. And 2008 was a year when interest in the news should have been relatively high.

Obama's success in using digital media during the election may have led some to expect that as president he would be able to do the same. The job, however, is different. Rallying your activist base may not be the best way to win marginal votes in Congress. What Obama needs to do to win those votes—for example, make concessions to moderate Democrats on health-care legislation—may, in fact, disappoint his most passionate supporters. Mobilizing public support as president, rather than as a candidate, is also a different challenge. Although digital communications have made reaching political supporters cheaper and easier, the fractured nature of the public makes it more difficult to reach both the less politically interested and the partisan opposition.

During what the political scientists Matthew A. Baum and Samuel Kernell refer to as the "golden age of presidential television" in the early postwar decades, close to half the households in the country would watch a primetime presidential TV appearance. As access to cable expanded in the 1980s, the audience started shrinking, and by 1995, only 6.5 percent of households watched one of Bill Clinton's news conferences. Obama started out with comparatively high ratings. According to Nielsen data, 31 percent of TV homes watched his first press conference, on February 9, though that dropped to 16 percent by his fifth, on July 22. His speeches to Congress have drawn a somewhat bigger audience, but the ratings have followed the same trajectory. Nonetheless, the president still has the ability to command wider attention than any other figure in American politics. Obama's health-care speech to Congress on September 9 drew an estimated 32 million viewers, which was down from 52 million for his first address to Congress in February but still far higher than any other political figure could hope to attract.

After a summer when the national debate on health-care reform seemed to be dominated by his opponents—thanks, in no small measure, to Fox News and its one-sided coverage of protests at congressional representatives' town-hall meetings—Obama was able to reverse the momentum. In any conflict, the president's voice can rise above the noise. In any national crisis, eyes will still turn to the president, and citizens will expect him to speak for the nation. On those occasions, if he uses the opportunity well, he remains the country's most important teacher. And that remains Obama's greatest strength in competing with Fox over the direction of the national conversation.

During his presidential campaign, Obama said he would try to repair America's bitter divisions, and he reached out to conservatives on various occasions, such as his visit to Rick Warren's Saddleback Church. American politics has become more polarized, however, for deep-seated historical reasons. With the shift of the South to the GOP, the Republicans have become a more purely conservative party, and the Democrats a more liberal one. If this change in the parties had occurred half a century ago, the dominant news media might have moderated polarizing tendencies because of their interest in appealing to a mass audience that crossed ideological lines. But the incentives have changed: on cable, talk radio, and the Internet, partisanship pays.

Not since the 19th century have presidents had to deal with partisan media of this kind, and even that comparison is imperfect. Today the media saturate everyday life far more fully than they did in early American history. Fox News, in particular, is in a league by itself. In the absence of clear national leadership in the Republican Party, Fox's commentators (together with Rush Limbaugh) have effectively taken over that role themselves. Although they have their liberal counterparts on MSNBC, the situation is not exactly symmetrical, because MSNBC's commentators do not have as strong a following and the network's reporting is not as ideologically driven as Fox's.

Of course, professional journalism, with its norms of detachment, hasn't disappeared, though it's in deep financial trouble. Leading newspapers, notably The New York Times, have a wider readership online and in print than they had before in print alone. Media-criticism blogs and Web sites from varied perspectives serve a policing function in the new world of public controversy. Partisan media are now firmly part of our national conversation, but counter-vailing forces—not just the political opposition and its supporters in the media, but professional journalists and other sources for authenticated facts—can keep partisanship from controlling that conversation. Although most American journalists assume that professionalism and partisanship are inherently incompatible, that is not necessarily so. Partisan media can, and in some countries do, observe professional standards in their presentation of the news. That is where civic groups and the scientific community, as well as media critics and others upholding those standards, should focus their pressure. Some commentators may be beyond embarrassment, but the news divisions of the partisan media are likely to be more sensitive to charges of unsubstantiated claims and loaded language. The yellow press of the 1890s looked equally immune from rebuke—and for a long time it was—but the growth of professional journalism in the 20th century did bring about a significant degree of restraint, even in the tabloids.

No one can put the old public back together again. Walter Cronkite's death last July provoked nostalgia for a time when it seemed all Americans had someone they could trust, and that person was a journalist. But it's not just Cronkite that's gone; the world that made a Cronkite possible is dead. Now we have a fighting public sphere, which has some compensating virtues of its own. As in the early 19th century, a partisan press maybe driving an increase in political involvement. After a long decline, voter turnout in the 2004 and 2008 elections returned to levels America hadn't seen in 40 years. Fox News and MSNBC stir up the emotions not just of their devoted viewers but of those who abhor them; liberals and conservatives alike may be more inclined to vote as a result. Democracy needs passion, and partisanship provides it. Journalism needs passion, too, though the passion should be for the truth. If we can encourage some adherence to professional standards in the world of partisan journalism, not via the government but by criticism and force of example, this republic of ours—thankfully no longer fragile—may yet flourish.

Critical Thinking

1. Why are national mass news media—including broadcast networks and newspapers—increasingly unable to fulfill their traditional roles as government watchdogs?

2. Which three historical stages of media have American presidents interacted with?

3. Why has Barack Obama's success with digital media during his campaign not translated to his presidency?

4. How might partisan journalism be compatible with professionalism in the news media?

PAUL STARR is a professor of sociology and public affairs at Princeton University and the author of most recently The Creation of the Media and Freedom's Power.

UNIT 4

Products of American Politics

Unit Selections

Learning Outcomes

After reading this unit you should be able to:

- Rank the six listed policy issues facing the United States from *most* to *least* important and explain the order in which you put them: energy and environmental problems, comprehensive immigration reform, homeland security against terrorism, the war in Afghanistan, the economy, the space program.

- Identify the tension or dilemma between, on the one hand, increased government spending aimed at a generally sluggish economy with high unemployment rates and other problems, and, on the other hand, huge national government budget debts and rising national debt. Decide how you would resolve this policy dilemma and explain why.

- Identify the tension or dilemma between, on the one hand, the desirability of making the United States more energy self-sufficient and limiting greenhouse gas emissions and, on the other hand, the U.S.'s economic woes and the need to continue to use energy to fuel economic growth. Recommend how you would try to resolve this dilemma.

- Summarize the reasons that the United States and other countries engage in military combat against or in foreign countries and the goals of such military combat. Then summarize the costs of war—broadly conceived (that is, not just economic costs)—for a nation such as the United States. Appraise current United States combat operations in light of your two summaries, doing, in effect, a cost/benefit analysis.

- Explain the growing overlap between what was traditionally thought to be domestic policy (the economy, health care, environment, agriculture, etc.) and what was traditionally thought to be foreign and national security policy (diplomacy, treaties, military combat operations, etc.).

- Bearing in mind the growing financial problems associated with Medicare and Social Security, identify and explain various options for what ought to be done about these two programs that are so central to the well-being of elderly Americans. Recommend what you think ought to be done.

- Compare and contrast the overall policy performance of the American national government during the George W. Bush years (2001–2009) and during the Obama years (2009 to date).

Student Website

www.mhhe.com/cls

"**P**roducts" refer to the government policies that the American political system produces. The first three units of this book have paved the way for fourth unit because the products of American politics are very much the consequences of the rest of the political system.

The health of the American economy is almost always a prominent policy issue in the American political system. One of the most remarkable consequences of 12 years (1981–1993) under President Reagan and the first President Bush was enormous growth in budget deficits and the national debt. During the Clinton presidency, the country enjoyed the longest period of continuous economic growth in U.S. history, accompanied by low unemployment and low inflation rates. Continuing economic growth and increased tax revenues to such an extent that the long-sought goal of a balanced budget was reached in 1998, amid predictions that the entire national debt would be eliminated within a decade or so. In the last months of the Clinton administration, however, some signs of an economic slowdown appeared. President George W. Bush pushed tax cuts through Congress early in his presidency, the country entered a recession in the second half of President Bush's first year in office, and the September 11 terrorist attacks accelerated the economic downturn. Large budget deficits returned and the national debt grew accordingly. By 2007, with the costs of the war in Iraq continuing to mount and the retirement of baby boomers drawing ever nearer, the country's fiscal situation was a cause for serious concern.

In 2008, home mortgage and other financial market problems shook the foundations of the nation's credit and banking systems, bringing Wall Street woes and a recession. Meanwhile, the national government's budget deficit soared, and growth in the national debt exceeded including that which had occurred during the Reagan administration and the first Bush presidency. By late 2008, it was unclear whether the traditional mainstays of American industry, the Big Three automakers, would avoid bankruptcy, as they publicly sought a bail-out from Washington in order to survive. Economic problems in the United States reverberated around the globe and many observers suggested that the economic downturn was going to be the worst since the Great Depression.

In its first months in office, the Obama administration concentrated on the country's economic woes. The second half of the $700-billion dollar Troubled Asset Relief Program (TARP), enacted in the last months of the Bush administration, was used to prop up failing financial institutions as well as General Motors and Chrysler. Moreover, President Obama pushed Congress for a stimulus package to try to get the economy growing again, and the result was passage of a $787 billion dollar Recovery Act in February 2009.

By late 2009, economic growth had returned amidst high unemployment rates that threatened "a jobless recovery." TARP and stimulus spending, combined with the costs of America's wars in Iraq and Afghanistan, and other costs associated with the recession made national government budget deficits reach the highest levels since the end of World War II. While Obama supporters claimed that his policies had saved the country from another Great Depression, Obama's critics expressed concern about the huge budget deficits, the mounting national debt, and when prosperity and economic stability would return to the United States. By the late summer of 2010, the "recovery" continued to be weak, with high unemployment figures, an extremely slow housing market, minimal economic growth, and fears of a so-called double-dip recession growing. In this context, it was unsurprising that President Obama's public approval ratings declined to below 50%, and that Republicans were expected to fare very well in the November 2010 congressional elections and perhaps even regain majority control of one or both houses of Congress.

Domestic public policy typically involves "trade-offs" among competing uses of scarce resources. During his 1992 campaign, Bill Clinton called attention to many such trade-offs in the area of health care. As president,

© C. Sherburne/PhotoLink/Getty Images

Clinton introduced a comprehensive health care reform proposal late in 1993. Congress never voted on that proposal, and, while minor changes were made in the nation's health care delivery system during the Clinton years, no comprehensive overhaul was ever achieved. In his 2007 State of the Union address, President Bush presented several proposals relating to health care, including a change in relevant tax code provisions, but no significant legislation ensued. In 2008, health care reform was a major priority of the two leading candidates for the Democratic presidential nomination, Hillary Clinton and Barack Obama, and Obama's victory over Republican opponent John McCain would seem to make major health care reform of some sort probable, if not inevitable.

After focusing on pressing economic and financial troubles in the first few months of the Obama administration, Congress and the president turned their attention to health care reform more publicly in the summer of 2009. The legislative process seemed to drag on interminably. Not until March 2010 was major health care reform enacted, with Democrats using a parliamentary maneuver called "reconciliation" to sidestep opposition in the Senate from the 41 Republican senators, a number large enough to mount a successful filibuster and thwart comprehensive reform efforts.

The final health care reform enactments included countless trade-offs and compromises among competing ideas about what ought to be in the bill, the final price tag, and how to pay for it. Moreover, trade-offs occurred outside the health reform bill itself. By urging Congress to work on passing a health care reform bill as a priority, President Obama and congressional leaders delayed efforts to pass cap-and-trade legislation to reduce greenhouse gas emissions and to enact immigration reform in favor of getting health care reform enacted. In the summer of 2010, Congress enacted the Dodd-Frank Wall Street Reform and Consumer Protection Act. Aimed at curbing financial market practices blamed for the 2008–09 financial meltdown, this bill was the most comprehensive financial regulatory package since the Great Depression. With congressional elections coming in November, however, Congress and the administration abandoned efforts to enact a major energy and environment bill as well as comprehensive immigration reform. Once again, trade-offs had been at work.

For most of the last half of the twentieth century, the United States and the Soviet Union each had the capacity to end human existence as we know it. Not surprisingly, the threat of nuclear war with the Soviet Union often dominated American foreign policy and diplomacy. During that same period, however, the United States used conventional military forces in a number of places, including Korea, Vietnam, Grenada, and Panama.

The demise of the Soviet Union in 1991 left the United States as the world's sole superpower, profoundly affecting world politics and U.S. foreign policy ever since. Questions about the appropriateness of U.S. intervention in such disparate places as Bosnia-Herzegovina, Somalia, Haiti, Iraq, Kosovo, and even Russia were at the forefront of foreign policy concerns during the Clinton administration. The George W. Bush administration and the nation as a whole, of course, became preoccupied with anti-terrorism efforts and homeland security after the September 11 terrorist attacks.

The foreign and defense policy process in the United States raises a host of related issues, including continuing struggle between legislative and executive branches for control. In 1991, after Iraq invaded Kuwait, Congress authorized war against Iraq, which was the first time since World War II that there has been explicit and formal congressional approval before commencement of U.S. military combat operations. In late 1995, President Clinton committed the United States to sending troops to Bosnia-Herzegovina as part of a multinational peacekeeping force. Despite some opposition, Congress passed resolutions supporting the troops. Toward the end of 1997, President Saddam Hussein of Iraq obstructed UN weapons inspection teams in his country, and President Clinton responded by increasing the readiness of U.S. military forces in the Persian Gulf. In late 1998, several days of U.S. air strikes on Iraq followed what was viewed as further provocation.

In the aftermath of the 9/11 terrorist attacks in 2001, Congress supported President George W. Bush in pursuing the perpetrators and launching an assault on Al Qaeda sites in Afghanistan. In the fall of 2002, Congress authorized President Bush to wage war against Iraq if he deemed it necessary to safeguard American security. Early in 2003, U.S. forces invaded Iraq, and critics in Congress and elsewhere suggested that President Bush had made insufficient attempts to gain international support. The initial military success in toppling Saddam Hussein's government has been followed by years of violent insurgency that threatened the legitimacy of Iraqi self-government, killed more than 4,000 U.S. troops and many multiples of that number of Iraqis, and cost billions and billions of dollars. Americans' dissatisfaction with the Iraq war seemed a major factor in Democrats' winning majority control of the the House and Senate in November 2006, which in turn set the stage for a sharp debate between President Bush and Congress about what to do next and about the proper role of each branch in shaping national security policy.

Barack Obama made his early opposition to the Iraq war, a cornerstone of his 2008 presidential candidacy, and promised to remove American troops from Iraq in a timely manner if he became president. By late 2008, the Iraqi government declared that American troops should be removed from Iraq within three years. During the transition period between his election and his taking the oath of office on January 20, 2009, Obama announced that he would keep President Bush's Secretary of Defense, Robert Gates, one of whose responsibilities would be to oversee the safe withdrawal of American troops from Iraq. This move suggested that, at long last, American policy-makers and the American public were moving toward a bipartisan consensus about ending American military involvement in Iraq. In the second month of his presidency, President Obama announced his plan to withdraw American combat troops from Iraq by August 2010, and the planned withdrawal occurred on schedule 18 months later. But even as his Iraq withdrawal plan was being met with approval by most Americans, in the fall of 2009 President Obama found himself wrestling with various military options in Afghanistan, which ranged, according to some observers, from "bad" to "worse." U.S. military forces in Afghanistan faced a growing Taliban insurgency, and the corrupt Afghanistan government led many Americans to wonder whether mounting American casualties in Afghanistan were justified. In December 2009 the commander-in-chief announced a new plan that would increase the number of U.S. troops in Afghanistan and change tactics used to fight the Taliban. By the end of American combat troop withdrawals from Iraq in August 2010, the additional U.S. troops were in place in Afghanistan, and the nation and the world waited to see whether the new strategy would be successful.

The traditional distinction between domestic and foreign policy is becoming more and more difficult to maintain, since so many contemporary policy decisions have important implications on both fronts. President Clinton's emphasis on the connection between domestic and international economic issues in maintaining what he called national economic security was reinforced at this point. In turn, he worked hard to pass the NAFTA accord of 1993, which dramatically reduced trade barriers among Canada, Mexico, and the United States. Similarly, President George W. Bush has repeatedly noted the connection between, on the one hand, military and diplomatic activities with respect to faraway places like Afghanistan, Iraq, Iran, and North Korea and, on the other, homeland security in the post-September 11 era. In his second inaugural address in 2005, President Bush declared that the liberty and security of Americans at home depends on the "expansion of freedom in all the world."

Two prominent policy challenges facing the Obama administration, economic recovery and global warming, further illustrate the convergence between domestic and foreign policy. With an increasingly globalized economy, the economic health of the United States is inevitably tied to economic conditions around the world. Similarly, no unilateral action by the United States or any other nation to fight global warming can be successful on its own; strategies to combat climate change can succeed only if pursued on a multilateral, or global level.

Internet References

American Diplomacy
www.unc.edu/depts/diplomat/

Cato Institute
www.cato.org/research/ss_prjct.html

Foreign Affairs
www.foreignaffairs.org

International Information Programs
http://usinfo.state.gov

STAT-USA
www.stat-usa.gov/stat-usa.html

Tax Foundation
www.taxfoundation.org/index.html

The Realities of Immigration

LINDA CHAVEZ

What to do about immigration—both legal and illegal—has become one of the most controversial public-policy debates in recent memory. But why it has occurred at this particular moment is something of a mystery. The rate of immigration into the U.S., although high, is still below what it was even a few years ago, the peak having been reached in the late 1990s. President Bush first talked about comprehensive immigration reform almost immediately after assuming office, but he put the plan on hold after 9/11 and only reintroduced the idea in 2004. Why the current flap?

By far the biggest factor shaping the popular mood seems to have been the almost daily drumbeat on the issue from political talk-show hosts, most prominently CNN's Lou Dobbs and the Fox News Channel's Bill O'Reilly and Scan Hannity (both of whom also have popular radio shows), syndicated radio hosts Rush Limbaugh, Laura Ingraham, Michael Savage, and G. Gordon Liddy, and a plethora of local hosts reaching tens of millions of listeners each week. Stories about immigration have become a staple of cable news, with sensational footage of illegal crossings featured virtually every day.

Media saturation has led, in turn, to the emergence of immigration as a wedge issue in the still-nascent 2008 presidential campaign. Several aspiring Republican candidates—former House Speaker Newt Gingrich, Senate Majority Leader Bill Frist, and Senator George Allen—have worked to burnish their "get tough" credentials, while, on the other side of the issue, Senator John McCain has come forward as the lead sponsor of a bill to allow most illegal aliens to earn legal status. For their part, potential Democratic candidates have remained largely mum, unsure how the issue plays with their various constituencies.

And then there are the immigrants themselves, who have shown surprising political muscle, especially in response to legislation passed by the House that would turn the illegal aliens among them into felons. Millions of mostly Hispanic protesters have taken to the streets in our big cities in recent months, waving American flags and (more controversially) their own national flags while demanding recognition and better treatment. Though Hispanic leaders and pro-immigrant advocates point to the protests as evidence of a powerful new civil-rights movement, many other Americans see the demonstrators as proof of an alien invasion—and a looming threat to the country's prosperity and unity.

In short, it is hard to recall a time when there has been so much talk about immigration and immigration reform—or when so much of the talk has been misinformed, misleading, and ahistorical. Before policy-makers can decide what to do about immigration, the problem itself needs to be better defined, not just in terms of costs and benefits but in relation to America's deepest values.

Contrary to popular myth, immigrants have never been particularly welcome in the United States. Americans have always tended to romanticize the immigrants of their grandparents' generation while casting a skeptical eye on contemporary newcomers. In the first decades of the 20th century, descendants of Northern European immigrants resisted the arrival of Southern and Eastern Europeans, and today the descendants of those once unwanted Italians, Greeks, and Poles are deeply distrustful of current immigrants from Latin America. Congressman Tom Tancredo, a Republican from Colorado and an outspoken advocate of tighter restrictions, is fond of invoking the memory of his Italian immigrant grandfather to argue that he is not anti-immigrant, just anti-illegal immigration. He fails to mention that at the time his grandfather arrived, immigrants simply had to show up on American shores (or walk across the border) to gain legal entry.

With the exception of the infamous Alien and Sedition Acts of 1798, there were few laws regulating immigration for the first hundred years of the nation's history. Though nativist sentiment increased throughout the later decades of the 19th century, giving rise to the 1882 Chinese Exclusion Act, it was not until 1917 that Congress began methodically to limit all immigration, denying admission to most Asians and Pacific Islanders and, in 1924, imposing quotas on those deemed undesirable: Jews, Italians, and others from Southern and Eastern Europe. These restrictions remained largely in effect until 1952, when Congress lifted many of them, including the bar on Asians.

The modern immigration era commenced in 1965 with the passage of the Immigration and Nationality Act, which abolished all national-origin quotas, gave preference to close relatives of American citizens, refugees, and individuals with certain skills, and allowed for immigrants from the Western hemisphere on a first-come, first-served basis. The act's passage drew a huge wave, much of it from Latin America and Asia. From 1970 to 2000, the United States admitted more than 20 million persons as permanent residents.

By 2000, some 3 million of these new residents were formerly illegal aliens who had gained amnesty as part of the 1986 Immigration Reform and Control Act (IRCA). This, Congress's first serious attempt to stem the flow of illegal immigration, forced employers to determine the status of their workers and imposed heavy penalties on those hiring illegal entrants. But from the beginning, the law was fraught with problems. It created huge bureaucratic burdens, even for private individuals wanting to hire someone to cut their lawn or care for their children, and spawned a vast new document-fraud industry for immigrants eager to get hold of the necessary paperwork. The law has been a monumental failure. Today, some 11.5 million illegal aliens reside in the U.S.—quadruple the population of two decades ago, when IRCA was enacted—and the number is growing by an estimated 500,000 a year.

The status quo has thus become untenable, and particularly so since the attacks of 9/11, which prompted fears of future terrorists sneaking across our sieve-like borders as easily as would-be busboys, janitors, and construction workers. Though virtually all Americans agree that something must be done, finding a good solution has proven elusive. The Bush administration has significantly increased border enforcement, adding nearly 30-percent more border-patrol agents since 2001 and increasing funding by 66 percent. The border patrol now employs nearly as many agents as the FBI, over 12,000 by the end of this fiscal year (not counting the additional 6,000 proposed by the President in May). But with some 6,000 miles of land border to monitor, that figure represents only one agent per mile (assuming eight-hour, 'round-the-clock shifts). Still, there has been progress: illegal immigration has actually slowed a bit since its peak during the boom economy of the late 1990s—a fact rarely noted in the current debate—though it has begun climbing again.

The latest suggestion is to build a wall along the border with Mexico. Some sections of the border already have 10-foot-high steel fences in place, and bills recently passed by the House and Senate authorize the construction of hundreds of additional miles of fencing along the border in California, Arizona, New Mexico, and Texas. The President, too, has endorsed the idea of a more formidable barrier. The Minuteman Project, a group that fashions itself a citizens' patrol, has volunteered to build the fence on private property along the Arizona/Mexico border. But unless the United States is prepared to build fences on its southern and northern borders, illegal entry will continue, albeit in diminished numbers. (Some 200,000 illegal immigrants—the equivalent of 1.8 million in U.S. terms—now live in Canada; most are Asians, but they are increasingly being joined by Latin Americans who in many cases are hoping to make the United States their ultimate destination.) More problematic for advocates of a fence is that an estimated 45 percent of all illegal aliens enter lawfully and simply overstay the terms of their visas.

So what might alleviate the current situation? Restrictionists claim that better internal enforcement, with crackdowns on employers who hire illegal aliens, would deter more from coming. This might work if we were willing to adopt a national identification card for every person in the country and a sophisticated instant-check system to verify the employment eligibility of each of the nation's 150 million workers. But concern over immigration seems unlikely on its own to spark sufficient support for such a system. Even after 9/11, when some experts recommended national ID's as a necessary security measure, Americans were reluctant to endorse the idea, fearing its implications for privacy.

President Bush has now proposed a tamper-proof card that all foreign workers would be required to carry, though one can envision grave "profiling" difficulties with this, not least when native-born Hispanic and Asian workers are selectively asked to produce such identification. Moreover, an experimental version of a program to require instant checks of work eligibility—now included in both the House and the Senate immigration bills—produced a nearly 30-percent error rate for legal immigrants who were denied employment.

The real question is not whether the U.S. has the means to stop illegal immigration—no doubt, with sufficient resources, we could mostly do so—but whether we would be better off as a nation without these workers. Restrictionists claim that large-scale immigration—legal and illegal—has depressed wages, burdened government resources, and acted as a net drain on the economy. The Federation for American Immigration Reform (FAIR), the most prominent of the pressure groups on the issue, argues that, because of this influx, hourly earnings among American males have not increased appreciably in 30 years. As the restrictionists see it, if the U.S. got serious about defending its borders, there would be plenty of Americans willing to do the jobs now performed by workers from abroad.

Indeed, FAIR and other extremists on the issue wish not only to eliminate illegal immigration but drastically to reduce or halt legal immigration as well. Along with its public-policy arm, the Center for Immigration Studies (CIS), FAIR has long argued that the U.S. should aim for a population of just 150 million persons—that is, about half the current level. If such an agenda sounds suspiciously like views usually found on the Left, that is no accident.

One of the great ironies of the current immigration debate is the strange ideological bedfellows it has created. The founder of the modern anti-immigration movement, a Michigan physician named John Tanton, is the former national president of Zero Population Growth and a long-time activist with Planned Parenthood and several Left-leaning environmentalist groups. Tanton came to the issue of immigration primarily because of his fears about overpopulation and the destruction of natural resources. Through an umbrella organization, U.S. Inc., he has created or funded not only FAIR and CIS but such groups as NumbersUSA, Population-Environment Balance, Pro-English, and U.S. English.[1] The Social Contract Press, another of Tanton's outfits, is the English-language publisher of the apocalyptic—and frankly racist—1975 novel *Camp of the Saints,* written by the French right-wing author Jean Raspail. The book, which apparently had a considerable influence in shaping Tanton's own views, foretells the demise of Europe at the hands of hordes of East Indians who invade the continent, bringing with them disease, crime, and anarchy.

As for the more conventional claims advanced by restrictionists, they, too, are hard to credit. Despite the presence in our workforce of millions of illegal immigrants, the U.S. is currently creating slightly more than two million jobs a year and boasts an unemployment rate of 4.7 percent, which is lower than the average in each of the past four decades. More to the point perhaps, when the National Research Council (NRC) of the National Academy of Sciences evaluated the economic impact of immigration in its landmark 1997 study The New Americans: Economic, Demographic, and Fiscal Effects of Immigration, it found only a small negative impact on the earnings of Americans, and even then, only for workers at lower skill and education levels.

Moreover, the participation of immigrants in the labor force has had obvious positive effects. The NRC estimated that roughly 5 percent of household expenditures in the U.S. went to goods and services produced by immigrant labor—labor whose relative cheapness translated into lower prices for everything from chicken to new homes. These price advantages, the study found, were "spread quite uniformly across most types of domestic consumers," with a slightly greater benefit for higher-income households.

Many restrictionists argue that if Americans would simply cut their own lawns, clean their own houses, and care for their own children, there would be no need for immigrant labor. But even if this were true, the overall economy would hardly benefit from having fewer workers. If American women were unable to rely on immigrants to perform some household duties, more of them would be forced to stay home. A smaller labor force would also have devastating consequences when it comes to dealing with the national debt and government-funded entitlements like Social Security and Medicare, a point repeatedly made by former Federal Reserve Board Chairman Alan Greenspan. As he told a Senate committee in 2003, "short of a major increase in immigration, economic growth cannot be safely counted upon to eliminate deficits and the difficult choices that will be required to restore fiscal discipline." The following year, Greenspan noted that offsetting the fiscal effects of our own declining birthrate would require a level of immigration "much larger than almost all current projections assume."

The contributions that immigrants make to the economy must be weighed, of course, against the burdens they impose. FAIR and other restrictionist groups contend that immigrants are a huge drain on society because of the cost of providing public services to them—some $67 to $87 billion a year, according to one commonly cited study. Drawing on numbers from the NRC's 1997 report, FAIR argues that "the net fiscal drain on American taxpayers [from immigration] is between $166 and $226 a year per native household."

There is something to these assertions, though less than may at first appear. Much of the anxiety and resentment generated by immigrants is, indeed, a result of the very real costs they impose on state and local governments, especially in border states like California and Arizona. Providing education and health care to the children of immigrants is particularly expensive, and the federal government picks up only a fraction of the expense. But, again, there are countervailing factors. Illegal immigrants are hardly free-riders. An estimated three-quarters of them paid federal taxes in 2002, amounting to $7 billion in Social Security contributions and $1.5 billion in Medicare taxes, plus withholding for income taxes. They also pay state and local sales taxes and (as homeowners and renters) property taxes.

Moreover, FAIR and its ilk have a penchant for playing fast and loose with numbers. To support its assessment of immigration's overall fiscal burden, for instance, FAIR ignores the explicit cautions in a later NRC report about cross-sectional analyses that exclude the "concurrent descendants" of immigrants—that is, their adult children. These, overwhelmingly, are productive members of the workforce. As the NRC notes, when this more complete picture is taken into account, immigrants have "a positive federal impact of about $1,260 [per capita], exceeding their net cost [$680 per capita on average] at the state and local levels." Restrictionists also argue that fewer immigrants would mean more opportunities for low-skilled native workers. Of late, groups like the Minuteman Project have even taken to presenting themselves as champions of unemployed American blacks (a curious tactic, to say the least, considering the views on race and ethnicity of many in the anti-immigrant camp[2]).

But here, too, the factual evidence is mixed. Wages for American workers who have less than a high-school education have probably been adversely affected by large-scale immigration; the economist George Borjas estimates a reduction of 8 percent in hourly wages for native-born males in that category. But price competition is not the only reason that many employers favor immigrants over poorly educated natives. Human capital includes motivation, and there could hardly be two more disparately motivated groups than U.S.-born high-school dropouts and their foreign-born rivals in the labor market. Young American men usually leave high school because they become involved with drugs or crime, have difficulty with authority, cannot maintain regular hours, or struggle with learning. Immigrants, on the other hand, have demonstrated enormous initiative, reflecting, in the words of President Reagan, "a special kind of courage that enabled them to leave their own land, leave their friends and their countrymen, and come to this new and strange land."

Just as important, they possess a strong desire to work. Legal immigrants have an 86-percent rate of participation in the labor force; illegal immigrant males have a 94-percent rate. By contrast, among white males with less than a high-school education, the participation rate is 46 percent, while among blacks it is 40 percent. If all immigrants, or even only illegal aliens, disappeared from the American workforce, can anyone truly believe that poorly skilled whites and blacks would fill the gap? To the contrary, productivity would likely decline, and employers in many sectors would simply move their operations to countries like Mexico, China, and the Philippines, where many of our immigrants come from in the first place.

Of equal weight among foes of immigration are the cultural changes wrought by today's newcomers, especially those from Mexico. In his book *Who Are We? The Challenges to National Identity* (2004), the eminent political scientist Samuel P. Huntington warns that "Mexican immigration is leading toward the demographic reconquista of areas Americans took from Mexico by force in the 1830s and 1840s." Others have fretted about the aims of militant Mexican-American activists, pointing to "El Plan de Aztlan," a radical Hispanic manifesto hatched in 1969, which calls for "the control of our barrios, campos, pueblos, lands, our economy, our culture, and our political life," including "self-defense against the occupying forces of the oppressors"—that is, the U.S. government.

To be sure, the fantasy of a recaptured homeland exists mostly in the minds of a handful of already well-assimilated Mexican-American college professors and the students they manage to indoctrinate (self-described "victims" who often enjoy preferential admission to college and subsidized or free tuition). But such rhetoric understandably alarms many Americans, especially in light of the huge influx of Hispanic immigrants into the Southwest. Does it not seem likely that today's immigrants—because of their numbers, the constant flow of even more newcomers, and their proximity to their countries of origin—will be unable or unwilling to assimilate as previous ethnic groups have done?

There is no question that some public policies in the U.S. have actively discouraged assimilation. Bilingual education, the dominant method of instruction of Hispanic immigrant children for some 30 years, is the most obvious culprit, with its emphasis on retaining Spanish. But bilingual education is on the wane, having been challenged by statewide initiatives in California (1998), Arizona (2000), and Massachusetts (2004), and by policy shifts in several major cities and at the federal level. States that have moved to English-immersion instruction have seen test scores for Hispanic youngsters rise, in some cases substantially.

Evidence from the culture at large is also encouraging. On most measures of social and economic integration, Hispanic immigrants and their descendants have made steady strides up the ladder. English is the preferred language of virtually all U.S.-born Hispanics; indeed, according to a 2002 national survey by the Pew Hispanic Center and the Kaiser Family Foundation, 78 percent of third-generation Mexican-Americans cannot speak Spanish at all. In education, 86 percent of U.S.-born Hispanics complete high school, compared with 92 percent of non-Hispanic whites, and the drop-out rate among immigrant children who enroll in high school after they come here is no higher than for the native-born.

It remains true that attendance at four-year colleges is lower among Hispanics than for other groups, and Hispanics lag in attaining bachelor's degrees. But neither that nor their slightly lower rate of high-school attendance has kept Hispanic immigrants from pulling their economic weight. After controlling for education, English proficiency, age, and geographic location, Mexican-born males actually earn 2.4 percent more than comparable U.S.-born white males, according to a recent analysis of 2000 Census data by the National Research Council. Hispanic women, for their part, hold their own against U.S.-born white women with similar qualifications.

As for the effect of Hispanic immigrants on the country's social fabric, the NRC found that they are more likely than other Americans to live with their immediate relatives: 88.6 percent of Mexican immigrant households are made up of families, compared with 69.5 percent of non-Hispanic whites and 68.3 percent of blacks. These differences are partially attributable to the age structure of the Hispanic population, which is younger on average than the white or black population. But even after adjusting for age and immigrant generation, U.S. residents of Hispanic origin—and especially those from Mexico—are much more likely to live in family households. Despite increased out-of-wedlock births among Hispanics, about 67 percent of American children of Mexican origin live in two-parent families, as compared with 77 percent of white children but only 37 percent of black children.

Perhaps the strongest indicator of Hispanic integration into American life is the population's high rate of intermarriage. About a quarter of all Hispanics marry outside their ethnic group, almost exclusively to non-Hispanic white spouses, a rate that has remained virtually unchanged since 1980. And here a significant fact has been noted in a 2005 study by the Population Reference Bureau—namely, that "the majority of inter-Hispanic children are reported as Hispanic." Such inter-marriages themselves, the study goes on, "may have been a factor in the phenomenal growth of the U.S. Hispanic population in recent years."

It has been widely predicted that, by mid-century, Hispanics will represent fully a quarter of the U.S. population. Such predictions fail to take into account that increasing numbers of these "Hispanics" will have only one grandparent or great-grandparent of Hispanic heritage. By that point, Hispanic ethnicity may well mean neither more nor less than German, Italian, or Irish ethnicity means today.

How, then, to proceed? Congress is under growing pressure to strengthen border control, but unless it also reaches some agreement on more comprehensive reforms, stauncher enforcement is unlikely to have much of an effect. With a growing economy and more jobs than our own population can readily absorb, the U.S. will continue to need immigrants. Illegal immigration already responds reasonably well to market forces. It has increased during boom times like the late 1990's and decreased again when jobs disappear, as in the latest recession. Trying to determine an ideal number makes no more sense than trying to predict how much steel or how many textiles we ought to import; government quotas can never match the efficiency of simple supply and demand. As President Bush has argued—and as the Senate has now agreed—a guest-worker program is the way to go.

Does this mean the U.S. should just open its borders to anyone who wants to come? Hardly. We still need an orderly process, one that includes background checks to insure that terrorists and criminals are not being admitted. It also makes sense to require that immigrants have at least a basic knowledge of English and to give preference to those who have advanced skills or needed talents.

Moreover, immigrants themselves have to take more responsibility for their status. Illegal aliens from Mexico now pay significant sums of money to "coyotes" who sneak them across the border. If they could come legally as guest workers, that same money might be put up as a surety bond to guarantee their return at the end of their employment contract, or perhaps to pay for health insurance. Nor is it good policy to allow immigrants to become welfare recipients or to benefit from affirmative action: restrictions on both sorts of programs have to be written into law and stringently applied.

A market-driven guest-worker program might be arranged in any number of ways. A proposal devised by the Vernon K. Krieble Foundation, a policy group based in Colorado, suggests that government-licensed, private-sector employment agencies be put in charge of administering the effort, setting up offices in other countries to process applicants and perform background checks. Workers would be issued tamper-proof identity cards only after signing agreements that would allow for deportation if they violated the terms of their contract or committed crimes in the U.S. Although the Krieble plan would offer no path to citizenship, workers who wanted to change their status could still apply for permanent residency and, ultimately, citizenship through the normal, lengthy process.

Do such schemes stand a chance politically? A poll commissioned by the Krieble Foundation found that most Americans (except those with less than a high-school education) consider an "efficient system for handling guest workers" to be more important than expanded law enforcement in strengthening the country's border. Similarly, a CNN tracking poll in May found that 81 percent of respondents favored legislation permitting illegal immigrants who have been in the U.S. more than five years to stay here and apply for citizenship, provided they had jobs and paid back taxes. True, other polls have contradicted these results, suggesting public ambivalence on the issue—and an openness to persuasion.

Regardless of what Congress does or does not do—the odds in favor of an agreement between the Senate and House on final legislation are still no better than 50–50—immigration is likely to continue at high levels for the foreseeable future. Barring a recession or another terrorist attack, the U.S. economy is likely to need some 1.5 to 2 million immigrants a year for some time to come. It would be far better for all concerned if those who wanted to work in the U.S. and had jobs waiting for them here could do so legally, in the light of day and with the full approval of the American people.

In 1918, at the height of the last great wave of immigrants and the hysteria that it prompted in some circles, Madison Grant, a Yale-educated eugenicist and leader of the immigration-restriction movement, made a prediction:

The result of unlimited immigration is showing plainly in the rapid decline in the birth rate of native Americans because the poorer classes of colonial stock, where they still exist, will not bring children into the world to compete in the labor market with the Slovak, the Italian, the Syrian, and the Jew. . . . The man of the old stock is being crowded out of many country districts by these foreigners, just as he is today being literally driven off the streets of New York City by the swarms of Polish Jews. These immigrants adopt the language of the native American, they wear his clothes, they steal his name, and they are beginning to take his women, but they seldom adopt his religion or understand his ideals, and while he is being elbowed out of his own home, the American looks calmly abroad and urges on others the suicidal ethics which are exterminating his own race.

Today, such alarmism reads as little more than a historical curiosity. Southern and Eastern European immigrants and their children did, in fact, assimilate, and in certain cases—most prominently that of the Jews—they exceeded the educational and economic attainments of Grant's "colonial stock."

Present-day restrictionists point to all sorts of special circumstances that supposedly made such acculturation possible in the past but render it impossible today. Then as now, however, the restrictionists are wrong, not least in their failure to understand the basic dynamic of American nationhood. There is no denying the challenge posed by assimilating today's newcomers, especially so many of them in so short a span of time. Nor is there any denying the cultural forces, mainly stemming from the Left, that have attenuated the sense of national identity among native-born American elites themselves and led to such misguided policies as bilingual education. But, provided that we commit ourselves to the goal, past experience and progress to date suggest the task is anything but impossible.

As jarring as many found the recent pictures of a million illegal aliens marching in our cities, the fact remains that many of the immigrants were carrying the American flag, and waving it proudly. They and their leaders understand what most restrictionists do not and what some Americans have forgotten or choose to deny: that the price of admission to America is, and must be, the willingness to become an American.

Notes

1. I was briefly president of U.S. English in the late 1980s but resigned when a previously undisclosed memo written by Tanton was published. In it, he warned of problems related to the "educability" of Hispanics and speculated that an influx of Catholics from south of the border might well lead the U.S. to "pitch out" the concept of church-state separation. Tanton was forced to resign as chairman of U.S. English and no longer has any affiliation with the group.

2. As the author and anti-immigration activist Peter Brimelow wrote in his 1995 book *Alien Nation,* "Americans have a legitimate interest in their country's racial balance . . . [and] a right to insist that their government stop shifting it." Himself an immigrant from England, Brimelow wants "more immigrants who look like me."

Critical Thinking

1. Why has immigration become such a hot topic within the past decade?

2. Why is border security only a partial solution to the immigration problem?

3. What is the restrictionist position on immigration?

4. What are some of the contributions immigrants make to the U.S. economy? What are some of the burdens they impose?

5. Describe how a market-based approach to immigration policy might work. Is this type of approach feasible to implement?

LINDA CHAVEZ, the author of *Out of the Barrio* (1991), among other books, is the chairman of the Center for Equal Opportunity in Washington, D.C. She is at work on a new book about immigration.

The *Real* Infrastructure Crisis

The nation's roads and bridges are in pretty good shape. It's the national will that is suspect.

BURT SOLOMON

It's a frighteningly familiar catastrophe to imagine. An earthquake in Northern California ruptures 30 levees along the converging Sacramento and San Joaquin rivers, and 300 billion gallons of saltwater rush inland from San Francisco Bay, flooding 16 islands and ruining the supply of fresh water across two-thirds of the nation's most populous state. Or picture this: In southern Kentucky, the 55-year-old Wolf Creek Dam (where water has seeped through the foundations for years) gives way. The breach lets loose the largest man-made reservoir east of the Mississippi River, flooding the communities along the Cumberland River and shorting out the electric guitars in Nashville.

These were the top two horror stories—"5 Disasters Coming Soon If We Don't Rebuild U.S. Infrastructure"—that *Popular Mechanics* conjured up for its readers last fall, after the collapse of a bridge in Minnesota killed 13 innocents on their way home from work. The stunning sight of an interstate highway plunging into the Mississippi River, just two weeks after a steam pipe exploded beneath Lexington Avenue in Midtown Manhattan—and less than two years after Hurricane Katrina brought New Orleans to its knees—dramatically brought the nation's fallible infrastructure to the public's attention. So, too, did the overwhelmed levees along the Midwestern rivers during the recent rains. And so did the garden-variety failures, such as the water main break on June 16 in Montgomery County, Md., bordering Washington that forced some of the capital's bigwigs to boil water before brushing their teeth.

In the mammoth but aging networks of roads, bridges, railroads, air traffic, sewers, pipelines, supplies of fresh water, and electricity grids that helped turn the United States into the world's economic superpower, other dangers lurk. All over the country, clean-water and wastewater facilities are wearing out. The combined sewers that 40 million people in 772 cities use could disgorge their raw contents into waterways when the next storm passes through. Every summer brings the possibility of blackouts.

Traffic gridlock has become a fact of life, jamming the highways and airways and creating bottlenecks of goods through the ports, especially around Los Angeles and New York City. The American Society of Civil Engineers has classified 3,500 of the nation's 79,000 dams as unsafe; in a 2005 report card

How Bad Is It?

- The total amount of money spent on infrastructure has **consistently been increasing,** mainly because of state and local investments.
- Even so, on a global scale, American infrastructure is **no longer on the cutting edge.**
- Both John McCain and Barack Obama have highlighted **infrastructure spending as an issue** in the presidential campaign.

on the nation's infrastructure, the society assigned grades that ranged from C+ (for the proper disposal of solid waste) down to D− (for the supply of drinking water and the treatment of wastewater).

Talk of the "crisis" in the nation's physical infrastructure has leapt beyond think-tank forums and earnest editorials. It has quickened legislators' interest, generated heartfelt lobbying on Capitol Hill—expected to climax next year when Congress must reauthorize the pork-laden highway program—and nosed its way into the presidential campaign.

Experts, however, consider "crisis" an overblown description of the perils that America's infrastructure poses. Federal investigators have tentatively concluded that the ill-fated Interstate-35W in Minnesota collapsed not because it was structurally deficient—although it was—but because of a design defect: The gusset plates connecting the steel beams were half as thick as they should have been. Nationwide, bridges are in better structural condition than they were 20 years ago, and the most critical of the nation's 4 million miles of roadways are in pretty good shape. In the transportation system, "the physical condition has not noticeably deteriorated . . . in the past two decades," said Katherine A. Siggerud, the managing director of physical infrastructure issues at the determinedly nonpolitical Government Accountability Office. "The condition of the most-traveled roads and bridges in the United States, the interstates and the national highways, [has] improved in quality."

The more serious problem is the lack of roads and the traffic congestion that this shortage creates, especially around major cities. In the nation's airways, too, congestion has become chronic, especially at airports in the Northeast. But Gerald Dillingham, the GAO's director of civil aviation issues, doesn't see a crisis in the near- or midterm, and he is hopeful that better technology and new ways of structuring the airways can stave off disaster for at least the next 15 years. The Transportation Department has calculated the overall economic cost of congestion at $200 billion a year, surely a drag on the nation's commerce, not to mention a vexation to anyone stuck in traffic. Still, in a $14 trillion economy, that amounts to 1.4 percent—a pittance.

Fixing the nation's infrastructure is "a matter of fine-tuning the economic production system," said Kenneth A. Small, an economist who specializes in transportation at the University of California (Irvine), "not a matter of moral outrage." Rudolph G. Penner, a senior fellow at the Urban Institute, said, "I'd call it a problem, not a crisis." Even the lobbyists who urge more spending on the nation's infrastructure acknowledge that the assertions of impending doom are an exaggeration. Janet F. Kavinoky, the director of transportation infrastructure at the U.S. Chamber of Commerce, is the executive director of Americans for Transportation Mobility, an alliance of construction companies and labor unions. "If you don't say it's a crisis," she explained, "nobody shows up at your press conference."

> **Even the lobbyists who urge more spending acknowledge that the assertions of impending doom are an exaggeration. "If you don't say it's a crisis, nobody shows up at your press conference."**
>
> —Janet F. Kavinoky, director of transportation infrastructure at the U.S. Chamber of Commerce

Nor is the country ignoring the issue. The nation's spending on infrastructure continues to rise; New Orleans is rebuilding the levees that Katrina breached. "The things that need to get done are getting done, by and large," said Timothy P. Lynch, the American Trucking Associations' senior vice president for federal relations and strategic planning.

This isn't to say, of course, that all is hunky-dory. The future of U.S. infrastructure could be grim indeed if too little is done. At the core, it's a question of cost. Bridges and roads are expensive—to build or to fix—and so are mass transit, airport runways, and almost everything else. The civil engineers issued a widely invoked price tag of $1.6 trillion over five years to do what needs to be done, but even champions of a strong infrastructure find such a number inflated—"a compilation of a wish list," the ATA's Lynch said.

Moreover, investment bankers say that plenty of capital is available for work that is critical to the nation's well-being. What may be missing, however, is the political will to spend this capital. Increasingly, legislators and local governments are trying to arrange infrastructure financing in ways that conceal

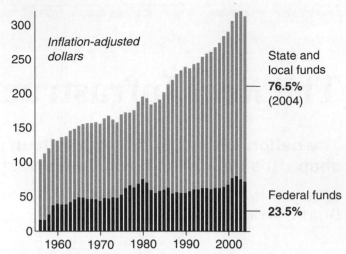

$350 billion

Inflation-adjusted dollars

State and local funds
76.5%
(2004)

Federal funds
23.5%

The Big Picture Spending on the nation's infrastructure has increased, but state and local governments are footing a larger share of the bill.

Total Public infrastructure Spending, 1956–2004.

Source: Congressional Budget Office.

the true costs from taxpayers, who are reluctant to foot the bill, and that may transfer the financial burdens to future generations. If the measure of a society's responsibility is its willingness to invest for the long run, then the crisis in infrastructure is this: Do Americans possess the national will to pay for what their children and their children's children are going to need?

Ancient Rome Meets Reagan

Only occasionally has a civilization made its infrastructure an emblem of its ambition or greatness. Consider, notably, the marvels of ancient Rome—its roads, its aqueducts, its public baths and lavatories, its Colosseum and other sites of public entertainment. Conceived as a military necessity to assure the movement of troops through a far-flung empire, Rome's extravagant and enduring infrastructure took on other functions, too. As a public benefaction, it gave the state a way to justify its own existence, according to Garrett G. Fagan, a historian at Pennsylvania State University, and the many amenities that wealthy families financed served as "a kind of social compact between the upper classes and the poorer classes." The boldness and breadth of Roman infrastructure, Fagan said, "go a long way to explain why the empire lasted so long."

The United States has often shown a similar ambition. In 1808, after Thomas Jefferson's Louisiana Purchase added a vast wilderness that stretched as far as the future Montana, Treasury Secretary Albert Gallatin proposed a national transportation network of roads, rivers, and ports.

In the following decades, Henry Clay of Kentucky lent his legislative weight in the House, and then in the Senate, to the "internal improvements" of canals and railroads. Abraham Lincoln, even as he struggled to win the Civil War, pursued plans for a transcontinental railroad. Theodore Roosevelt, so fond of proclaiming the needs of "future generations," convened a conference of governors that resulted in water projects that irrigated the West and generated electricity cheaply; his list of ventures-still-undone gave TR's fifth cousin, Franklin D. Roosevelt, a starting point when he tried to spend the nation out of the Great Depression. Then, in the postwar boom of the 1950s, President Eisenhower pressed for a system of interstate highways that knitted the nation together and bolstered its economy. As late as the 1970s, after the Cuyahoga River in Cleveland caught fire in 1969, the federal government invested tens of billions of dollars in sewer systems and wastewater treatment plants.

Taxpayers' generosity toward the nation's infrastructure, however, took a dive during the 1980s. President Reagan's aversion to using taxes for domestic spending, exacerbated by Wall Street's obsession with quarterly earnings, encouraged a shortsightedness in assessing the public good. According to Sherle R. Schwenninger, the director of the New America Foundation's economic growth program, the money that government at all levels has devoted to infrastructure, as a proportion of the nation's total economic output, slipped from 3 percent during the 1950s and 1960s to only 2 percent in recent years.

"We've just not reinvested," former Council of Economic Advisers Chairman Martin N. Baily complained at a Brookings Institution forum last fall, "because nobody wanted to raise the taxes to do that." Even in Katrina-devastated Louisiana, when the Army Corps of Engineers announced in 2006 that its estimate for fixing the levees had ballooned from $3.5 billion to $9.5 billion, the state's politicians and editorial writers wailed.

Not to Worry

It wouldn't take many years, or so it is said, before the weeds poked up through a neglected interstate highway. Not to worry. Even as the nation's enthusiasm for long-term investments has flagged, the total amount of money spent on its infrastructure has continued to grow. As the federal share has shrunk (from 32 percent in 1982 to less than 24 percent in 2004, according to the Congressional Budget Office), state and local governments have picked up the slack. Counting all levels of government, public entities spent $312 billion on the nation's transportation and water infrastructure in 2004, three times as much—after taking inflation into account—as in 1956, when Eisenhower's heyday began. *(See chart.)*

Has the U.S. underfunded its infrastructure, on which its economy rests? "Compared to what we really need, I think so," said Penner, a former CBO director, "but relatively slightly."

Consider, for example, the state of the nation's bridges. Last summer's tragedy in Minnesota cast a spotlight on the Federal Highway Administration's alarming conclusion that, as of last December, 12 percent of the nation's bridges were structurally deficient. But less attention was paid to the fact that this proportion had shrunk from 13 percent in 2004 and nearly 19 percent in 1994. Nor was it widely noticed that the label of "structurally deficient" covered a range of poor conditions, from serious to far less so. Fewer than a tenth of the tens of thousands of bridges deemed deficient are anywhere close to falling down. (A Federal Highway Administration spokeswomen said the agency

does not have summary information about the location and size of the worst bridges.)

The surge of bridge inspections that followed the disaster in Minnesota turned up a second bridge with bowed gusset plates across the Mississippi in Minneapolis-St. Paul—it was immediately closed and slated for repairs—and another one in Duluth. The Minnesota Legislature found numerous shortcomings in the state inspectors' work on the I-35 bridge that had been tagged as structurally deficient for some cracking and fatigue. According to the National Transportation Safety Board's investigators, however, the inspectors were not the problem. Indeed, the investigators cited the effort to repair the bridge, which entailed piling construction supplies and equipment on its overburdened deck, and the thin gusset plates as the likely leading causes of the I-35 collapse. The more that they have learned about the disaster, the less it has served as a morality tale.

As for a fear of falling bridges, "I don't really think we're in a crisis," said economist Small. He also mentioned the "pretty strong" system of bridge inspections and placed the 13 deaths in Minnesota into the context of all U.S. traffic fatalities, which average 120 a day. "If you plot the statistics," he noted, "you might not notice the bump."

On the roads, too, drunk drivers or malfunctioning vehicles cause many more deaths than potholes or crumbling concrete. The roads are OK, but there aren't enough of them to hold the traffic, and building more will only increase demand. The gridlock is worst of all around Los Angeles, the San Francisco Bay area, Chicago, New York City, Atlanta, and Washington, but it has also spread into unlikelier venues. A third lane is being built along certain truck-clogged stretches of Interstate 80 in Iowa and Nebraska. The GAO's Siggerud pointed to "bottlenecks in every mode of transportation," which stand to get worse. The Federal Aviation Administration has predicted that air traffic may triple during the next two decades, and the American Road & Transportation Builders Association has forecast that the volume of cargo on U.S. roads will double. In Los Angeles, the freight volume is expected to triple as the population grows by 60 percent, producing strains that the U.S. chamber's Kavinoky warned "will paralyze the city."

Ian Grossman, the FHWA's associate administrator for public affairs, lamented the Little League games unattended and the volunteerism in decline because of congestion. "It shouldn't be a fact of life," he said.

The economic impact of the bottlenecks has been "woefully understudied," according to Robert Puentes, an expert in infrastructure at the Brookings Institution, who regards transportation policy as "a fact-free zone." But Clifford Winston, an economist at Brookings, has tried. His calculation of the annual economic cost of congestion is just a third of DOT's—$15 billion in air traffic and nearly $50 billion on the roads, counting the shipping delays, the higher inventories required, the wasted fuel, the value of gridlocked motorists' time, and other not-quite-tangible factors. The impediments are numerous, Winston said, but "none of them are big. That's why they persist."

The problem of congestion is, to a degree, self-limiting. It could injure the economy of a gridlocked metropolis, but by no more than 5 to 10 percent, according to Small, by driving business to the suburbs, exurbs, and smaller cities that stand to benefit from the big cities' pain.

Nor has congestion in the air been neglected. The air traffic system, in which 25 percent of last year's flights arrived late, has added runways in recent years in Atlanta, Boston, Cincinnati, Minneapolis, and St. Louis; starting this November it will add another runway at Chicago's O'Hare. The $13 billion that the FAA spends annually on infrastructure development for civil aviation falls a mere $1 billion short—pocket change, really—of what GAO analyst Dillingham believes it should spend. The next generation of air traffic control, based on a global positioning system instead of on radar, has been delayed—not because of the immense cost or the technology, Dillingham said, but because of the difficulty of integrating it into the existing system.

Scarier, perhaps, for the nation's economic future is the possibility that congestion or other strains on an elderly infrastructure will damage America's already shaky competitive position in global markets. The American business executives who leave South Korea's luxurious Incheon International Airport or Shanghai's modern, half-empty airport to arrive at New York's seedy JFK are bound to feel repulsed. Today, that is nothing more than inconvenience, but eventually, economists say, it could count.

"In a globalized economy," the New America Foundation's Schwenninger said, "there are only a few ways you can compete." Asian countries can claim lower wage rates and taxes, and Europe boasts governmental subsidies and an educated workforce. This leaves infrastructure, Schwenninger ventured, as American businesses' best hope for a competitive edge—more so than 20 to 30 years ago, and more important than education. Silicon Valley, he reported, has lost some of its silicon-wafer manufacturing to Texas and countries overseas because producers fear brownouts in California.

Yet the threat to U.S. competitiveness shouldn't be exaggerated, for other countries face similar problems with congestion. Gaining permission to build a new road or runway is even harder in cramped, environmentally conscious Europe. China and India are spending 9 percent and 5 percent, respectively, of their gross domestic product on infrastructure. The U.S., however, has an overwhelming advantage: Its elaborate infrastructure—4 million miles of roads, 600,000 bridges, 26,000 miles of commercially navigable waterways, 11,000 miles of transit lines, 500 train stations, 300 ports, 19,000 airports, 55,000 community drinking water systems, and 30,000 wastewater plants—is already built.

Ducking the Costs

Still, on matters of infrastructure, the United States is losing ground. "It would be an overstatement to say our system is in crisis," Brookings's Winston said. "At the same time, the annual costs of the inefficiencies [because of congestion] are large, growing, and unlikely to be addressed by the public sector."

No longer is American infrastructure on the cutting edge. "I think we are falling behind the rest of the world," Rep. Earl Blumenauer, an earnest veteran Democrat from Portland, Ore., said in an interview. He is pushing legislation to create a

blue-ribbon commission that would frame a coherent national vision for dealing with the country's disparately owned and operated infrastructure, variously the responsibility of federal, state, or local governments or—for a majority of dams and many recent water systems—private owners. Besides the existing bottlenecks in the movement of goods, Blumenauer foresees "real problems with the backlog of projects"—for sewers, roads, water, bridges, etc.—within five to 10 years. And deferring maintenance, he noted, increases the costs, which is one reason he thinks that the astronomical price tags "tend to be understated, not overstated."

America was once on the cutting edge of infrastructure, but no more. "I think we are falling behind the rest of the world. . . . In the end, there's no substitute for making systematic investment."

—Rep. Earl Blumenauer, D-Ore., who wants to create a blue-ribbon commission on infrastructure

The GAO, among others, is more skeptical, not only of the civil engineers' $1.6 trillion, $300-billion-plus-a-year cost projection but also of a congressionally created panel's recommendations. The National Surface Transportation Policy and Revenue Study Commission announced in January that the nation must spend $225 billion annually—$140 billion more than at present—on its roads, waterways, and railroads. "Most of the needs assessments," the Urban Institute's Penner explained, "are very much influenced by special interests," using unrealistic assumptions and self-serving estimates.

How much the nation must spend, however, is certain to rise. For fresh water and wastewater alone, by the GAO's calculations, the infrastructure costs over the next 20 years will range between $400 billion and nearly $1.2 trillion to correct past underinvestment. The existing facilities, if not repaired or replaced, would probably take 10 to 20 years to deteriorate, an offical said, not two or three.

Given the presumed reluctance of American taxpayers to pay up front, such projections have quickened the search for politically palatable alternatives to financing infrastructure projects—artful ways of ducking the costs. Hence the rising popularity of public-private partnerships, "or as we called them, business deals," Everett M. Ehrlich, an expert on infrastructure financing, told the House Transportation and Infrastructure Committee in June. On May 19, Pennsylvania Gov. Ed Rendell had announced the winning $12.8 billion bid (submitted by a Spanish toll-road company and a division of Citigroup) for a 75-year lease of the Pennsylvania Turnpike. The idea wasn't original. The city of Chicago signed a $1.8 billion lease for the Chicago Skyway in 2005 and has received a half-dozen bids for privatizing Midway Airport. The Indiana Toll Road was leased in 2006 for $3.8 billion. A private company built and runs the Dulles Toll Road in Northern Virginia, and the Texas Legislature has imposed a two-year moratorium on a planned network of private toll roads out of concern that the deals were too lucrative for the operators.

A private operator, the thinking goes, can raise tolls with an abandon that would give politicians the willies, and investment banks are salivating at the prospect of jumping in. But the criticism has mounted. "Deferred maintenance will become a big part of creating profits for shareholders," Allen Zimmerman, a resident of South Whitehall Township, Pa., warned about leasing the turnpike, in a letter to *The Morning Call* of Allentown, Pa. Economists worry that a private operator might milk the drivers along the popular routes while ignoring the boondocks.

By the GAO's lights, the value of any given deal depends on the particulars, such as the quality of the management, the assurances of proper maintenance, and the uses to which a state will put the newfound revenues. Indiana is spending its bump in revenue on a 10-year transportation plan; Chicago, on the other hand, has pointedly refrained from any allocation. Pennsylvania officials have vowed to spend their windfall on transportation but have been "evasive," the ATA's Lynch said, about specifics.

At least so far, the greatest hindrance to an influx of private capital for the nation's infrastructure, according to Penner of the Urban Institute, is the paucity of investment opportunities. He also lacks faith in the other ideas being pitched on Capitol Hill that seek to lure capital while dodging the costs—notably, proposals to establish an infrastructure "bank" to leverage private investments and to institute a separate capital budget for the federal government. Nor does the direct approach—the possibility of federal appropriations—give him reason to hope. He fears that the entitlement programs (Social Security, Medicare, and Medicaid) will squeeze the budget, shrinking the discretionary spending on infrastructure projects.

Where, then, will the money come from? At Brookings, infrastructure expert Puentes thinks that relatively small, targeted investments can relieve the worst bottlenecks—those of national importance, such as the congestion at the port of Long Beach, Calif. In any event, simply relying on the construction of new highways and airport terminals won't suffice, in Small's view: "It's just too expensive."

Many economists favor another solution—congestion pricing. London, Stockholm, and Singapore now charge vehicles that drive into the central cities at busy times of the day. Michael Bloomberg, New York City's businessman-turned-mayor, pursued the idea until the state Legislature shot it down. Pure congestion pricing, a high-tech means of raising or lowering the toll depending on the traffic, is being tested on a highway north of San Diego, where the price of driving changes every few minutes. Such pricing would be one way for Americans to pay their way.

The Political Marketplace

On the night that Sen. Barack Obama of Illinois claimed the Democratic nomination for the presidency, he spoke to the nation about, among a litany of intentions, "investing in our crumbling infrastructure." Of course, he happened to be in Minnesota, less than 10 miles from where the I-35 bridge had collapsed. But

then he spoke of the problem again two days later while campaigning in Virginia and, later, at a roundtable with 16 Democratic governors. In trying to bolster his appeal to working-class voters in Flint, Mich., on June 16, Obama promised to use the money he would save from ending the war in Iraq on a National Infrastructure Reinvestment Bank that would spend $60 billion over 10 years. Stressing the issue helps Obama look sober and serious about the nation's long-term needs, which is useful for a candidate who is criticized for being inexperienced.

24% of infrastructure spending in 2004 was federally funded.

Sen. Hillary Rodham Clinton of New York, whom Obama bested for the nomination, demonstrated the versatility of infrastructure as a political issue. A week after the bridge fell in Minnesota, she delivered a speech in New Hampshire on infrastructure as "a silent crisis." She showed a thorough understanding of the issue ("Today nearly half the locks on our waterways are obsolete.") and offered a detailed plan of attack, including a $10 billion emergency repair fund, $1.5 billion for public transit, $1 billion for intercity passenger railways, and sundry other millions for additional projects. Nine months later, however, facing political death as Indiana Democrats readied to vote, she climbed onto the back of a pickup truck and appealed to voters beleaguered by the soaring price of fuel. Her idea? Suspend the federal gasoline tax, which pays for the upkeep on the nation's pivotal highways. Economists gagged at the thought, but Indiana Democrats rewarded her with a narrow victory.

The presumed Republican nominee, Sen. John McCain of Arizona, who agreed with Clinton on the gasoline tax, has also used infrastructure as a political football. It's a word he reveres. In campaign speeches, he has applied "infrastructure" to public health, alternative fuels, "the infrastructure of civil society," and "the Republican infrastructure." But in the conventional sense, he has linked it to one of his trademark issues. "The problem with roads and infrastructure and bridges and tunnels in America can be laid right at the doorstep of Congress," he said in May, four months after federal investigators blamed the Minnesota bridge collapse on a design flaw, "because the pork-barrel, earmark spending, such as the 'Bridge to Nowhere' in Alaska, has diverted people's hard-earned tax dollars that they pay at the gas pump." This charge drew a public rebuke from Tim Pawlenty, Minnesota's Republican governor, who is a national co-chairman of McCain's campaign and is often mentioned as a possible running mate. "I don't know what he's basing that on," Pawlenty said, "other than the general premise that projects got misprioritized throughout time."

One legislator's pork, of course, is another's infrastructure. Such criticism of "pork," as a result, has not dampened Congress's enthusiasm for spending money on highways and such. The 2005 highway legislation (known, improbably, as SAFETEA-LU) authorized $286 billion over six years, $32 billion more than the Bush administration wanted. But this amount was miserly compared with the House-approved $380 billion.

Members of Congress earmarked just one-tenth of the money for particular projects back home, and not all of those were considered boondoggles. An earmark, for instance, funded the newly built Woodrow Wilson Bridge along the Capital Beltway between Virginia and Maryland.

The lobbyists for the labor unions and the contractors that stand to benefit from road construction are already gearing up for next year's effort to reauthorize the highway bill. The pot will surely grow bigger—reportedly to $500 billion over six years—especially if a Democratic president works with a Democratic Congress. Spending on infrastructure has recently been touted by Rockefeller Foundation President Judith Rodin, among others, as a Keynesian response to an impending recession. And even if earmark-happy highway bills inevitably waste money, they may be worthy of praise for paying up front for whichever roads and bridges—to nowhere or to somewhere— the democratic system has deemed worthy. "In the end, there's no substitute for making systematic investment," Rep. Blumenauer said.

As a political issue, infrastructure is the kind that democracies have a hard time with—a chronic, usually invisible problem that only occasionally becomes acute. For better or worse, however, politics has become inseparable from the battles over infrastructure, sometimes to the point of amusement. When members of the House Transportation and Infrastructure Committee discussed the fateful gusset plates in Minnesota, the Republicans stressed the arbitrary nature of such a failure, which money would never have averted, while the Democrats kept mentioning the bridge's wear and tear, for which more money would have mattered. Partisan positions on gusset plates—who knew?

Still, the politics of infrastructure are far from straightforward. Earmarks and pork find enthusiasts and critics within both political parties. Congestion pricing has produced odd bedfellows. Both Bush administration conservatives and environmental activists approve of such a market mechanism that would save fuel and improve economic efficiency, while some Democrats worry about the effect of "Lexus lanes" on the poor.

The true political divide may lie between Americans who'll be willing and able to pay up front for the nation's needs— whether through taxes or tolls—and those who would rather skimp or burden their children. This sort of decision, between a world-class infrastructure and muddling through, will be made in the political marketplace. If Americans get disgusted enough, they'll do what it takes. Otherwise, they won't.

Critical Thinking

1. What is the most serious problem with physical U.S.infrastructure? Is the situation best classified as a problem or a crisis?

2. Is funding available to improve physical infrastructure? What are the political barriers to spending money on such improvements?

3. What effects might the U.S.'s neglect of air-based infrastructure have on the nation's economic future?

4. How have public-private partnerships been used as a solution to infrastructure improvement? What are some criticisms of this approach?

5. How did key figures in the 2008 presidential election address the issue of physical infrastructure improvements?

The Other National Debt

$14 Trillion in the Red? We Should Be So Lucky

KEVIN D. WILLIAMSON

About that $14 trillion national debt: Get ready to tack some zeroes onto it. Taken alone, the amount of debt issued by the federal government—that $14 trillion figure that shows up on the national ledger—is a terrifying, awesome, hellacious number: Fourteen trillion seconds ago, Greenland was covered by lush and verdant forests, and the Neanderthals had not yet been outwitted and driven into extinction by *Homo sapiens sapiens,* because we did not yet exist. Big number, 14 trillion, and yet it doesn't even begin to cover the real indebtedness of American governments at the federal, state, and local levels, because governments don't count up their liabilities the same way businesses do.

Accountants get a bad rap—boring, green-eyeshades-wearing, nebbishy little men chained to their desks down in the fluorescent-lit basements of Corporate America—but, in truth, accountants wield an awesome power. In the case of the federal government, they wield the power to make vast amounts of debt disappear—from the public discourse, at least. A couple of months ago, you may recall, Rep. Henry Waxman (D., State of Bankruptcy) got his Fruit of the Looms in a full-on buntline hitch when AT&T, Caterpillar, Verizon, and a host of other blue-chip behemoths started taking plus-size writedowns in response to some of the more punitive provisions of the health-care legislation Mr. Waxman had helped to pass. His little mustache no doubt bristling in indignation, Representative Waxman sent dunning letters to the CEOs of these companies and demanded that they come before Congress to explain their accounting practices. One White House staffer told reporters that the writedowns appeared to be designed "to embarrass the president and Democrats."

A few discreet whispers from better-informed Democrats, along with a helpful explanation from *The Atlantic*'s Megan McArdle under the headline "Henry Waxman's War on Accounting," helped to clarify the issue: The companies in question are required by law to adjust their financial statements to reflect the new liabilities: "When a company experiences what accountants call 'a material adverse impact' on its expected future earnings, and those changes affect an item that is already on the balance sheet, the company is required to record the negative impact—'to take the charge against earnings'—as soon as it knows that the change is reasonably likely to occur,"

McArdle wrote. "The Democrats, however, seem to believe that Generally Accepted Accounting Principles are some sort of conspiracy against Obamacare, and all that is good and right in America." But don't be too hard on the gentleman from California: Government does not work that way. If governments did follow normal accounting practices, taking account of future liabilities today instead of pretending they don't exist, then the national-debt numbers we talk about would be worse— far worse, dreadfully worse—than that monster $14 trillion–and–ratcheting–upward figure we throw around.

Beyond the official federal debt, there is another $2.5 trillion or so in state and local debt, according to Federal Reserve figures. Why so much? A lot of that debt comes from spending that is extraordinarily stupid and wasteful, even by government standards. Because state and local authorities can issue tax-free securities—municipal bonds—there's a lot of appetite for their debt on the marketplace, and a whole platoon of local special-interest hustlers looking to get a piece. This results in a lot of misallocated capital: By shacking up with your local economic-development authority, you can build yourself a new major-league sports stadium with tax-free bonds, but you have to use old-fashioned financing, with no tax benefits, if you want to build a factory—which is to say, you can use tax-free municipal bonds to help create jobs, so long as those jobs are selling hot dogs to sports fans.

Also, local political machines tend to be dominated by politically connected law firms that enjoy a steady stream of basically free money from legal fees charged when those municipal bonds are issued, so they have every incentive to push for more and more indebtedness at the state and local levels. For instance, the Philadelphia law firm of Ballard Spahr kept Ed Rendell on the payroll to the tune of $250,000 a year while he was running for governor—he described his duties at the firm as "very little"—and the firm's partners donated nearly $1 million to his campaign. They're big in the bond-counsel business, as they advertise in their marketing materials: "We have one of the premier public finance practices in the country, participating since 1987 in the issuance of more than $250 billion of tax-exempt obligations in 49 states, the District of Columbia, and three territories." Other Pennsylvania bond-counsel firms were big Rendell donors, too, and they get paid from 35 cents to 50 cents per $1,000 in municipal bonds issued, so they love it when the local powers borrow money.

So that's $14 trillion in federal debt and $2.5 trillion in state-and-local debt: $16.5 trillion. But I've got some bad news for you, Sunshine: We haven't even hit all the big-ticket items.

One of the biggest is the pension payments owed to government workers. And here's where the state-and-local story actually gets quite a bit worse than what's happening in Washington—it's the sort of thing that might make you rethink that whole federalism business. While the federal government runs a reasonably well-administered retirement program for its workers, the states, in their capacity as the laboratories of democracy, have been running a mad-scientist experiment in their pension funds, making huge promises but skipping the part where they sock away the money to pay for them. Every year, the pension funds' actuaries calculate how much money must be saved and invested that year to fund future benefits, and every year the fund managers ignore them. In 2009, for instance, the New Jersey public-school teachers' pension system invested just 6 percent of the amount of money its actuaries calculated was needed. And New Jersey is hardly alone in this. With a handful of exceptions, practically every state's pension fund is poised to run out of money in the coming decades. A federal bailout is almost inevitable, which means that those state obligations will probably end up on the national balance sheet in one form or another.

The states have been running a mad-scientist experiment in their pension funds, making huge promises but skipping the part where they sock away the money to pay for them.

"We're facing a full-fledged state-level debt crisis later this decade," says Prof. Joshua D. Rauh of the Kellogg School of Management at Northwestern University, who recently published a paper titled "Are State Public Pensions Sustainable?" Good question. Professor Rauh is a bit more nuanced than John Boehner, but he comes to the same conclusion: Hell, no. "Half the states' pension funds could run out of money by 2025," he says, "and that's assuming decent investment returns. The federal government should be worried about its exposure. Are these states too big to fail? If something isn't done, we're facing another trillion-dollar bailout."

The problem, Professor Rauh explains, is that pension funds are used to hide government borrowing. "A defined-benefit plan is politicians making promises on time horizons that go beyond their political careers, so it's really cheap," he says. "They say, 'Maybe we don't want to give you a pay raise, but we'll give you a really generous pension in 40 years.' It's a way to borrow off the books." The resulting liability runs into the trillions of dollars.

Ground Zero for the state-pension meltdown is Springfield, Ill., and D-Day comes around 2018: That's when the state that nurtured the political career of Barack Obama is expected to be the first state to run out of money to cover its retirees' pension checks. Eight years—and that's assuming an 8 percent average return on its investments. (You making 8 percent a year lately?) Under the same projections, Illinois will be joined in 2019 by Connecticut, New Jersey, and Indiana. If investment returns are 6 percent, then 31 U.S. states will run out of pension-fund money by 2025, according to Rauh's projections.

States aren't going to be able to make up those pension short-falls out of general tax revenue, at least not at current levels of taxation. In Ohio, for instance, the benefit payments in 2031 would total 55 percent of projected 2031 tax revenues. For most states, pension payments will total more than a quarter of all tax revenues in the years after they run out of money. Most of those pensions cannot be modified: Illinois, for instance, has a constitutional provision that prevents reducing them. Unless there is a radical restructuring of these programs, and soon, states will either have to subsidize their pension systems with onerous new taxes or seek a bailout from Washington.

So how much would the states have to book to fully fund those liabilities? Drop in another $3 trillion. Properly accounting for these obligations, that takes us up to a total of $19.5 trillion in governmental liabilities. Bad, right? You know how the doctor looks at you in that recurring nightmare, when the test results come back and he has to tell you not to bother buying any green bananas? Imagine that look on Tim Geithner's face right now, because we still have to account for the biggest crater in the national ledger: entitlement liabilities.

The debt numbers start to get really hairy when you add in liabilities under Social Security and Medicare—in other words, when you account for the present value of those future payments in the same way that businesses have to account for the obligations they incur. Start with the entitlements and those numbers get run-for-the-hills ugly in a hurry: a combined $106 trillion in liabilities for Social Security and Medicare, or more than five times the total federal, state, and local debt we've totaled up so far. In real terms, what that means is that we'd need $106 trillion in real, investable capital, earning 6 percent a year, on hand, today, to meet the obligations we have under those entitlement programs. For perspective, that's about twice the total private net worth of the United States. (A little more, in fact.)

Suffice it to say, we're a bit short of that $106 trillion. In fact, we're exactly $106 trillion short, since the total value of the Social Security "trust fund" is less than the value of the change you've got rattling around behind your couch cushions, its precise worth being: $0.00. Because the "trust fund" (which is not a trust fund) is by law "invested" (meaning, not invested) in Treasury bonds, there is no national nest egg to fund these entitlements. As Bruce Bartlett explained in *Forbes,* "The trust fund does not have any actual resources with which to pay Social Security benefits. It's as if you wrote an IOU to yourself; no matter how large the IOU is it doesn't increase your net worth . . . Consequently, whether there is $2.4 trillion in the Social Security trust fund or $240 trillion has no bearing on the federal government's ability to pay benefits that have been promised." Seeing no political incentives to reduce benefits, Bartlett calculates that an 81 percent tax increase will be necessary to pay those obligations. "Those who think otherwise are either grossly ignorant of the fiscal facts, in denial, or living in a fantasy world."

There's more, of course. Much more. Besides those monthly pension checks, the states are on the hook for retirees' health care and other benefits, to the tune of another $1 trillion. And, depending on how you account for it, another half a trillion or so (conservatively estimated) in liabilities related to the government's guarantee of Fannie Mae, Freddie Mac, and securities supported under the bailouts. Now, these aren't perfect numbers, but that's the rough picture: Call it $130 trillion or so, or just under ten times the official national debt. Putting Nancy Pelosi in a smaller jet isn't going to make that go away.

Critical Thinking

1. What explains the large amount of state and local debt in the United States?

2. Explain how state pension systems are potentially a large liability.

3. Why is there such a large difference between the stated federal debt figure of $14 trillion and the calculation of $140 trillion cited by the author?

From *The National Review*, June 21, 2010. Copyright © 2010 by National Review, Inc, 215 Lexington Avenue, New York, NY 10016. Reprinted by permission.

In Defense of Deficits

A big deficit-reduction program would destroy the economy two years into the great crisis.

JAMES K. GALBRAITH

The Simpson–Bowles Commission, just established by the president, will no doubt deliver an attack on Social Security and Medicare dressed up in the sanctimonious rhetoric of deficit reduction. (Back in his salad days, former Senator Alan Simpson was a regular schemer to cut Social Security.) The Obama spending freeze is another symbolic sacrifice to the deficit gods. Most observers believe neither will amount to much, and one can hope that they are right. But what would be the economic consequences if they did? The answer is that a big deficit-reduction program would destroy the economy, or what remains of it, two years into the Great Crisis.

For this reason, the deficit phobia of Wall Street, the press, some economists, and practically all politicians is one of the deepest dangers that we face. It's not just the old and the sick who are threatened, we all are. To cut current deficits without first rebuilding the economic engine of the private credit system is a sure path to stagnation, to a double-dip recession—even to a second Great Depression. To focus obsessively on cutting future deficits is also a path that will obstruct, not assist, what we need to do to re-establish strong growth and high employment.

To put things crudely, there are two ways to get the increase in total spending that we call "economic growth." One way is for government to spend. The other is for banks to lend. Leaving aside short-term adjustments like increased net exports or financial innovation. Governments and banks are the two entities with the power to create something from nothing. If total spending power is to grow, one or the other of these two great financial motors—public deficits or private loans—has to be in action.

For ordinary people, public budget deficits, despite their bad reputation, are much better than private loans. Deficits put money in private pockets. Private households get more cash. They own that cash free and clear, and they can spend it as they like. If they wish, they can also convert it into interest-earning government bonds or they can repay their debts. This is called an increase in "net financial wealth." Ordinary people benefit, but there is nothing in it for banks.

And this, in the simplest terms, explains the deficit phobia of Wall Street, the corporate media, and the right-wing economists.

Bankers don't like budget deficits because they compete with bank loans as a source of growth. When a bank makes a loan, cash balances in private hands also go up. But now the cash is not owned free and clear. There is a contractual obligation to pay interest and to repay principal. If the enterprise defaults, there may be an asset left over—a house or factory or company—that will then become the property of the bank. It's easy to see why bankers love private credit but hate public deficits.

All of these should be painfully obvious, but it is deeply obscure. It is obscure because legions of Wall Streeters—led notably in our time by Peter Peterson and his front man, former comptroller general David Walker, and including the Robert Rubin wing of the Democratic Party and numerous "bipartisan" enterprises like the Concord Coalition and the Committee for a Responsible Federal Budget—have labored mightily to confuse the issues. These spirits never uttered a single word of warning about the financial crisis, which originated on Wall Street under the noses of their bag men. But they constantly warn, quite falsely, that the government is a "super subprime" "Ponzi scheme," which it is not.

We also hear, from the same people, about the impending "bankruptcy" of Social Security, Medicare—even the United States itself. Or of the burden that public debts will "impose on our grandchildren." Or about "unfunded liabilities" supposedly facing us all. All of these form part of one of the great misinformation campaigns of all time.

The misinformation is rooted in what many consider to be plain common sense. It may seem like homely wisdom, especially, to say that "just like the family, the government can't live beyond its means." But it's not. In these matters the public and private sectors differ on a very basic point. Your family needs income in order to pay its debts. Your government does not.

Private borrowers can and do default. They go bankrupt (a protection civilized societies afford them instead of debtors' prisons). Or if they have a mortgage, in most states they can simply walk away from their house if they can no longer continue to make payments on it.

With government, the risk of nonpayment does not exist. Government spends money (and pays interest) simply by typing numbers into a computer. Unlike private debtors, government does not need to have cash on hand. As the inspired amateur economist Warren Mosler likes to say, the person who writes Social Security checks at the Treasury does not have the phone number of the tax collector at the IRS. If you choose to pay taxes in cash, the government will give you a receipt—and shred the bills. Since it is the source of money, government can't run out.

It's true that government can spend imprudently. Too much spending, net of taxes, may lead to inflation, often via currency depreciation—though with the world in recession, that's not an immediate risk. Wasteful spending—on unnecessary military adventures, say—burns real resources. But no government can ever be forced to default on debts in a currency it controls. Public defaults happen only when governments don't control the currency in which they owe debts—as Argentina owed dollars or as Greece now (it hasn't defaulted yet) owes euros. But for true sovereigns, bankruptcy is an irrelevant concept. When Obama says, even offhand, that the United States is "out of money," he's talking nonsense—dangerous nonsense. One wonders if he believes it.

Nor is public debt a burden on future generations. It does not have to be repaid, and in practice it will never be repaid. Personal debts are generally settled during the lifetime of the debtor or at death, because one person cannot easily encumber another. But public debt does not ever have to be repaid. Governments do not die—except in war or revolution, and when that happens, their debts are generally moot anyway.

So the public debt simply increases from one year to the next. In the entire history of the United States it has done so, with budget deficits and increased public debt on all but about six very short occasions—with each surplus followed by a recession. Far from being a burden, these debts are the foundation of economic growth. Bonds owed by the government yield net income to the private sector, unlike all purely private debts, which merely transfer income from one part of the private sector to another.

Nor is that interest a solvency threat. A recent projection from the Center on Budget and Policy Priorities, based on Congressional Budget Office assumptions, has public-debt interest payments rising to 15 percent of GDP by 2050, with total debt to GDP at 300 percent. But that can't happen. If the interest were paid to people who then spent it on goods and services and job creation, it would be just like other public spending. Interest payments so enormous would affect the economy much like the mobilization for World War II. Long before you even got close to those scary ratios, you'd get full employment and rising inflation—pushing up GDP and, in turn, stabilizing the debt-to-GDP ratio. Or the Federal Reserve would stabilize the interest payouts, simply by keeping short-term interest rates (which it controls) very low.

What about indebtedness to foreigners? True, foreigners do us a favor by buying our bonds. To acquire them, China must export goods to us, not offset by equivalent imports. That is a cost to China. It's a cost Beijing is prepared to pay, for its own reasons: export industries promote learning, technology transfer, and product quality improvement, and they provide jobs to migrants from the countryside. But that's China's business.

For China, the bonds themselves are a sterile hoard. There is almost nothing that Beijing can do with them. China already imports all the commodities and machinery and aircraft it can use—if it wanted more, it would buy them now. So unless China changes its export policy, its stock of T bonds will just go on growing. And we will pay interest on it, not with real effort but by typing numbers into computers. There is no burden associated with this, not now and not later. (If the Chinese hoard the interest, they also don't help much with job creation here. So the fact that we're buying a lot of goods from China simply means we have to be more imaginative, and bolder, if we want to create all the jobs we need.) Finally, could China dump its dollars? In principle it could, substituting Greek bonds for American and overpriced euros for cheap dollars. On brief reflection, no Beijing bureaucrat is likely to think this a smart move.

What is true of government as a whole is also true of particular programs. Social Security and Medicare are government programs; they cannot go bankrupt, and they cannot fail to meet their obligations unless Congress decides—say on the recommendation of the Simpson–Bowles Commission—to cut the benefits they provide. The exercise of linking future benefits and projected payroll tax revenues is an accounting farce, done for political reasons. That farce was started by FDR as a way of protecting Social Security from cuts. But it has become a way of creating needless anxiety about these programs and of precluding sensible reforms, like expanding Medicare to those 55 and older, or even to the whole population.

As government programs, Social Security, and Medicare cannot go bankrupt—unless Congress cuts the benefits they provide.

Social Security and Medicare are transfer programs. What they do, mainly, is move resources around within our society at a given time. The principal transfer is not from the young to the old, since even without Social Security the old would still be around and someone would have to support them. Rather, Social Security pools resources, so that the work of the young collectively supports the senior population. The effective transfer is from parents who have children who would otherwise support them (a fairly rare thing) to seniors who don't. And it is from workers who do not have parents to support, to workers who would otherwise have to support their parents. In both cases this burden sharing is fair, progressive, and sustainable. There is a healthcare cost problem, as everyone knows, but that's not a Medicare problem. It should not be solved by cutting back on healthcare for the old. Social Security and Medicare also replace private insurance with cheap and efficient public administration. This is another reason these programs are the hated targets, decade after decade, of the worst predators on Wall Street.

Public deficits and private lending are reciprocal. Increased private lending generates new tax revenue and smaller deficits; that's what happened in the 1990s. A credit collapse kills the tax base and generates more spending; that's what's happening now, and our big deficits are the accounting counterpart of the massive decline, last year, in private bank loans. The only choice is what kind of deficit to run—useful deficits that rebuild the country, as in the New Deal, or useless ones, with millions kept unnecessarily on unemployment insurance when they could instead be given jobs.

If we could revive private lending, should we do it? Well, yes, up to a point there is good reason to have a robust private lending sector. Government is by nature centralized and policy driven. It works by law and regulation. Decentralized and competitive private banks have much more flexibility. A good banking system, run by capable people with good business judgment who know their clients, is good for the economy. The fact that you have to pay interest on a loan is also an important motivator of investment over consumption.

But right now, we don't have functional big banks. We have a cartel run by an incompetent plutocracy, with its long fingers deep in the pockets of the state. For functional credit to return, we'll have to reduce the unpayable private debts now outstanding, to restore private incomes (meaning: create jobs) and collateral (meaning: home values), and we'll have to restructure the big banks. We need to break them up, shrink the financial sector overall, expose and prosecute frauds, and create incentives for profitable lending in energy conservation, infrastructure, and other sectors. Or we could create a new parallel banking system, as was done in the New Deal with the Re construction Finance Corporation and its spinoffs, including the Home Owners' Loan Corporation and later Fannie Mae and Freddie Mac.

Either way, until we have effective financial reform, public budget deficits are the only way toward economic growth. You don't have to like budget deficits to realize that we must have them, on whatever scale necessary to restore growth and jobs. And we will need them not just now but for a long while, until we've shaped a strategic program for investment, energy and the environment, financed in part by a reformed, restored, and disciplined financial sector.

It's possible, of course, that all the deficit hysteria is intended to divert attention from the dysfunctions of private banking, and so to help thwart calls for financial reform. Is that giving them too much credit? Maybe. Maybe not.

Critical Thinking

1. Why are public budget deficits better than private loans for ordinary people?
2. How does government differ from private borrowers? Why is there no risk of non-payment?
3. How can public debt be a source of economic growth?
4. Why are interest and indebtedness to foreigners not an insolvency threat?
5. What is a "transfer program," and how does the author explain Social Security and Medicare using this term?

JAMES K. GALBRAITH is the author of *The Predator State: How Conservatives Abandoned the Free Market and Why Liberals Should Too*. He teaches at the LBJ School of Public Affairs at the University of Texas and is a senior scholar at the Levy Economics Institute.

Meet the Real Death Panels

Health care reform is done, but the battle over "entitlement reform" is just beginning—and already, deficit hawks are suggesting that geezers like me need to pull the plug on ourselves for the good of society. Are they looking out for future generations—or just the bonuses of health care execs?

JAMES RIDGEWAY

There's a certain age at which you cease to regard your own death as a distant hypothetical and start to view it as a coming event. For me, it was 67–the age at which my father died. For many Americans, I suspect it's 70–the age that puts you within striking distance of our average national life expectancy of 78.1 years. Even if you still feel pretty spry, you suddenly find that your roster of doctor's appointments has expanded, along with your collection of daily medications. You grow accustomed to hearing that yet another person you once knew has dropped off the twig. And you feel more and more like a walking ghost yourself, invisible to the younger people who push past you on the subway escalator. Like it or not, death becomes something you think about, often on a daily basis.

Actually, you don't think about death, per se, as much as you do about dying–about when and where and especially *how* you're going to die. Will you have to deal with a long illness? With pain, immobility, or dementia? Will you be able to get the care you need, and will you have enough money to pay for it? Most of all, will you lose control over what life you have left, as well as over the circumstances of your death?

These are precisely the preoccupations that the right so cynically exploited in the debate over health care reform, with that ominous talk of Washington bean counters deciding who lives and dies. It was all nonsense, of course-the worst kind of political scare tactic. But at the same time, supporters of health care reform seemed to me too quick to dismiss old people's fears as just so much paranoid foolishness. There are reasons why the death-panel myth found fertile ground–and those reasons go beyond the gullibility of half-senile old farts.

While politicians of all stripes shun the idea of health care rationing as the political third rail that it is, most of them accept a premise that leads, one way or another, to that end. Here's what I mean: Nearly every other industrialized country recognizes health care as a human right, whose costs and benefits are shared among all citizens. But in the United States, the leaders of both political parties along with most of the "experts" persist in treating health care as a commodity that is purchased, in one way or another, by those who can afford it. Conservatives embrace this notion as the perfect expression of the all-powerful market; though they make a great show of recoiling from the term, in practice they are endorsing rationing on the basis of wealth. Liberals, including supporters of President Obama's health care reform, advocate subsidies, regulation, and other modest measures to give the less fortunate a little more buying power. But as long as health care is viewed as a product to be bought and sold, even the most well-intentioned reformers will someday soon have to come to grips with health care rationing, if not by wealth then by some other criteria.

In a country that already spends more than 16 percent of each GDP dollar on health care, it is easy to see why so many people believe there's simply not enough of it to go around. But keep in mind that the rest of the industrialized world manages to spend between 20 and 90 percent less per capita and still rank higher than the US in overall health care performance. In 2004, a team of researchers including Princeton's Uwe Reinhardt, one of the nation's best known experts on health economics, found that while the US spends 134 percent more than the median of the world's most developed nations, we get less for our money—fewer physician visits and hospital days per capita, for example—than our counterparts in countries like Germany, Canada, and Australia. (We do, however, have more MRI machines and more cesarean sections.)

Where does the money go instead? By some estimates, administration and insurance profits alone eat up at least 30 percent of our total health care bill (and most of that is in the private sector—Medicare's overhead is around 2 percent). In other words, we don't have too little to go around—we overpay for what we get, and we don't allocate our spending where it does us the most good. "In most [medical] resources we have a surplus," says Dr. David Himmelstein, co-founder of Physicians for a National Health Program. "People get large amounts of care that don't do them any good and might cause them harm [while] others don't get the necessary amount."

Looking at the numbers, it is pretty safe to say that with an efficient health care system, we could spend a little less than we do now and provide all Americans with the most spectacular care the world has ever known. But in the absence of any serious challenge to the health-care-as-commodity system, we are doomed to a battlefield scenario where Americans must fight to secure their share of a "scarce" resource in a life-and-death struggle that pits the rich against the poor, the insured against the uninsured—and increasingly, the old against the young.

For years, any push to improve the nation's finances—balance the budget, pay for the bailout, or help stimulate the economy—has been accompanied by rumblings about the greedy geezers who resist entitlement "reforms" (read: cuts) with their unconscionable demands for basic health care and a hedge against destitution. So, too, today: Already, President Obama's newly convened deficit commission looks to be blaming the nation's fiscal woes not on tax cuts, wars, or bank bailouts, but on the burden of Social Security and Medicare. (The commission's co-chair, former Republican senator Alan Simpson, has declared, "This country is gonna go to the bow-wows unless we deal with entitlements.")

Old people's anxiety in the face of such hostile attitudes has provided fertile ground for Republican disinformation and fear mongering. But so has the vacuum left by Democratic reformers. Too often, in their zeal to prove themselves tough on "waste," they've allowed connections to be drawn between two things that, to my mind, should never be spoken of in the same breath: *death* and *cost*.

Dying Wishes

The death-panel myth started with a harmless minor provision in the health reform bill that required Medicare to pay in case enrollees wanted to have conversations with their own doctors about "advance directives" like health care proxies and living wills. The controversy that ensued, thanks to a host of right-wing commentators and Sarah Palin's Facebook page, ensured that the advance-planning measure was expunged from the bill. But the underlying debate didn't end with the passage of health care reform, any more than it began there. If rationing is inevitable once you've ruled out reining in private profits, the question is who should be denied care, and at what point. And given that no one will publicly argue for withholding cancer treatment from a seven-year-old, the answer almost inevitably seems to come down to what we spend on people—*old* people—in their final years.

As far back as 1983, in a speech to the Health Insurance Association of America, a then-57-year-old Alan Greenspan suggested that we consider "whether it is worth it" to spend so much of Medicare's outlays on people who would die within the year. (Appropriately, Ayn Rand called her acolyte "the undertaker"—though she chose the nickname because of his dark suits and austere demeanor.)

Not everyone puts the issue in such nakedly pecuniary terms, but in an April 2009 interview with the *New York Times Magazine,* Obama made a similar point in speaking of end-of-life care as a "huge driver of cost." He said, "The chronically ill and those toward the end of their lives are accounting for potentially 80 percent of the total health care bill out here."

The president was being a bit imprecise. Those figures are actually for Medicare expenditures, not the total health care tab, and more important, lumping the dying together with the "chronically ill"—who often will live for years or decades—makes little sense. But there is no denying that end-of-life care is expensive. Hard numbers are not easy to come by, but studies from the 1990s suggest that between a quarter and a third of annual Medicare expenditures go to patients in their last year of life, and 30 to 40 percent of *those* costs accrue in the final month. What this means is that around one in ten Medicare dollars—some $50 billion a year-are spent on patients with fewer than 30 days to live.

Pronouncements on these data usually come coated with a veneer of compassion and concern: How *terrible* it is that all those poor dying old folks have to endure aggressive treatments that only delay the inevitable; all we want to do is bring peace and dignity to their final days! But I wonder: If that's really what they're worried about, how come they keep talking about money?

At this point, I ought to make something clear: I am a big fan of what's sometimes called the "right to die" or "death with dignity" movement. I support everything from advance directives to assisted suicide. You could say I believe in one form of health care rationing: the kind you choose for yourself. I can't stand the idea of anyone—whether it is the government or some hospital administrator or doctor or Nurse Jackie—telling me that I must have some treatment I don't want, any more than I want them telling me that I can't have a treatment I *do* want. My final wish is to be my own one-member death panel.

A physician friend recently told me about a relative of hers, a frail 90-year-old woman suffering from cancer. Her doctors urged her to have surgery, followed by treatment with a recently approved cancer medicine that cost $5,000 a month. As is often the case, my friend said, the doctors told their patient about the benefits of the treatment, but not about all the risks—that she might die during the surgery or not long afterward. They also prescribed a month's supply of the new medication, even though, my friend says, they must have known the woman was unlikely to live that long. She died within a week. "Now," my friend said, "I'm carrying around a $4,000 bottle of pills."

Perhaps reflecting what economists call "supplier-induced demand," costs generally tend to go up when the dying have too *little* control over their care, rather than too much. When geezers are empowered to make decisions, most of us will choose less aggressive—and less costly—treatments. If we don't do so more often, it's usually because of an overbearing and money-hungry health care system, as well as a culture that disrespects the will of its elders and resists confronting death.

> You could say I believe in one form of health care rationing: the kind you choose for yourself. When geezers are empowered to make choices about our dying days, most of us will choose less aggressive—and less costly—treatments.

Once, when I was in the hospital for outpatient surgery, I woke up in the recovery area next to a man named George, who was talking loudly to his wife, telling her he wanted to leave. She soothingly reminded him that they had to wait for the doctors to learn the results of the surgery, apparently some sort of exploratory thing. Just then, two doctors appeared. In a stiff, flat voice, one of them told George that he had six months to live. When his wife's shrieking had subsided, I heard George say, "I'm getting the fuck out of this place." The doctors sternly advised him that they had more tests to run and "treatment options" to discuss. "Fuck that," said George, yanking the IV out of his arm and getting to his feet. "If I've got six months to live, do you think I want to spend another minute of it here? I'm going to the Alps to go skiing."

I don't know whether George was true to his word. But not long ago I had a friend, a scientist, who was true to his. Suffering from cancer, he anticipated a time when more chemotherapy or procedures could only prolong a deepening misery, to the point where he could no longer recognize himself. He prepared for that time, hoarding his pain meds, taking care to protect his doctor and pharmacist from any possibility of legal retribution. He saw some friends he wanted to see, and spoke to others. Then he died at a time and place of his choosing, with his family around him. Some would call this euthanasia, others a sacrilege. To me, it seemed like a noble end to a fine life. If freedom of choice is what makes us human, then my friend managed to make his death a final expression of his humanity.

My friend chose to forgo medical treatments that would have added many thousands of dollars to his health care costs—and, since he was on Medicare, to the public expense. If George really did spend his final months in the Alps, instead of undergoing expensive surgeries or sitting around hooked up to machines, he surely saved the health care system a bundle as well. They did it because it was what they wanted, not because it would save money. But there is a growing body of evidence that the former can lead to the latter—without any rationing or coercion.

One model that gets cited a lot these days is La Crosse, Wisconsin, where Gundersen Lutheran hospital launched an initiative to ensure that the town's older residents had advance directives and to make hospice and palliative care widely available. A 2008 study found that 90 percent of those who died in La Crosse under a physician's care did so with advance directives in place. At Gundersen Lutheran, less is spent on patients in their last two years of life than nearly any other place in the US, with per capita Medicare costs 30 percent below the national average. In a similar vein, Oregon, in 1995, instituted a two-page form called Physician Orders for Life-Sustaining Treatment; it functions as doctor's orders and is less likely to be misinterpreted or disregarded than a living will. According to the *Dartmouth Atlas of Health Care,* a 20-year study of the nation's medical costs and resources, people in Oregon are less likely to die in a hospital than people in most other states, and in their last six months, they spend less time in the hospital. They also run up about 50 percent less in medical expenditures.

It is possible that attitudes have begun to change. Three states now allow what advocates like to call "aid-in-dying" (rather than assisted suicide) for the terminally ill. More Americans than ever have living wills and other advance directives,

and that can only be a good thing: One recent study showed that more than 70 percent of patients who needed to make end-of-life decisions at some point lost the capacity to make these choices; yet, among those who had prepared living wills, nearly all had their instructions carried out.

Here is the ultimate irony of the deathpanel meme: In attacking measures designed to Promote advance directives, conservatives were attacking what they claim is their core value—the individual right to free choice.

The QALY of Mercy

A wonkier version of the reform-equals-rationing argument is based less on panic mongering about Obama's secret euthanasia schemes and more on the implications of something called "comparative effectiveness research." The practice got a jump start in last year's stimulus bill, which included $1.1 billion for the Federal Coordinating Council for Comparative Effectiveness Research. This is money to study what treatments work best for which patients. The most obvious use of such data would be to apply the findings to Medicare, and the effort has already been attacked as the first step toward the government deciding when it's time to kick granny to the curb. Senate minority leader Mitch McConnell (R-Ky.) has said that Obama's support for comparative effectiveness research means he is seeking "a national rationing board."

Evidence-based medicine, in itself, has absolutely nothing to do with age. In theory, it also has nothing to do with money—though it might, as a by-product, reduce costs (for example, by giving doctors the information they need to resist pressure from drug companies). Yet the desire for cost savings often seems to drive comparative effectiveness research, rather than the other way around. In his *Times Magazine* interview last year, Obama said, "It is an attempt to say to patients, you know what, we've looked at some objective studies concluding that the blue pill, which costs half as much as the red pill, is just as effective, and you might want to go ahead and get the blue one."

Personally, I don't mind the idea of the government promoting the blue pill over the red pill, as long as it really is "just as effective." I certainly trust the government to make these distinctions more than I trust the insurance companies or pharma representatives. But I want to know that the only target is genuine waste, and the only possible casualty is profits.

There's nothing to give me pause in the health care law's comparative effectiveness provision, which includes $500 million a year for comparative effectiveness research. The work is to be overseen by the nonprofit Patient-Centered Outcomes Research Institute, whose 21-member board of governors will include doctors, patient advocates, and only three representatives of drug and medical-device companies.

Still, there is a difference between comparative effectiveness and comparative *cost* effectiveness—and from the latter, it's a short skip to outright cost-benefit analysis. In other words, the argument sometimes slides almost imperceptibly from comparing how well the blue pill and the red pill work to examining whether some people should be denied the red pill, even if it demonstrably works better.

The calculations driving such cost-benefit analyses are often based on something called QALYs—quality-adjusted life years. If a certain cancer drug would extend life by two years, say, but with such onerous side effects that those years were judged to be only half as worth living as those of a healthy person, the QALY is 1.

In Britain, the National Health Service has come close to setting a maximum price beyond which extra QALYs are not deemed worthwhile. In assessing drugs and treatments, the NHS's National Institute for Health and Clinical Excellence usually approves those that cost less than 20,000 pounds per QALY (about $28,500), and most frequently rejects those costing more than 30,000 pounds (about $43,000).

It's not hard to find examples of comparative effectiveness research—complete with QALYs—that hit quite close to home for almost anyone. Last year I was diagnosed with atrial fibrillation, a disturbance in the heart rhythm that sometimes leads to blood clots, which can travel to the brain and cause a stroke. My doctor put me on warfarin (brand name Coumadin), a blood-thinning drug that reduces the chances of forming blood clots but can also cause internal bleeding. It is risky enough that when I go to the dentist or cut myself shaving, I have to watch to make sure it doesn't turn into a torrent of blood. The levels of warfarin in my bloodstream have to be frequently checked, so I have to be ever mindful of the whereabouts of a hospital with a blood lab. It is a pain in the neck, and it makes me feel vulnerable. I sometimes wonder if it's worth it.

It turns out that several comparative effectiveness studies have looked at the efficacy of warfarin for patients with my heart condition. One of them simply weighed the drug's potential benefits against its dangerous side effects, without consideration of cost. It concluded that for a patient with my risk factors, warfarin reduced the chance of stroke a lot more than it increased the chance that I'd be seriously harmed by bleeding. Another study concluded that for a patient like me, the cost per QALY of taking warfarin is $8,000—cheap, by most standards.

Prescription drug prices have more than doubled since the study was done in 1995. But warfarin is a relatively cheap generic drug, and even if my cost per QALY was $15,000 or $20,000, I'd still pass muster with the NHS. But if I were younger and had fewer risk factors, I'd be less prone to stroke to begin with, so the reduction in risk would not be as large, and the cost per QALY would be correspondingly higher about $370,000. Would I still want to take the drug if I were, say, under 60 and free of risk factors? Considering the side effects, probably not. But would I want someone else to make that decision for me?

Critics of the British system say, among other things, that the NHS's cost-per-QALY limit is far too low. But raising it wouldn't resolve the deeper ethical question: Should anyone but the patient get to decide when life is not worth living? The Los Angeles Times' Michael Hiltzik, one of the few reporters to critically examine this issue, has noted that "healthy people tend to overestimate the effect of some medical conditions on their sufferers' quality of life. The hale and hearty, for example, will generally rate life in a wheelchair lower than will the wheelchair-bound, who often find fulfillment in ways 'healthier' persons couldn't imagine."

Simone de Beauvoir wrote that fear of aging and death drives young people to view their elders as a separate species, rather than as their future selves: "Until the moment it is upon us old age is something that only affects other people." And the more I think about the subject, the more I am sure of one thing: It's not a good idea to have a 30-year-old place a value on my life.

Whose Death Is It Anyway?

Probably the most prominent advocate of age-based rationing is Daniel Callahan, co-founder of a bioethics think tank called the Hastings Center. Callahan's 1987 book, *Setting Limits: Medical Goals in an Aging Society,* depicted old people as "a new social threat," a demographic, economic, and medical "avalanche" waiting to happen. In a 2008 article, Callahan said that in evaluating Medicare's expenditures, we should consider that "there is a duty to help young people to become old people, but not to help the old become still older indefinitely . . . One may well ask what counts as 'old' and what is a decently long lifespan? As I have listened to people speak of a 'full life,' often heard at funerals, I would say that by 75-80 most people have lived a full life, and most of us do not feel it a tragedy that someone in that age group has died (as we do with the death of a child)." He has proposed using "age as a specific criterion for the allocation and limitation of care," and argues that after a certain point, people could justifiably be denied Medicare coverage for life-extending treatments.

You can see why talk like this might make some old folks start boarding up their doors. (It apparently, however, does not concern Callahan, who, last year at age 79, told the *New York Times* that he had just had a life-saving seven-hour heart procedure.) It certainly made me wonder how I would measure up.

One prominent advocate of rationing has suggested that society doesn't have a duty to help those in their 70s and 80s "become still older indefinitely." You can see why talk like that might lead old folks to start boarding up their doors.

So far, I haven't cost the system all that much. I take several different medicines every day, which are mostly genetics. I go to the doctor pretty often, but I haven't been in the hospital overnight for at least 20 years, and my one walk-in operation took place before I was on Medicare. And I am still working, so I'm paying in as well as taking out.

But things could change, perhaps precipitously. Since I have problems with both eyesight and balance, I could easily fall and break a bone, maybe a hip. This could mean a hip replacement, months of therapy, or even long-term immobility. My glaucoma could take a turn for the worse, and I would face a future of near blindness, with all the associated costs. Or I could have that stroke, in spite of my drug regimen.

I decided to take the issue up with the Australian philosopher Peter Singer, who made some waves on this issue with a *New York Times* op-ed published last year, titled "Why We Must Ration Health Care." Singer believes that health care is a scarce resource that will inevitably be limited. Better to do it through a public system like the British NHS, he told me, than covertly and inequitably on the private US model. "What you are trying to do is to get the most value for the money from the resources you have," he told me.

In the world he imagines, I asked Singer over coffee in a Manhattan café, what should happen if I broke a hip? He paused to think, and I hoped he wouldn't worry about hurting my feelings. "If there is a good chance of restoring mobility," he said after a moment, "and you have at least five years of mobility, that's significant benefit." He added, "Hip operations are not expensive." A new hip or knee runs between $30,000 and $40,000, most of it covered by Medicare. So for five years of mobility, that comes out to about $7,000 a year—less than the cost of a home-care aide, and exponentially less than a nursing home.

But then Singer turned to a more sobering thought: If the hip operation did not lead to recovery of mobility, then it might not be such a bargain. In a much-cited piece of personal revelation, Obama, in 2009, talked about his grandmother's decision to have a hip replacement after she had been diagnosed with terminal cancer. She died just a few weeks later. "I don't know how much that hip replacement cost," Obama told the *Times Magazine.* "I would have paid out of pocket for that hip replacement just because she's my grandmother." But the president said that in considering whether "to give my grandmother, or everybody else's aging grandparents or parents, a hip replacement when they're terminally ill . . . you just get into some very difficult moral issues."

Singer and I talked about what choices we ourselves might make at the end of our lives. Singer, who is 63, said that he and his wife know "neither of us wants to go on living under certain conditions. Particularly if we get demented. I would draw the line if I could not recognize my wife or my children. My wife has a higher standard—when she couldn't read a novel. Yes, I wouldn't want to live beyond a certain point. It's not me anymore." I'm 10 years older than Singer, and my own advance directives reflect similar choices. So it seems like neither one of us is likely to strain the public purse with our demands for expensive and futile life-prolonging care.

You can say this is all a Debbie Downer, but people my age know perfectly well that these questions are not at all theoretical. We worry about the time when we will no longer be able to contribute anything useful to society and will be completely dependent on others. And we worry about the day when life will no longer seem worth living, and whether we will have the courage—and the ability—to choose a dignified death. We worry about these things all by ourselves—we don't need anyone else to do it for us. And we certainly don't need anyone tallying up QALYs while our overpriced, underperforming private health care system adds a few more points to its profit margin.

Let It Bleed

What happened during the recent health care wars is what military strategists might call a "bait-and-bleed" operation: Two rival parties are drawn into a protracted conflict that depletes both their forces, while a third stands on the sidelines, its strength undiminished. In this case, Republicans and Democrats alike have shed plenty of blood, while the clever combatant on the sidelines is, of course, the health care industry.

In the process, health care reform set some unsettling precedents that could fuel the phony intergenerational conflict over health care resources. The final reform bill will help provide coverage to some of the estimated 46 million Americans under 65 who live without it. It finances these efforts in part by cutting Medicare costs—some $500 billion over 10 years. Contrary to Republican hysteria, the cuts so far come from all the right places—primarily from ending the tip-offs by insurers who sell government-financed "Medicare Advantage" plans. The reform law even manages to make some meaningful improvements to the flawed Medicare prescription drug program and preventive care. The legislation also explicitly bans age-based health care rationing.

Still, there are plenty of signs that the issue is far from being put to rest. Congress and the White House wrote into the law something called the Independent Payment Advisory Board, a presidentially appointed panel that is tasked with keeping Medicare's growth rate below a certain ceiling. Office of Management and Budget director Peter Orszag, the economics wunderkind who has made Medicare's finances something of a personal project, has called it potentially the most important aspect of the legislation: Medicare and Medicaid, he has said, "are at the heart of our long-term fiscal imbalance, which is the motivation for moving to a different structure in those programs." And then, of course, there's Obama's deficit commission: While the president says he is keeping an open mind when it comes to solving the deficit "crisis," no one is trying very hard to pretend that the commission has any purpose other than cutting Social Security, Medicare, and probably Medicaid as well.

> **I'd be willing to give up some expensive, life-prolonging medical treatment for my Gen X son, and maybe even for the good of humanity. But I'm certainly not going to do it so some WellPoint executive can take another vacation.**

Already, the commission is working closely with the Peter G. Peterson Foundation, headed by the billionaire businessman and former Nixon administration official who has emerged as one of the nation's leading "granny bashers"—deficit hawks who accuse old people of bankrupting the country.

In the end, of course, many conservatives are motivated less by deficits and more by free-market ideology: Many of them want to replace Medicare as it now exists today with a system of vouchers, and place the emphasis on individual savings and tax

ANNUAL EDITIONS

breaks. Barring that, Republicans have proposed a long string of cuts to Medicaid and Medicare, sometimes defying logic—by, for example, advocating reductions in in-home care, which can keep people out of far more expensive nursing homes.

The common means of justifying these cuts is to attack Medicare "waste." But remember that not only are Medicare's administrative costs less than one-sixth of those of private insurers, Medicare pays doctors and hospitals less (20 and 30 percent, respectively) than private payment rates; overall, Medicare pays out less in annual per capita benefits than the average large employer health plan, even though it serves an older, sicker population.

That basic fact is fully understood by the health care industry. Back in January 2009, as the nation suited up for the health care wars, the Lewin Group—a subsidiary of the health insurance giant United Health—produced an analysis of various reform proposals being floated and found that the only one to immediately reduce overall health care costs (by $58 billion) was one that would have dramatically expanded Medicare.

Facts like these, however, have not slowed down the granny bashers. In a February op-ed called "The Geezers' Crusade," commentator David Brooks urged old people to willingly submit to entitlement cuts in service to future generations. Via Social Security and Medicare, he argued, old folks are stealing from their own grandkids.

I'm as public spirited as the next person, and I have a Gen X son. I'd be willing to give up some expensive, life-prolonging medical treatment for him, and maybe even for the good of humanity. But I'm certainly not going to do it so some Well-Point executive can take another vacation, so Pfizer can book $3 billion in annual profits instead of $2 billion, or so private hospitals can make another campaign contribution to some gutless politician.

Here, then, is my advice to anyone who suggests that we geezers should do the right thing and pull the plug on ourselves: Start treating health care as a human right instead of a profit-making opportunity, and see how much money you save. Then, by all means, get back to me.

Critical Thinking

1. How is health care treated as a commodity in the United States?
2. What factors indicate that the U.S. healthcare system is inefficient?
3. What are "advance directives"? How did discussion of advance directives evolve into the rumor of "death panels"?
4. What is a QALY? How are QALYs used as calculations in cost-benefit analysis for health care?
5. How does free-market ideology drive political views on health care? Does the author ultimately agree with this approach?

Clean, Green, Safe and Smart

Why the United States needs a new national energy policy.

Michael T. Klare

If the ecological catastrophe in the Gulf of Mexico tells us anything, it is that we need a new national energy policy—a comprehensive plan for escaping our dangerous reliance on fossil fuels, and creating a new energy system based on climate-safe alternatives. Without such a plan, the response to the disaster will be a hodgepodge of regulatory reforms and toughened environmental safeguards but not a fundamental shift in behavior. Because our current energy path leads toward greater reliance on fuels acquired from environmentally and politically hazardous locations, no amount of enhanced oversight or stiffened regulations can avert future disasters like that unfolding in the gulf. Only a dramatic change in course—governed by an entirely new policy framework—can reduce the risk of catastrophe and set the nation on a wise energy trajectory.

By far the most important part of this strategy must be a change in the overarching philosophy that steers decisions on how much energy the United States should seek to produce, of what sorts and under what conditions. It may not seem as if we operate under such a philosophy today, but we do—one that extols growth over all other considerations, that privileges existing fuels over renewables and that ranks environmental concerns below corporate profit. Until we replace this outlook with one that places innovation and the environment ahead of the status quo, we will face more ecological devastation and slower economic dynamism. Only with a new governing philosophy—one that views the development of climate-friendly energy systems as the engine of economic growth—can we move from our current predicament to a brighter future.

One way to appreciate the importance of this shift is to consider the guiding policies of other countries. In March, I had the privilege of attending an international energy conference at Fuenlabrada, just outside Madrid. I sat transfixed as one top official after another of Spain's socialist government spelled out their vision of the future— one in which wind and solar power would provide an ever-increasing share of the nation's energy supply and make Spain a leader in renewable energy technology. Other speakers described strategies for "greening" old cities—adding parks, farms, canals, and pedestrian plazas in neglected neighborhoods. Around me were a thousand university students—enthralled by the prospect of creative and rewarding jobs in architecture, engineering, technology, and the sciences. This, I thought, is what our own young people need to look forward to.

Instead, we are governed by an obsolete, nihilistic energy philosophy. To fully comprehend the nature of our dilemma, it is important to recognize that the gulf disaster is a direct result of the last governing blueprint adopted by this country: the National Energy Policy of May 17, 2001, better known as the Cheney plan. This framework, of which

the former vice president was the lead author, called for increased drilling in wilderness areas, such as the Arctic National Wildlife Refuge, as well as in the deep waters of the Gulf of Mexico. Congress did not permit drilling in ANWR, but it wholeheartedly embraced wider exploitation of the deepwater gulf. To speed these efforts, the Bush administration encouraged the Minerals Management Service to streamline the issuing of permits to giant oil firms like BP to operate in these waters. BP clearly took shortcuts when drilling offshore—thus inviting the blowout on April 20—but it did so in a permissive atmosphere established by the 2001 policy framework.

The 2001 energy plan was devised with substantial input from the energy industry—no representatives of the environmental community were invited to the secret meetings held by Dick Cheney to prepare it— and was widely viewed as a payoff to Bush/Cheney supporters in the oil industry. But it was far more than that: at its core, the plan embodied a distinctive outlook on the role of energy in the economy and how that energy should be supplied. This outlook held that cheap and abundant energy is an essential driver of economic growth and that the government's job is to ensure that plentiful energy is endlessly available. As noted by President Bush at the time, "The goals of this strategy are clear: to ensure a steady supply of affordable energy for America's homes and businesses and industries." But not just any sort of energy. In deference to the executives of Chevron, Enron, ExxonMobil, and the other energy giants that helped elect Bush in 2000, the plan aimed to extend the life of the nation's existing energy profile, with its overwhelming reliance on oil, coal, natural gas, and nuclear power.

However, a strategy aimed at producing more energy while maintaining reliance on traditional fuels was inherently problematic. Although the concept of "peak oil" was not then in widespread circulation, energy experts were becoming increasingly aware of the impending scarcity of conventional oil—i.e., liquid crude acquired from easily accessible reservoirs. Concerns were also growing about the future availability of easily accessible coal and natural gas. The only way to supply more energy while preserving the existing energy profile, Cheney and his allies concluded, was to increase the level of environmental and political risk, whether by drilling in wilderness areas and the deepwater gulf of by procuring more energy from dangerous and unfriendly areas, such as the Middle East, Africa and the former Soviet Union. This became the underlying premise of the 2001 energy plan and underlies much of the global violence and environmental devastation unleashed by Bush during his eight years in office.

Adherence to the Cheney plan has had another significant downside: it has focused energy investment on the extension of the existing energy paradigm rather than on introducing renewable energy systems. Far greater funds have been devoted to, say, deep offshore drilling and the extraction of gas from shale rock than to advancing wind and solar power. As a result, the United States has fallen behind China, Germany, Japan, and Spain in developing next-generation energy systems, jeopardizing our future competitiveness in the global economy.

The philosophy that produced these disasters—"more energy of the existing types at whatever the risk"—must now be repudiated and replaced by a new, forward-looking alternative that stresses innovation and environmental protection. Such an outlook would replace each component of the Bush/Cheney philosophy with its opposite. Instead of growth at any price, it would emphasize energy sufficiency—the minimum amount needed to accomplish vital tasks. Instead of clinging to existing environmentally damaging fuels, it would harness America's ingenuity in the development of new, climate-friendly fuels. And instead of embracing environmental and political risk as a solution to scarcity and excessive greed, it would favor domestically produced, renewable systems that largely eliminate the element of risk. To compress this into a nutshell, the new outlook would favor energy that is "clean, green, safe, and smart."

The philosophy that produced this disaster—'more energy at whatever the risk'—must be replaced with a forward-looking alternative.

What, in practice, would this entail?

First, let's take a closer look at "sufficiency"—the basis for all else. By energy sufficiency, I mean enough energy to meet basic consumer and industrial needs without succumbing to a bias for waste and inefficiency, as is now the case. For example, if X number of American commuters must drive Y number of miles every day to work, sufficient energy would be the amount needed to power the most fuel-efficient personal or public-transit vehicles available, rather than the most inefficient. Likewise, sufficient heating energy would be the amount needed to heat American homes and businesses if all were equipped with the most efficient heating and insulation systems. A wise energy policy would aim to provide whatever is needed when all reasonable measures for efficiency have been factored in—and no more than that. Of course, the transition from inefficient to efficient transportation, heating and industrial systems will be costly at first (the costs will go way down over time), so a wise policy would provide subsidies and incentives to facilitate the transition.

Defining what constitutes sufficient energy will require considerable time and effort. But thanks to visionaries like Amory Lovins of the Rocky Mountain Institute, enough is known about the potential energy savings of various conservation and efficiency initiatives to be confident that our economy can produce more in the years ahead using far less energy. Likewise, Americans can lead equally satisfying lives with less energy use. For example, if every car owner in America drove a gas/electric hybrid or superefficient conventional vehicle instead of one getting about 20 miles per gallon (the current national average), we could reduce our daily oil intake by as much as 4–5 million barrels per day (of a total consumption of approximately 20 million barrels). And if the hybrids were of a plug-in type that could recharge their batteries at night when power plants have surplus capacity, the oil requirement could be reduced by several million more barrels without requiring additional power plants. Clearly, we don't need more oil to satisfy our transportation needs; we need more efficiency.

By seeking energy sufficiency instead of constant growth, we free ourselves of a tremendous burden. It is impossible to keep expanding the net supply of energy and reduce our dependence on fossil fuels and uranium-powered fission; the only sure way to achieve growth is to supply more of every fuel available. Once you abandon the commitment to growth, however, it is possible to begin the truly critical task: reducing our reliance on traditional fuels while significantly increasing the share of energy provided by alternatives.

To put things in perspective, fossil fuels now provide about 84 percent and nuclear power about 8.5 percent of America's net energy supply; renewables, including hydropower, provide a mere 8 percent. Although the amount of energy provided by renewables is expected to grow in the years ahead, the United States is projected to need so much more energy under its current path—114.5 quadrillion British thermal units per year in 2035, compared with approximately 100 quadrillion today—that it will need much larger amounts of oil, gas, and coal to supply the necessary increase. As a result, says the Energy Department, we will rely more on fossil fuels in 2035 than we do today, and will be emitting greater quantities of carbon dioxide.

Clearly, the existing path leads us ever closer to environmental catastrophe. Only by freezing (and eventually reducing) the total amount of energy consumed and reversing the ratio between traditional and alternative fuels can disaster be averted. A progressive energy policy would aim to achieve a ration of 50:50 between traditional and renewable fuels by 2030, and by 2050 would confine fossil fuels and nuclear power to a small "niche" market.

Accepting the necessity of switching to noncarbon alternatives, what are the "clean, green, and safe" fuels that America should rely on? Any source of energy chosen to meet the nation's future requirements should meet several criteria: it must be renewable, affordable, available domestically, and produce zero or very low amounts of greenhouse gas emissions. Several fuels satisfy two or three of these qualities, but only one—wind power—meets all of them. When located at reliably windy spots and near major transmission lines, wind turbines are competitive with most existing sources of energy and have none of their disadvantages. Solar power comes close to wind in its appeal, possessing great utility for certain applications (such as rooftop water heating); still, electricity derived from existing photovoltaic cells remains uncompetitive with other fuels in most situations. Geothermal, tidal, and wave energy show great promise but will need considerable development to be commercially applicable on a large scale. Biofuels derived from cellulose or algae also look promising, but they, too, require more work. Further out on the development path are hydrogen and nuclear fusion; it will take at least another generation or two before they will achieve widespread commercial utility.

Some within the environmental community argue for short-term reliance on some combination of natural gas, nuclear fission and coal, using the carbon capture and storage process as a "bridge" to renewable fuels, recognizing America's slow start in adopting the latter. While a case can be made for each of these, not one is clean, green, and safe. Natural gas, while emitting less carbon dioxide than other fossil fuels, is increasingly being derived from shale rock through the environmentally risky process known as "hydraulic fracturing" [see Kara Cusolito, "The Next Drilling Disaster?" June 3]. Nuclear fission produces radioactive waste that cannot be stored safely. Likewise, there is no assurance that carbon separated from coal can be stored safely for long periods of time. It follows that a wise policy would seek to leapfrog these technologies and move as rapidly as possible to renewable sources of energy.

With this in mind, the basic goal of a new national energy policy should be to minimize the use of existing fuels while ramping up the development and use of truly green alternatives—which requires not just technological innovation but a concerted effort to bring the new technologies to scale in the market, as Christian Parenti argues in the following article. The transition will also require a change in the way energy is distributed. At present a large share of our energy, in the form of oil, natural gas, and coal, is delivered by pipeline, rail, and truck. Most renewables, however, will be delivered in the form of electricity. This will require a massive expansion of the nation's electrical system—and its transformation into a "smart grid" that can rapidly move energy from areas of strong wind or sun (depending on weather conditions) to areas of peak need. A smart grid would also allow people to install their own energy-generating systems—solar panels, wind turbines, hydrogen fuel cells—and sell surplus energy back to the system.

Specifically, this policy would seek to:

- dramatically increase the use of wind power by adding more turbines and by increasing links to an expanded national electrical grid;

- increase the efficiency and cost-effectiveness of solar energy, especially photovoltaics and solar-thermal power;

- accelerate the development of geothermal, tidal, and wave power as well as biofuels derived from cellulose and algae, and expand research on hydrogen fuel cells and nuclear fusion;

- create a national "smart grid" capable of absorbing a vast increase in wind, solar, geothermal, and wave power and delivering it to areas of greatest need;

- spur the development, production, and acquisition of super-energy-efficient vehicles, buildings, appliances and industrial processes;

- accelerate the transition from conventional vehicles to hybrids, from regular hybrids to plug-in hybrids and from hybrids to all-electric automobiles;

- encourage and facilitate greater personal reliance on intercity rail, public transit, bicycles, and walking.

To achieve these goals, the government will have to assemble policy tools and funding devices. All incentives and subsidies for fossil fuel extraction and nuclear fission should be phased out, and like amounts directed toward the development of promising renewables and the further modernization and expansion of the electrical grid. Liberal tax breaks should be awarded to households and small businesses that invest in energy-saving heating, cooling, and lighting systems; similar breaks should be offered for the purchase of hybrid and electric vehicles. Many key initiatives, such as the construction of regional high-speed rail lines, will be costly. To finance such endeavors, taxes on gasoline and other carbon-based fuels should be increased as payroll taxes are decreased, thus encouraging job growth while discouraging carbon pollution; rebates should also be given to cushion the effect on low-income people. In addition, a ten-year, $250 billion energy innovation fund should be established to provide low-interest loans for commercializing promising new technologies being developed at universities and start-up firms around the country; once repaid, these funds could then be used to fund other such endeavors.

The Cheney plan envisioned, among other goals, building 1,000 new nuclear power plants by 2030. By contrast, the new energy policy envisioned here would have the following goals:

- create 5 million jobs through the pursuit of a green energy revolution, with a focus on the construction and manufacturing sectors, as outlined by the nonprofit group Apollo Alliance;

- maximize the nation's energy efficiency—in transportation, heating, electricity, and all other sectors—such that total energy demand declines by at least 50 percent by 2050, as documented in a comprehensive study by Greenpeace International and the European Renewable Energy Council;

- phase out oil consumption, except in niche markets, by 2030;

- formalize the current de factor moratorium on constructing new coal-fired power plants, phase out existing plants as well and halt all coal use by 2020;

- supply at least 75 percent of US electricity from wind, solar, and other renewable sources by 2030 and 99 percent by 2050, as described in the Greenpeace-EREC study;

- shift the US vehicle fleet to all-electric cars by 2035, to be powered with renewable energy;

- reduce US greenhouse gas emissions (from 1990 levels) by at least 90 percent by 2050, as described in the Greenpeace-EREC study.

There is not enough space here to argue the case for each of these specifics, but the essential elements of the new energy policy our nation needs are these: a guiding philosophy, a vision of the intended outcome, an assessment of the possible energy sources, and an outline of tools for implementation. Each of the final three can be modified as necessary to account for global events and scientific advances; but adherence to the first is critical. Adopting an enlightened new philosophy to guide our nation's future energy plans is the single most valuable thing we can do in the wake of the Deepwater Horizon tragedy.

Critical Thinking

1. Why does the United States need a new national energy strategy?

2. What was the outlook of the 2001 National Energy Policy, known as the "Cheney Plan," on the role of energy in the economy and how energy should be supplied? What have been the drawbacks of following this plan?

3. What is "energy sufficiency," and why is it an important concept in a forward-thinking energy plan?

4. What should be the basic goal of a new national energy strategy, according to the author? What would some of its key points include?

5. What policy and funding devices does the author suggest as a means to implement his vision of a national energy policy?

MICHAEL T. KLARE, The Nation's defense correspondent, is professor of peace and world security studies at Hampshire College. His latest book is Rising Powers, Shrinking Planet: The New Geopolitics of Energy.

Reprinted by permission from the August 2/9, 2010 issue of *The Nation*. Copyright © 2010 by The Nation. For subscription information, call 1-800-333-8536. Portions of each week's Nation magazine can be accessed at www.thenation.com

A Flimsy Trust
Why Social Security Needs Some Major Repairs

ALLAN SLOAN

I n Washington these days, the only topics of discussion seem to be how many trillions of dollars to throw at health care and the recession, and whom on Wall Street to pillory next. But watch out. Lurking just below the surface is a bailout candidate that may soon emerge like the great white shark in "Jaws"—Social Security.

Perhaps as early as this year, Social Security, which at $680 billion is the nation's biggest social program, will be transformed from an operation that's helped finance the rest of the government for 25 years into a cash drain that will need money from the Treasury. In other words, a bailout.

I've been writing about Social Security's problems for more than a decade, arguing that having the government borrow several trillion dollars to bail out the program so it can pay its promised benefits would impose an intolerable burden on our public finances. But I've changed my mind about what "intolerable" means. With the government spending untold trillions to bail out incompetent banks and the auto industry, it should damn well bail out Social Security recipients, too. But in a smart way.

Why am I talking about Social Security now, when health care is sucking up nearly all the oxygen in our nation's capital? Because Social Security is a big deal, providing a majority of the income for more than half of Americans 65 and up and also supporting millions of people with disabilities and survivors of deceased workers. And because the collapse of stock prices and home values makes Social Security retirement benefits far more important than they were during the highs of a few years ago. And because the problems aren't that hard to solve if we look at Social Security realistically instead of treating it as a sacred, untouchable program (liberals) or a demonic plot to make people dependent on government (conservatives).

Finally, this is a good time to discuss Social Security because the Obama folks say it's next on the agenda, after health care. No one at the White House, the Treasury Department or the Social Security Administration would discuss specifics, however.

It ought to tell you something that Peter Orszag, director of the White House Office of Management and Budget, is a noted Social Security scholar. Alas, he wouldn't tell me what he plans to propose. "Health care first" was all he'd say.

I'd like to show you that Social Security has a real and growing cash problem even as its trust fund is getting bigger than ever, explain how the program really works, and—immodest though it may seem—propose a few solutions.

Social Security has a real—and growing—cash problem.

The Cash Problem

How can Social Security possibly need a bailout when, by Washington rules, it's "solvent" for another 26 years? To understand the problem, look at me. I'll turn 66 next year, which makes me and my wife eligible for full Social Security benefits. They'll be about $42,000 a year for the both of us starting Jan. 1, 2011, and are scheduled to rise as the consumer price index does.

Social Security, which analyzed my situation, values those promised (but not legally binding) benefits at a bit more than $600,000. That is a lot of money, but Social Security is way ahead of us because the value of our benefits is far less than the Social Security taxes we and our employers will have paid by the end of next year, plus the interest Social Security will have earned on that money in the decades since we started working. Those taxes and interest will total more than $800,000 by Dec. 31, 2010. For example, the $5.18 my employer and I paid in 1961—the year I got my card—will have grown to $140 by next year.

I don't have a problem with this disparity. One of the principles of Social Security is that higher-paid folks like me support the lower-paid. That's as it should be, given that the Social Security tax (12.4 percent of covered wages, split equally between employer and employee) is regressive, far more costly as a percentage of income to a $40,000-a-year worker than it is to me. According to the Tax Policy Institute, five of six U.S. workers pay more in Social Security tax (including the employer's portion) than in federal income tax—something that makes it especially important (and only fair) to preserve the program for lower earners, who get old-age benefits of up to 90 percent of their covered wages, while I get only 28 percent.

How can my wife and I pose a problem to Social Security when our benefits are valued at $600,293, while our tax payments plus interest will total $804,686? Answer: Because the obligation is real, but the $800,000-plus asset is illusory, consisting solely of government IOUs to itself.

Now, let's step back a bit—to 1935, actually—to see how we got into this mess. President Franklin D. Roosevelt set up Social Security as an intergenerational social-insurance plan, under which today's workers support their parents (and those with disabilities and workers' survivors) in the hope that their children will in turn support them. It's not a pension fund. It's not an insurance company.

Social Security exists in its own world. In this world, taxes are called "contributions," though they're certainly not voluntary. "Trust funds," which in the outside world connote real wealth bestowed on beneficiaries, are nothing but IOUs from one arm of the government (the Treasury) to another (the Social Security Administration). And "solvency," which in the real world means that assets are greater than liabilities, means only that the Social Security trust fund has a positive balance.

Alas, the trust fund is a mere accounting entry, albeit one with a moral and political claim on taxpayers. It currently holds about $2.5 trillion in Treasury securities and is projected to grow to more than $4 trillion, even as Social Security begins to take in far less cash in taxes than it spends in benefits. For instance, it projects a cash deficit of $234 billion for 2023. But the trust fund will grow—on paper—because it will get $245 billion in Treasury IOUs as interest. The Treasury pays its interest tab with paper, not cash.

"The trust fund has no financial significance," says David Walker, former head of the Government Accountability Office and now president of the Peter G. Peterson Foundation, which advocates fiscal responsibility. "If you did [bookkeeping like] that in the private sector, you'd go to jail."

Let me show you why the Social Security trust fund isn't social or secure, has no funds, and can't be trusted, by returning to my favorite subject: myself.

The cash that Social Security has collected from me and my wife and our employers isn't sitting at Social Security. It's gone. Some went to pay benefits, some to fund the rest of the government. Since 1983, when it suffered a cash crisis, Social Security has been collecting more in taxes each year than it has paid out in benefits. It has used the excess to buy the Treasury securities that go into the trust fund, reducing the Treasury's need to raise money from investors. What happens if Social Security takes in less cash than it needs to pay benefits? Watch.

Let's say that late next year, Social Security realizes that it's short the $3,486 it needs to pay me and my wife for our Jan. 1, 2011, benefit. It gets that money by having the Treasury redeem $3,486 in trust-fund Treasury securities. The Treasury would get the necessary cash by selling $3,486 in new Treasury securities to investors. That means that $3,486 has been moved from the national debt that the government owes itself, which almost no one cares about, to the national debt it owes investors, which almost everyone—and certainly the bond market—takes very seriously.

This example shows you that the trust fund is of no economic value to the government as a whole (which is what really matters), because the government has to borrow from private investors the money it needs to redeem the securities. It would be the same if the trust fund sold its Treasury securities directly to investors—the government would be adding to the publicly held national debt to fund Social Security checks.

Social Security's "solvency" calculations—and the insistence by the status quo's supporters that there's "no problem" until 2036 because the trust fund will have assets until then—assumes that the Treasury can and will borrow the necessary money to redeem the trust fund's Treasury securities. There is also the assumption that our children, who by then will be running the country, will allow all this money to be diverted from other needs. I sure wouldn't assume that.

This whole problem of Social Security posting huge surpluses for years, using proceeds from a regressive tax to fund the rest of the government and then needing a Treasury bailout to pay its bills, is an unanticipated consequence of the 1983 legislation that supposedly fixed the system.

In order to show 75 years of "solvency" as required by law, Congress, using the bipartisan 1983 Greenspan Commission report as political cover, sharply raised Social Security taxes, cut future benefits and boosted the retirement age (then 65, currently 66, rising to 67).

The changes transformed Social Security from an explicitly pay-as-you-go program into one that produced huge cash surpluses for years followed by huge cash deficits. No one in authority seems to have realized that the only way to really save the temporary surpluses was to let the trust fund invest in non-Treasury debt securities, such as high-grade mortgages (yes, such things exist) or corporate bonds. That way, interest and principal repayments from homeowners and corporations would have been covering Social Security's future cash shortfalls, rather than the Treasury's having to borrow money to cover them.

This problem has been metastasizing for 25 years. Now I'll show you why the day of reckoning may finally be here.

Just last year, Social Security was projecting a cash surplus of $87 billion this year and $88 billion next year. These were to be the peak cash-generating years, followed by a cash-flow decline, followed by cash outlays exceeding inflows starting in 2017.

But in this year's Social Security trustees report, the cash flow projections for 2009 and 2010 have shrunk by almost 80 percent, to $19 billion and $18 billion, respectively. How did $138 billion of projected cash go missing in one year? Stephen Goss, Social Security's chief actuary, says the major reason is that the recession has cost millions of jobs, reducing Social Security's tax income below projections.

But $18 billion is still a surplus. So why do I say Social Security could go cash-negative this year? Because unemployment is far worse than Social Security projected. It assumed that unemployment would rise gradually this year and peak at 9 percent in 2010. Now, of course, the rate is 9.5 percent and rising—and we're still in 2009.

Social Security's having negative cash flow this year would be a relatively minor economic event—what's a few more billion dollars when the government's already borrowing more than $1 trillion?—but I think it would be a really important psychological and political event.

Orszag pooh-poohed my thinking when I met with him. He says I'm wrong to harp on Social Security's near-term cash flow—a term, by the way, that he won't use. "I think the real question of Social Security is how we bring long-term revenues in line with long-term expenses," he said, "not whether the primary surplus within Social Security turns negative within the next few years." I guess we'll see.

When you look back at numbers from previous years, you suddenly realize that Social Security's finances have been deteriorating for a long time. Social Security's cash flow (and thus its trust fund balances) has fallen well below earlier projections. Seven years ago, the projected 2009 cash flow was $115 billion. That fell to $87 billion by last year and is now $19 billion. Ten years ago, the trust fund was projected to be $3 trillion at the end of this year, rather than the currently projected $2.56 trillion.

In 1983, the system was projected to be "solvent" until the 2050s. This year it's only until 2036. Social Security's Goss says the major reason is that over the past two decades, the wages on which Social Security collects taxes have grown more slowly than projected. He said Social Security projected them to grow at 1.5 percent above inflation, but they've been growing at only 1.1 percent above it.

The scariest thing, at least to me, is that even as its financials erode, Social Security is as important as ever—maybe more so. Let me elaborate on what I said earlier, about how older people depend heavily on Social Security. It accounts for more than half the income of 52 percent of married couples over 65, and 72 percent of that of 65-and-up singles, according to the Social Security Administration.

What's more, this dependence—which Goss says isn't projected to change—comes despite 30 years of broadly popular self-directed retirement accounts such as 401(k)s, IRAs, 403(b)s and such.

Why haven't those savings accounts reduced dependence on Social Security? Part of the reason is that it takes a lot of money to generate serious retirement income: about $170,000 for a $1,000-a-month lifetime annuity. Inflation protection, if you can find it, is ultra-expensive. Vanguard, which offers a lifetime inflation-adjusted annuity in conjunction with an AIG insurance company called American General, quoted me a staggering price for an annuity mimicking my wife's and my Social Security benefit. Would you believe $774,895?

Another problem is that the stock market has been stinko. Stocks are below their level of April 2000, when the great bull market (August 1982 to March 2000) ended. It's hard to make money in stocks when they've been down for nine years. The Employee Benefit Research Institute estimates that the average retirement account balance of people 65 to 74 was $266,000 in 2007 but had fallen to $217,000 as of mid-June.

Then there's the problem of lost home equity. According to a study conducted for Fortune by the Center for Economic and

Good Numbers Gone Bad

Social Security will soon take in less cash than it spends, partly because of rising unemployment. Its cash flow will shrink to a projected $19 billion this year, compared with the $115 billion predicted seven years ago.

Shrinking projections of Social Security cash flow for 2009 (in billions)

2009 cash flow as projected in 2002

$115

$87 ... as projected in 2008

$19 ... as projected in 2009

Number of Social Security beneficiaries per 100 workers

Sources: Fortune magazine. Social Security administration

Policy Research, people in the lower-income to upper-middle-income ranges have lost a far greater proportion of their net worth as a result of the housing bust than the most wealthy people have.

The bottom line is that many older people who felt reasonably well fixed for retirement a few years ago now need Social Security more than ever. That makes it even more important to come up with a way to sustain it and to show our children a realistic plan to give them benefits, rather than to rely on the trust fund and the supposed political clout of the geezer class to keep benefits flowing when cash flow goes negative.

So how do we fix these problems? Let me divide it into three categories: what to do, what to change and what not to do.

What to Do

Many of the old standbys: raising the "covered wage" limit, but not to outrageous levels; tweaking the benefit formulas so that high-end people like me get a little less bang for the buck; modifying cost-of-living increases for us high-end types; and, most important, raising the retirement age to 70, with a special earlier-retirement provision for manual laborers, who can't be expected to work that long.

What to Change

- **The law requiring 75-year solvency.** It's hard to predict what will happen 75 days from now, let alone 75 years from now. But the obsession with 75-year solvency and the status of the trust fund has obscured what's really going on.

This requirement forces Social Security's actuaries—who are among the best and smartest public servants I know—to make all sorts of impossible projections. As we've seen, even one faulty projection—such as overestimating wage growth—can cause substantial problems.

- **The trust fund.** Before the Greenspan Commission-related changes in 1983, the trust fund was a checking account. The workings of Social Security since 1983 have turned it into something it was never intended to be: an investment account. Let's gradually draw down the trust fund by having the Treasury redeem $100 billion or so annually (less than the current interest the fund earns) by giving the fund cash rather than Treasury IOUs, gradually increasing the redemptions. That will let the fund buy assets that will be useful when serious cash-flow deficits hit, assets such as high-grade mortgage securities and high-grade bonds.

That way we'll be bailing out Social Security a bit at a time, which is realistic, rather than in huge chunks, which isn't. Combine that with the lower costs and higher revenues, and today's kids could see that there really is a way they'll get benefits someday.

What Not to Do

- **Depend on taxing "the rich."** One solution you hear in Washington is restoring "covered wage" levels to the good old Greenspan Commission days, when 90 percent of wages were subject to Social Security tax, compared with 83 percent now. Sounds simple and fair, doesn't it? But that would increase the Social Security wage base to about $170,000 from the current $106,800, according to Andrew Biggs of the American Enterprise Institute—at 12.4 percent, a huge new tax to middle-class workers. (And yes, that's middle-class income, not rich-person income, in large parts of the country.)

During his campaign, President Obama proposed (and then dropped) a plan to leave the Social Security wage cap where it is but to apply the 12.4 percent Social Security tax to all wages above $250,000. That—like the 90-percent-level-of-income idea—would be a huge new tax that would weaken support for

Social Security among higher-income people. I'm not saying "rich people," because truly rich people generally have huge amounts of investment income, which isn't subject to Social Security tax.

- **Means-test benefits.** It's being done. We'd be making a terrible mistake to means-test Social Security by saying that people above a certain income level can't get it. That would violate the social compact that everyone pays Social Security taxes and everyone gets something.

Besides, Social Security is already means-tested, indirectly. That's because if you have enough non-Social Security income—about $23,000 a year in my case—you pay federal income tax on 85 percent of your benefit.

Given the three pensions I stand to collect from previous employers, I think I hit that level. So, for the final time, let's run my numbers. If my wife and I are in the 28 percent federal tax bracket when we start collecting benefits, we'll be giving almost a quarter of our benefit right back to Social Security.

It would also mean that the $600,000 benefit I talked about earlier would cost Social Security only about $450,000—just 55 percent or so of the $800,000-plus value of our taxes.

I don't mind that big haircut, but I'd be furious if the government decided to just confiscate all the money my wife and I put in over the decades by saying we were "rich" and had no right to any benefits. And I wouldn't be alone.

Given the way health-care reform has bogged down, Social Security may not make it onto the agenda until next year. But it's going to show up sooner or later, probably sooner, because the numbers are so bad that something's going to have to be done. As I hope I've shown, we're going to have to bail out Social Security or risk hurting a lot of low-income older people or putting the whole program at risk by gouging and alienating upper-income Social Security sympathizers like me.

So let's fix this already. By the numbers. And by the right numbers, not fantasy ones.

Critical Thinking

1. Why are Social Security "trust funds" of no economic value to government as a whole?

2. How did the 1983 Social Security cash crisis and resulting legislation implemented to solve it inadvertently lead to the transformation of the system from "pay as you go" into a surplus-deficit cycle, leading to an impending crisis?

3. Explain the reasons why people are becoming increasingly dependent on Social Security income.

4. What does the author suggest the government specifically do or change to fix the problems with Social Security?

5. What does the author suggest the government to avoid doing in reforming Social Security?

With reporting by Doris Burke of *Fortune*. **ALLAN SLOAN** is *Fortune* magazine's senior editor at large. His e-mail address is asloan@fortunemail.com.

How Globalization Went Bad

From terrorism to global warming, the evils of globalization are more dangerous than ever before. What went wrong? The world became dependent on a single superpower. Only by correcting this imbalance can the world become a safer place.

STEVEN WEBER ET AL.

The world today is more dangerous and less orderly than it was supposed to be. Ten or 15 years ago, the naive expectations were that the "end of history" was near. The reality has been the opposite. The world has more international terrorism and more nuclear proliferation today than it did in 1990. International institutions are weaker. The threats of pandemic disease and climate change are stronger. Cleavages of religious and cultural ideology are more intense. The global financial system is more unbalanced and precarious.

It wasn't supposed to be like this. The end of the Cold War was supposed to make global politics and economics easier to manage, not harder. What went wrong? The bad news of the 21st century is that globalization has a significant dark side. The container ships that carry manufactured Chinese goods to and from the United States also carry drugs. The airplanes that fly passengers nonstop from New York to Singapore also transport infectious diseases. And the Internet has proved just as adept at spreading deadly, extremist ideologies as it has e-commerce.

The conventional belief is that the single greatest challenge of geopolitics today is managing this dark side of globalization, chipping away at the illegitimate co-travelers that exploit openness, mobility, and freedom, without putting too much sand in the gears. The current U.S. strategy is to push for more trade, more connectivity, more markets, and more openness. America does so for a good reason—it benefits from globalization more than any other country in the world. The United States acknowledges globalization's dark side but attributes it merely to exploitative behavior by criminals, religious extremists, and other anachronistic elements that can be eliminated. The dark side of globalization, America says, with very little subtlety, can be mitigated by the expansion of American power, sometimes unilaterally and sometimes through multilateral institutions, depending on how the United States likes it. In other words, America is aiming for a "flat," globalized world coordinated by a single superpower.

That's nice work if you can get it. But the United States almost certainly cannot. Not only because other countries won't let it, but, more profoundly, because that line of thinking is faulty. The predominance of American power has many benefits, but the management of globalization is not one of them. The mobility of ideas, capital, technology, and people is hardly new. But the rapid advance of globalization's evils is. Most of that advance has taken place since 1990. Why? Because what changed profoundly in the 1990s was the polarity of the international system. For the first time in modern history, globalization was superimposed onto a world with a single superpower. What we have discovered in the past 15 years is that it is a dangerous mixture. The negative effects of globalization since 1990 are not the result of globalization itself. They are the dark side of American predominance.

The world is paying a heavy price for the instability created by globalization and unipolarity, and the United States is bearing most of the burden.

The Dangers of Unipolarity

A straightforward piece of logic from market economics helps explain why unipolarity and globalization don't mix. Monopolies, regardless of who holds them, are almost always bad for both the market and the monopolist. We propose three simple axioms of "globalization under unipolarity" that reveal these dangers.

Axiom 1: *Above a certain threshold of power, the rate at which new global problems are generated will exceed the rate at which old problems are fixed.*

Power does two things in international politics: It enhances the capability of a state to do things, but it also increases the number of things that a state must worry about. At a certain point, the latter starts to overtake the former. It's the familiar law of diminishing returns. Because powerful states have large spheres of influence and their security and economic interests touch every region of the world, they are threatened by the risk of things going wrong—anywhere. That is particularly true for the United States, which leverages its ability to go anywhere and do anything through massive debt. No one knows exactly when the law of diminishing returns will kick in. But, historically, it starts to happen long before a single great power dominates the entire globe, which is why large empires from Byzantium to Rome have always reached a point of unsustainability.

That may already be happening to the United States today, on issues ranging from oil dependency and nuclear proliferation to pandemics and global warming. What Axiom 1 tells you is that more U.S. power is not the answer; it's actually part of the problem. A multipolar world would almost certainly manage the globe's pressing problems more effectively. The larger the number of great powers in the global system, the greater the chance that at least one of them would exercise some control over a given combination of space, other actors, and problems. Such reasoning doesn't rest on hopeful notions that the great powers will work together. They might do so. But even if they don't, the result is distributed governance, where some great power is interested in most every part of the world through productive competition.

Axiom 2: In an increasingly networked world, places that fall between the networks are very dangerous places—and there will be more ungoverned zones when there is only one network to join.

The second axiom acknowledges that highly connected networks can be efficient, robust, and resilient to shocks. But in a highly connected world, the pieces that fall between the networks are increasingly shut off from the benefits of connectivity. These problems fester in the form of failed states, mutate like pathogenic bacteria, and, in some cases, reconnect in subterranean networks such as al Qaeda. The truly dangerous places are the points where the subterranean networks touch the mainstream of global politics and economics. What made Afghanistan so dangerous under the Taliban was not that it was a failed state. It wasn't. It was a partially failed and partially connected state that worked the interstices of globalization through the drug trade, counterfeiting, and terrorism.

Can any single superpower monitor all the seams and back alleys of globalization? Hardly. In fact, a lone hegemon is unlikely to look closely at these problems, because more pressing issues are happening elsewhere, in places where trade and technology are growing. By contrast, a world of several great powers is a more interest-rich environment in which nations must look in less obvious places to find new sources of advantage. In such a system, it's harder for troublemakers to spring up, because the cracks and seams of globalization are held together by stronger ties.

Axiom 3: Without a real chance to find useful allies to counter a superpower, opponents will try to neutralize power, by going underground, going nuclear, or going "bad."

Axiom 3 is a story about the preferred strategies of the weak. It's a basic insight of international relations that states try to

balance power. They protect themselves by joining groups that can hold a hegemonic threat at bay. But what if there is no viable group to join? In today's unipolar world, every nation from Venezuela to North Korea is looking for a way to constrain American power. But in the unipolar world, it's harder for states to join together to do that. So they turn to other means. They play a different game. Hamas, Iran, Somalia, North Korea, and Venezuela are not going to become allies anytime soon. Each is better off finding other ways to make life more difficult for Washington. Going nuclear is one way. Counterfeiting U.S. currency is another. Raising uncertainty about oil supplies is perhaps the most obvious method of all.

Here's the important downside of unipolar globalization. In a world with multiple great powers, many of these threats would be less troublesome. The relatively weak states would have a choice among potential partners with which to ally, enhancing their influence. Without that more attractive choice, facilitating the dark side of globalization becomes the most effective means of constraining American power.

Sharing Globalization's Burden

The world is paying a heavy price for the instability created by the combination of globalization and unipolarity, and the United States is bearing most of the burden. Consider the case of nuclear proliferation. There's effectively a market out there for proliferation, with its own supply (states willing to share nuclear technology) and demand (states that badly want a nuclear weapon). The overlap of unipolarity with globalization ratchets up both the supply and demand, to the detriment of U.S. national security.

It has become fashionable, in the wake of the Iraq war, to comment on the limits of conventional military force. But much of this analysis is overblown. The United States may not be able to stabilize and rebuild Iraq. But that doesn't matter much from the perspective of a government that thinks the Pentagon has it in its sights. In Tehran, Pyongyang, and many other capitals, including Beijing, the bottom line is simple: The U.S. military could, with conventional force, end those regimes tomorrow if it chose to do so. No country in the world can dream of challenging U.S. conventional military power. But they can certainly hope to deter America from using it. And the best deterrent yet invented is the threat of nuclear retaliation. Before 1989, states that felt threatened by the United States could turn to the Soviet Union's nuclear umbrella for protection. Now, they turn to people like A.Q. Khan. Having your own nuclear weapon used to be a luxury. Today, it is fast becoming a necessity.

North Korea is the clearest example. Few countries had it worse during the Cold War. North Korea was surrounded by feuding, nuclear-armed communist neighbors, it was officially at war with its southern neighbor, and it stared continuously at tens of thousands of U.S. troops on its border. But, for 40 years, North Korea didn't seek nuclear weapons. It didn't need to, because it had the Soviet nuclear umbrella. Within five years of the Soviet collapse, however, Pyongyang was pushing ahead full steam on plutonium reprocessing facilities. North Korea's founder, Kim Il Sung, barely flinched when former

U.S. President Bill Clinton's administration readied war plans to strike his nuclear installations preemptively. That brinkmanship paid off. Today North Korea is likely a nuclear power, and Kim's son rules the country with an iron fist. America's conventional military strength means a lot less to a nuclear North Korea. Saddam Hussein's great strategic blunder was that he took too long to get to the same place.

How would things be different in a multipolar world? For starters, great powers could split the job of policing proliferation, and even collaborate on some particularly hard cases. It's often forgotten now that, during the Cold War, the only state with a tougher nonproliferation policy than the United States was the Soviet Union. Not a single country that had a formal alliance with Moscow ever became a nuclear power. The Eastern bloc was full of countries with advanced technological capabilities in every area except one—nuclear weapons. Moscow simply wouldn't permit it. But today we see the uneven and inadequate level of effort that non-superpowers devote to stopping proliferation. The Europeans dangle carrots at Iran, but they are unwilling to consider serious sticks. The Chinese refuse to admit that there is a problem. And the Russians are aiding Iran's nuclear ambitions. When push comes to shove, nonproliferation today is almost entirely America's burden.

The same is true for global public health. Globalization is turning the world into an enormous petri dish for the incubation of infectious disease. Humans cannot outsmart disease, because it just evolves too quickly. Bacteria can reproduce a new generation in less than 30 minutes, while it takes us decades to come up with a new generation of antibiotics. Solutions are only possible when and where we get the upper hand. Poor countries where humans live in close proximity to farm animals are the best place to breed extremely dangerous zoonotic disease. These are often the same countries, perhaps not entirely coincidentally, that feel threatened by American power. Establishing an early warning system for these diseases—exactly what we lacked in the case of SARS a few years ago and exactly what we lack for avian flu today—will require a significant level of intervention into the very places that don't want it. That will be true as long as international intervention means American interference.

> If there were rival great powers with different cultural and ideological leanings, globalization's darkest problem of all—terrorism—would look different.

The most likely sources of the next ebola or HIV-like pandemic are the countries that simply won't let U.S. or other Western agencies in, including the World Health Organization. Yet the threat is too arcane and not immediate enough for the West to force the issue. What's needed is another great power to take over a piece of the work, a power that has more immediate interests in the countries where diseases incubate and one that is seen as less of a threat. As long as the United States remains the world's lone superpower, we're not likely to get any help.

Even after HIV, SARS, and several years of mounting hysteria about avian flu, the world is still not ready for a viral pandemic in Southeast Asia or sub-Saharan Africa. America can't change that alone.

If there were rival great powers with different cultural and ideological leanings, globalization's darkest problem of all—terrorism—would also likely look quite different. The pundits are partly right: Today's international terrorism owes something to globalization. Al Qaeda uses the Internet to transmit messages, it uses credit cards and modern banking to move money, and it uses cell phones and laptops to plot attacks. But it's not globalization that turned Osama bin Laden from a small-time Saudi dissident into the symbolic head of a radical global movement. What created Osama bin Laden was the predominance of American power.

A terrorist organization needs a story to attract resources and recruits. Oftentimes, mere frustration over political, economic, or religious conditions is not enough. Al Qaeda understands that, and, for that reason, it weaves a narrative of global jihad against a "modernization," "Westernization," and a "Judeo-Christian" threat. There is really just one country that both spearheads and represents that threat: the United States. And so the most efficient way for a terrorist to gain a reputation is to attack the United States. The logic is the same for all monopolies. A few years ago, every computer hacker in the world wanted to bring down Microsoft, just as every aspiring terrorist wants to create a spectacle of destruction akin to the September 11 attacks inside the United States.

Al Qaeda cells have gone after alternate targets such as Britain, Egypt, and Spain. But these are not the acts that increase recruitment and fundraising, or mobilize the energy of otherwise disparate groups around the world. Nothing enhances the profile of a terrorist like killing an American, something Abu Musab al-Zarqawi understood well in Iraq. Even if al Qaeda's deepest aspirations lie with the demise of the Saudi regime, the predominance of U.S. power and its role supporting the house of Saud makes America the only enemy really worth fighting. A multipolar world would surely confuse this kind of clear framing that pits Islamism against the West. What would be al Qaeda's message if the Chinese were equally involved in propping up authoritarian regimes in the Islamic, oil-rich Gulf states? Does the al Qaeda story work if half its enemy is neither Western nor Christian?

Restoring the Balance

The consensus today in the U.S. foreign-policy community is that more American power is always better. Across the board. For both the United States and the rest of the globe. The National Security Strategy documents of 2002 and 2006 enshrine this consensus in phrases such as "a balance of power that favors freedom." The strategy explicitly defines the "balance" as a continued imbalance, as the United States continues "dissuading potential competitors . . . from challenging the United States, its allies, and its partners."

In no way is U.S. power inherently a bad thing. Nor is it true that no good comes from unipolarity. But there are significant downsides to the imbalance of power. That view is hardly revolutionary. It has a long pedigree in U.S. foreign-policy thought. It was the perspective, for instance, that George Kennan brought to the table in the late 1940s when he talked about the desirability of a European superpower to restrain the United States. Although the issues today are different than they were in Kennan's time, it's still the case that too much power may, as Kennan believed, lead to overreach. It may lead to arrogance. It may lead to insensitivity to the concerns of others. Though Kennan may have been prescient to voice these concerns, he couldn't have predicted the degree to which American unipolarity would lead to such an unstable overlap with modern-day globalization.

America has experienced this dangerous burden for 15 years, but it still refuses to see it for what it really is. Antiglobalization sentiment is coming today from both the right and the left. But by blaming globalization for what ails the world, the U.S. foreign-policy community is missing a very big part of what is undermining one of the most hopeful trends in modern history—the reconnection of societies, economies, and minds that political borders have kept apart for far too long.

America cannot indefinitely stave off the rise of another superpower. But, in today's networked and interdependent world, such an event is not entirely a cause for mourning. A shift in the global balance of power would, in fact, help the United States manage some of the most costly and dangerous consequences of globalization. As the international playing field levels, the scope of these problems and the threat they pose to America will only decrease. When that happens, the United States will find globalization is a far easier burden to bear.

Critical Thinking

1. How did the fall of the Soviet Union and other geopolitical events of the 1990s affect the global balance of power? How are the side effects of globalization a negative by-product of this power shift?

2. How would a multipolar world handle global problems more effectively than a unipolar one?

3. Why is nuclear proliferation an effective deterrent to dominant U.S. military power in a globalized world? How would the situation differ in a multipolar world?

4. What are the implications of globalization for global public health?

5. How would a shift in the global balance of power ultimately benefit the United States, according to the authors?

STEVEN WEBER is professor of political science and director of the Institute of International Studies at the University of California, Berkeley. **NAAZNEEN BARMA, MATTHEW KROENIG,** and **ELY RATNER** are PhD candidates at U.C., Berkeley, and research fellows at its New Era Foreign Policy Center.

Reprinted in entirety by McGraw-Hill with permission from *Foreign Policy,* January/February 2007, pp. 48+. www.foreignpolicy.com. © 2007 Washingtonpost.Newsweek Interactive, LLC.

Worth Fighting—or Not

In judging which of its dozen major wars America should have fought, *unintended consequences* often outweigh the intended ones.

BURT SOLOMON

War is hell, but it can also be useful as hell. Even if that isn't always obvious at the time. Ponder, for a moment, the War of 1812. When the fledgling United States of America repulsed the British—again—in 1815, the war "felt like a loss or a tie," according to Allan Millett, a military historian at the University of New Orleans. The torch had been put to the Capitol and the White House, and the Battle of Baltimore produced the lyrics of a National Anthem that generations of Americans would struggle to sing. The Americans hadn't won; the British had lost.

Only as the years passed did it become clear that the war had truly served the United States as a Second War of Independence. It forced Britain to respect its former colony's sovereignty; helped to nudge the Spanish out of Florida; persuaded the European colonial powers to accept the Louisiana Purchase and to stop aiding the Indians, thereby opening the way to Western expansion; and prepared the geopolitical groundwork for the Monroe Doctrine. Not for another 186 years, until September 11, 2001, would the continental United States suffer a foreign attack.

"In the long run," Millett judged, "it worked out."

Unintended consequences can also work in the other direction, of course. Consider the following zigzag of events. The humiliating American defeat in the Vietnam War may have encouraged the Soviet Union's adventurism, notably its invasion of Afghanistan in 1979, four years after North Vietnamese troops seized control of South Vietnam. The Afghan mujahedeen eventually drove the Soviets out, with the covert support of the United States, as dramatized in the 2007 movie *Charlie Wilson's War.* The playboy member of Congress, a Texas Democrat, prevailed upon Israel, Egypt, Saudi Arabia, Pakistan, and the U.S. Congress to cough up billions of dollars and untraceable weaponry.

But recall the movie's penultimate scene, when Wilson fails to persuade his fellow House appropriators to spend a pittance to rebuild Afghan schools, in hopes of reconstructing a land left broken by war and occupation. The resulting power vacuum allowed the Taliban to emerge as the mountainous nation's militantly Islamic rulers, offering sanctuary and succor to Al Qaeda as it prepared its terrorist attacks on New York City and Arlington, Va., on 9/11. Surely, the best and brightest who botched the Vietnam War hadn't given the slightest thought to backward Afghanistan or to the World Trade Center's twin towers, which were dedicated just six days after the last U.S. troops withdrew from Vietnam in 1973.

Bunker Hill to Baghdad

Revolutionary War
War of 1812
Mexican War
Civil War
Spanish-American
WWI
WWII
Korean War
Vietnam War
Persian Gulf War
War in Afghanistan
War in Iraq

- All wars, in a sense, are **wars of choice.**
- The smaller wars the U.S. has fought often turned out pretty well: **low cost with high impact.**
- Vietnam is the war from which the **fewest benefits** seem to have flowed, historians say.

Sometimes, the desirability of a particular war will rise and fall over time. When Chou En-lai, the Chinese premier, was asked to assess the French Revolution fought nearly two centuries before, he famously replied: "It is too early to say." Consider the oscillating historical verdicts on the Mexican War. President Polk and Mexican dictator Santa Anna "were as combustible a combo as [Bush] 43 and Saddam," said Philip Zelikow, a historian at the University of Virginia who was a foreign-policy adviser for both Presidents Bush. When the war ended in 1848, it was counted as a clear-cut American success, assuring that Texas would remain part of the United States and adding territories that became the states of Arizona, California, and New Mexico. But after 1850, this territorial expansion reignited the political battles over slavery that the war's opponents (including a one-term member of Congress named Abraham Lincoln) had feared, thereby accelerating the descent into civil war. But that was then. Now, with the Civil War long past, it is hard to imagine the United States without the former chunks of Mexico. At least it was—until Texas Gov. Rick Perry, a Republican, raised the possibility recently that his state might want to secede from the U.S.

With occasional exceptions, the minor wars that the United States has waged from time to time have worked out pretty much as hoped. From the Barbary pirates to Grenada to Bosnia and Kosovo, clear objectives and a sufficiency of military force led to success at a low cost. But in America's 12 major wars during its 233 years of independence, things have rarely played out as expected, in the aftermath of the conflicts if not during them.

Historians, probably wisely, are wary of balancing the costs and benefits of America's past wars and delivering a bottom-line judgment. But if pressed, they'll divide them into a few "good" wars, especially the American Revolution, the Civil War, and World War II; several muddled wars; and a real stinker, Vietnam, the only one that America has lost outright.

Which brings us, of course, to the two wars that the United States is fighting now. There are reasons for hope and reasons for skepticism about the likely outcome of both. The war in Afghanistan, which President Obama has escalated, threatens to become the first war of necessity that the United States loses, especially if the nation next door, nuclear-armed Pakistan, devolves into chaos. In Iraq, the prospect of a reasonably stable, tolerably democratic regime has grown. But even in the unlikelier event that Iraq becomes a beacon of democracy for a mostly despotic Middle East, because of the high costs—including the encouragement of a nuclear-armed Iran and an ebb in American influence—some foreign-policy experts doubt that history will ever judge the Iraq war as worth the fight.

Apples and Oranges

How to judge a war? Let us count the ways.

Thucydides, the historian of ancient Greece who chronicled the Peloponnesian War, categorized wars by the aggressor's motivation for starting them—namely, fear, honor, and interests. In judging the importance of the national interest, "most people put it first, and they're mostly wrong," said Donald Kagan, a professor of classics and history at Yale University. "It's way down the list." Alarm at foreigners' intentions and, especially, feelings of dishonor are more often the main reasons that nations go to war, he says.

Another way of judging the usefulness of a war is by assessing the need for it. In *War of Necessity, War of Choice: A Memoir of Two Iraq Wars,* published in May, Richard Haass distinguishes between a necessary Persian Gulf war, in 1991, when he served on the staff of President George H.W. Bush's National Security Council, and an unnecessary invasion of Iraq begun in 2003, while he directed the State Department's policy planning. A war of necessity, in his thinking, is one that involves a vital national interest and in which military force is the only option that might succeed—judgments that entail "elements of subjectivity," Haass, who is now president of the Council on Foreign Relations, noted in an interview. Rare, after all, is the war that its proponents don't try to sell to the public as essential, even when it isn't. Zelikow, who served as the executive director of the bipartisan commission that examined 9/11, is skeptical of the distinction. "It takes a post facto argument and makes it sound like objective history," he said. "The only war we did not choose is the one that was brought to New York City on 9/11."

Maybe the purest way of judging a war is to contemplate whether it is just or unjust to fight, an exercise most usefully pursued before the shooting starts. Michael Walzer, a political philosopher and professor emeritus at the Institute for Advanced Study in Princeton, N.J., is the author of *Just and Unjust Wars,* published in 1977 in the wake of Vietnam. The factors in figuring a war's justice are a mix of morality and fact, taking into account whether a nation was attacked or is (credibly) about to be attacked; its efforts to find peaceful solutions; the international or legal legitimacy of its military response; its likelihood of success; and, once a war has begun, the conduct of the fighting.

But these judgments, too, are "different," Walzer acknowledged in an interview, from the practical considerations—measured in lives, treasure, territory, security, and power—that determine whether a nation benefits, on balance, from starting or entering a war. Indeed, neither the justice nor the necessity of a war bears more than an incidental correlation to whether, in hindsight, it was worth fighting. Walzer regards the Mexican War, for instance, as an "unjust war that worked out well," for the United States at least. In Haass's mind, the American Revolution probably ought to be counted as a war of choice, though a "warranted" one that should have been fought. Even a war of choice can be worth fighting—it's just that "the standards are higher," he said—if its benefits sufficiently exceed its costs, measured both in the short and longer term.

"Each had benefits," said Mackubin Owens, a professor of strategy and force planning at the U.S. Naval War College, referring to the major wars that the United States has fought. The problem for decision makers, of course, is that neither costs nor benefits can be known with any certainty—or even good guesswork—in advance. A war's consequences, more often than not, are unfathomable. Even afterward, as any fair-minded historian will attest, it is no easy task to judge. Start with the impossibility of placing a value on the lives lost and disrupted; take into account the improbability of divining the future; and imagine the necessarily speculative character of the counterfactuals—what would have happened had the war not broken out. This is far beyond the reach of any mathematical or actuarial formulation.

Worse, weighing the costs and benefits of a war is an exercise in comparing apples and oranges. Consider the war in Korea, which lasted from 1950 to '53. The U.S.-led combat to repel Communist North Korea's invasion of anti-communist (though autocratic) South Korea proved popular with the American public at first. But that support soured, especially when an armistice settled on virtually the same boundary between the two Koreas that existed when the war began, at the cost of 36,574 American lives. Nonetheless, as the Cold War went on, it became clear that in this first test of resolve after World War II, the U.S. willingness to stand up to Communist aggressiveness cooled Soviet strongman Joseph Stalin's geopolitical ambitions and kept South Korea—and Japan—allied with the West. "I thought it was a just war at the time," Walzer recounted, and "I think it probably helped in the eventual victory over communism."

Andrew Bacevich, a professor of international relations at Boston University, agrees—up to a point. "The initial U.S. response to Korea was a war that we needed to fight," he said. But a crucial mistake was made in conducting it: President Truman's decision to acquiesce in Gen. Douglas MacArthur's desire to invade the North drew Communist China into the war and ultimately produced a stalemate. The consequences, Bacevich said, went beyond the estimated 30,000 additional American Millet to include two decades of enmity between the United States and China—until President Nixon opened the door in 1972—and a failure to exploit the Sino-Soviet schism in a manner that might have weakened the Soviet

U.S. Wars: Worth Fighting?

Historians, if pressed, will divide America's wars into a few "good" wars—especially the American Revolution, the Civil War, and World War II; several muddled wars; and a real stinker, Vietnam.

	Revolutionary War (1775–83)	War of 1812 (1812–15)	Mexican War (1846–48)	Civil War (1861–65)	Spanish-American War (1898–99)	World War I (1917–18*)	World War II (1941–45*)	Korean War (1950–53)	Vietnam War (1964–73)	Persian Gulf War (1990–91)	War in Afghanistan (2001–)	War in Iraq (2003–)
Strategic Benefits	Won independence	Gained recognition of Louisiana Purchase, lessened Indian threat, laid groundwork for Monroe Doctrine	Assured Texas as a state, seized New Mexico, Arizona, California	Preserved the Union, ended slavery	Incorporated Puerto Rico and Hawaii, assured U.S. predominance in Americas	Emerged as world power	Defeated Nazi Germany and Japan	Discouraged Communist aggression, kept Japan and South Korea as U.S. allies	None	Blocked Saddam Hussein from threatening Saudi oil	Ousted Al Qaeda from camps	Created U.S. ally in Arab Middle East
Strategic Cost	Tories punished, Indians harmed	Failed to gain control of Canada	Inflamed debate over slavery	Devastation	Annexation of the Philippines brought conflict with Japan	Diplomatic aftermath led to World War II	Enabled Soviet hegemony in Eastern Europe, Cold War	Led to two decades of antipathy with mainland China	First U.S. defeat, reduced diplomatic influence, caused domestic discord	Left Saddam in power	Destabilized Pakistan	Diminished American influence, emboldened Iran
American Deaths (total serving)	25,324 (290,000)	2,260 (286,730)	13,283 (78,718)	498,332 (3,713,363)	2,446 (306,760)	116,516 (4,734,991)	405,399 (16,112,566)	36,574 (1,789,000**)	58,209 (3,403,000**)	382 (694,550**)	685† (More than 1.9 million troops have served in these wars since 9/11)	4,294†
Financial Cost (in billions of constant 2008 dollars)	$1.8	$1.2	$1.8	$60.4	$6.8	$253	$4,114	$320	$686	$96	$189††	$642††

* Duration of U.S. involvement.

** In war zone only.

† As of May 30, 2009.

†† Does not include $75.5 billion in supplemental war funding requested in April 2009.

Sources: Oxford Companion to American Military History; Defense Department; Congressional Research Service.

214

Union and bolstered the West. "It sent us down a path," he pointed out, "that cast the decision to go in in a different light." Bacevich cautioned against trying to arrive at "concise judgments" about the desirability of the Korean—or any—War.

The "Good" Wars

The nation's first war, for its independence, was probably its most essential—and successful. King George III had committed "a long Train of Abuses and Usurpations," as Thomas Jefferson detailed in the Declaration of Independence, even as the Founding Draftsman glossed over perhaps the most threatening of the British monarchy's tyrannical acts. Yale's Kagan cited Britain's efforts, from 1763 on, to impose taxes and restrictions that suppressed the commercial ambitions of an entrepreneurial people. Hence the impulse for independence.

Still, only a third of the colonists, historians estimate, supported a rebellion against their British masters; a third remained loyal to the Crown and the rest were ambivalent or indifferent. Many of the Tories paid a price for their loyalty, Bacevich noted, in having to knuckle under or flee. The continent's aboriginal inhabitants likewise did not fare well. Conceivably, the colonists might have acted like their neighbors to the north—Canada waited until 1867 to obtain self-government from Britain without shedding blood—although it is daunting to find anyone who would make that case today.

The Civil War, pitting brother against brother, produced a more vehement diversity of opinion, at the time and ever since. The war was probably unavoidable, most historians say, given the conflicts between the North and the South in their economies—with or without slavery—and their cultures. Had the conflict not broken out in 1861, they suppose, it would have happened later. And by the time the Civil War ended, it accomplished more than its participants had imagined. Early on, President Lincoln declared that he was willing to keep slavery or to end it, in whole or in part, as long as the Union was preserved; the Emancipation Proclamation referred to abolition in the rebellious states as a matter of "military necessity."

Had the South successfully seceded, historians debate whether slavery would have faded out on its own as the soil in the cotton fields was depleted, or, rather, would have spread to states farther west and into Latin America. A popular theme in counterfactual histories posits that the Confederacy and the Union would have reunited eventually. In any event, slavery would presumably have ended sometime (Brazil became the last country in the Western Hemisphere to abolish it, in 1888), although maybe not quickly enough for a slow-changing electorate to choose an African-American president in 2008. But was an earlier end of slavery "worth 600,000 deaths? It's hard to say," concluded Max Boot, a senior fellow at the Council on Foreign Relations. "There wasn't a lot of whooping for joy in 1865. Wars look better when the human costs have faded into history."

> **"There wasn't a lot of *whooping for joy* in 1865. Wars look better when the human costs have faded into history."**
> —Max Boot

The classic "good" war, fought by the Greatest Generation, was good ol' Double-U-Double-U-Two. The United States had to be dragged into the Second World War—until the Japanese bombed Pearl Harbor—over the isolationists' objections that the fighting in Europe and Asia was, for a nation protected by oceans, a war of choice. Before it ended, the human costs were staggering, estimated at more than 72 million deaths worldwide, including 405,399 Americans. But the benefits, historians say, were mightier still: the defeat of Hitler's Germany, with its ambitions to control Europe and beyond, and the end of Japan's brutal imperialism across the Far East.

Nonetheless, World War II can be blamed for an unintended consequence—and it was a biggie. The defeat of Nazi Germany left a power vacuum, especially in Eastern Europe, that for nearly a half-century allowed the Soviet Union to have its way. A strong Germany, BU's Bacevich said, would have restrained Soviet aggression, but America's entry ensured Germany's defeat. The United States was drawn into the Cold War, featuring an Iron Curtain, a nuclear arms race, the Berlin airlift, hot wars in Korea and Vietnam, the Cuban missile crisis, and decades of living on the brink of World War III. So which would have better served U.S. interests after World War II: victory by a hegemonic Stalin, or by a genocidal Hitler? Pick your poison.

Wars of Confusion

Something else troubles historians in recounting World War II: It might have been avoided. Winston Churchill, Britain's wartime prime minister and a historian in his own right, described it as a necessary war that shouldn't have been fought.

But it was, and historians blame the sloppy diplomacy that marked the end of World War I. The United States, had it accepted the Treaty of Versailles, would have joined with Britain and France in policing the European peace, presumably to block Hitler from remilitarizing the Rhineland in 1936. That would have prompted the German generals to fire him as chancellor, Kagan said, and "Hitler would never have risen to power." An intransigent President Wilson, unwilling to accept Senate skeptics' reservations about the treaty, is usually accorded the bulk of the blame.

For historians with a taste for slapstick, World War I is the classic case of diplomatic bungling that leads to an unnecessary war. In Lenin's view, both sides were engaged in an imperialist war, trying to carve up spheres of influence. For the European powers, the war proved pointlessly destructive.

But not necessarily for the United States. "The U.S. might have limited the damage of World War I if it had credibly prepared to intervene in 1916 and used that threat to mediate negotiations that leaders on both sides wanted," according to Zelikow. It didn't. But by entering the war in 1917, almost three years after it started in Europe, American troops ended the military stalemate, defeating Kaiser Wilhelm's aggressiveness and bringing the conflict to a triumphal conclusion.

Historians disagree over what might have happened had Germany prevailed. Years later, a German historian found archival evidence that the kaiser's ambitions for a "Greater Germany" extended into Russia and France. The power of a militarily mighty, scientifically advanced, boldly affluent Germany might have blocked—or at least complicated—the emergence of America as a world power. But Walter McDougall, a professor of history and international relations at the University of Pennsylvania, contends that it also would have meant "no Bolshevism, no Holocaust, perhaps no World War II, atomic weapons, or Cold War."

As it happened, WWI fell laughably short of Wilson's idealistic hopes for a war that would end all wars and would make the world safe for democracy. Yet America benefited greatly. Its 19 months at war "gave the U.S. more diplomatic leverage than it probably deserved," military historian Millett said. The war's devastation in Europe held an extra benefit for the United States: It ensured an economic superiority over Germany and Britain, the strongmen of the prewar world, that America has never relinquished.

America's emergence onto the international scene had begun during its previous war. As with World War I, the Spanish-American War of 1898 has given historians fits. Driven by domestic politics in the United States as well as in Spain, it was set off by the typically American blur between idealism and naked self-interest. The Spanish brutalities in Cuba spurred William Randolph Hearst to sell his newspapers by inspiring American intervention in a situation on its doorstep. On a Friday afternoon, after his boss had knocked off for the weekend, the imperialist-minded assistant Navy secretary—Theodore Roosevelt, by name—ordered some battleships moved closer to the Philippines. The result was a quick and relatively bloodless conflict that was "clearly a war of expansion," said Edward (Mac) Coffman, a retired military historian at the University of Wisconsin. It freed Cuba from Spanish rule and, according to Owens at the Naval War College, "basically made it clear that we're the dominant power in the Western Hemisphere. Now we had a seagoing Navy capable of projecting power and an ability to defend the Monroe Doctrine."

The war against Spain probably benefited, on balance, the inhabitants of Puerto Rico and Hawaii by bringing them under U.S. control. But some historians discern a downside in America's trophy of the war. "The annexation of the Philippines created a 'hostage' that the Japanese could attack at will," Millett said. "Long-term, it was a political and strategic disaster," one that put the United States "crosswise" with Japan, fueling an antipathy that exploded on December 7, 1941. The Bataan Death March, in 1942, was another unintended consequence.

Julian Zelizer, a historian at Princeton University, posits a longer-term cost of the Spanish-American War. It was a turning point for the United States, he said, in establishing an "expansionist model" for wielding its influence overseas. He sees in it the roots of another, sadder war seven decades later in Vietnam.

"The annexation of the Philippines created a 'hostage' that the Japanese could attack at will. Long-term, it was a *political and strategic disaster*."

—Allan Millett, on the Spanish-American War

The Ugliest War

The widely ridiculed "domino effect," so often invoked by Lyndon Johnson in making his case for the Vietnam War, wasn't in itself a stupid idea. "A number of dominoes fell," Graham Allison, a professor of government at Harvard University and former Pentagon adviser, pointed out. Communism's advance in Vietnam ushered in a Communist regime in Laos (which remains in power, as it does in Vietnam) and another, far more virulent version in Cambodia.

Yeah, so? Even if the United States had won in Vietnam, historians say, the benefits wouldn't have been worth the costs. A pro-Western regime in South Vietnam wouldn't have mattered. Thailand and Indonesia would be just about the same. "I lost 58,000 colleagues," said Owens, a Marine veteran of Vietnam who was wounded twice. Tallying up the economic costs and the turmoil in the streets at home, he now concludes that the war probably wasn't worth fighting. ("Though who could say that [the turmoil] wouldn't have happened anyway?") Internationally, the defeat in Vietnam contributed to the image of the United States, which had never lost a war, as a paper tiger.

The miscalculations made in conducting the war are legendary, starting with the "ludicrous" assumption (as Allison put it) among U.S. decision makers that North Vietnam was acting as an agent for China, its enemy of many centuries' standing. A tour of the Hanoi Hilton that showcases John McCain's Navy uniform at the end begins with a guillotine dating from the 19th-century days of French colonial rule. The Americans who decided on the war failed to understand the enemy, a mistake they would make again in Iraq.

"The threat was not real, the death toll was so big, and it affected the U.S. role in the world," Princeton's Zelizer said. "A pretty big catastrophe."

Who was to blame? President Eisenhower comes in for the greatest share from historians. By backing the French as they were being driven out of Vietnam and committing Washington to support a corrupt and unpopular government in Saigon, Yale's Kagan said, Eisenhower made it politically dangerous for Presidents Kennedy and Johnson to back away from Vietnam without seeming soft on communism. In private (though taped) conversations with Sen. Richard Russell, D-Ga., who was a friend, Johnson sounded far more ambivalent about a war that ultimately ruined his presidency and drove him from the White House.

Two Iraq Wars

After the moral morass of Vietnam came the clarity of the Persian Gulf War. When Iraqi troops invaded Kuwait in 1990 and British Prime Minister Margaret Thatcher prevailed on Bush 41 not to go "wobbly," the carefully planned and well-executed war fulfilled Bush's vow: "This will not stand." Kuwait regained its freedom, and Saddam Hussein's forces were forced back across the border into Iraq. With only 382 Americans killed, the United States accomplished a lot at a relatively low cost.

"It would have been a disaster if Saddam Hussein had kept Kuwait," because it would have furthered his progress toward development of a nuclear bomb and destabilized the Middle East, according to Boot of the Council on Foreign Relations. For the United States, something even more vital was at stake. "It was about oil," said Harvard's Allison, citing the fear that the Iraqi dictator would march his troops beyond Kuwait and into Saudi Arabia, in hopes of manipulating the world's—and America's—oil supply. The invasion did not stand. Threat undone.

Yet Bush's famed prudence, reflected in his decision not to chase the Iraqi army back to Baghdad or to oust Saddam from power, took on a different cast during his son's presidency a dozen years later. With a half-million U.S. troops already on the scene, the elder

Bush might have had an easier time changing the Baghdad regime than George W. Bush did. The unfinished business of the first Iraq war led, as events (and perhaps a father-and-son psychodrama) unfolded, to the second, harder war.

The two military ventures showed that the political appeal of a war bears little relationship to its utility. "Iraq I passed the Senate by only five votes and was absolutely right," Zelikow said. "Iraq II passed the Senate by 50 votes and was iffy."

The younger Bush might have tried other, less costly ways to alter Iraqi behavior. An assassination or a coup could have sufficed to change the leadership. Or, Haass wrote, "the United States could well have accomplished a change in regime behavior and a change in regime threat without regime change." The costs of the six-year-long war have exceeded 4,300 American military deaths, a price tag of nearly $1 trillion or beyond—and something less tangible but perhaps more consequential. "Iraq contributed to the emergence of a world in which power is more widely distributed than ever before," Haass maintained, "and U.S. ability to shape this world much diminished."

So, will the potential benefits of the second Iraq war ever be judged worth the price? On that, the jury is out. It could take 10 or 20 or 30 years, foreign-policy experts say, to determine whether the Iraqi government functions as a democracy that is able to bring stability, without a dictator's iron hand, to a nation of sectarian hatreds. Proponents say that the odds of a tolerably good outcome are about even.

But *how* good an outcome is still possible seems harder to gauge. The neoconservative enthusiasts for the Iraq war (along with the likes of *New York Times* columnist Thomas Friedman) envisioned a shining democracy in a reborn nation that would inspire the undoing of Islamic autocracies across the Middle East. Haass believes that such a goal has become "unreachable." Whether anything less would produce enough benefits to make the war ultimately worth fighting will depend, at least in part, on the price. Haass said he sees no plausible scenario by which the direct and indirect costs of the war wouldn't outweigh its benefits. U.S. mistreatment of Iraqi insurgents at Abu Ghraib prison and the indefinite detention of accused enemy combatants at Guantanamo Bay sullied America's good-guy image across the Muslim world (and elsewhere) and surely led to the recruitment of additional terrorists.

Potentially, the most perilous of these costs extend beyond Iraq's borders. The chaos of war and the rise to power of Iraq's Shiite majority have emboldened the imperial ambitions of Shiite-dominated Iran. Moises Naim, the editor of *Foreign Policy,* fears that the Iraq war has encouraged Iran to develop nuclear weaponry, which in turn could inspire Egypt, Saudi Arabia, and possibly Arab Gulf states to do the same. "Is a shining, democratic Iraq," he asked, "worth a neighborhood full of nuclear bombs?"

War(s) of Necessity

Another cost of the Iraq war has been the distractions it has caused, not only in Iran and North Korea, which is pursuing a nuclear program of its own, but also Afghanistan. Barack Obama repeatedly leveled such a charge about the neglect of America's other ongoing war during his 2008 campaign. As president, he has announced the deployment of an additional 17,000 troops to Afghanistan, ousted his top general on the scene, and—in next year's budget, for the first time—has proposed to spend more Defense Department money in Afghanistan than in Iraq. Invading Afghanistan after 9/11 was widely considered necessary, not only to clean out Al Qaeda's camps but also to ensure a stable government that wouldn't give terrorists safe haven again.

"We had to do it, no matter what," Boot said. "Even if it doesn't work, no one will fault Bush [for invading], though maybe for how he fought it." Experts on all sides say that the war is "losable," as Kagan put it, but they're hopeful that it isn't too late to change tactics and win. This was evidently the Obama administration's motivation in recently replacing the cautious American commander in the field with an advocate of counterinsurgency.

Haass, for one, no longer regards the war in Afghanistan as essential to U.S. national security. As long as the American military continues to strike at terrorist-related targets, the United States could accept a "messy outcome" in Afghanistan, he said, one that allows the Taliban to make some political inroads in a civil war. Afghanistan has evolved from a war of necessity, Haass said, into "Mr. Obama's war of choice."

But there is plenty of reason to worry about the deteriorating situation just beyond Afghanistan's borders. In the muddled Afghan war, "what's at stake is Pakistan anyway," military historian Millett said. The nuclear-armed nation, with its shaky democratic government, is facing the Taliban on the doorstep of Islamabad, the Pakistani capital. Should Pakistan's government collapse or if any of its nuclear weapons fall into the wrong hands, the United States could well find itself in yet another war of necessity, one that would prove treacherous to lose.

Critical Thinking

1. What has been the most common result of the small wars the U.S. has fought? What has been the predominant outcome of the large wars it has fought?

2. Why is calculating the potential and actual costs and benefits of a war so difficult? How do "unintended consequences" often overshadow intentions?

3. What wars are widely considered to be "good wars" in U.S. history? What characterizes these wars?

4. What are some of the potential long-term costs and benefits of the current U.S. war in Iraq? What is a war of necessity versus a war of choice?

bsolomon@nationaljournal.com.

The Carbon Footprint of War

Bruce E. Johansen

The pentagon's recent announcement that global warming poses a national-security risk should have set off the irony alarms.

The Pentagon has as many as 1,000 bases in other countries, and maintaining these bases (and sending troops to and from them) leaves a gigantic carbon footprint.

The U.S. armed forces consume about 14 million gallons of oil per day, half of it in jet fuel. Humvees average 4 miles per gallon, while an Apache helicopter gets half a mile per gallon.

The Iraq War, which George W. Bush launched in part to protect vital oil supplies, consumed oil at a phenomenal rate.

At the start, in 2003, the United Kingdom Green Party estimated that the United States, Britain, and the minor parties of the "coalition of the willing" were burning the same amount of fuel as the 1.1 billion people of India.

U.S. forces in Iraq during 2007 consumed 40,000 barrels of oil a day, all of which was transported into the war zone from other countries.

The U.S. Air Force uses 2.6 billion gallons of jet fuel a year, 10 percent of the U.S. domestic market.

By the end of 2007, according to a report from Oil Change International by Nikki Reisch and Steve Kretzmann, the Iraq, war had put at least 141 million metric tons of carbon dioxide equivalent into the air, as much as adding 25 million cars to the roads. The Iraq war by itself added more greenhouse gases to the atmosphere than 60 percent of the world's nations.

When we are really serious about carbon footprints, we will know the amount of greenhouse gases generated by each platoon sent to war, each bomb dropped, each tank deployed. However, today we know the carbon footprint of a bag of British potato chips from a Tesco grocery store in England, but war—that elephant in the greenhouse—remains unmeasured.

Consider this one fact: More than 1.4 million liters of bottled water per day are used by our troops, who need them to stay hydrated during Baghdad's 115-degree summer days. How much fuel has been burned to get the water bottles into the war zone?

When the Pentagon trumpets its efforts to save energy—as when it announced in January that it was replacing 4,200 fluorescent lights with light-emitting diode (LED) lights, saving 22 percent of the energy of the old ones—it's a bad joke. Likewise, the solar array posted on the Pentagon roof is a mirage that is aimed at passengers in cars driving on nearby highways.

The business of the Pentagon is still war, and the making of war destroys the Earth.

So it has been since the dawn of the industrial age. Less than a hundred years ago, at the beginning of World war I, the main motive force in battle was the horse and shoe leather, as troops in Europe marched off to battle on foot or horseback. World war I quickly witnessed a dramatic escalation in war's carbon dioxide production with the advent of aerial bombardment, however, as well as increasing use of tanks. War is often a powerful technological motor, and carbon-consumption innovator. World war II began with quarter-century old biplanes, and ended with jet-propelled fighters. Compared with World war II, the U.S. military in Iraq and Afghanistan is using 16 times more fuel per soldier, according to the Pentagon.

The mechanization of the military provided many more opportunities to increase carbon dioxide production during the world wars of the early twentieth century. World war II's Sherman tank, for example, got 0.8 miles per gallon. Seventy-five years later, tank mileage had not improved: the 68-ton Abrams Tank got 0.5 miles per gallon. Fighter jets' typical subsonic fuel consumption is 300 to 400 gallons per hour at full thrust (or 100 gallons per hour at cruising speed) during hundreds of hours' training, or combat missions. Blasting to supersonic speed on its afterburners, an F-15 Fighter can burn as much as four gallons of fuel per second.

During the 1950s and 1960s, U.S. B-52s were in the air at all times, on the theory that an airborne fleet would prevent the Soviet Union from obliterating the entire U.S. nuclear-armed armada on the ground. Each of these B-52s burned hundreds of gallons of fossil fuel per hour while aloft. The B-52 Stratocruiser, with eight jet engines, consumes 500 gallons of jet fuel per minute, or 3,000 per hour. In a few minutes, a B-52 consumes what an average automobile driver uses in a year.

What I'd like to know is, how many years of riding a bike to work would it take for me to offset one F-15 flying for an hour? Assuming that my bike replaces a car that gets 25 miles per gallon, my daily commute of five miles would use a gallon a week. That's nearly seven years to fuel a fighter jet at top thrust for one hour.

We don't have that kind of time. Thermal inertia delivers the results of atmospheric change roughly a half century after our burning of fossil fuels provokes them. the weather today is reacting to greenhouse gas emissions from about 1960. Since then, the world's emissions have risen roughly 400 percent. The Cold War, the Vietnam War, the Gulf War, the Iraq War, and the Afghanistan War have all played their part. But we haven't even felt their full environmental effects yet.

Global warming has already accelerated beyond even the predictions of pessimistic scientists. The polar ice caps are dissolving and the permafrost is melting, injecting more carbon dioxide and methane into the air. And as the ice caps melt, the sun reflects off the dark water instead of the white snow, and the atmosphere heats all the faster. This summer, large swaths of tundra have been burning, adding still more greenhouse gases to the atmosphere.

Before the hot wind blows in our face, we need to recognize the environmental insanity of war.

The Pentagon wants to go "green," though—and not only with its light bulbs. It is also using solar energy at some of its bases, and is even trying to manufacture a synthetic fuel for the B-1 bomber. But we don't need a "green" military with high-mileage tanks, or bombers flying on biofuel. Anyway, war, for the foreseeable future, will depend largely on fossil fuels. As the Pentagon now tells us, we have no national security without climate security. War has become the ultimate environmental oxymoron.

Instead, we need to address the reasons countries and groups go to war: nationalism, religious fanaticism, tribalism, poverty—and scarcity of resources, like oil. And we can't do that by consuming that oil in spasms of nationalism.

Peacemakers are often assumed to be naive dreamers. Given the environmental circumstances, however, a timely end to war is not naive, but necessary. The Earth can no longer afford war.

Critical Thinking

1. How does the U.S. military's fuel consumption contribute to carbon production?

2. What other non-fuel-related consumption patterns contribute to the military's greenhouse gas emissions?

3. How has the mechanization of the military in the past century increased the carbon footprint of wars?

BRUCE E. JOHANSEN is a professor of communication at the University of Nebraska at Omaha and author of "Hard Science and Hot Air: Dissecting the Global Warming Debate" (due in January 2010) and the two-volume "Encyclopedia of Global Warming Science and Technology," published in 2009.

Test-Your-Knowledge Form

We encourage you to photocopy and use this page as a tool to assess how the articles in *Annual Editions* expand on the information in your textbook. By reflecting on the articles you will gain enhanced text information. You can also access this useful form on a product's book support website at www.mhhe.com/cls.

NAME: _____   DATE: _____

TITLE AND NUMBER OF ARTICLE: _____

BRIEFLY STATE THE MAIN IDEA OF THIS ARTICLE:

_____

_____

LIST THREE IMPORTANT FACTS THAT THE AUTHOR USES TO SUPPORT THE MAIN IDEA:

_____

_____

_____

_____

WHAT INFORMATION OR IDEAS DISCUSSED IN THIS ARTICLE ARE ALSO DISCUSSED IN YOUR TEXTBOOK OR OTHER READINGS THAT YOU HAVE DONE? LIST THE TEXTBOOK CHAPTERS AND PAGE NUMBERS:

_____

_____

_____

_____

_____

LIST ANY EXAMPLES OF BIAS OR FAULTY REASONING THAT YOU FOUND IN THE ARTICLE:

_____

_____

_____

_____

LIST ANY NEW TERMS/CONCEPTS THAT WERE DISCUSSED IN THE ARTICLE, AND WRITE A SHORT DEFINITION:

We Want Your Advice

ANNUAL EDITIONS revisions depend on two major opinion sources: one is our Advisory Board, listed in the front of this volume, which works with us in scanning the thousands of articles published in the public press each year; the other is you—the person actually using the book. Please help us and the users of the next edition by completing the prepaid article rating form on this page and returning it to us. Thank you for your help!

ANNUAL EDITIONS: American Government 11/12

ARTICLE RATING FORM

Here is an opportunity for you to have direct input into the next revision of this volume.
We would like you to rate each of the articles listed below, using the following scale:

1. **Excellent: should definitely be retained**
2. **Above average: should probably be retained**
3. **Below average: should probably be deleted**
4. **Poor: should definitely be deleted**

Your ratings will play a vital part in the next revision.
Please mail this prepaid form to us as soon as possible.
Thanks for your help!

RATING	ARTICLE
	1. The Declaration of Independence
	2. The History of the Constitution of the United States
	3. Federalist No. 10
	4. Federalist No. 51
	5. Can America Fail?
	6. The Right Bite
	7. The Purposes of Political Combat: Why Obama Has Been Blindsided by the Strength and Vitality of His Opposition
	8. These People Have No Shame
	9. The Crisis Comes Ashore
	10. Over Time, a Gay Marriage Groundswell
	11. It Is Time to Repair the Constitution's Flaws
	12. Is Judicial Review Obsolete?
	13. A Triumph for Political Speech: An Important Supreme Court Decision May Mark the End of Misbegotten Campaign-Finance "Reform"
	14. Corporations Aren't Persons; Amend the Constitution
	15. A Title IX for Health Care
	16. Misremembering Reagan
	17. Small Ball after All?
	18. The Founders' Great Mistake
	19. Happy Together?
	20. Veto This!
	21. Dear Leader
	22. The Obama Enigma: Disconnection from the Main Currents of American Life Turns Out to Be a Political Disadvantage
	23. When Congress Stops Wars: Partisan Politics and Presidential Power
	24. How to Get Our Democracy Back: There Will Be No Change Until We Change Congress
	25. The Case for Congress

RATING	ARTICLE
	26. The Case for Busting the Filibuster
	27. Roberts versus Roberts
	28. Court under Roberts Is Most Conservative in Decades
	29. Marking Time: Why Government Is Too Slow
	30. Legislation Is Just the Start
	31. Teaching a Hippo to Dance
	32. The 'Enduring Majority'—Again
	33. Polarized Pols versus Moderate Voters?
	34. The Tea Party Paradox
	35. America Observed
	36. Six Myths about Campaign Money
	37. The American Presidential Nomination Process: The Beginnings of a New Era
	38. Don't Call Them Lobbyists
	39. Born Fighting
	40. Why They Lobby
	41. Tea Minus Zero
	42. The Revolution Will Not Be Published
	43. Build the Wall
	44. A See-Through Society
	45. Governing in the Age of Fox News
	46. The Realities of Immigration
	47. The Real Infrastructure Crisis
	48. The Other National Debt
	49. In Defense of Deficits
	50. Meet the Real Death Panels
	51. Clean, Green, Safe and Smart
	52. A Flimsy Trust: Why Social Security Needs Some Major Repairs
	53. How Globalization Went Bad
	54. Worth Fighting—or Not
	55. The Carbon Footprint of War

ABOUT YOU

Name   Date

_____

Are you a teacher? ☐ A student? ☐
Your school's name

_____

Department

_____

Address   City   State   Zip

_____

School telephone #

_____

YOUR COMMENTS ARE IMPORTANT TO US!

Please fill in the following information:
For which course did you use this book?

_____

Did you use a text with this ANNUAL EDITION? ☐ yes ☐ no
What was the title of the text?

_____

What are your general reactions to the Annual Editions concept?

_____

Have you read any pertinent articles recently that you think should be included in the next edition? Explain.

_____

Are there any articles that you feel should be replaced in the next edition? Why?

_____

Are there any World Wide Websites that you feel should be included in the next edition? Please annotate.

_____

May we contact you for editorial input? ☐ yes ☐ no
May we quote your comments? ☐ yes ☐ no